Techniques of
Program Structure
and Design

Techniques of Program Structure and Design

EDWARD YOURDON

President
YOURDON inc.

PRENTICE-HALL, INC., *Englewood Cliffs*, *New Jersey*

Library of Congress Cataloging in Publication Data

YOURDON, EDWARD.
   Techniques of program structure and design.

   Includes bibliographies.
   1. Electronic digital computers—Programming.
I. Title.
QA76.6.Y68   001.6′42   75-9728
ISBN 0-13-901702-X

10 9 8 7 6 5 4 3 2 1

Printed in the United States of America

PRENTICE-HALL INTERNATIONAL, INC., *London*
PRENTICE-HALL OF AUSTRALIA, PTY. LTD., *Sydney*
PRENTICE-HALL OF CANADA, LTD., *Toronto*
PRENTICE-HALL OF INDIA PRIVATE LIMITED, *New Delhi*
PRENTICE-HALL OF JAPAN, INC., *Tokyo*
PRENTICE-HALL OF SOUTHEAST ASIA (PTE.) LTD., *Singapore*

To JENNY

CONTENTS

PREFACE

"We build systems like the Wright brothers built airplanes—build the whole thing, push it off a cliff, let it crash, and start over again."

Professor R. M. Graham
Software Engineering, page 17

"Of course 99 percent of computers work tolerably well, that is obvious. There are thousands of respectable Fortran-oriented installations using many different machines and lots of good data processing applications running quite steadily; we all know that! The matter that concerns us is the sensitive edge, which is socially desperately significant."

Professor J. N. Buxton
Software Engineering, page 119

"I think it is inevitable that people program, and will continue to program, poorly. Training will not substantially improve matters. Using subsets of languages doesn't help because people always step outside the subset. We have to learn to live with it."

Professor A. J. Perlis
Software Engineering Techniques, page 33

"There is a widening gap between ambitions and achievements in software engineering. This gap appears in several dimensions: between promises to users and performance by software, between what seems to be ultimately

Preface opening quotes from *Softwave Engineering*, P. Naur and B. Randell, (eds.), NATO Scientific Affairs Division, Brussels 39, Belgium, January 1969 and *Software Engineering Techniques*, J. N. Buxton and B. Randell, (eds.), NATO Scientific Affairs Division, Brussels 39, Belgium, April 1970.

possible and what is achievable now and between estimates of software costs and expenditures. This gap is arising at a time when the consequences of software failures in all its aspects are becoming increasingly serious. Particularly alarming is the seemingly unavoidable fallibility of large software, since a malfunction in an advanced hardware-software system can be a matter of life and death, not only for individuals, but also for vehicles carrying hundreds of people, and ultimately for nations as well."

Dr. E. E. David and Mr. A. G. Fraser
Software Engineering, page 120

In 1970 I made the terrible mistake of writing a set of notes for a seminar entitled ADVANCED PROGRAMMING TECHNIQUES. I say "mistake" because I quickly discovered that I knew almost nothing about that advanced state of witchcraft that we call programming, despite the fact that I had been gainfully employed in the field for several years. Nevertheless, I persisted: from 80 pages of almost incoherent scribblings in 1970, the notes went through ten major revisions and slowly grew to 900 typewritten pages. At several points in this process, common sense dictated that I throw all ten versions of the manuscript away and cease inflicting my ideas upon my students; unfortunately, pride and sheer orneriness have prevailed. Pity the poor students who suffered through this period: Nearly 3000 programmers in 12 countries have forgiven my bugs and overlooked some of my more absurd ideas; more important, they have all patiently communicated to me what *they* know about programming—a privilege that must be experienced to be appreciated.

It has been especially interesting to me during this period to watch the transformation through which the computer field has been struggling. The emergence of such prophets as Edsger Dijkstra, Niklaus Wirth, and Gerald Weinberg encourages one to think that perhaps programmers will eventually be taught to write good programs from the very beginning.

If this turns out to be the case, some of the suggestions and warnings in this book may turn out to be unnecessary. Both in my seminars and in this book, I have made the basic assumption that the student has been exposed to some of the rudiments of programming, but that he has not been exposed to any significant ideas on "good" programming. I think this is a very reasonable assumption when one is dealing with the vast majority of programmers working in industry. As long as basic training courses continue to stress the mechanics of a particular programming language (as is usually the case with most FORTRAN and COBOL courses) this will continue to be true. It is particularly encouraging to see the recent trend in university courses toward teaching students the elements of good programming.

In any case, that is what this book attempts to discuss: "good" programming. However, my experience has been that it is very difficult to tell someone how to design a good program if he (or she) violently disagrees with me as to what a good program is. Hence, the first chapter in the book is a discussion of the characteristics of a good program. I must admit that this chapter is aimed at the experienced programmer; a college freshman would probably not have any preconceived ideas about the relative merits of maintainability, flexibility, and efficiency in a program.

The next logical question is: How do we go about designing such a good program? Chapter 2 provides answers in the form of *top-down design*. There seems to be some controversy concerning the order in which some of these ideas are presented. Many people argue that the concept of structured programming should be presented first, after which the programmer is more likely to comprehend and accept the principle of top-down design. Perhaps this is so; indeed, when I am confronted with a group of particularly impatient programmers in a seminar, I find it helpful to present the more tangible concepts of structured programming first, before moving on to the more abstract concept of top-down design. Nevertheless, from a logical point of view, it makes much more sense to talk about the *design* of a program before one talks about a coding discipline.

Chapter 3 contains a discussion of modular programming. It represents a nice transition from the abstract discussion of top-down design to the more detailed discussion of structured programming. Nearly everyone seems to consider modular programming the precursor to the currently fashionable structured programming. I find it ironic that when I began these notes in 1970, modular programming was considered somewhat radical by many programmers; in today's world of structured programming, modular programming is considered passé. Oddly enough, it is just this area of modularity that will probably see the greatest advances in the next few years. Larry Constantine's paper on "Structured Design" in the May 1974 *IBM Systems Journal* will probably be as responsible for generating new interest in modular design as Terry Baker's article in the January 1972 *IBM Systems Journal* was in the field of structured programming.

In any case, structured programming certainly deserves ample discussion in any modern textbook on programming; Chapter 4 discusses this topic at length. One section of the chapter deserves special mention: Section 4.3.3 discusses the conversion of unstructured programs into structured programs. A number of people have objected to the emphasis I have placed on this area, but I submit that the usefulness of this material is a direct function of the students' programming experience. A new programmer, with no previous exposure to GO-TO-ridden "rat's nest" programs, probably requires none of the material in Section 4.3.3—indeed, it may actually be harmful! An experienced programmer, on the other hand, is in desperate need of these conversion techniques, because they help him convert his unstructured *thinking* into structured *thinking*. It is somewhat naive to argue that the programmers currently being trained in universities will learn structured programming from the beginning; that is roughly comparable to the argument that, since FORTRAN lacks the control structures required to conveniently implement structured programs, people should instantly cease programming in FORTRAN. Things don't work that way in the real world. For better or for worse, people are going to continue programming in FORTRAN for the next several years until we can begin to shift them towards more civilized languages. In the meantime, it is eminently practical to teach people how to accomplish some reasonable approximation of structured programming in FORTRAN. By the same token, we currently have several *hundred thousand* experienced programmers in the world, each of whom probably has another twenty years of "rat's nest" programming before he drops from exhaustion. If we wait for the newly trained university students to rectify the situation with the magic of structured programming, most of our current computer systems will collapse.

After all this preaching about structured programming, I must admit that I temporarily ran out of energy. Chapters 5 and 6—a discussion of programming style and defensive programming—probably do not get the attention they deserve. I offer the following excuse: If the philosophies in Chapters 1–4 are followed faithfully, there is a reasonable chance that the programmer will already have accomplished what is suggested in Chapters 5 and 6. Perhaps a more substantial excuse is that a thorough treatment of programming style would require a book in itself. I highly recommend both *The Elements of FORTRAN Style* (Schneiderman and Kreitzberg; Harcourt, Brace, Jovanovich, 1971) and *The Elements of Programming Style* (Kernighan and Plauger, McGraw-Hill, 1974) in this area.

For various reasons, I felt that a discussion of testing and debugging should accompany a discussion of top-down design, modular programming, and structured programming; hence Chapters 7 and 8. I still insist on making a distinction between testing and debugging, despite the feeling of many of my students that I am belaboring the issue. I must admit to a sense of frustration at the end of the chapter on testing: I have the feeling that the majority of programmers don't really know how to test a program properly. Most computer scientists probably agree that a great deal more work needs to be done before we have achieved the same level of discipline in testing that we have in structured programming. Maybe we need "structured testing?"

If structured testing, why not structured debugging? The major objective of Chapter 8 has been to present some debugging strategies that are quite distinct from the usual approach of dumps and traces. I have always felt that these strategies represented the *art* of debugging, and that if some students found it difficult to apply the strategies, it was because they lacked the inborn artistic talents required of a good debugger. Perhaps this is an oversimplified view; some friends of mine at Shell Oil in Melbourne tell me that their programmers are being given courses in general problem-solving in an attempt to improve their debugging skills. Perhaps this is the beginning of structured debugging.

At the end of the book I have included four major programming exercises that may be used to illustrate many of the principles of program design. The problems in Appendix A and Appendix B were intended to be designed by a *team* of programmers; a group of three or four seems to be the optimal size. Appendix C and Appendix D are small enough to be attacked by an individual programmer.

Acknowledgments

In addition to the thousands of students who read through the manuscript of this book and suggested improvements and corrections, I would like to give special thanks to Brian Kernighan of Bell Labs and Peter Neely of the University of Kansas for their thorough review. My colleagues Bill Plauger, Trish Sarson, and Bob Abbott also deserve thanks for using the material in several training courses and giving me recommendations for improvements in the manuscript. During the production of the book, Lynne Sadkowski retained her composure while continually trying to track me down in some far-distant part of the world to review critical galleys, while Wendy Eakin provided invaluable assistance by copyediting and proofreading my manuscript to the point where it resembled proper English.

In the final analysis, though, I owe this book to Sam, who, more than all the others, believed in me.

Techniques of
Program Structure
and Design

1

THE
CHARACTERISTICS
OF A "GOOD"
COMPUTER PROGRAM

In fact, the central concept in all software is that of a program, and a generally satisfactory definition of a program is still needed. The most frequently used definition—that a program is a sequence of instructions—forces one to ignore the role of data in the program. A better definition is that a program is a set of transformations and other relationships over sets of data and container structures. At least this definition guides the designer to break up a program design problem into the problems of establishing the various data and container structures required, and defining the operators over them. The definition requires that attention be given to the properties of the data regardless of the containers (records, words, sectors, etc.).

KENNETH K. KOLENCE
Software Engineering, page 50

There is no theory which enables us to calculate limits on the size, performance or complexity of software. There is, in many instances, no way even to specify in a logically tight way what the software product is supposed to do, or how it is supposed to do it.

EDWARD E. DAVID
Software Engineering, page 69

One of the problems that is central to the software production process is to identify the nature of progress and to find some way of measuring it. Only one

Chapter opening quotes from *Software Engineering*, P. Naur and B. Randell (eds.), NATO Scientific Affairs Division, Brussels 39, Belgium, January 1969 and *Software Engineering Techniques*, J. N. Buxton and B. Randell (eds.), NATO Scientific Affairs Division, Brussels 39, Belgium, April 1970.

thing seems to be clear just now. It is that program construction is not always a simple progression in which each act of assembly represents a distinct forward step and that the final product can be described simply as a sum of many sub-assemblies.

A. G. FRASER
Software Engineering, page 86

Programming management will continue to deserve its current poor reputation for cost and schedule effectiveness until such time as a more complete understanding of the program design process is achieved.

KENNETH K. KOLENCE
Software Engineering, page 123

Any large program will exist during its lifetime in a multitude of different versions, so that in composing a large program we are not so much concerned with a single program, but with a whole family of related programs, containing alternative programs for the same job and/or similar programs for similar jobs. A program therefore should be conceived and understood as a member of a family; it should be so structured out of components that various members of this family, sharing components, do not only share the correctness demonstrated of the shared components but also of the shared substructure.

E. W. DIJKSTRA
Software Engineering Techniques, page 31

1.0 Introduction

Throughout this book, we assume that you are already familiar with the basic elements of computer hardware, operating systems, and programming languages; you are now ready to direct your attention to the finer points of computer programming. Which area of programming would you like to explore first? Shall it be list structures? Dynamic memory allocation? Decision tables? Or perhaps searching and sorting algorithms?

If you chose *any* of these areas, you may be suffering from a weakness common to almost all programmers: a fatal fascination with *techniques* of programming. You may be assured that we will eventually discuss a number of important programming techniques, but only after we agree on some *philosophies* of programming.

Philosophical discussions of this type are generally unpopular with programming students; they seem too vague and general, and the programmers would prefer to spend their time discussing more "practical," "useful" subjects. On the other hand, it should be remembered that programmers are, in many cases, a somewhat stubborn, unrealistic, and uncompromising breed: They often seem to think that their primary function is to invent clever new algorithms, rather than to perform useful work.

Without meaning to be unnecessarily cruel, I feel that I must remind you of an important fact: *As a programmer, you will always be working for an employer.* Unless you are very rich and very eccentric, you will not enjoy the luxury of having a computer in your own home; unless you plan to remain a perpetual student, you cannot expect to spend your life dazzling your awe-stricken professors with your programming virtuosity. In short, you cannot be an artist, separate and aloof; it is highly unlikely that the programming community will ever generate a Michelangelo or Rembrandt. As a programmer, you will be expected to do whatever is necessary to make the computer provide some useful service. This is true whether you are a business programmer, a scientific programmer, or involved in research activities for a computer manufacturer.

I thus feel that it is eminently practical to discuss some philosophies of programming. What things should you do to make yourself useful as a programmer? What aspects of your programs will be of most concern to your employer? These topics may seem rather trifling to you, but they can ensure your success as a programmer. To ignore the philosophies presented in this chapter will certainly cost you dearly in terms of promotions and salary increases, and it may even cost you your job. What could be more practical?

The basic purpose of this chapter is to present a checklist of good program design. We will begin by making some general comments on the qualities of a good *programmer*, as well as the qualities of a good *program*; this will be followed by a more specific list of seven characteristics of a good program. After writing a computer program, you should ask yourself if your program satisfies these "rules" of good programming; *before* writing a program, you should ask yourself how you can best satisfy these rules.

1.1 What Are the Qualities of a Good Programmer?

During the past several years, I have had the opportunity to teach advanced programming courses to thousands of students in several different countries around the world. The students, in general, have been experienced programmers in banks, insurance companies, government agencies, manufacturing organizations, scientific installations, universities, and every other conceivable background. More for my own amusement than anything else, I have often begun each course with the question, "What are the qualities of a good programmer?" The answers have been as varied as the students' backgrounds, and some of them are worth repeating:

1. A good programmer writes good programs (or efficient programs, or well-documented programs, etc.).
2. A good programmer works well with other people.
3. A good programmer communicates well with the users of his program.
4. A good programmer takes a bath at least once a week.
5. A good programmer shows up for work on time.
6. A good programmer *never* shows up for work on time.

7. A good programmer doesn't cause trouble.
8. A good programmer works well under pressure.
9. A good programmer likes classical music.

An argument often breaks out about the first answer to the question, i.e., the statement that a good programmer is anyone who writes good programs. It is pointed out that managers are usually required to evaluate the "goodness" of a programmer, yet they seem to be singularly incapable of determining the quality of a good program. We will see during this chapter that *none* of us is really in a good position to quantitatively determine the quality of a program, so a manager should not be blamed too much in this difficult situation.

Nevertheless, it seems that some programmers have a reputation in their organization for being "superprogrammers": The word will spread that Tom can turn out a large complex program in a single day, or that Alice always manages to debug her programs with a maximum of one test shot. Given this natural situation, I have occasionally amended my original question and asked my programming classes:

> Is a superprogrammer—i.e., someone who can code faster than a speeding bullet, leap over reams and reams of printout in a single bound, and generally out-program everyone else in the organization—looked upon with favor and respect by the management?

Though there is often a tremendous amount of heated debate and controversy on this point, it has been surprising how many people—especially programming supervisors and managers—have emphatically said "No!" A programmer in a large bank in Montreal put it rather well: "If my programs are outrageously inefficient, so inefficient that even my manager can tell, then I'm in trouble. Similarly, if I take ten times longer to write a program than other people in my department, I will be in trouble. For the most part, though, my manager is more interested in my ability to function as a human being in a human organization; my relationship with the computer is my own business. My manager wants me to work reasonably regular hours, interface well with other programmers and computer users, and most of all, not to cause trouble." The same management attitude seems to be quite prevalent in large insurance companies, government agencies, and banks; less prevalent in medium-sized manufacturing organizations; and generally not true in universities, research organizations, and computer manufacturing companies.

To the extent that this management attitude is true, the subject of advanced programming, and indeed this entire book, may be rather academic. What is the point of writing the most efficient program in the world if you lack other traits that make you an accepted, if not popular, member of your organization? Fortunately, the situation is generally not quite that extreme. Management *would* like to see programs with all of the "good" qualities that we will be discussing later in this chapter; still, it is important to remember that they are often not willing to tolerate the popular image of the "computer bum" for the sake of obtaining highly efficient programs.

Note that there are different reasons for disliking the so-called "super-programmer." Some superprogrammers can develop working programs very quickly, or can write extremely efficient programs—but they are undocumented, impossible to understand, maintain, or modify. On the other hand, there are some superprogrammers who turn out truly superlative code—and yet they are unsociable or, in the words of one manager, "a bit like Allen Ginsberg."

The most interesting point about discussing the merits of good and bad programmers is that we seem unable to measure their merits in any reasonable quantitative fashion. That is, the superprogrammer *seems* to write much better programs than his mortal colleagues—but how much better? We are at a loss in this area, for we have no way of knowing whether he is twice as good, 3.14 times as good, or ten times as good as the other programmers.

This fact was dramatically illustrated by a study made by Messrs. H. Sackman, W. J. Erickson, and E. E. Grant.[1] During a study to compare the advantages of an on-line (i.e., time-sharing) programming approach versus the standard batch programming approach,[2] a group of twelve experienced programmers were given two different programming problems to solve: One was an algebraic problem, and the other was a program that could find its way out of a "rat's maze." Careful records were kept to determine how long it took to code and debug the program. Debugging time was considered to have begun when the programmer had removed all of the "serious" compilation errors, and the debugging was considered to be finished when the program could successfully process some standard test input.

The results of the experiment are shown in Table 1.1. Note the startling ratio between the best and worst performances in the areas of coding and debugging. The ratios on all other areas of measurement, while not quite as dramatic, are still large enough to cause problems for a manager attempting to plan and schedule a programming project. As the authors pointed out in their conclusions:

> When a programmer is good,
> He is very, very good,
> But when he is bad,
> He is horrid.

[1]"Exploratory Experimental Studies Comparing Online and Offline Programming Performance," H. Sackman, W. J. Erickson, and E. E. Grant, *Communications of the ACM*, January 1968, pages 3–11.

[2]As a point of interest, the researchers *did* find that time-sharing enabled a programmer to finish his work more quickly, though more computer time was consumed in the development process.

Table 1.1. RANGE OF INDIVIDUAL DIFFERENCES
IN PROGRAMMING EXPERIMENT

Performance Measure	Worst	Best	Ratio
1. Debugging hours—algebra program	170	6	28:1
2. Debugging hours—maze problem	26	1	26:1
3. CPU sec. for program development—algebra problem	3075	370	8:1
4. CPU sec. for program development—maze problem	541	50	11:1
5. Coding hours—algebra program	111	7	16:1
6. Coding hours—maze problem	50	2	25:1
7. Program size—algebra problem	6137	1060	6:1
8. Program size—maze problem	3287	650	5:1
9. Run time (CPU sec.)—algebra problem	7.9	1.6	5:1
10. Run time (CPU sec.)—maze problem	8.0	0.6	13:1

They also pointed out that

> The observed pattern was one of substantial correlation with . . . test scores with programmer trainee class grades, but of no detectable correlation with experienced programmers' performance.

Their final conclusion was that

> This situation suggests that general programming skill may dominate early training and initial on-the-job experience, but that such skill is progressively transformed and displaced by more specialized skills with increasing experience.

What conclusions may one draw from all of this? Not much—except that we know very little about what makes programmers tick, what makes them good, or how to measure just how talented they really are. The seeming tautology that "a good programmer is one who writes good programs" is not necessarily true, according to those who hand out the raises and promotions. In addition to knowing OS and JCL on the IBM System/360, it seems that a good programmer must have a number of qualities that have nothing to do with a computer.

1.2   What Are the Qualities of a Good Program?

As I mentioned before, I often begin a course on advanced programming by asking the students for their definition of a good programmer. Not too surprisingly, I often follow this up with the question, "What are the qualities of a good computer program?" Once again, there is a variety of definitions; some of the more interesting ones are:

1. It works.
2. It works according to specifications.
3. It is flexible.

4. It is ready on time.
5. It has no bugs.
6. The bugs, which are inevitable, can be fixed quickly.
7. It is well-documented.
8. It executes quickly.
9. It makes efficient use of memory.

Clearly, we could compile a number of other desirable characteristics of a program, but the list above seems fairly representative. However, we should be able to organize and standarize these desirable qualities so that everyone will have a common metric with which to judge his programs. What follows is a list of seven desirable qualities of a program, listed in what I personally feel to be decreasing order of importance. Following this discussion, we will comment on our ability to *quantify* these desirable characteristics.

1.2.1   The Program Works and Is Readily Observable

It is irteresting to note that many of my programming students have already realized, with one or two years of experience, *that the most important quality of a program is that it work*. It is truly incredible to see the number of times that two programmers (or two software houses, or two computer manufacturing companies) will enter into the following debate about their programs, which are both supposed to do the same thing: Programmer A tells Programmer B, "My program is ten times faster than yours—and it takes up three times less memory!" . . . to which Programmer B replies, "Yes, but your program doesn't work, and mine does!"[3]

In some cases, it is meaningful to distinguish between a program that works and a program that works according to specifications. For a number of obvious reasons, the programmer may ultimately develop a subset of the original specifications, or possibly something quite different from what the specifications called for: The programmer may have misunderstood the specifications, the specifications may have been vague and imprecise (decision tables are often a solution to this problem), the specifications may have changed as the program was being developed, or the programmer may have discovered that he promised more than he could deliver—so he delivered a subset of the original specifications.

As programs and programming systems continue to grow more complex in the future, we may find that it is no longer sufficient for a program to simply work; it may be necessary for the program (and possibly the programmer) to have some way of *verifying* that the program is working correctly. Note the subtle difference between *testing* a program and providing some kind of

---

[3]For a particularly amusing story along these lines, and for a number of other brilliant insights into the psychology of programming, see *The Psychology of Computer Programming*, by Gerald Weinberg, D. Van Nostrand Co., 1971.

continual verification of the correctness of the program. The first activity is primarily for the benefit of the programmer and the person who has to accept the finished program (e.g., the programmer's manager, or possibly a user-oriented person). The second activity gives a continual psychological reassurance to the person who has to use the output from the program that it is indeed correct.

This kind of verification may not be necessary for many straightforward applications, but it would be useful where the program's computations are so complex that they are not immediately obvious to the user. Consider, for example, an engineering application, where the user requires computations to help determine the physical dimensions and characteristics of a bridge, an airplane, or any other expensive and complex mechanism. The computations performed by the program may involve thousands of differential equations, numerical integrations, simultaneous equations, and so forth, and yet the output may be a simple statement like, "the airplane's wings should be 972.34567 feet long." The engineer may be very suspicious of such an answer, since he has never seen an airplane with such huge wings, and yet the answer may be correct. In such a situation, it would indeed be helpful if the program could give some evidence to indicate *how* it arrived at such an answer; it might do this by giving the results of intermediate calculations.

Again, such considerations may not be necessary for many simple applications; however, for the complex business-oriented and scientific-oriented applications that are beginning to exceed the user's ability to perform his own verification, this characteristic of a computer program should be considered the most important.

1.2.2   Minimize Testing Costs

The testing and debugging of a computer program is undoubtedly the programming manager's greatest headache; it often becomes the programmer's greatest headache as well. A standard rule of thumb in the computer industry is that testing and debugging of a computer program occupies between $\frac{1}{3}$ and $\frac{1}{2}$ of the total project time. Clearly, anything that can decrease this inordinate amount of time is of great value.

From a philosophical point of view, you must remember that if you write a program so clever, so intricate, and so complicated that only you can understand it, then the program is worthless; if your program makes use of undocumented, esoteric features of the hardware, it is worthless; if your program is not commented and documented, it is worthless. All of these practices lead to a worthless program because they make it *much* more difficult to test. As a result, the program becomes unnecessarily expensive in terms of time and money.

Speaking of time and money, we should note that it is possible to quantify this characteristic of a program; that is, we can measure the "goodness" of a program with respect to testing by recording the length of time required for the testing, the amount of CPU time for test shots, the amount of extra equipment (e.g., sophisticated hardware simulators of real-time systems, or expensive parallel runs) for testing, and the cost of lost customer confidence due to untested programs. As shown in Table 1.1, there can be a tremendous range between the amounts of time spent by programmers in testing.

There are a number of common practices that make a program more difficult to debug; some of the worst ones are mentioned below.

Uncommented Code. In my opinion, there is nothing in the programming field more despicable than an uncommented program. A programmer can be forgiven many sins and flights of fancy, including many of those listed in the sections below; however, *no* programmer, no matter how wise, no matter how experienced, no matter how hard-pressed for time, no matter how well-intentioned, should be forgiven an uncommented and undocumented program.

If this seems an unreasonably venomous attack, you are invited to debug, maintain, or change someone else's uncommented program; you will usually find that it is worse than having no program at all. An abundance of comments is also imperative to test your own program quickly and painlessly. Only a fool would venture into an unknown forest without leaving trail-markers behind. Writing an uncommented program is roughly the same as crawling blindfolded into the jungles of the Amazon. Though there are no firm rules in this area, a good guideline to follow is four to five lines of comment for every subroutine (or COBOL section, etc.), and an average of one comment for every two or three lines of source code.

Of course, it is important to point out that comments are not an end unto themselves. As Messrs. Kernighan and Plauger point out in their excellent book, *The Elements of Programming Style,* good comments cannot substitute for bad code. However, it is not clear that good code can substitute for comments. That is, I do not agree that it is unnecessary for comments to accompany "good" code: The code obviously tells us *what* the program is doing, but the comments are often necessary for us to understand *why* the programmer has used those particular instructions.

In my experiences as a programmer and programming supervisor, I have had the opportunity to hear (and occasionally use) some of the following objections (a polite euphemism for *excuses*) for not putting comments into the program:

1. I don't have enough time to put in any comments.
2. I have to do my own keypunching, and I don't type well—so I can't bother with a lot of comments.

3. I type my programs into a time-sharing terminal, and I get charged for connect time—and since I don't type well, I can't afford to put in a lot of comments.

4. My program is self-documenting.

5. Any *competent* programmer can understand my code without comments.

6. My program is only going to be used once, so documentation is not necessary.

7. The program will certainly be changed drastically during the testing and debugging phase, so the documentation will be obsolete by the time the program is finished.

8. I understand perfectly well what my program does—so why should I have to document it?

9. I don't like to document or comment.

10. It's not good to have too many comments—it obscures the important ones.

11. If I put in too many comments, my program will take longer to compile.

12. My source program will take up too much room on the disk (or on punched paper tape on some minicomputer systems) if I have a large number of comments.

13. Who reads the documentation anyway?

Nonexistent comments are an obvious problem; a more subtle problem can exist if the program is heavily laden with comments, but:

1. The comments are redundant.
2. The comments are obsolete.
3. The comments are (and always were) incorrect.
4. The comments are vague and imprecise.
5. The comments are correct, but incomplete.
6. The comments cannot be understood by anyone else.

Indeed, it is this aspect of comments that makes them so potentially dangerous. A comment that gives incorrect or misleading information about the program statement it accompanies is probably worse than no comment at all; a comment that is redundant (e.g., a comment that says "now we are moving A to B" accompanying the COBOL statement MOVE A TO B) will probably so discourage the maintenance programmer that he won't bother looking for useful comments elsewhere in the program. Indeed, it is not surprising that some experiments have shown that it is faster and easier to fix bugs in someone else's program by first removing all the comments.

Unfortunately, many programmers seem to write comments as personal messages to themselves, that is, to remind themselves of the purpose of the particular instruction or program statement they used. The personal note, though, may be completely indecipherable to anyone else, and even the original programmer may have difficulty understanding the meaning of the comment (as well as the statement that it accompanies, of course) at some later time. An interesting example of this occurred several years ago when a lone superprogrammer single-handedly developed a FORTRAN II compiler for a well-known computer manufacturer. After he tested the compiler and turned it over to his manager, the programmer disappeared for several days,[4] during which time the manager discovered that there were some bugs that required immediate attention. The junior programmer assigned to find and fix the bugs discovered, to his horror, that the entire compiler contained only *one* comment, which accompanied an octal constant in the following manner:

```
CONST23:      3443        ; R.I.P.L.V.B.
```

Since the superprogrammer had a reputation for brevity as well as brilliance, the junior programmer began to think that perhaps this single comment would unlock all of the mysteries of the compiler. After several hours of pondering the meaning of the comment, he finally hit on the answer—the number 3443, in octal, is equivalent to the number 1827 in decimal. Being a classical music fan (recall the earlier list of characteristics of a good programmer) and a collector of trivial information, the junior programmer happened to remember that 1827 was the year Beethoven died! As one might imagine, the programming manager was quite unamused by all of this, and when the superprogrammer reappeared, he was asked to take his inestimable talents elsewhere.

Use of Assembly Language When a High-Level Language Will Do Just As Well. Assembly language programming seems to be a fetish among many of the so-called sophisticated programmers; the disease seems especially prevalent among undergraduate computer science students. Indeed, in the programming caste system that exists in many organizations, assembly language programmers seem to rank highest.

However, it must be remembered that assembly language programs are almost invariably more difficult to test than high-level language programs;

---

[4]It was later discovered that the superprogrammer had read in his local newspaper that a Harvard undergraduate student had ridden every New York City subway line (including all branches of the IRT, IND, and BMT lines) on a single subway token in a record time (since nobody had ever done it before) of 48 hours. An MIT graduate himself, the superprogrammer saw a chance for some healthy intercollegiate rivalry; so he wrote a program to calculate the fastest possible path through the subway lines, and organized a team of friends to attack the problem in a scientific fashion. The program, written in LISP and using some very complex heuristic algorithms to solve what amounted to a variation on the travelling salesman problem, ran out of memory on the night before the team was to travel to New York and attack the subways. Faced with a choice of optimizing an individual subway line, or "suboptimizing" the entire transit system, they chose to partially optimize their entire route. It was never determined whether the program actually worked, for after 27 hours on the subways, one team member fell asleep at a critical subway stop; as the other team members raced back into the train to retrieve their comrade, their connecting subway left without them—and they ultimately lost to the Harvard student by 5 minutes. Needless to say, the programming manager was not amused by all of this.

there are many more subtle ways for the unwary programmer to get himself into trouble. For most of the straightforward business and scientific applications, high-level languages are quite adequate; indeed, there is a growing feeling that even *systems programs*, e.g., compilers, assemblers, operating systems, etc., should be written in a high-level language.

For applications where extremely efficient coding is necessary, there may indeed be an argument for using assembly language. On the other hand, it often makes better sense to write an initial version of the program in FORTRAN, COBOL, or PL/I, determine which portions of the program require the greatest optimization, and then rewrite those portions in assembly language.

Multitasking, or Asynchronous Execution. Multitasking is one of several current "buzz-words" used to describe techniques that allow the programmer to initiate and control the execution of several different *tasks* within one application. It is a useful and important concept, especially in the real-time and on-line applications that are becoming more prevalent today.

However, because it allows the programmer to take on some of the functions normally performed only by the operating system (i.e., the concurrent execution of programs), it makes testing *much* more difficult. Unless you are writing an on-line or real-time application where efficiency is of the greatest importance, it is best to stay away from this concept; for other applications of multitasking, such as the overlapping of IO and computation in a batch program, you should convince yourself that the savings in machine time will be worth the extra 10–15% in testing time before committing yourself to a multitasking approach.

Shared Files Within a Multiprogramming Environment. Another difficult aspect of multiprogramming is the concept of shared files. Virtually all third-generation computer systems permit multiprogramming; indeed, they encourage it. Most also allow concurrently executing application programs to access the same files under reasonably well-controlled conditions.

Once again, we must realize that while this is a powerful concept, it is also a potentially dangerous one. For example, some operating systems allow one program to read a file while another is updating it. Figure 1.1 illustrates one of the potential problems that can occur: If one program is reading two or more logically related records while another program is updating them, the first program may receive inconsistent information.

Misuse of Instructions. A devious computer programmer can usually find some way to pervert, or misuse, any machine, any programming language, or any operating system. He will find a feature which, though not documented in any of the vendor's literature, seems to work for his application—and presumably saves a few microseconds and/or a few storage locations. On

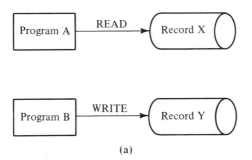

(a)

The problem begins when program A reads record X;
it will then read record Y. Meanwhile, program B has
begun updating record Y; it will then update record X.

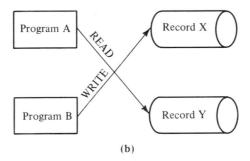

(b)

At this point, program A has read record Y and
has become very confused. Note that it has
read an "old" record X and a "new" record Y.

Figure 1.1. Shared-file problems in a multiprogramming environment.

many second-generation computers, for example, programmers could sometimes make use of the "undefined" machine language instructions, i.e., operation codes that were not defined in the assembly language manual and which
often had rather strange and unpredictable results. The IBM 7090/7094 was
one of the classic examples of a machine that could be misused by the programmer in such a way.

While most third-generation computers have eliminated these undefined
instructions, it is still possible for the programmer to misuse the instructions.
On some machines, for example, the programmer will use a "floating-point
normalized" instruction to find the first one-bit in a bit-map; others will find
some obscure use for unused bits in the computer's "program status word";
others may take advantage of the fact that a program accidentally sets a hardware condition code the first time through a loop, but not on subsequent
passes through the loop.

High-level-language programmers are not immune to such antics. Consider, for example, the following sequence of FORTRAN coding:

```
DIMENSION A(20), B(30)
    .
    .
    .

    DO 10 I = 1,50
10  A(I) = J
    .
    .
    .
    .
    .
```

In this case, the programmer has discovered that the two arrays are placed next to each other when the compiled FORTRAN program is loaded into memory. As a result, his DO loop passes entirely through the A array and falls into the B array, thus saving the overhead of a second DO loop to initialize the B array. While it *does* work on some machines (I first discovered it on CDC 6400 FORTRAN while preparing this book), and while it *does* save some CPU time and some memory, it should be considered as a perversion of the FORTRAN language.

FORTRAN lends itself to a few other perversions as well. On some older versions of FORTRAN, student programmers in a few universities discovered that the following sequence of coding would produce rather interesting results:

```
ASSIGN 10 TO I
    .
    .
    .

I = 12345
    .
    .
    .
    .

GO TO I
    .
    .
    .
```

Unless the FORTRAN compiler manages to flag this as an error (which most compilers do now), the GO TO statement would cause control to be transferred to memory location 12345. Such a trick was often quite useful for providing alternate entries into a subroutine.

COBOL programmers have also been known to misuse their language. One of the more common COBOL perversions is to use a record area as working storage after a file has been opened, but before it has been used—or conversely, after the input/output on the file has been finished, but before the file has been closed. COBOL and FORTRAN programmers alike have a tendency to assume that all variables, data-names, tables, and arrays will be initialized to zero before their program begins.

All of this is not only useless, but dangerous. The programmer will spend an inordinate amount of time forcing the machine (or the programming language, or the operating system) to obey his perverse commands, and will probably destroy the program logic.

Programs that Modify Themselves. We shall comment on this form of programming malpractice several times in subsequent chapters. Figure 1.2 illustrates a simple case of program modification; some programmers manage to carry this concept to incredible extremes. For example, instruction *A* (at the beginning of the program) may, under certain obscure conditions,

Figure 1.2. A COBOL Program that modifies itself.

```
         .
         .
         .
         .
    ALTER SWITCH1 TO PROCEED TO SWITCH2.
         .
         .
         .
         .
SWITCH1.
    GO TO INITIALIZATION-ROUTINE.
         .
         .
         .
         .
SWITCH2.
    ALTER SWITCH3 TO PROCEED TO SWITCH4.
         .
         .
         .
         .
```

Note: If these statements are scattered throughout a large program, it becomes extremely difficult to tell what the program is doing. In addition, it may prevent the program from being reentrant or serially reusable, as will be discussed again in Chapter 5.

change instruction B (in the middle of the program), which, in turn, modifies instruction C (at the end of the program). If the programmer is truly fiendish, he may arrange to have instruction C modify instruction A. The resulting program displays a remarkable chameleon-like effect and is almost impossible to debug.

Sharing Variables and Temporary Storage Among Many Subroutines. Many high-level languages allow the programmer to declare common blocks of temporary storage, and this can be a useful concept when working with large arrays, working storage areas, etc. The same concept is often used in assembly language programs: Two subroutines will often share the same memory locations for their temporary calculations. In many cases, this practice of sharing memory locations is a little more subtle than it looks. In FORTRAN, COBOL, and PL/I, for example, the programmer often uses the same variables I, J, and K for several different purposes within the same module.

As Fig. 1.3 illustrates, the practice of sharing storage locations works only as long as the two modules are independent of one another, i.e., as long as one subroutine does not call another, there will be no problem. However, the logical relationship of the subroutines (or paragraphs or sections within a COBOL program) may change during the implementation and testing of the entire program. Thus, it is very possible that subroutines that once cooperated with each other suddenly begin to have conflicts; these bugs are often *extremely* hard to find!

Even if the two subroutines are logically independent, there may still be a temporary storage conflict. As Fig. 1.4 illustrates, two subroutines executing in a multiprogramming environment may interrupt one another and destroy temporary storage locations. Since these interrupts are based on the timing characteristics of the system, these bugs are even more difficult to find

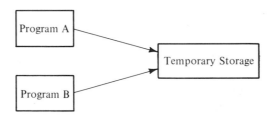

Program A and program B can share the same area of temporary storage as long as they are logically independent of one another That is, as long as A does not call B, and vice versa, there will be no conflict.

Figure 1.3. Sharing temporary storage between programs.

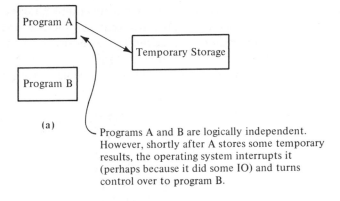

(a)

Programs A and B are logically independent. However, shortly after A stores some temporary results, the operating system interrupts it (perhaps because it did some IO) and turns control over to program B.

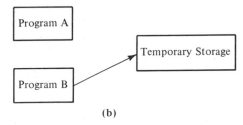

(b)

Program B now begins executing and, unaware that A had been interrupted, stores its own temporary results. When A regains control, its variables will have been destroyed.

Figure 1.4. Temporary storage conflicts in a real-time system.

(e.g., the problem occurs because, on rare occasions, one program's disk record is read *slightly* before the other's, or because one program receives its terminal input a millisecond before the other one does).

To avoid this problem, it is a good idea to give each module or subroutine its own temporary storage areas. This is a natural practice in a language like PL/I or ALGOL, but it often requires some conscious thought in FORTRAN, COBOL, and assembly language. Only when large amounts of memory can be saved (e.g., several hundred elements in an array) should storage be shared between different routines.

Complex Macros in Assembly Language Programs. Most of the medium-sized and large-sized computers have fairly sophisticated macro assembly languages. If you are not familiar with macros, please forget about this section for the time being; at this point, ignorance is bliss. If you *are* familiar with macros, you should try to use them in a limited, straightforward manner. Avoid nested macros, recursive macros, and macros which redefine themselves; these are interesting in graduate computer science courses, but they are of limited usefulness in the real world.

If you *must* use macros (to generate extremely complex tables or queue structures, for example), then it is imperative that you include several comments in the vicinity of your macro definition. You should also carefully examine the source code generated by the macro; if you define an *extremely* complicated macro, you may even find that the assembler does not process it properly.

Programs with an Excessive Number of GO-TO Statements. Whether in a high-level programming language (FORTRAN, COBOL, PL/I, etc.) or assembly language, an excessive number of GO-TO statements, or unconditional branch statements, makes a program extremely difficult to debug. Such programs tend to lack any recognizable structure or flow of control. Instead of a program based on GO-TO statements, the programmer should consider an organization based on decision tables, subroutines, or the BEGIN-END block structures that are found in PL/I and ALGOL.

Table 1.2 shows some statistics from a FORTRAN program that seems to use an excessive number of GO-TO statements. Note that while the overall average of GO-TO statements in the program is an astounding 24.2%, it is even higher in some of the larger subroutines and the main program. To make matters worse, most of the GO-TO statements are somewhat "random" in nature, that is, they branch several pages forward or backward in the program listing, so that it is extremely difficult to follow the logic of the program. As a result, the program took an extraordinarily long time to code and was very difficult to debug—and, in fact, it still does not work properly.[5] As a contrast, it is interesting to note that Knuth[6] has found that in the average FORTRAN program, only 13.0% of the statements are GO-TO statements.

In some cases, the excessive use of GO-TO statements is caused by sloppy programming. For example, one often sees the following sequence of FORTRAN code:

```
         .
         .
         .
      IF ( X .EQ. 0) GO TO 20
      A = 17
10    CONTINUE
         .
         .
         .
20    A = 23
      GO TO 10
```

[5] For a deeper analysis of this very interesting program, see "Measuring the 'Goodness' of a Computer Program," Edward Yourdon, *ACPA Thruput*, April 1972.

[6] "An Empirical Study of FORTRAN Programs," Donald E. Knuth, *Software—Practice and Experience*, Volume 1, Number 2 (April–June 1971), pages 105–133.

Table 1.2. ANALYSIS OF A BAD FORTRAN PROGRAM

	Main Prog.	Subroutines										TOTALS
		HDNG5	MESSET	MSFLD	CHECK	DSTCT	STTRPT	ANA	HDNG6	HDNG7	TWEEK	
Total cards in program	1354	54	346	78	141	152	128	170	39	49	67	2578
Total comment cards	626	27	159	45	61	60	58	74	16	19	38	1183
Blank comment cards	351	8	70	24	53	28	36	47	8	9	17	651
Nonblank comments	275	19	89	21	28	32	22	27	8	10	21	532
Cards with FORTRAN statements	728	27	187	33	80	88	70	96	23	30	29	1395
Declarative cards (COMMON, etc)	204	14	14	5	24	25	17	27	14	15	12	371
Cards with executable statements	525	13	173	28	56	63	53	69	9	15	17	1024
IO Statements (READ,WRITE)	25	6	0	0	14	11	5	15	5	6	3	90
DO Statements	27	0	26	5	2	1	3	5	0	0	2	71
IF Statements	67	3	3	4	12	7	7	8	1	2	3	117
GO-TO Statements	141	2	49	8	24	10	10	11	1	3	4	263
Assignment Statements (RETURN, etc.)	251	4	90	13	12	38	28	32	2	4	4	478
Control Statements	13	1	3	1	2	5	3	2	1	1	4	36
CALL Statements	14	0	0	0	0	2	4	5	0	0	0	25
Computed GO-TO Statements	2	1	1	0	0	0	0	0	0	0	0	4
Total executable statements	540	17	172	31	66	74	60	78	10	16	20	1084

Interesting statistics

46.0% of all cards in program were COMMENT cards.
55.0% of the comment cards were blank.
26.6% of all noncomment cards had declarative statements.
73.4% of all noncomment cards had executable statements.
8.3% of the executable statements were IO statements.
6.5% were DO statements.

10.8% were IF statements.
24.2% were GO-TO statements!
44.0% were assignment and computational statements.
3.3% were control statements.
2.3% were CALL statements.
0.4% were computed GO-TO statements.

which could be rewritten in the following way:

```
          .
          .
          .
     A = 17
     IF  (X .EQ.  0)  A  =  23
```

to tighten up the logic of the program and, incidentally, save two GO-TO statements. Note that the same example could have been developed in COBOL, PL/I, or ALGOL, though it is more likely that a programmer using one of the latter languages would avoid the entire problem by writing something like

```
          .
          .
          .
     IF X = 0 THEN A = 23 ELSE A = 17;
          .
          .
          .
```

Aside from these examples of simple inefficiencies, the really dangerous use of the GO-TO statement is in branching into areas of "common code." For instance, our original FORTRAN example is more likely to be written in the following way:

```
          .
          .
          .
     IF ( X .EQ. 0 )  GO TO 20
     A = 17
10   CONTINUE
          .
          .
          .
20   A = 23
     GO TO 30
          .
          .
          .
30   CALL  GRUMP(I,J,K)
     GO TO 10
          .
          .
          .
```

That is, when writing the code at statement 20, the programmer suddenly discovers he wants to do the same thing that was already being done for some other reason at statement 30. Thus an extra GO-TO statement is inserted, and the programmer congratulates himself for having saved two statements in his program. Unfortunately, it is now much harder to follow the logic of the program. In addition, the programmer may eventually forget that the code at statement 30 is also entered from the code near statement 20, and when he makes what appears to be an innocent change to the code at statement 30, the entire program may fall apart.

To avoid this problem, some organizations have gone to the extreme of forbidding the use of GO-TO statements in the application programs. While this is highly impractical in FORTRAN (because of the weakness of the logical IF statement and the lack of a block structure), it is feasible in COBOL and almost a natural programming approach in PL/I and ALGOL.

In the meantime, since you are probably not prepared to relinquish your beloved GO-TO statements completely, you should at least be aware that a program based on random, haphazard GO-TO statements is more difficult to debug than a program based on subroutines, decision tables, or some other modular structure. We will expand upon some of these ideas again in Chapter 4.

Nonmnemonic Variable Names. Finally, we should mention the distressing lack of imagination shown by most programmers when it comes to choosing names for variables, statement labels, file names, and record names. This includes those programmers who use the names of their girl friends or four-letter words (sometimes interchangeably) for various names. It is amusing to see the COBOL programmer who arranges his entire program so that he can write the one statement

    ADD GIN TO VERMOUTH GIVING MARTINI.

or the FORTRAN programmer who writes

    000000 = 2 + LOG(3*000000) = 000000

where all of the 000000 variables are distinct and unique variable names—but indistinguishable because the high-speed printer prints the same graphic for the *letter* o and the *number* 0.

More commonly though, we find that the programmer uses one-character variable names such as I, J, and K, or perhaps meaningless abbreviations such as ORK37. With languages like COBOL, PL/I, and ALGOL, it is possible for the programmer to define names that are 15, 31, or 63 characters long. As long as the programmer is not too lazy or clumsy to do a little extra keypunching, these languages should provide ample opportunity for reasonable mnemonics. Contrary to the heated feeling of some programmers, there is really nothing wrong with a subroutine named INITIALIZETHEPROGRAM or READTHEINPUTCARDSAND-CHECKFORERRORS.

1.2.3 Minimize Maintenance Costs

Any program that is worth anything at all will be around for a long time. There are a significant number of IBM 1401 programs, for example, that were originally written in the early 1960s. They have subsequently been simulated, emulated, and generally beaten into the ground on IBM 7040/7044s, 7090/7094s, System 360s and System 370s, but the original form and logic has remained virtually unchanged. There are even a few IBM 650 programs, originally written in the mid-1950s, that are still running today. On the other hand, there are a few programs—often scientific and engineering applications—that are truly used once or twice and then thrown away. However, these are extremely rare and should be considered as the exception rather than the rule.

Whether you, as the original programmer, continue to maintain your program, or whether you turn it over to someone else, the fact remains that there will almost always be ongoing development and maintenance. It has been only recently that data processing organizations have begun realizing the magnitude of this effort: a recent survey showed that the average American organization spends 50% of its EDP budget on maintenance.[7] Another informal survey taken by a major computer manufacturer in England suggested that a program written by an individual programmer was generally maintained by ten generations of subsequent maintenance programmers before being discarded and rewritten.

There are several aspects of the maintenance problem, some of which can be solved by proper design and some of which can not. The major problems facing a maintenance department seem to be the following:

1. Programs that are put into maintenance still have a significant number of bugs; so what is called maintenance is really just a continuation of the testing effort. This seems an obvious point, but it is often ignored. What is happening is that the maintenance programmers are suffering from the sins of the original programmers.
2. There is the continuing problem of upgrading the program for new compilers, new operating systems, and other new system software. It is not likely that this problem will cease in the immediate future.
3. Most significant programs require continuing maintenance to meet the needs of an evolving user community. There are very few programs that are so well-defined that they need never change.
4. When maintenance changes are required, the original programmer has often disappeared.
5. We face a basic problem that people generally don't like to do maintenance. It is not considered very glamorous work, often doesn't rate the same pay

[7]"That Maintenance Iceberg," *EDP Analyzer*, October 1972.

schedules, and suffers from the obvious frustrations of trying to fix up someone else's sloppy work.

6. A very basic problem is that most people have great difficulty understanding other people's code. Perhaps this is because most programmers seem to evolve their own personal programming style; a larger part of the problem, though, is that many programmers write their code in a relatively disorganized style.

7. The documentation that accompanies most programs is awful. Some experiments have indicated that maintenance programmers would be better off by first removing all of the comments that accompany a program, and *then* trying to find a bug or implement some improvements. Clearly, many organizations are now paying the price for poor documentation standards in the past.

It is obvious that good program design cannot solve *all* of the problems of maintenance; nevertheless, it is equally clear that such problems would be reduced drastically if we were able to design, code, and test programs more adequately. In any case, it suggests that when we write a program, we should plan things so that the maintenance work will be as simple as possible. As we do this, we should keep in mind that our program will almost certainly be maintained by someone else.

Most of the suggestions found elsewhere in this chapter and in subsequent chapters of this book should be of great help for the maintenance programmer. Presumably, if a program is easy to test and debug, it will be relatively simple to maintain—whether by the original programmer or someone else. The most important ideas in this area are the following:

1. Structured programming (as discussed in Chapter 4) or some form of modular programming. It is extremely important to avoid a random program organization; it is not clear that the *original* programmer can even understand such a program, but it *is* clear that most maintenance programmers cannot.

2. Simplicity of programming style is extremely important. As you program, keep asking yourself, "Would a typical maintenance programmer understand this?" Avoid the egotistical attitude of, "Any decent programmer ought to be able to understand this . . . ." Don't forget that the maintenance programmer may not be as brilliant as you are.

3. "Document unto others as you would have them document unto you." This gem is taken from the excellent book, *The Elements of FORTRAN Style*, by Kreitzberg and Schneiderman (Harcourt, Brace, Jovanovich, 1971).

Of course, if all programmers followed these suggestions (as well as the suggestions elsewhere in this book), we would have very few maintenance problems; the fact that they do *not* follow such suggestions is the major cause for maintenance headaches. This suggests that we may actually be dealing with a management problem: A program should not be accepted by the maintenance department until that department decides it is adequate. This is perhaps the greatest failing in many EDP organizations—as long as the program still has bugs in it, it might just as well be worked on by the programmers who know its characteristics, rather than dumping it on programmers who don't want it and don't understand it. Thus, before accepting a program for maintenance, there should be some verification that it has been adequately tested, adequately documented, written according to reasonable programming standards, and *accepted* by both the users and the maintenance department.

Many other suggestions concerning maintenance could be given, but they tend to fall into the category of "management suggestions," an area generally outside the realm of this book. On the other hand, it may be helpful to give some suggestions to those unfortunate programmers required to maintain a program that has *not* been adequately designed, tested, or documented. Such an activity is often referred to as maintaining "alien" code. The following suggestions may be helpful:

1. Study the program before you get into "emergency mode." Get to know it fairly well. If possible, find the original author of the program; try to get as much background information about it as possible. Ask him for any unofficial documentation that might exist.

2. Try to become familiar with the overall flow of control of the program; ignore the coding details at first. It may be very useful to draw your own high-level flowchart at this point, if one doesn't already exist.

3. Evaluate the reasonableness of the existing documentation. Insert your own comments into the listing if you think they will help.

4. Make good use of cross-reference listings, symbol tables, and other aids generally provided by the compiler and/or assembler. Make up your own tables if necessary.

5. Make changes to the program with the greatest caution. Respect the style and formatting of the program if at all possible. Don't change the program just for the sake of changing it, e.g., don't rewrite a whole subroutine just to eliminate one or two apparently useless instructions. *Always indicate, on the listing itself, which instructions you have changed.*

6. Don't eliminate code unless you are sure that it isn't used.

7. Don't try to share the use of temporary variables and working storage that already exist in the program. Insert your own local variables to avoid trouble.

8. Keep detailed records of the changes you have made, the bugs you have fixed, and the improvements you have made.

9. Avoid the irrational urge to throw the program away and rewrite it. Instead, keep good records to show the amount of effort that you have invested in maintenance, and try to extrapolate into the future. Make a reasonable effort to estimate the amount of time that it would take you to rewrite the program—and remember that your program will also require maintenance!

10. *Do* insert error-checking all around the code you are inserting, as well as around existing code wherever it looks reasonable to do so.

1.2.4 Flexibility—Ease of Changing, Expanding, or Upgrading the Program

Despite everyone's best intentions, most programs are changed during their lifetime. The requirements and specifications stated by the user or the customer are rarely "frozen," and you should always assume that your program will eventually have to be modified so that it will be bigger, faster, more extensive, etc.

This is a very difficult point to impress upon new programmers. Quite often, the junior programmer will argue that he is writing a "quick and dirty" program, one that he doesn't intend to keep around for any length of time. While this is sometimes true, it is nevertheless like an architect telling his client that the building he is designing is not intended to be permanent, but rather just a "quick and dirty" edifice. This analogy is not quite as extreme as it sounds: A number of shoddy wooden barracks and Quonset huts were erected during World War II and are still being used, much to the irritation of the present inhabitants.

To judge whether a program is easy to change or upgrade, you and your manager should constantly be asking yourselves, "What happens if we want to expand this table?" "What if we want to define new transaction codes someday?" "What if we have to change the format of that output report?" "What if someone decides to provide input to the program from a teletype instead of the card reader?"

In most cases, it is not difficult to discover what questions to ask; one simply has to attack a program with the philosophy that *everything* is liable to be changed, expanded, or modified. Thus, you simply have to train yourself to look at *every* program module, *every* subroutine, *every* table, and *every* data area with an eye toward its eventual revision. Of course, it may be rather difficult deciding how to best write the program with these considerations in mind. There are certainly some tradeoffs to be established, and you may need guidance from your manager or your analyst (if you find yourself completely indecisive in this area, your psychoanalyst may be of more assistance than your systems analyst) before deciding to implement an extremely general and flexible approach. On the other hand, a very large number of the problems that occur in this area could have been avoided with a trivial amount of work at the beginning of the design of the program. Hopefully, some of these problems will become clearer in the next few chapters.

1.2.5 Minimize Development Costs

One of the most important characteristics of a program is the ease with which it can be originally programmed. We recall from the experiment performed by Sackman *et al.* that the coding time and the testing time were the two areas that showed the widest variation among programmers. In most cases, the actual *elapsed project time* is the most critical factor—every day of delay in getting the program implemented incurs additional costs for the programmer salaries, overhead, and administrative support, as well as possible penalties or lost business on the part of the ultimate user of the computer program. We would also like to be able to develop computer programs that require a minimal amount of *machine time* for compilations, test shots, and so forth.

In addition to these considerations, a programming manager should be aware that on many medium-sized and large-sized programming projects, the key programmer may decide to leave rather abruptly—to get married, to avoid getting married, to have a baby, find another job, travel around the world, or various reasons. Thus, the manager should always ask himself whether each programmer is developing his programs in such a way that someone else could take over on short notice; obviously, a good programmer will always be asking *himself* the same questions.

Once again, this is simply a *philosophy*; putting it into practice is usually not too difficult if you keep it in mind at all times. It is a habit that programmers working for software houses and consulting organizations are usually forced to learn rather quickly: There is always the danger (or the opportunity, depending on one's point of view) that he will be reassigned tomorrow. For the success of the project, and in some cases the company, it is therefore necessary to always ensure that someone else can take over the work. For someone working in a more sanguine and stable job environment, this may seem an unnecessary precaution to take; however, most programmers *do* want to move on to the next project within a year or two, and the easiest way of ensuring that the program can be turned over to a new programmer is to design it from the beginning with that in mind.

As with so many of the other suggestions in this chapter, I would not be surprised to hear you complain that your program is so small and simple that you should not have to worry about such considerations. Remember that, if your program is of any value whatsoever, it will be around for a while. So even if you do manage to finish coding and debugging the program, someone else will eventually have to take it over for maintenance and/or revisions (and for the continuation of the debugging process, which usually goes on ad infinitum). One of the best ways of impressing this upon a programmer is to given him someone else's program to maintain, debug, or modify; if done early enough in his career, it can have a strong and beneficial effect on his programming habits.

1.2.6 Simplicity of Design

In a number of industries, manufacturers have discovered that the product with the smallest number of moving parts is often the most reliable. This maxim certainly holds true in the computer hardware business: Terminals, tape drives, card readers, and other peripheral devices with a minimum number of moving parts are likely to be more rugged and reliable.

All other things being equal, the same is true of software: The simple, straightforward approach, with a minimum number of esoteric features, is usually the most "solid." For example, given a choice between using a recursive, nested macro or straightforward assembly language, you would usually be better off with the latter; given a choice between a very tightly coded COBOL program with an intricate series of ALTER statements and GO-TO statements instead of PERFORMS, versus a slightly longer, slightly slower, but more straightforward COBOL program, you would be better off with the latter. Given a choice between a complex PL/I structure and a more simple one, you would be wise to choose the latter.

One can draw a simple analogy with cameras. An expensive Leica or Nikon camera has the potential to take better pictures, but a simple Kodak Instamatic or Polaroid camera is better in many ways: It is more rugged and can withstand being dropped on the floor or thrown against the wall; it still works after your daughter pours Coca-Cola on it; and you can take it to the beach without worrying about sand clogging up its inner works. Most important, it takes just as good a picture as the Leica for 90 % of the pictures that the average photographer wants to take.

The concept of simplicity is, to a large extent, implied by the previous sections of this chapter. That is, the most logical way, and in some cases, the *only* way, to make a program easy to test, easy to maintain, easy to upgrade, and easy for someone else to take over is to keep it simple and straightforward.

1.2.7 Efficiency

This area is normally considered by most programmers as the most important characteristic of a program. Many programmers, including some of the most talented and experienced, will spend hours, or even days, trying to speed up a subroutine by a few microseconds, trying to make the subroutine one instruction shorter, or making an array one word smaller. In many cases, it really isn't worth the effort.

If speed really is an important consideration, then you should attempt to speed up your program in a reasonable way. Rather than trying to make *every* subroutine optimally fast, you should concentrate on those subroutines that are executed most often. In many cases, it will be impossible to make such a determination until after the program has been written, because the nature of execution may depend on the type of input data received by the program, or on the manner in which the program is used by the customer. Thus, the best approach may be to write the program in straightforward FORTRAN or COBOL, gather statistics on the running program, and then *rewrite* the critical portions in assembly language.

Similarly, if you are attempting to save memory, you should attempt to go about it in a reasonable fashion. It is worthwhile attempting to eliminate buffers of several thousand characters or huge 5000×5000 arrays, but it is usually not worth spending much time on the smaller items. If memory space is a critical factor, then the suggestion made above should be followed:

Write the program in a reasonable and straightforward way, and *then* determine where the greatest savings can be made. If this is not feasible, you can sometimes estimate in advance which sections of your program will be the largest and, therefore, the most amenable to improvement.

This is not to suggest that you should write *stupid* code. It is fairly easy to identify a number of straightforward techniques that will lead to reasonably efficient programs without a great deal of work; this "bag of tricks" should solve the problem of writing efficient programs for most cases, and the tricky rewriting of subroutines should be left for the most critical cases. It is worth noting that Knuth's study of FORTRAN programs found that approximately 50% of the CPU time was consumed by 5% of the source statements in the program.[8]

In this area of efficiency, it may be desirable for the programming manager to try to establish a tradeoff between programmer time and computer time. For example, a number of studies have shown that the average programmer can generate about 10–20 debugged statements per day; other studies have shown that when a change is made to a working program, there is only a 50% chance that the changed program will work. If a programmer earns $12,000–$14,000 per year, then his total cost, including overhead, is close to $100 per day. Thus, you and your manager should ask yourselves whether you will actually save $100 in machine time by spending an extra day trying to speed up your program. This can be rather dangerous, however, for it may illustrate to your manager how overpaid you really are if you have a reputation for devoting a great deal of time and energy to this area; his solution may be to give you a reduction in salary!

1.3 Some Concluding Remarks About the "Goodness" of Computer Programs

All of the discussion in the preceding section has been rather *qualitative* in nature. While we have indicated that a program should be easy to test and debug, we have not indicated *how* easy or how we should go about measuring it. More important, we have said nothing of the tradeoffs between the various desirable characteristics of a program that were outlined in the previous section, that is, will a 10% increase in the efficiency of a program necessitate a 20% increase in the testing time?

Ideally, we would like to be able to assign a number V to a program to indicate its value or "goodness." V would be computed from the formula

$$V = a_1 \cdot (\text{testing costs}) + a_2 \cdot (\text{programming costs}) + \ldots + a_7 \cdot (\text{efficiency})$$

[8]"An Empirical Study of FORTRAN Programs," Donald E. Knuth, *Software— Practice and Experience*, Volume 1, Number 2 (April–June 1971), pages 105–133.

where the coefficients a_i would be chosen by the manager (or the programmer) for each program. The numbers involved should be normalized, so that V would have a value between 1 and 100; this would allow us to judge the effectiveness of the program and, of course, of the programmer who wrote it.

For some applications, efficiency might be of overriding concern; in judging that one program, then, the coefficient a_7 would be significantly larger than the other ones. In other cases, we might want to heavily weigh testing costs, flexibility, or ease of maintenance.

All of this sounds quite nice, but at the current time, it won't work. In some cases, we have no way of comparing two programs with respect to the desirable characteristics that were discussed above; that is, it is very difficult for me to say that my program is 3.14159 times more flexible than yours. I *can* say that my program is 6.7 times faster than yours, or that it is 3.2 times smaller, or that it took 2.78128 times less time to test it. On the other hand, none of these numbers can be computed before the program is written. We are not able to look at two flowcharts and predict which of them will take longer to code, longer to test, more CPU time, or more memory (at least not with any precision). We have no way of comparing a given program against an *absolute*—that is, we seem to be unable to calculate that a given program is 3.2 times slower than the fastest possible program for this application. Finally, as Sackman demonstrated so vividly in his experiment, we do not know how to compare two programmers—unless we give them the same program to work on!

In short, we really know very little about programs and programmers that can be quantified or measured; most of what we know consists of guidelines and philosophies. Some work *is* being done in this area, but there are no results to report yet. In the meantime, the best we can do is to pass on our experience to other programmers and hope that a Galileo or Newton will someday come along to organize that advanced state of witchcraft we call computer programming.

PROBLEMS

1. Give your own definition of a good programmer. Should the qualifications that are necessary to be hired as a programmer be the same as the ones to be considered for a generous salary increase?

2. How do you think your manager defines a good programmer? Is his definition significantly different from your definition? Is he aware of your definition? Have you discussed this area with him?

3. What are the distinguishing talents of the best programmer you have ever known? Do you think these talents can be taught or transferred to others? Do you think some of these talents come from experience? Or are they inborn?

4. How can one measure the "goodness" of a computer programmer? What are the weaknesses and limitations of using "number of debugged source statements per days" as a measure?

5. Give your own definition of a good computer program. Can such a program be achieved under normal working conditions?

6. How important do you consider efficiency to be in a program—relative to such characteristics as maintainability, etc.?

7. Find some output from at least one computer-generated bill (from the local telephone company, the tax bureau, etc.). Is it obvious that the indicated charges (especially taxes, finance charges, service charges, etc.) are correct? Indicate what you would have done to make the correctness of output obvious to the casual observer.

8. In addition to the reasons listed in this section, can you think of any other reasons (or excuses) for *not* providing documentation on the program listing?

9. (An experiment) Find a reasonably well-commented program with which you and several colleagues of approximately equal programming ability are *not* familiar. A good example of such a program might be a vendor-supplied program, package, operating system, or compiler. Decide upon some change to make to the program, e.g., an improvement, a new feature, or a bug to fix. Give one group of programmers an uncommented version of the program with which to work; the other group should work on the version with the original comments. Keep statistics and a diary with which to draw some conclusions about the *real* usefulness of comments in a program listing.

10. Write a program that can analyze a source program, and indicate the density of comments (e.g., number of comments per source statement, or per subroutine, or per module). Analyze a reasonably large sample of programs, e.g., all of the programs in your organization's library or within the vendor's library. What is the average density of comments? What variations do you find between different programs? (The author would be interested to see any statistics that are gathered in this fashion.)

11. Other than efficiency, can you suggest any good arguments for using assembly language instead of a high-level programming language? If so, try to rate the importance of these considerations.

12. Are programmers with assembly language experience and knowledge considered better programmers in your organization than those who know only a high-level programming language? Are they paid a higher salary? Do you think this is fair? How much recognition is given to those programmers who know two or more high-level languages?

13. If your computer system provides some kind of multitasking capability (e.g., with the ATTACH macro on the IBM System/370), find out how much CPU time overhead it causes. For what kind of programming situation is this overhead justified? Describe a possible application where the multitasking capability *could* be used, but where its use would be uneconomical.

14. List three reasons why multitasking functions might easily cause increased testing problems. If in doubt, consult *Design of On-Line Computer Systems* (by Edward Yourdon, Prentice-Hall, 1972) or *Design of Real-Time Computer Systems* (by James Martin, Prentice-Hall, 1967).

15. Describe another problem that can be caused by two programs accessing the same file at the same time. If in doubt, consult Chapter L of Edward Yourdon's *Design of On-Line Computer Systems.*

16. Describe five devious, perverse, illegal, and immoral programming practices in FORTRAN. Can you think of any situations in which these programming practices might be justified? In the situations where you have seen them used (or used them yourself), have you seen adequate documentation to warn the unwary maintenance programmer of the precise nature of the code?

17. Describe five devious, perverse, illegal, and immoral programming practices in COBOL. Can you think of any situations in which these programming practices might be justified? In the situations where you have seen them used (or used them yourself), have you seen adequate documentation to warn the unwary maintenance programmer of the precise nature of the code?

18. Describe five devious, perverse, illegal, and immoral programming practices in PL/I. Can you think of any situations in which these programming practices might be justified? In the situations where you have seen them used (or used them yourself), have you seen adequate documentation to warn the unwary maintenance programmer of the precise nature of the code?

19. Describe five devious, perverse, illegal, and immoral programming practices in ALGOL. Can you think of any situations in which these programming practices might be justified? In the situations where you have seen them used (or used them yourself), have you seen adequate documentation to warn the unwary maintenance programmer of the precise nature of the code?

20. Describe five devious, perverse, illegal, and immoral programming practices in assembly language. Can you think of any situations in which these programming practices might be justified? In the situations where you have seen them used (or used them yourself), have you seen adequate documentation to warn the unwary maintenance programmer of the precise nature of the code?

21. Extend the source program analyzer described in problem 10 above to examine a program for the perverse programming techniques mentioned in problems 16–20. Analyze several programs within your organization's program library to see how common these practices are; compare this with an analysis of programs written by your vendor; compare that with programs supplied by your computer's user association (e.g., SHARE, DECUS, CUBE, etc.). Do you think that such an analysis should be a necessary prerequisite before a programmer is allowed to put his program into a library?

22. What kind of standards should be developed concerning programs that modify themselves, e.g., with the ALTER statement in COBOL? Is it reasonable to completely forbid such statements?

23. Find three examples in programs you have written (or, if that should prove too embarrassing, find someone else's program) in which some variables were used as temporary storage by two or more portions of the program. Did this cause any problems? Why did you write the program that way—to save memory, or just out of laziness?

24. Discuss those features of FORTRAN which encourage or discourage the programmer from sharing the same areas of memory for temporary storage.

25. Discuss those features of COBOL which encourage or discourage the programmer from sharing the same areas of memory for temporary storage.

26. Discuss those features of PL/I which encourage or discourage the programmer from sharing the same areas of memory for temporary storage.

27. Discuss those features of ALGOL which encourage or discourage the programmer from sharing the same areas of memory for temporary storage.

28. Discuss those features of assembly language which encourage or discourage the programmer from sharing the same areas of memory for temporary storage.

29. Rank the five languages above in decreasing order of "safety" of preventing a programmer from carelessly using the same variable or memory for temporary storage in two or more modules.

30. Can the strict imposition of programming standards eliminate this problem of sharing areas of working storage?

31. Is it possible to develop a preprocessor (or analyzer) that could examine a program to see if it was sharing temporary storage areas? If so, how difficult would it be to write? Is it worth the effort?

32. (An experiment) Try to write a macro that is legal (according to the vendor's assembly language manual) but sufficiently complex that it
    (a) causes the assembler to go into an infinite loop or abort.
    (b) causes it to generate incorrect code.
    If you were successful, then:
    (a) send a trouble report to the vendor.
    (b) apologize to the operations staff.
    (c) discuss the possible practical applications of your complex macro.
    In any case, try to determine how much CPU time was spent *in the assembler* as it attempted to expand the macro and generate object code.

33. Write a program to analyze the type of statements used in a program (see the discussion of Knuth's program in Section 1.2.2). Use it to analyze a large sample of programs in your organization. Some of the areas you might investigate are:
    (a) How many GO-TO statements are used in the average program?
    (b) Does there appear to be a significant variation between different programmers in the use of different kinds of statements?
    (c) Does there appear to be a significant variation between different programming languages in the use of fundamental types of statements (e.g., GO-TO statements and subroutine-calling statements)? That is, are there

more GO-TO statements in the average FORTRAN program than in the average COBOL program?

(d) Does there appear to be a strong correlation between the number of GO-TO statements and

    (1) the efficiency of the program (often an excuse for using the GO-TO statement)?

    (2) modularity?

    (3) the number of test shots that were required to make the program work properly (What? You don't know how many test shots are required? See Chapter 7.)?

    (4) adequacy of documentation?

34. Section 1.2.2 discusses a simple FORTRAN example and concludes that some GO-TO statements could be eliminated by writing such code as

```
        .
        .
        .
    A = 17
    IF (X .EQ. 0) A = 23
        .
        .
        .
```

What are the possible disadvantages of this approach? Do you think that this type of programming style should be encouraged as a *standard* for FORTRAN programmers? Why or why not?

35. Extend the source program analyzer described in problems 10 and 21 to analyze the length of variable names and other labels in the programs written in your organization. There are two related areas you should investigate:

(a) What is the average length of the labels? Does it vary significantly from one programmer to another?

(b) Some programming languages—notably FORTRAN and many assembly languages—restrict the length of a variable to six or eight characters. How much of this label capacity is used by the programmer? For instance, if his labels have an average length of four characters, and if the maximum is eight characters, then he has used 50% of his label capacity. Is this significant?

36. Do you think it is reasonable to require that all labels have a minimum length of N characters? What is an appropriate value of N? Is it possible to extend the source program analyzer discussed in problems 10, 21, and 35 above to indicate violations of this minimum label length? Is it desirable?

37. In 1971, I had the opportunity to discuss the question of meaningful labels and mnemonics with one of the programmers working on some critical simulation programs for the NASA Manned Spacecraft Center. His feeling was that variables, subroutine names, and other labels should *not* be given "meaningful" names, because they might be misunderstood or misinterpreted by a subsequent maintenance programmer. As a result, he purposely chose such names as QRK17, GLOP42, and ZYX123—none of which had any relationship to the variable or subroutine being named. His feeling was that the maintenance programmer would then be forced to carefully study the program to learn the true meaning of the labels. Do you agree with this philosophy? Do you think it has any advantages?

38. How much of the data processing budget in your organization is devoted to maintenance? How many programs are currently under the supervision of a maintenance department? What is the oldest program in your library? (Don't be surprised if this information is not immediately available when you ask the appropriate authority. Many organizations simply do not know how much they spend in this area.) Does this tell you anything about the importance of maintenance and the importance of writing programs in such a way that they can be maintained more easily?

39. (An experiment) Find a willing colleague and choose two problems from any chapter in this book that require writing a program. You should take one of the problems; your colleagues should take the other. Each of you should proceed until you have reached one of the following milestones:
   (a) Top-level design has been completed (see Chapter 2 for a more detailed discussion of "top-down" programming).
   (b) Detailed design has been completed.
   (c) Coding has been finished.
   (d) The program assembles (or compiles) with no fatal errors.
   (e) One test case works properly.
   At this point, you and your colleague should swap programs, that is, you should attempt to complete the program begun by your colleague, and he should attempt to do the same with yours. Keep careful notes on the problems you encounter as you attempt to complete your partner's unfinished program. What could he have done to make your job easier? What could you have done to make his job easier?
   A variation: Begin working on the two problems as described above, but do *not* decide in advance when the programs should be swapped. A third party (an arbitrator) observes the progress of both programs and, without prior warning, orders the swap to take place at a point when it appears that it will cause the most confusion (thus simulating a common situation in the programming industry!).

40. Write a short essay *against* the concept of designing and writing simple programs. Do you sincerely believe in what you are writing?

41. Pick one small section of "clever" or extremely sophisticated code that you have written; it should be fairly short—no more than a page long. Show the program to five of your brighter colleagues and record the length of time until each has
   (a) indicated that he understands your code.
   (b) successfully made a nontrivial change or improvement to your program (a change which should be specified by you).

Is there a great discrepancy between the best and worst effort by your colleagues? Does this tell you anything about the virtues of simplicity?

42. Write a short essay giving your own ideas about:
   (a) How we ought to measure the quality of a program.
   (b) Why we can't do it now.
   (c) What work must be performed in order to develop a reasonable set of "metrics" for programs.

2

TOP-DOWN PROGRAM DESIGN

2.0 Introduction

Now that we have discussed some of the characteristics of a good computer program, it seems appropriate to ask: *How should we go about designing a program*? Is there some orderly process by which we can organize the solution to a programming problem and put it into a form that will be recognizable to the computer as well as to the maintenance programmer?

The theme of this chapter—and, indeed, of much of this volume—is that there *is* such a rational approach; the EDP profession refers to this approach as a *top-down* design. It is an intuitively appealing approach, and it has been discussed several times in the literature over the past several years. Some of the other names that have been used for top-down design are "constructive programming" (in Wulf [1]), "programming by stepwise refinement" (in Wirth [2]), "systematic programming" (in Wirth [3]), and "hierarchical design" (in Constantine [4]).

Indeed, it is interesting to see that many data processing organizations have made their own private attempt to develop what could be referred to as a "canonical form" for program *design* (a canonical form for internal logic organization, known as structured programming, is discussed in Chapter 4). These organizations have realized that many of their applications perform similar types of processing, and therefore they should have the same form and structure. Thus, some organizations have said, "All of our programs have an initialization module, a basic set of READ/WRITE modules, a processing module, and a set of termination routines; hence all of our programs should be structured so that these modules take on a recognizable form."

The result of this is often a directive to the programmers that their programs must take the form shown in Fig. 2.1; it is the lower-level modules (represented by X, Y, and Z in Fig. 2.1) that distinguish one application from another. Other organizations have gone even further and said, "All of our commercial applications consist of an edit (and sort) of transactions, followed by an update of the master file, followed by the printing of one or more reports; therefore, all of our programs should have a form where these modules are recognizable." Thus, the programmers are told that whatever they do must fit into the overall structure shown in Fig. 2.2. Once again, it is the low-level modules X, Y, and Z that distinguish one application from another.

Other EDP organizations have not been so fortunate as to find that all of their applications fall into such a narrow category. Nevertheless, they have

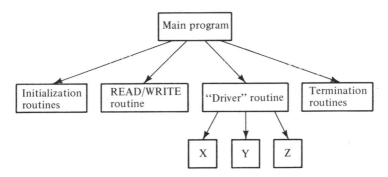

Figure 2.1. A standard form of program organization.

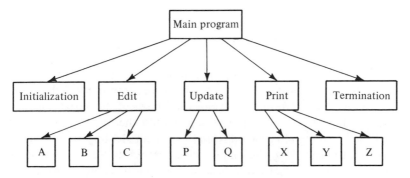

Figure 2.2. A standard form for commercial programs.

attempted to formalize the design of their programs, acting on the belief that most of their programs are *somewhat* similar, even if not as nearly identical as the edit-update-sort-print variety shown in Fig. 2.2. In a more general sense, these organizations have attempted to encourage their programmers to follow what has variously been called "mainline design," "design by explosion," and so forth.

To a large extent, the design methodology that we propose in this chapter is similar to these ad hoc methodologies which have been developed by individual organizations to cope with their specialized applications. The basic philosophy behind top-down design can be applied to *any* application; in special cases, it may take the form shown in Fig. 2.1 or Fig. 2.2. Rather than issuing the edict that "All programs written in this organization *must* fit into the edit-update-sort-print framework," it is important that we understand the underlying principles behind such a canonical form. Without these underlying principles, the lower-level module may be designed randomly by the programmer, resulting in a Frankenstein product whose "intelligent" top structure has been arbitrarily joined to a disorganized, poorly designed body of the program. Since the body of the program usually represents the major part of the coding, it is important that we allow the ideas that were begun in Fig. 2.1 and Fig. 2.2 to be carried into the lower levels of the program structure.

This concept of top-down design is discussed in more detail in the next section. Following that, we discuss the related concepts of *top-down coding* and *top-down testing*. It should be recognized that all of these ideas are being presented as *philosophies*, or *strategies*—but strategies that can hopefully be used as tools in program design. It is important to realize that they are not universal laws of nature, nor are they to be considered the ten commandments of some new religion. Indeed, common sense will dictate some variations from the basic principles of top-down design in special cases. Some of these variations are discussed in Section 2.4. Finally, a case study is presented in Section 2.5 to illustrate the principles.

2.1 Top-Down Design

One of the natural approaches to program design is the *top-down* approach. Though called by such names as "systematic programming," "hierarchical program design," and "design by explosion," most of the variations on top-down design have the same objective: to identify the major functions to be accomplished, and then to proceed from there to an identification of the lesser functions that derive from the major ones. Though the basic philosophy is quite simple, there are many ramifications, as will be shown below.

2.1.1 The Basic Concept of Top-Down Design

Indeed, the basic concept of top-down design *is* simple—at least in theory. Consider a program—any program; let us call it GLOP. We begin designing our program by imagining that we have a machine with a hardware instruction that will perform GLOP (an idea that is not beyond the realm of possibility with today's microprogrammable computers!). Thus, to write program GLOP, we merely write the instruction

```
GLOP
```

and we are done! Not only are we finished, but we are relatively certain that the resulting program is correct—assuming that the hardware primitive GLOP performs correctly (and if it doesn't, we can always blame it on the vendor).

Unfortunately, there are not many machines in current use that have a GLOP instruction; thus, we must break the problem, and hence the program, into slightly smaller pieces. We realize that the performance of GLOP consists of some initialization, some computation, and some concluding activities (e.g., closing of files, printing of summary reports). Thus, we rewrite our GLOP program as

```
INITIALIZEGLOP
PERFORMGLOPCOMPUTATIONS
TERMINATEGLOP
```

where INITIALIZEGLOP, PERFORMGLOPCOMPUTATIONS, and TERMINATEGLOP may again be thought of as primitives in the hypothetical machine upon which we are programming. The process then continues: each of the above operations is broken into smaller primitives until we finally define primitives that are small enough and simple enough to be implemented easily on a *real* machine.

2.1.2 An Example of Top-Down Design

To further illustrate the concept of top-down design, we will proceed through a few steps in the design of a management information system that is often referred to as a *financial model*. Consider the dilemma of a manager trying to decide whether he should enter a new business. He wants to know how much profit he will enjoy each month, how much cash he will have to invest in the business before he begins to make a profit, and so forth. All of this must be based on some estimate of the number of salesmen that will be employed by his new business; the number of customers that can be acquired by those salesmen; the revenues that will be generated by those customers; the costs associated with manufacturing, distributing, and servicing the product; and so forth. All of this can be programmed into what amounts to a *simulation* of a new business.

For a brief description of such a simulation of a time-sharing service bureau business (in which the author came to the conclusion that one time-sharing system would lose money regardless of the number of customers it had!), see reference 5. A more precise specification of the problem is given in Appendix A of this volume. This problem has been used in several programming courses throughout the United States, Europe, and Australia, and well over 35 different project teams have attacked it in a variety of ways.

Suppose we were to design and write such a program according to the specifications in Appendix A; for lack of a better name, we have decided to call the program MONEY. Our first step, as we saw above, is to imagine that there is a machine whose machine language repertoire includes a MONEY instruction. To write the program, then, we simply write

    MONEY

Since this is not likely to get us very far in the real world, we must carry our design one step further. It occurs to us that, in order to perform the financial simulation desired by the manager, we must have some *input parameters* that specify such things as the manager's estimates of the number of salesmen, the productivity of the salesmen, the revenue to be expected from each customer, etc.; indeed, Appendix A lists some 48 different input parameters. In fact, we notice from the specification that the manager may want to vary some of the parameters much in the fashion of a FORTRAN DO-loop—he may want to examine the profits and cash flow with 5 salesmen; he may then want to examine the situation with all other parameters held constant, but with the number of salesmen increased to 10; he may wish to repeat the calculations again with 15 salesmen, and so forth until, say, 50 salesmen are reached.

Thus, we can imagine that our program begins by performing some initialization work (the precise nature of which is not known at this point). It will then read the parameter cards which must be edited to ensure that there are no catastrophic errors. Assuming that this is the case, we should perform our basic calculations (e.g., of customers, revenue, costs, and profit); the calculations should be repeated as long as we can generate more permutations of input parameters. This gives us the program shown in Fig. 2.3(a). Unfortunately, many students in the author's programming courses have objected to the program being shown in ALGOL, so we are often forced to show it in COBOL, as in Fig. 2.3(b)—and, of course, one can see just how significant the differences are at this stage!

Where do we go from here? Ideally, we would like to have a machine upon which all of the statements in Fig. 2.3(a) or Fig. 2.3(b) could be implemented as primitives, but it is obvious that we have several stages of design

Figure 2.3(a). Top-level logic for the MONEY program.

```
COMMENT this is the main program;
BEGIN
INITIALIZETHEWORLD;
READPARAMETERCARDS;
EDITPARAMETERCARDS;
IF CARDSAREOKFLAG THEN
    WHILE MOREPARAMETERSTOWORKONFLAG
        BEGIN
            PRINTREPORTS;
            EVALUATEPARAMETERS;
        END;
ELSE PRINTERRORMESSAGE;
FINISHOFFEVERYTHING;
END;
```

Figure 2.3(b). COBOL Version of top-level logic for MONEY program.

```
MAIN-PROGRAM SECTION.
PERFORM INITIALIZETHEWORLD.
PERFORM READPARAMETERCARDS.
PERFORM EDITPARAMETERCARDS.
IF CARDSOKFLAG = 1 THEN
    PERFORM PROCESSCARDS
        UNTIL MORECARDSFLAG = 0
ELSE
    PERFORM PRINTERRORMESSAGE.
PERFORM FINISHOFFEVERYTHING.
STOP RUN.
```

to go before we will find such a machine. Thus, we must continue in the same fashion. Each of the statements in Fig. 2.3(a) or Fig. 2.3(b) must be thought of as an abstraction, which we must now attempt to realize in lower-level primitives. However, it does not always make sense to do this in strict sequential order, as can be seen in this example: We don't yet know what things need to be initialized, so it makes no sense to "refine" the INITIALIZE statement. We *can*, though, try to expand the READPARAMETERCARDS statement, since it appears likely that we will have to read all 48 cards and store them in a table of some kind for future use.

Similarly, the PRINTREPORTS primitive that was shown in Fig. 2.3(a) and Fig. 2.3(b) can be expanded in the form shown in Fig. 2.4(a) or Fig. 2.4(b). Note that we are performing all of the basic calculations on a monthly basis, starting in month 1 and proceeding until we reach a month where, according to the specifications, we are supposed to stop. At that point, we invoke another primitive, EVALUATEPARAMETERS, to see if there are any more permutations of parameters left to be evaluated.

It is of particular interest to see how the students in my programming courses proceed at this point; it should be pointed out that most such students have experience in the EDP field ranging from 2 years to 15 years. For the most part, they accept the top-level structure suggested by Fig. 2.3(a) [or Fig. 2.3(b)] and Fig. 2.4(a) [or Fig. 2.4(b)] as a reasonable starting point. With this suggested *beginning* to the problem, they retreat into their workshop sessions to develop a complete design and implementation of the problem.

Naturally, their attention is drawn to the calculations in the BASIC-CALCULATIONS primitive, for it is there, as they all point out, that the

Figure 2.4(a). Expansion of top-level coding in Fig. 2.3(a).

```
PROCEDURE PRINTREPORTS;
BEGIN
INTEGER I;
FOR I: = 1 STEP 1 UNTIL N47 DO
    BEGIN
        CALCULATESALESMEN(I);
        CALCULATECUSTOMERS(I);
        CALCULATEREVENUE(I);
        CALCULATECOSTS(I);
        CALCULATEPROFITLOSS(I);
        PRINTOUTPUT(I);
    END;
END PRINTREPORTS;
```

Figure 2.4(b). Expansion of top-level coding in Fig. 2.3(b).

```
PROCESSCARDS SECTION.
    PERFORM BASIC-CALCULATIONS VARYING
        T FROM 1 BY 1 UNTIL T GREATER
        THAN N47.
    PERFORM EVALUATEPARAMETERS.
    EXIT.
BASIC-CALCULATIONS.
    PERFORM CALCULATESALESMEN.
    PERFORM CALCULATECUSTOMERS.
    PERFORM CALCULATEREVENUE.
    PERFORM CALCULATECOSTS.
    PERFORM CALCULATEPROFITLOSS.
    PERFORM PRINTREPORTS.
    EXIT.
```

"meat of the problem" lies. Since the first item within BASICCALCULA-TIONS is CALCULATESALESMEN, it naturally occurs to them that they should, in fact, determine how to calculate the number of salesmen in the corporation. A quick glance through the specifications tells them that a certain number of salesmen will be employed when the hypothetical company begins operation; additional salesmen will be hired in subsequent months until some maximum number of salesmen are on the payroll; and finally, it is specified that a certain percentage of the sales force can be expected to quit in any given month.

For some reason, the students' attention seems to be drawn to the portion of the specifications dealing with salesmen who quit. The fact that it is a *percentage* who quit makes a strong impression on many; they point out that this means that, unless careful precautions are taken, a *fraction* of a salesman might quit. Since salesmen are assumed to be human beings, and since human beings are assumed to be integers, it naturally occurs to the students that there might be some terrible problems if their financial model allows 3.14159 salesmen to quit at the end of the first month of business. This tempts many into suggesting that any fraction of a salesman who wants to quit in month N should be carried over into month $N + 1$, when he can be combined with some other fraction of a salesman—thus forming a whole salesman who can be allowed to leave the company. Naturally, this leads to some discussion as to the means of representing the number of salesmen in the program. Should it be single precision floating point, double precision floating point, or integer? What about truncation problems? Should all salesmen-oriented calculations be rounded?

While the whole situation might appear rather ludicrous, it has often been the case that programming teams spend *hours* arguing about this part of the programming exercise. In fact, the argument often extends to the problem of programmers and other employees in the company who might, under certain conditions, be fired from the company. Once again, there is the question: How do we deal with a fraction of a programmer? How can we fire 2.78128 programmers? Indeed, if one has the appropriate political inclinations, he can go so far as to argue that programmers ought not to be fired at all! After two hours of heated debate on this topic, I found that one of my programming groups had gotten into a debate on Eastern religions and alternative forms of social organization; they were not to be tempted back into a discussion of such mundane things as programming until the next day!

The fact that, in a financial simulation, the user is not likely to care about fractions of programmers does not seem to occur to these students; the idea that the number of programmers (or salesmen) could be truncated, rounded up, or rounded down does not seem to occur to them. The possibility that the user will be dissatisfied no matter which approach they take and request a change (e.g., rounding up instead of rounding down) apparently has not occurred to them. Of course, the fundamental point is this: *Whether the number of salesmen is kept as a single precision floating point variable is utterly irrelevant at this stage of the design*! At some later point, it will obviously have to be specified, but that is the least of the design problems at this point.

If the programming groups have recognized this point (or, more likely, if they have finally come to some tentative agreement about the nature of the salesmen variable), they continue with their design of the BASICCALCULATIONS algorithm. It occurs to them to try to express the number of salesmen as some kind of mathematical formula, e.g., by writing a FORTRAN-like statement of the form

NUMBEROFSALESMEN = A + B + C + D

Of course, it strikes them very quickly that the number of salesmen in month N is, according to the specifications, a function of the number of customers in month $N - 1$. Hence, to calculate salesmen, it appears to be necessary to calculate customers. Unfortunately, the situation is complicated by the fact that the number of customers is a function of the number of salesmen, which obviously leads to some confusion!

The confusion usually escalates because another programmer in the group is simultaneously attempting to figure out how much revenue will be generated by the hypothetical company in a given month. Attempts to express this in a FORTRAN-like statement of the form

REVENUE = A + B + C + D

lead to hopeless complexity—especially because nearly every programmer seems to have a fanatical urge to perform the entire computation in one incredibly complex statement! This in turn leads to complaints from the students that, "I can't solve this problem because I didn't study differential equations in college." Those who *did* study differential equations in college find it equally difficult to cope with the problem, and their complaint is usually something of the form, "I can't solve the problem because I didn't study accounting and finance in college." Apparently a college degree has its limitations!

It is interesting to note that some groups of programmers never even get to the BASICCALCULATIONS module because they run into difficulties with the EVALUATEPARAMETERS module that was suggested to them as part of the top-down design in Fig. 2.4(a) and Fig. 2.4(b). While they may understand *what* the EVALUATEPARAMETERS module is supposed to accomplish, they often don't understand *how* it can be accomplished; in other words, they can't figure out how to write the module. Since they have no faith in their ability to design the details of the module, they are concerned that the overall design of the MONEY program may be questionable—and they often attempt to cope with this by scrapping the design and searching for an alternative means of doing what the EVALUATEPARAMETERS module was doing (occasionally with such clumsy techniques as arranging the program with 48 nested levels of loops).

This kind of concern about the design of a program is certainly understandable, though it is somewhat surprising that they should have such trouble with EVALUATEPARAMETERS, since it requires only three or four FORTRAN or COBOL statements to be implemented. However, there is another aspect of this design difficulty that I find even more surprising: In some cases, I have suggested to the students that they not worry about the implementation of EVALUATEPARAMETERS—that I will code it for them. All I ask is that they tell me what kind of input they will give my module, and what kind of output they want. The *function* to be accomplished is assumed to be known (but the fact that it is not really understood seems to be the source of the trouble in many cases). I have found on two or three occasions that the programmers have rejected the offer. They have indicated that until they can satisfy themselves that they understand the details of the EVALU-ATEPARAMETERS module, they are not willing to continue with the design. No matter how many times I try to reassure them that the module *can* be coded and that I *will* do it, they are reluctant to continue. "It just doesn't feel right," they say, "attempting to design a program with a module so mysterious that we don't even know how it works."

Obviously, not every group stumbles into all of the problems mentioned above; some even manage to come up with a good solution in a reasonable amount of time. Nevertheless, it is interesting, as well as educational, to see how many difficulties *are* encountered by some of the groups. More than one group has been forced to admit at the end of several days of work that they have no solution at all.

It seems, though, that the concept of top-down design is not so simple after all. Perhaps we should take a closer look at what appeared to be an intuitively obvious principle of design.

2.1.3 A Closer Look at Top-Down Design

As we have seen, top-down design involves breaking a large problem into smaller subproblems that can be dealt with individually. It may be appropriate at this point to make a few important suggestions concerning the successful application of top-down design:

1. The key to successful top-down design seems to be a formal and rigorous effort on the part of the designer to specify the *input*, the *function*, and the *output* of each module in a program or system. Many of the difficulties I have observed in

program design occurred because the designer(s) worked too informally, e.g., "Oh, well, if we need to accomplish *X*, we'll just CALL a module that will do it for us."

2. Once you have convinced yourself that a particular portion of the problem *can* be encapsulated within a module, then try to forget about it, i.e., don't worry too much about *how* it will be implemented.

3. Be especially careful that you don't allow yourself (or a group of designers) to become embroiled in a trivial aspect of the problem.

4. At each level of the design, try to express the implementation of a module in a single page of coding or flowcharting. If a single sheet of paper is insufficient to express the implementation of a module in primitive terms (e.g., in simple COBOL statements), then express it in terms of lower-level modules to be designed at some later stage.

5. Pay as much attention to the design of data as to the design of processes or algorithms. In many cases, the data consists of *interfaces* between modules, and the design of the modules cannot proceed very far until those interfaces have been carefully specified.

Several of these suggestions are discussed in more detail below.

Specification of Interfaces. Previously, we suggested that one of the most important elements of successful top-down design is a formal approach to the specification of inputs, functions, and outputs to be accomplished by a module. As one programming student ruefully told me of his attempt at top-down design in COBOL, "This was my first attempt to do anything with subroutines—and I had the feeling that if I invented a module that could be PERFORMed from the main program, everything would take care of itself."

Obviously, things *don't* just take care of themselves—on the contrary, a sloppy approach to top-down design can give the programmer a false sense of confidence. It is apparently because of this problem that several organizations have made serious attempts to *formalize* the steps of a top-down design. It is interesting that many of these attempts have been buried in project organization guidelines used by EDP project managers to control and organize the overall development of a data processing project. One of the more interesting and widely known examples of such a formal top-down approach is IBM's HIPO system, an acronym for Hierarchical-Input-Processing-Output diagrams. HIPO requires that the overall system structure be shown in an overview diagram of the nature shown in Fig. 2.5(a). Each module in the overview diagram is described further in a diagram of the form shown in Fig. 2.5(b). Additional levels of detailed diagrams can be drawn if required. An even more formal approach to the graphical representation of system structure has been suggested in a recent article by Stevens, Myers, and Constantine [6]. This is not to suggest that HIPO is the only tool to be used, or that Constantine's graphical representation is the only approach. The major point here is that *some* formal (and standardized) approach to the documentation of a top-down design is required; otherwise, programmers and designers have a tendency to be far too informal.

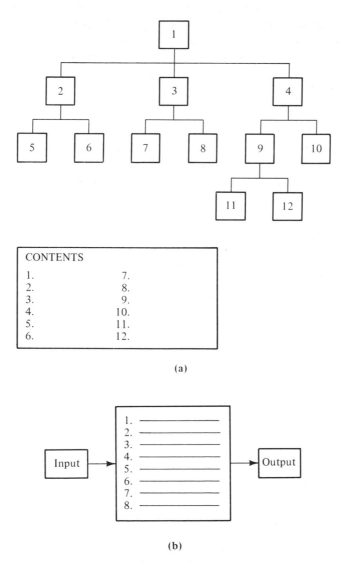

(a)

(b)

Figure 2.5. HIPO Diagrams. (a) An overview. (b) Detailed diagrams. Each item in this diagram may refer to an even lower-level diagram.

It is interesting to note the weaknesses of various programming languages at this point. The COBOL programmer often thinks of interfaces between program modules in terms of the PERFORM verb—and yet the PERFORM verb does not require any explicit argument list. One would think that the FORTRAN programmer *would* be required to formally specify the arguments to be passed to the called subroutine, since the subroutine-calling mechanism is generally of the form

```
CALL GLOP(A,B,C)
```

and yet it is interesting to note how often the FORTRAN programmer passes his arguments through COMMON because he is too lazy to specify the arguments in a formal argument list. Obviously, the same comments can apply to PL/I and other high-level languages as well.

A number of programmers complain that the process of designing a program or computer system *cannot* be treated in such a formal manner, that it is a series of informal fumbling attempts at developing a solution. They often argue that it is an iterative process, that the problems discovered at the second level of design often require a rethinking of the first level of design. Of course, some portions of a design process *are* of this type—nobody really thinks of a complete design in one blinding flash of genius. Especially when the design is being performed by a group of people, we would expect to see some cases of the "two steps forward, one step back" phenomenon; we would expect people to change their minds about their implementation of some module; we would expect the first attempt at developing a design of a program to be somewhat fuzzy and vague. None of this invalidates the basic philosophy of top-down design. After a reasonable amount of informal discussion and brainstorming about the design of a particular level of a program, it is still reasonable to ask that the design be formalized (in terms of inputs, processes, and outputs) before the design of the next level commences. If indeed a problem encountered at the $(N + 1)$th level causes a redesign of the Nth level, so be it; it still seems that this is an organized way of attacking a problem.

Try to Ignore the Details of Lower-Level Modules. It was suggested in the previous discussion that many programmers become involved in trivial details when they should be concentrating on the higher levels of design. It may be appropriate to ask at this point: Why does this problem occur? What can be done about it? Having watched several programming groups flounder in this area, and having asked them *why* they became so immersed in trivia, I will suggest three major reasons:

1. Some programmers find that the trivial details are the only tangible things they can talk about. They find much of the high-level design too abstract, too vague.

Since they have often not had much experience in this kind of design (indeed, one often wonders if they have had *any* experience in program design!), they find it difficult to communicate with one another. At least with the trivial details of the problem, they all agree that they have something to argue about.

2. Many of the programming groups admit that their main problem was one of discipline. Even though they knew that they were wasting their time on a trivial aspect of the design, they found that their attention was continually being drawn to it. In many cases, this reflected a management problem: Nobody in the group was strong enough to insist that the trivial item be postponed.

3. Finally, some groups claim that the success of the entire design may depend on their ability to invent a proper solution to a low-level module. I have heard this comment, for example, from designers of real-time programs: "If I can't be assured that my low-level module X can perform its processing in 43 microseconds, then the entire system is no good." While this may be true in isolated examples, it is usually a somewhat exaggerated fear; in any case, *after* the critical low-level module has been designed, there is no reason why the designer should not return to the top-down approach. What concerns me is that many program designers become engrossed in the design of the critical low-level module and *forget* to return to the overall design of the program or system.

What can be done to solve this problem? In most cases, it is sufficient to repeat the warning of the previous section: Force yourself to carefully and formally specify the interface between the higher-level portion of the program and the low-level module whose existence you have just become aware of, and whose implementation you are concerned about. In most cases, it should become immediately obvious to you that the low-level module *can* be implemented; it may very well have been the fuzziness of the module's definition that caused the problems in the first place. Even if the implementation of the module is not immediately obvious, common sense should tell you whether its implementation is possible by someone other than a superprogrammer. If the implementation looks extraordinarily difficult—or if its implementation is critical, as was suggested in the example of real-time systems above—then perhaps it would be a good idea to pursue its implementation. The key point, again, is that the top-down process should be resumed once you have finished dealing with the difficulties of the low-level problem.

Limit the Size of a Module in Your Top-Down Design. It is also a good idea to limit the extent of your design to a page or so of work at a time. At any stage of your design of a program, you should be attempting to express the implementation of a module whose inputs are known, whose functions are known, and whose required outputs are known. If it is not immediately obvious how to implement the module in thirty or forty primitive statements (e.g., COBOL statements, FORTRAN statements, and PL/I statements), then try to identify the major *subfunctions* to be accomplished. Though you may find it somewhat tedious, it is almost always true that any given module can be implemented in a relatively small number of submodules. Having done this

somewhat informally (just to organize your thoughts), you may wish to
expand each of the submodules so that you end up with a collection of primitive statements and calls to lower-level modules.

For example, suppose we were concerned with the overall design of a
typical program. Rather than getting immersed in a tremendous amount of
detail, we might try to organize our thoughts by writing:

```
CALL  INITIALIZATION
CALL  READINPUT
CALL .EDITINPUT
CALL  PROCESSINPUT
CALL  TERMINATION
```

While the design might appear trivial at this level, it has nevertheless helped
us to organize our thinking—just as it is helpful to write down a list of main
topics before attempting to write a report or memorandum. A somewhat
more critical look at the code we have written above might even tempt us to
write it in the form:

```
CALL  INITIALIZATION
CALL  READINPUT
CALL  EDITINPUT
IF FATALERRORFLAG = 0 THEN
      CALL PROCESSINPUT
ELSE
      CALL PRINTERRORMESSAGE
CALL  TERMINATION
```

At this point, it might occur to us that the process of initialization is
rather trivial; it might involve opening only two files, and initializing FATAL-
ERRORFLAG. Similarly, the termination module might be equally trivial,
being responsible only for closing the two files. Thus, we might feel like
expressing our design in the following form:

```
OPEN  FILEA
OPEN  FILEB
FATALERRORFLAG = 0
CALLREADINPUT
CALL  EDITINPUT
IF FATALERRORFLAG = 0 THEN
      CALL PROCESSINPUT
ELSE
      CALL PRINTERRORMESSAGE
CLOSE FILEA
CLOSE FILEB
```

Note that the example above has violated—in a very fundamental way—
an earlier suggestion of formally specifying the inputs, functions, and outputs

of a module. We have not, for example, formally specified the function of the READINPUT module, nor its inputs, nor its outputs. However, as an abstract example, it illustrates that we can express the overall design of a program in approximately ten lines of primitive statements and calls to lower-level subroutines.

Pay Close Attention to the Design of Data. Finally, it should be emphasized that the design of *data* is just as important as the design of algorithms in a typical design effort. In most cases, we find that the concept of top-down design applies just as much to the design of data as it does to the design of algorithms, though there may be a great deal of variation from one project to another. For example, some project organization guidelines advocate a top-down design of the system modules. At the same time, they suggest that the system designer first identify the *files* that he will require in his system, followed in a separate stage of design by an identification of the records within the files, followed finally by a precise specification of the format of each field within each record.

Similarly, some system designers argue that the major structure of the data base is already known. It is obvious to them, for example, that their commercial application requires a master file, a transaction file, and various other types of files. What remains to be designed, as far as they are concerned, is the relationship of one record to another (e.g., how the file is to be sorted), the detailed contents of each record, and so forth. The fact that the overall file design is obvious is similar to the discovery on the part of many system designers that their program structure is of the standard form shown in Fig. 2.1 or Fig. 2.2.

In a more general situation, though, we must recognize that the data of which we speak consists of the input to the entire program, the output from the program, and the various files, tables, and other intermediate pieces of information that are transmitted from one module to another within the program. We can usually assume that the output has been specified. After all, this is one of the primary functions of the systems analyst who works with the ultimate user of the computer program—and if he has done a good job, the overall function of the program should also have been specified. We are often in a position to tell the user what kind of input he must provide in order for our program to generate the kind of output he wants to see. In any case, it is usually the internal files, tables, and other variables that we are free to design as we see fit.

It would seem that if the top-down design of the program modules is to proceed successfully, some aspects of the data design must be done in *complete* detail at a relatively early stage. For example, consider a payroll system whose overall structure is represented by Fig. 2.6(a). We would assume at this point that both the input and the output for the program have been fully

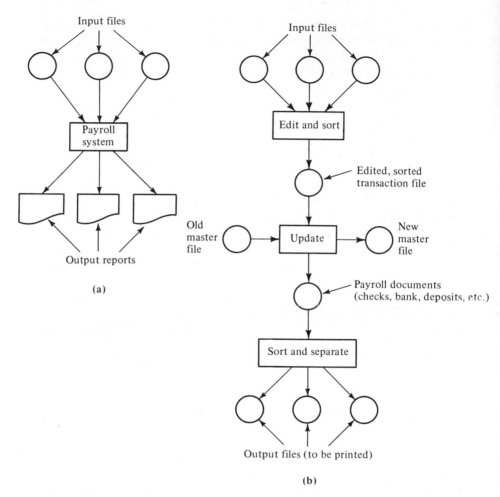

Figure 2.6. Payroll system. (a) Top-level structure for a hypothetical payroll system. (b) An expanded view of the payroll system.

specified—otherwise, we cannot be sure that the user is satisfied with the output or that he is capable of creating the proper input. Furthermore, if we expanded the design of our hypothetical payroll system to the form shown in Fig. 2.6(b), we would assume that the various intermediate files would have to be fully specified, down to the last bit in each record, before the design of the edit module and the update module could proceed any further.

It is important that we see the distinction between *detailed* data design and *inflexible* data design. The major objective of top-down design has been to allow us to break a large problem into smaller problems, *so that each portion of the problem can be dealt with separately.* Thus, in order for the edit module and the update module of our payroll example to be designed separately, we must have a sufficiently detailed description of the interface so that (in theory) the designer of the edit module and the designer of the update module will not have to speak to each other again. However, this does not prevent us from designing that interface in a flexible manner; thus, we might tell the designers of both modules that they should be prepared for new types of taxes, new methods of salary payment (e.g., on a daily basis instead of a weekly basis), and so forth.

2.1.4 Developing Structured Specifications for Design

Having discussed the problems of top-down design for the last several pages, we should conclude by mentioning the largest problem of all: *It is extremely difficult to develop an organized top-down design from incoherent, incomplete, disorganized specifications.* Unfortunately, it often seems that that is precisely the type of specifications we are most likely to receive!

From whom do we typically receive program specifications and system specifications? If they come from a non-computer-oriented user, we probably have no right to expect the specifications to be well-organized; that is part of our job as computer professionals. On the other hand, if we are given a specification by a systems analyst who worked with the user to find out what he really wanted, then we *do* have a right to expect something fairly organized. Indeed, we might almost ask for the specification itself to be presented to us in a top-down fashion.

Clearly, this can be a significant problem. Without intending to insult the large number of competent systems analysts in the world, it should nevertheless be pointed out that the following problems have been observed:

1. Some systems analysts are the result of the well-known Peter Principle: they were excellent programmers and were therefore promoted to the position of systems analyst—a job at which they are incompetent.

2. Some analysts weren't even good programmers, at least not by today's standards. They may have been able to make an IBM 1401 stand on its head and spit wooden nickels, but they may *not* have been familiar with (or even aware of) today's important concepts of top-down design, modular design, structured programming, and so forth. As analysts, their specifications are therefore often a reflection of their previous disorganized programs.

3. Some analysts have had *no* exposure to programming; for example, they may have drifted into the position of systems analyst from a "user-oriented" position. As a result, they may be totally unfamiliar with the program design concepts we have been discussing; they may even be unfamiliar with *any* concepts of logical thinking!

Naturally, one would expect analysts to make similar rude remarks about programmers, and we might expect to find such remarks in a book on systems analysis! Nevertheless, it does seem that the programmer's attempt (or the system designer's attempt) at a good top-down design may be strongly influenced by the nature of the specifications with which he is working.

The first suggestion to be made here, of course, is that systems analysts (and in some cases, perhaps even users) should be made aware of some of the concepts and philosophies of top-down design. This is even more important when we begin discussing top-down testing in Section 2.3. Naturally, this presumes that the analyst has a basic knowledge of computer hardware and programming—a suggestion with which many analysts still seem to violently disagree! In addition, the analyst should help the programmer by providing his specifications in a top-down fashion; in fact most of our discussion of top-down design can be applied to the concept of top-down development of specifications.

It has also been argued rather strongly that specifications should be written in a structured form, as opposed to the usual ambiguous narrative English style. This has even led to the development of "structured English," a form of writing consisting only of imperative statements, IF-THEN-ELSE clauses, and DO-WHILE clauses; this idea goes hand in hand with the structured programming concepts discussed at length in Chapter 4. Meanwhile, other system designers have begun to ask that specifications be documented in the form of decision tables, or with the HIPO diagram approach that we discussed earlier in this section.

2.2 Top-Down Coding

Having discussed top-down design at length, we turn now to a closely related concept: top-down coding. We will first define the concept, then give some arguments in favor of using it, and then discuss some coding details.

2.2.1 Definition

Top-down coding basically refers to the concept of writing code in parallel with the various stages of design of a program. The terminology does not seem to have been standardized yet in the literature. Some use the phrase "top-down programming" to describe what we have called "top-down design"; others use the phrase "top-down programming" to refer to the collective idea of "top-down design," "top-down coding," and "top-down testing." To help avoid some of the confusion, we will use the phrase "top-down coding" to refer to the act of writing code; what we are interested in discussing is *when* that code should be written.

The simplest form of top-down coding suggests that all of the design should be completed before *any* code is developed. Having finished the design, we first write the code for the main program; when that is complete, we write the code for the next lower level, then for the next lower level, and so forth. While this may seem a rather trivial idea, there are some reasonable arguments in its favor, as we will see in the next section.

Most people have something more ambitious in mind when they talk about top-down coding. In its extreme form, it suggests that the top level of the program should be designed—*and then, before any further design is accomplished, that top level should be coded.* The second level of the program is then designed and coded; then the third level, and so forth. Obviously, this means that we are writing code at a point in time when the design is not complete.

As might be expected, the extreme form of top-down coding strikes terror in the hearts of many programmers; it is considered sufficiently radical by most of the EDP organizations that have been exposed to it that they are extremely reluctant to even try it. Nevertheless, there *are* some good arguments in its favor, as we will see in the following section.

2.2.2 Arguments in Favor of Top-Down Coding

The arguments in favor of top-down coding can be summarized as follows:

1. Flowcharts, block diagrams, and other techniques are often a poor means of communicating a design. In many cases, code is more precise, more concise, and more convenient.
2. The act of coding may point out some problems in the design of the lower levels of the program logic, simply because the act of coding generally forces the programmer to think more carefully about what he is doing. It is a good idea to be aware of any such design problems as early as possible, while they can still be easily changed.
3. Top-down coding facilitates top-down testing, the subject of Section 2.3.

Even if the first two arguments were untrue or irrelevant, the relationship between top-down coding and top-down testing would be a strong argument in its favor; indeed, it is usually considered the *strongest* argument in favor of top-down coding. As we will see in more detail in Section 2.3, the concept of top-down testing suggests that we begin testing a program before it has even been completely designed. This allows us to begin exercising the major interfaces between modules, as well as ensuring that the program is basically meeting the user's needs. In order to perform this kind of testing, it is necessary to write the code for the higher levels of design before the lower levels of design have been accomplished.

The other two arguments are considered by many programmers to be equally important. It may be noticed that much of our discussion of top-down design was accomplished using actual code (or, as it is sometimes called, "computer Esperanto") to communicate the design. On the other hand, there are programmers who argue that a *graphical* approach, such as a flowchart or block diagram, has much more impact on the person to whom the design is being shown. The fact that flowcharts often do not convey very much information is perhaps not a reason to eliminate a graphic approach. Perhaps what we need is a more structured approach to the graphical representation of programs, such as the approach taken by Constantine *et al.* in [6].

There may be some argument as to the usefulness of flowcharts for *communicating* ideas; on the other hand, many programmers agree that flowcharts are often a very poor way of *documenting* the structure of a program for the simple reason that flowcharts are rarely maintained with any enthusiasm after the program has been finished. Indeed, most programmers will admit that they rarely bother writing the flowchart until the program has been finished (and then only because the manager insisted on it), so there is no guarantee that there is a one-to-one relationship between the flowchart and the program. On the other hand, it is obvious that the code *is* kept up-to-date as the program undergoes normal maintenance and upgrading.

Thus, our argument is that code *may* be a better means of communicating the design of a program to another person, and that it is almost always a better form of long-term documentation. The ease of communication is especially apparent at the higher levels of design: What the programmer normally describes in the flowchart shown in Fig. 2.7(a) could just as easily be shown in the coding of Fig. 2.7(b). This is often true even at the lower levels

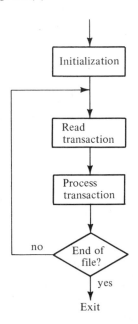

Figure 2.7(a). A high-level flow chart.

Figure 2.7(b). Coding for flowchart in Fig. 2.7(a).

```
      PERFORM  INITIALIZATION.
      PERFORM  MAIN-LOOP  UNTIL
               END-OF-FILE-FLAG  =  1.
      STOP  RUN.
  MAIN-LOOP.
      READ  TRANSACTION-FILE  AT  END
            MOVE  1  TO  END-OF-FILE-FLAG.
      PERFORM  PROCESS-TRANSACTION.
      EXIT.
```

of program logic, *especially if the programmer follows the suggestion of never designing something that requires more than one page.*

It is the opinion of many programmers, including the author, that flowcharts are often a good way of organizing one's thoughts, especially during the formative stages of program design when most of one's brilliant ideas are being scribbled on the back of an envelope or some other handy scrap of paper. Once having organized our thoughts, we should be able to present them to others in the form of neat, tidy code—just as programmers currently communicate their designs in the form of neat, tidy flowcharts. There is good reason to suggest that future programmers may not need flowcharts at all: their first act of design may be to write a few tentative lines of code. In any case, it is probably a very good idea to separate "private" design—the kind of program design done on the back of an envelope—from "public" design. How a programmer approaches his private design should be known only to himself and to God; how he presents his design to a public audience is an entirely different matter.

There is one other aspect of top-down coding that should be discussed briefly. Assuming that we have *designed* the program in a top-down fashion, how should we arrange the code for the various modules in our program listing? For example, suppose we have designed a program as shown in Fig. 2.8(a); we might consider arranging the code in a horizontal manner, as shown in Fig. 2.8(b), or in a vertical manner, as shown in Fig. 2.8(c). If we want an overview of the program, the horizontal approach is likely to be convenient: having looked at the main program, we are likely to want to examine the code for modules A, B, and C—which appear one after the other in the listing. Similarly, having examined module B, we are likely to be interested in modules B1, B2, and B3,—all of which appear together.

From a debugging or maintenance point of view, the vertical approach may be more convenient. If we are tracing the flow of logic through the program, it is likely that we will want to see the main program, then the code for module A, then the code for module A1, then X, then Y, then Z, then A2,

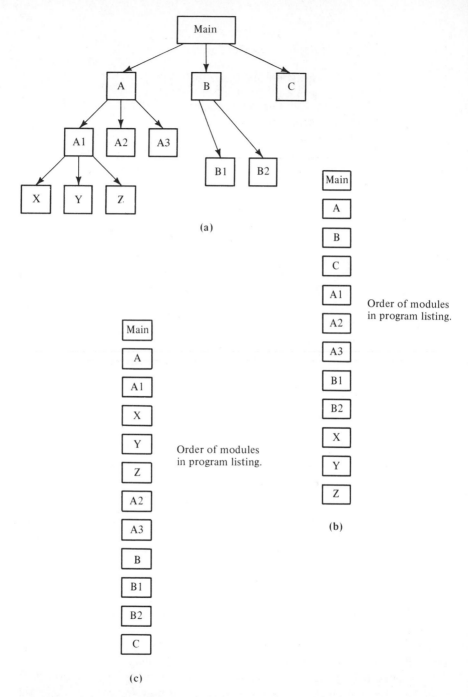

Figure 2.8. (a) A typical program. (b) Horizontal arrangement of modules. (c) Vertical arrangement of modules.

and so forth. If we had arranged the modules as shown in Fig. 2.8(c),[1] the appropriate modules would appear in the proper order.

Of course, the general problem with which we are faced is this: If we are looking at an arbitrary module X somewhere in the middle of our program listing, and we see that module X refers to module Y, how do we know where module Y is located? With the horizontal approach, for example, if we are looking at module B, how can we tell where module B1 is located in the listing? Similarly, if we are following the vertical approach, and if we are looking at module A, how can we find module A3 easily? Various attempts have been made to number modules or to introduce alphabetical prefixes [as has been implied in Fig. 2.8(a) itself], and they generally work if a little common sense is applied. For example, if we know that the programmer arranged his listing in a vertical fashion, then we know that all of the A modules appear in the listing before any of the B modules. We usually don't mind searching through the various subordinate A modules for the one we want. Naturally, this process is simplified if the programmer is consistent in the arrangement of his modules—and even more so if *all* of the programmers on a common project are consistent in their approach.

2.3 Top-Down Testing

The next major concept to be discussed is that of *top-down testing*. As in the previous section, we will begin by describing the nature of top-down testing; we will then discuss its advantages; finally we will discuss some variations on top-down testing that have been practiced in some programming projects.

2.3.1 The Basic Concept of Top-Down Testing

The classic approach to testing, now referred to as "bottom-up" testing, is shown in Fig. 2.9(a), Fig. 2.9(b), and Fig. 2.9(c). The first stage of testing is often referred to as "module testing" or "program testing" or "unit testing"; subsequent stages of testing are referred to as "run testing" or "subsystem testing"; the final stage of testing may be referred to as "system testing," "integration," "user testing," or "field testing." It seems to be regarded as the standard approach to testing in many organizations and has been recommended in a number of programming textbooks and project organization guidelines.

Instead of the usual bottom-up approach, a number of computer scien-

[1] In the study of data structures, this ordering scheme is usually referred to as "preordering." See Knuth's *The Art of Computer Programming*, Volume 1.

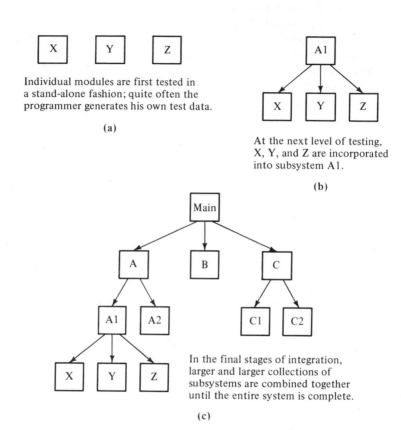

Individual modules are first tested in
a stand-alone fashion; quite often the
programmer generates his own test data.

(a)

At the next level of testing,
X, Y, and Z are incorporated
into subsystem A1.

(b)

In the final stages of integration,
larger and larger collections of
subsystems are combined together
until the entire system is complete.

(c)

Figure 2.9. Bottom-up testing.

tists are now suggesting that testing should be approached in a top-down fashion—in parallel with the top-down design and top-down coding concepts suggested earlier in this chapter. The basic concept is rather simple. As shown in Fig. 2.10(a), we begin with the main program and one or two lower levels of modules. After we have tested this skeleton sufficiently to convince ourselves that the major interfaces are working, we add another level of logic as shown in Fig. 2.10(b). When we have added the last low-level module to the system, as shown in Fig. 2.10(c), we are effectively finished, that is, there is no system testing to be done at this stage.

The top-down testing scheme requires the use of dummy modules, or "program stubs." As shown in Fig. 2.10(a), only the top few levels of the program have been implemented; the lower levels are not present. That is, the higher-level modules are CALLing or PERFORMing low-level modules

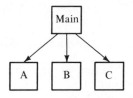

All of the modules *called* by A, B, and C
are dummy modules, e.g., they exit immediately.

(a)

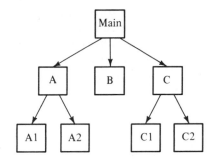

Modules called by A1, A2, C1, and C2 are dummies.

(b)

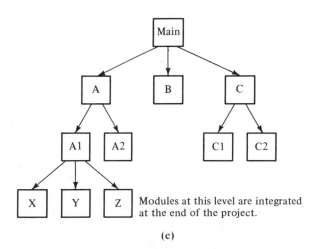

Modules at this level are integrated
at the end of the project.

(c)

Figure 2.10. Top-down testing.

which will be implemented in the following manner:

1. Exit immediately if the function to be performed is not critical.
2. Provide a constant output.
3. Provide a random output.
4. Print a debugging message so that the programmer will know that the module has been entered.
5. Provide a primitive version of the final form of the module. Suppose, for example, that one of the low-level modules is required to compute a square root; the final version would probably be written in assembly language using an algorithm to minimize the number of arithmetic operations required, but the "primitive" version could be clumsily coded in FORTRAN, using Heron's method.

In theory, we could begin the top-down testing with only the main program, and with all lower-level modules implemented as program stubs; in practice, of course, this would be rather clumsy. Common sense will usually dictate the number of levels that must be implemented to form a reasonable skeleton; subsequent testing can then be thought of as adding flesh to the skeleton until the entire program has been finished.

It should be clear that top-down testing is intended to go hand in hand with top-down design and top-down coding. In its extreme form, it suggests that we should design the main program, code it, and test it; then design the next level of modules, code them, and add them to the existing skeleton for testing; and so on until the last level has been designed, coded, and integrated into the program. As we will discuss further in Section 2.3.3, there are a number of variations on this approach that may be required in some projects.

Naturally, it is impossible to perform a *complete* test of the program when it is still in the skeleton form shown in Fig. 2.10(a). However, we *can* begin to exercise the interfaces between the major modules in the program to see that the output from one module is indeed capable of being accepted as input by the next module. When we have added the next lower level of modules, as shown in Fig. 2.10(b), we should be able to perform a substantially more thorough test, since each major module of the program will be capable of carrying out a more complete version of its ultimate function. Our goal at each level of testing is to pass some data through the entire program, so that we can be relatively sure that all of the interfaces are working together.

Figure 2.11 shows an example that illustrates the concept of top-down testing. As we can see, the EDIT module is responsible for accepting four different types of transaction files; its purpose is to edit the transactions for possible errors, and then sort them into a predetermined sequence. The output from the EDIT module (assumed to be a file, though not necessarily so) is input to the UPDATE module; the UPDATE combines the transactions produced by EDIT with records on a master file to produce a new master file. The new master file, in turn, is used as input to another program called SELECT. As its name implies, SELECT extracts various records from the

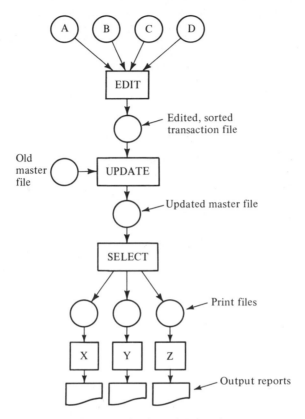

Figure 2.11. An example of top-down testing.

master file, sorts them (possible in different sequences), and generates three output files. For example, the SELECT program might select from the master file all records of type X and sort those records alphabetically. Similarly, it might select all records of type Y and sort them numerically on one key within the record; records of type Z might be extracted and sorted numerically on another key. Finally, some report-writing programs read the output files from SELECT and produce the appropriate reports.

Without knowing anything more about the nature of processing within each of the major modules, we can already begin to plan our top-down testing approach. Every programmer may have a slightly different approach, and obviously common sense should dictate the exact sequence of testing to be done. As an example, though, we might suggest the following seven steps:

1. The control cards for all of the modules, or all of the programs, should be developed. The entire program should be run with null files and null modules, that

is, the EDIT program should exit immediately, as should the UPDATE, SELECT, and print programs. While this may seem a trivial step, generating the correct control cards can be a major problem area on equipment like IBM's System/360 and System/370. For those who argue that this is a trivial operation, our answer is: If it is trivial, we should be able to do it in a few minutes—and since we will have to do it eventually, why not do it now, so we will have a skeleton for the next step?

2. The purpose of the next step is to demonstrate that some input—*any* input—can be passed through the entire program. We might develop enough of the EDIT program, for example (*in a top-down fashion*), to accept only type-A transactions—and only if those transactions have been presorted and have no errors in them. That is, we would expect that none of the editing and sorting functions have been implemented in EDIT, and that it is not even capable of reading type-B, type-C or type-D transactions. Similarly, the UPDATE program should be designed and coded to a low enough level that it is capable of recognizing type-A transactions, as well as reading records from the old master file. We would not expect UPDATE to even recognize other types of transactions, nor would we expect it to process type-A transactions. All it has to do is read type-A transactions and ignore them—as well as reading old master file records and passing them immediately onto the output master file. Similarly, we might be able to write the SELECT program so that it is capable of reading master file records and perhaps selecting type-X records to be sorted (since most computer systems have sort packages available, we might as well implement the sort at this stage). The output from the SELECT program would be read by a dummy version of the report-writing program that would simply dump the records onto the printer.

3. The next step would expand all of the programs so that all types of transactions could be read by EDIT—but only if they were error-free, and only if they had been presorted. Similarly, we would expect UPDATE to recognize all types of transactions and call the appropriate processing modules—but those modules would still be program stubs. Since we would expect the SELECT program to be relatively simple compared to the others, we might have a dummy version of *all* of the report-writing programs, though there would be no urgent need to actually produce the report (assuming that there is no need to show a preliminary version of the report to the ultimate user of the program for his approval).

4. Having gotten this far, perhaps the next step would be to expand the EDIT so that it is capable of sorting the various transactions it reads. We still would not bother actually editing the transactions, which means that any testing would require the programmer to supply "clean" transactions. Similarly, the UPDATE program could be expanded so that it checks the sequence of the transactions.

5. The next logical step would be to develop the code in EDIT to perform all of the editing functions for type-A transactions; type-B, type-C, and type-D transactions would remain unedited. Similarly, we might develop the code in UPDATE to actually process a type-A transaction. It should not be necessary at this stage to make any changes to the SELECT module, and it should still not be necessary to write final versions of the report-writing modules.

6. Having successfully processed type-A transactions, we would then add the code to EDIT and UPDATE type-B, type-C, and type-D transactions.

7. Finally, we could develop the code to write the reports. It may be convenient to do this at some earlier stage if it seems that a simple dump of the output files from SELECT (which was suggested in stage 2 above) is difficult to read.

One of the pleasant aspects of top-down testing is that it can usually be planned in advance, i.e., for most types of programs, it is not too difficult to identify the stages of testing, as we did for the example above. The major point to recognize here is that we can do this planning at the beginning of the project. Indeed, it does not seem very difficult to build a schedule around the testing stages, that is, at the beginning of the project we should be able to assess the extent of work to be done at each stage and determine that stage one will be finished on the first of January, stage two on the first of February, and so forth. Several programming projects have been quite successful in doing this kind of planning.

2.3.2 Advantages of Top-Down Testing

Some programmers find the top-down testing approach intuitively appealing; indeed, some point out that they have been following this approach for quite some time. On the other hand, some organizations find the entire concept rather radical and fail to understand why anyone would want to practice top-down testing. Several programming projects have demonstrated the following benefits of top-down testing:

1. System testing, in its classical sense, is virtually eliminated.
2. Major interfaces of the program are tested first. As a result, major bugs are discovered early in the project, while trivial bugs are discovered toward the end of the project.
3. The users can be given a preliminary version of the program at a relatively early stage.
4. If it is not possible to finish the entire program by the time a deadline has arrived, it is likely that a usable subset of the program will have been finished.
5. It is often much easier to find bugs (i.e., debugging as opposed to testing) with a top-down testing approach.
6. Testing time is distributed more evenly throughout the project, thus eliminating the requirements for large amounts of computer time toward the end of the project.
7. The programmers' morale is improved considerably when they can see the results of a successful test of a skeleton of the final program.
8. Top-down testing provides a natural "test harness" for the testing of lower-level modules.

Elimination of System Testing. It has been observed in several programming projects that system testing can consume between one third and one half of the total project time. It is important to note that very little tangible progress is observed during this period of time—the programmers have demonstrated that their individual modules work (or at least they *claim* that they have done such testing), and yet the overall system does not work. To the non-computer-oriented outsider (e.g., the user, and perhaps management as well), it is not obvious that the programmers are actually *doing* anything during this period.

And while the same outsiders may well feel that programmers *never* do anything constructive, it is a much more serious issue during this "fuzzy" period of system testing. We should remember that system testing has taken as long as two or three *years* on several projects—and during this period of time, the entire project may well be vulnerable to various political calamities, including complete cancellation.

To some extent, this problem can be eliminated with top-down testing. Tangible milestones, with demonstrable results that even the most non-computer-oriented user can understand, can be scheduled at fairly close intervals. Even if the top-down testing approach took as long as the bottom-up approach (which it usually does not), we would still have the advantage of having tangible milestones throughout the testing period.

Major Interfaces Are Tested First. It is obvious tautology that if we had no bugs in our computer programs, there would be no need for testing. We *do* have bugs, some of which are significant and some of which are relatively trivial. It makes sense that, if we have a major logic flaw that could affect the overall design of our program, we should discover it as quickly as possible. If we have a trivial coding error that only affects one module, it matters very little when the bug is actually found. Top-down testing encourages this kind of testing; bottom-up testing does just the opposite.

For example, consider the hypothetical program in Fig. 2.11. In a classical bottom-up approach, one programmer might be assigned to develop the EDIT module, while another is assigned to the UPDATE module. Having defined the interface between the two modules, each programmer could theoretically continue to work without talking to the other. Unfortunately, they might discover after several months of work that they had had a misunderstanding as to the nature of the interface, and this might well mean that the UPDATE module is incapable of reading the output from the EDIT. Though this may seem extreme, it *has* happened in several projects—often after a year or more of work by scores of programmers! In one such major project undertaken by an insurance company in Australia, the entire project had to be scrapped after two years of work because two major subsystems (which had been designed and coded separately and tested in a bottom-up fashion) were totally incapable of communicating with each other.[2]

With the top-down approach, an attempt is made to begin exercising these major interfaces as early as possible. We recall that the first stage of testing with the example in Fig. 2.11 was to ensure that the job control state-

[2]George Mealy, who was deeply involved in the development of some of the early IBM OS/360 software, made a very perceptive remark in this area when he pointed out that the interface between major subsystems of a project usually reflects the interface between the organizations that develop the subsystems.

ments were correct. As we pointed out then, a number of serious problems have been caused by errors at this level. The next stage of testing required a minimal interaction between the EDIT, UPDATE, SELECT, and report-writing programs; the objective at this point is simply to ensure that if the EDIT program is writing 200-character output records, the UPDATE program is indeed capable of reading 200-character input records, not that the data within those records is correct. Similarly, we recall that stage 4 of the testing required the EDIT program to sort its transactions. Since we are presumably passing sorted transactions across the interface to UPDATE, it thus makes sense for UPDATE to *test* that the transactions are indeed sorted. If a bug is discovered within the UPDATE module at a relatively late stage of testing (e.g., in stage 5 or stage 6), we would be relatively confident that it could be fixed without requiring any changes to the EDIT program.

Users Can Be Given a Preliminary Version of the Program. It will be immediately obvious to many programmers that it is highly desirable to show the users a preliminary version of a program during the top-down testing procedure. If the entire project is behind schedule, or if the user is suspicious that it may not be finished on time, a demonstrable preliminary version of the program can be an extremely important public relations tool. Similarly, if the user is not quite sure of what he wants, it may be extremely valuable to show him a preliminary version of the program as early as possible. His reactions may cause a number of lower-level modules to be designed differently than they would otherwise have been.

Of course, it is usually necessary to show the users some *output* in order to convince them that the program is doing what they wanted it to do. Thus, with our example in Fig. 2.11, it would be necessary to develop enough of the report-writing programs to convince the users that the programs were accomplishing a reasonable amount of work. Indeed, many programmers point out that users tend to be extremely finicky about the format of output reports. Having accomplished this, though, we could eventually show them that a particular kind of transaction was processed correctly—long before the various editing functions had been designed or coded. It should be clear from the example in Fig. 2.11 that the influence of users can have a significant influence on the nature of the stages of testing that the programmer plans at the beginning of the project.

Deadline Problems Can Sometimes Be Circumvented. Having conducted courses, lectures, and seminars for several thousand programmers in various countries, I am continually amazed at the number of projects that are developed with a schedule that the programmers consider totally unrealistic. "We've been given six months to do this job," the programmer will say, "when it's obvious that it's going to take at least three years to finish it."

Having worked in a consulting capacity on many of these projects, I tend to sympathize with the programmers; it *is* obvious that the project will take considerably longer than the management has allowed. Regardless of the reasons for this absurd situation, the point is that it *does* occur. A substantial number of projects are organized in such a way that the programmer knows he is six months behind schedule on the day he begins work! Even if the schedule looks reasonable, there is always the possibility that the project may fall behind the projected schedule.

With these potential problems, the top-down approach can turn a major political disaster into a minor political embarrassment. If the user thinks the project will be finished in six months and the programmer thinks it will take twelve months, the significant question is: How much will actually be finished after six months? It is very frustrating to tell a non-computer-oriented user, "I've finished all of my coding, and some of the module testing is finished"; after all, he probably doesn't even know what a module is, let alone what module testing is. On the other hand, if we can tell him, "We can process a type-A transaction, assuming you don't give us any bad input; we'll have the type-B, type-C and type-D transactions finished next month," he can probably understand what we are telling him. Obviously, he will still be unhappy that we did not finish the entire program on schedule, but at least there is *something* that he can use (of course, it requires reasonably good judgment to choose the critical functions to implement first).

Top-Down Testing Makes Debugging Easier. Though it may not be immediately obvious, most programmers find that debugging is considerably easier with the top-down approach. It is very important that we distinguish between *testing* and *debugging* at this point (a distinction that is discussed at greater length in Chapters 7 and 8). We assume at this point that the programmer is aware that his program does not work correctly and that his major difficulty is finding the precise nature and location of the bug.

To understand the problems of debugging, consider the bottom-up example originally shown in Fig. 2.9(a), Fig. 2.9(b), and Fig. 2.9(c). If there are any bugs in the module testing carried out in Fig. 2.9(a), we assume that the programmer will not have any unusually difficult debugging problems. After all, since the programmer is carrying out module testing, he can assume that any bugs he encounters will be in the module he is testing (obviously, this ignores potential bugs in the test data itself, and various other peculiarities that occasionally make debugging a nightmare). However, when we have reached the level of subsystem testing, as shown in Fig. 2.9(b), the situation is considerably more difficult. Suddenly, three or four modules have been thrown together for the first time. If there is a bug in any one of the modules, its nature might not be immediately obvious to the programmer, especially if each module has been written by a different programmer! The fact that any one of the modules may have caused the bug makes debugging that much more difficult—we really don't know where to start looking for the bug. The situation can be even more difficult when we reach the system testing stage shown in Fig. 2.9(c). At this stage, we may have several hundred or even several thousand modules interacting with one another, and any one of them may have caused a bug whose nature may not be immediately clear to the programmer(s). Once again, what makes the situation difficult is the fact that a large number of modules are suddenly being combined for the first time—and if one of them doesn't work, it may not be obvious *which* one it is.

The top-down approach tends to be considerably simpler. In most cases, we are starting from a known skeleton that performs certain functions correctly; our testing consists of adding one new module to the system to see if it works correctly. If, for some reason, the new version of our program does not work, then it is reasonable (though occasionally incorrect) to assume that the difficulties were associated with the new module, or with its interface with an existing high-level module, or in the high-level module itself. The advantage is that of a controlled scientific experiment: We begin with a known quantity and introduce one new element (namely, the new low-level module that is to be tested). If the new version of the program does not work, it is fairly obvious where to begin looking for the problem. In the worst case, we can always remove the nonworking module and retreat to the previous skeleton version of the system!

Better Distribution of Testing Time. A number of programmers and project leaders have expressed some concern that the top-down testing approach might lead to increased requirements for testing time. The reason for the concern is fairly clear: At first glance, it appears that we are performing a full system test every time we add a new module to the existing skeleton of the program. In practice, though, this concern is groundless; in most cases, the top-down approach requires substantially *less* testing time, and in any case, the testing time is distributed more evenly throughout the project.

Top-Down Testing Improves Morale. Programmer morale should not be ignored on major programming projects. It is extremely frustrating to spend several months (or years) designing and coding without seeing tangible results, especially if the project is in danger of being cancelled because the users and/or management think it is too far behind schedule! Even during the testing period of a bottom-up project, progress often seems difficult to measure; as a result, the morale of the overall project often suffers.

In the case of a top-down project, though, we find that there are tangible milestones—and they are achieved at an early stage in the project. All of the programmers (not to mention the users and management) can see that their program has actually accomplished what they promised it would accomplish.

The improvement in morale often leads to harder work to achieve the next milestone, and so forth.

Top-Down Testing Provides a Natural Test Harness. In most cases, it is extremely difficult to test a module in a total vacuum. The module requires input from some other source; it often requires records from a data base; it may require access to various tables, control blocks, and other global data. With the bottom-up approach, the programmer is often forced to *simulate* the environment in which his module expects to operate; this is occasionally done by providing a test harness (see Section 7.8.3 for a more detailed discussion) of module testing.

With top-down testing, the program skeleton provides a natural test harness within which the newly coded module can execute. Of course, the modules *beneath* the new module are still program stubs; nevertheless, we would expect the global environment to exist when our new module begins to execute, and this can make testing considerably easier. Some degree of common sense should be used here. It may make sense to ensure that the new module is at least capable of executing from beginning to end without aborting *before* it has been inserted into the existing program skeleton.

On some occasions, programmers have argued that it is *more* difficult to perform module testing with the top-down approach. Their argument is that the top-down approach requires that test data for a new module be introduced at the beginning of the program, e.g., by introducing the appropriate type-A transactions in our example in Fig. 2.11. In some cases, it may be extremely difficult to generate all of the different types of type-A transactions which will eventually generate all of the different types of calls to our new low-level module. It may be far easier, according to some programmers, to use a test-data generator that is capable of generating all of the different inputs to our new module. There does not seem to be anything wrong with this approach; however, once the module testing has been accomplished with a test-data generator, the new module should still be inserted into the overall program skeleton to ensure that the skeleton is capable of generating input that the new module is willing to accept.

2.3.3   Variations in Top-Down Testing

As we suggested in the previous section, programmers occasionally find it difficult to follow the pure form of top-down testing. We must emphasize again that the approach being suggested here is not to be considered a religion with rigid, unbreakable rules; it should be considered as a *philosophy*, with minor variations as required by individual projects.

For example, we pointed out earlier that the extreme form of top-down testing would suggest that when the main portion of a program has been designed, it should immediately be coded and tested—before *any* low-level modules have been implemented. In practice, this is not likely to get us very far, since it is difficult to make the program do anything when *all* of its modules are program stubs (on the other hand, it may allow us to ensure that our job control cards are correct, which is a worthwhile activity on many projects). In most cases, we require the main program and one or two lower levels to be implemented before any nontrivial testing can be done; this should not be considered a violation of the top-down testing philosophy.

Indeed, the situation may require some portions of the program to be implemented almost completely while other major portions of the program remain as dummy modules. Figure 2.12 illustrates an example. Module A and all of its subsidiary modules have been fully designed, coded, and tested while modules B, C, and D remain as program stubs. One common example of this approach is the development of input/output modules with dummy IO routines; the rest of the program will not be able to do anything at all! Similarly, in the example shown in Fig. 2.11, it appeared that the SELECT module should be developed rather fully, while the EDIT, UPDATE, and report-writing modules were still largely unimplemented.

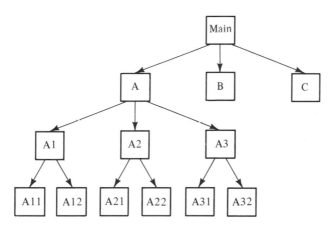

Figure 2.12. A variation in top-down testing.

The same philosophical problem can be viewed in a slightly different way. When we first illustrated the concept of top-down testing at the beginning of section 2.3.1, we used Fig. 2.10(a), Fig. 2.10(b), and Fig. 2.10(c) to show that modules were being developed and tested a level at a time. A number of programmers have interpreted this as meaning that they must proceed *strictly* on a level-by-level approach, that is, they think that *all* of the modules at level 2 must be designed, coded, and tested before any of the modules at level 3 can be designed.

As a *philosophy*, this is indeed what we are suggesting; in practice, though, it may occasionally be necessary or desirable to zigzag through the program structure. In Fig. 2.13(a), for example, we see that the programmer has developed his main program and the code for modules A, B, C, and D; everything below that is a dummy. In Fig. 2.13(b), though, we see that he has expanded the A module two more levels, while leaving B, C, and D alone. We assume that practical considerations dictated this approach. Similarly, Fig. 2.13(c) shows that he has now expanded B, C, and D one more level, and Fig. 2.13(d) indicates that the programmer found it expedient to expand the D module two more levels. The basic approach here is still that of a top-down test; the zigzag variations, if done sensibly, should not cause any problems.

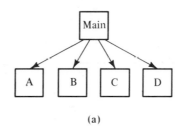

(a)

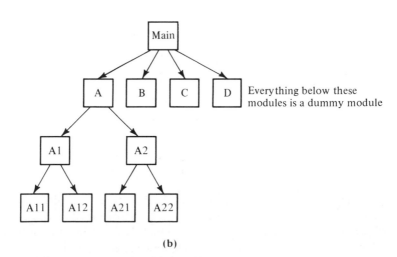

(b)

Figure 2.13. Zigzag top-down development.

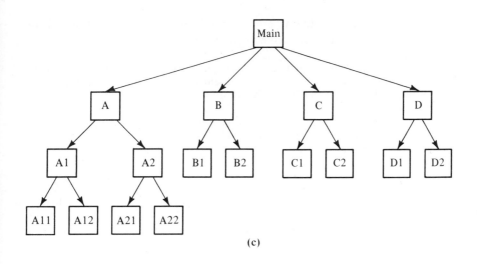

(c)

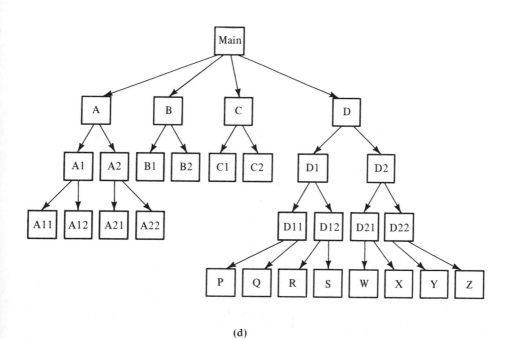

(d)

Figure 2.13 Continued.

We may also find that a certain amount of bottom-up testing will be necessary. There are several reasons why this may be true:

1. Lack of adequate testing time may persuade the programmer to make a "quick-and-dirty" test of a module in a stand-alone manner. When satisfied that the module will at least execute from beginning to end, he will put it into the skeleton for top-down testing.

2. As we suggested in the previous section, the programmer may find that it is difficult to generate an adequate amount of test data for his module in a top-down fashion. It may be much easier to use a test-data generator and perform stand-alone testing of the module.

3. Lack of adequate testing time may prevent the programmer from doing as much top-down testing as he wants. In Fig. 2.11, for example, the programmer may add a new low-level module to the UPDATE portion of the program. Ideally, he would test this by passing transactions through the EDIT program into the UPDATE program to see if his new module is working. However, if adequate testing time is not available, he may decide to take a sorted transaction file (i.e., the output from EDIT) from some previous test run and use that for testing his new UPDATE module.

4. Organizational, management, and staffing problems (which we will discuss in more detail in Section 2.4) may have caused a number of junior programmers to develop low-level modules before the top-level skeleton is finished. Thus, a certain amount of stand-alone module testing and bottom-up integration may be necessary until such time as the top-level skeleton is ready; unfortunately, this kind of situation often degenerates into a complete bottom-up test.

Again, these considerations are of a *practical* nature. The programmer may want to do top-down testing, but he may not have any control over the amount of computer time he is given for testing.

2.3.4   Structured Walk-Throughs

One of the more interesting variations on top-down testing is the concept of *structured walk-throughs* developed by IBM as part of its "chief programmer team" approach to project organization. Other organizations have referred to the same concept as "team debugging" and a variety of other terms. Structured walk-throughs can be thought of as a set of formal procedures for reviews—by the entire programming team—of program specifications, program design, actual code, and adequacy of testing. If implemented properly, structured walk-throughs go hand in hand with the other top-down concepts discussed in this chapter, as well as the structured programming concepts discussed in Chapter 4.

As we have already seen, design and coding of a program should proceed in a top-down fashion. This means that a programmer should have the top levels of logic designed and coded at a relatively early stage in the project. As each successive level of the program is designed and coded, the programmer can subject it to a group review by other programmers on the same project and/or other programmers in his organization. The purpose of the team review is to "walk through" the program, that is, to go through all of the logic, step by step, to ensure that:

   1. The logic is correct, i.e., it accomplishes what it is supposed to accomplish.
   2. The logic meets all of the appropriate standards of the organization, i.e., it is sufficiently clear, simple, efficient, modular, structured (in the sense of the discussion in Chapter 4), well-documented, and so forth.

Since the dawn of the computer age, programmers have been urged to perform extensive desk-checking before running their programs on the computer; however, desk-checking began to be enforced less and less as scarce computer time became more and more plentiful in the 1960s. In some organizations, the advent of time-sharing virtually eliminated the concept of desk-checking altogether. Structured walk-throughs are, in a sense, a return to the old philosophy of desk-checking, but with an important difference: Now we are suggesting that a *group* of programmers should review the design and coding of an individual programmer.

   The real importance of the structured walk-through concept lies in its connection to top-down design and coding. At a very early stage in a programming project, the programmer should be able to show to his peers or to other members of his team his design of the *entire* program. A great deal of the program may be in the form of dummy modules, but the overall logic and structure should be present. The purpose of the team review is to ensure that the overall logic of the program is correct, *assuming that the dummy modules, when implemented, will work correctly.* Rather than worrying about the details of low-level modules, the team concentrates its efforts, at the beginning of the project, on a review of the high-level structure of the program, thus exposing any major flaws that the programmer may have overlooked.

   In several organizations, the concept of a structured walk-through has been formalized as part of the overall project management and control. Project management and project control are not the primary concern of this textbook; rather than dwell on this area, we will simply note some of the more interesting procedural aspects of structured walk-throughs:

   1. Assuming that a team of programmers is working on a common project, an individual programmer will arrange for a structured walk-through of his program by scheduling a formal meeting. Copies of his design and/or code and/or test data are distributed to the other programmers a day or two before the meeting, and they are expected to be familiar with these by the time the meeting begins.
   2. The project manager is often barred from the structured walk-through. Many organizations feel that the presence of the project manager (whose responsibilities are assumed to be primarily administrative rather than technical) would inhibit the frank and open exchange of ideas about the program being reviewed.
   3. In some cases, it is necessary to include in the meeting an impartial mediator who can resolve any arguments and disputes among the programmers. Some-

times there is the danger than an overly aggressive group will totally demolish the design of a programmer who was never very sure of his work anyway; in other cases, an overly aggressive programmer will overwhelm the suggestions and criticisms of the rest of the team. Indeed, some groups have found it as important to concentrate on their personality problems—by discussing them in a group therapy fashion—as on their technical problems.

4. Formal notes are taken in the meeting (often by a program librarian) and distributed to everyone the next day. The programmer whose program was subjected to the structured walk-through is required to make a formal response to the group's suggestions and criticisms.

5. The structured walk-through specifically *avoids* redesigning a program. The purpose of the meeting is to find problems and/or to ensure that the program is working correctly. If problems are found, it is assumed that the programmer will fix them. Attempts at spontaneous group design are usually disastrous.

6. The entire team is considered responsible for any bugs or flaws that may eventually be discovered in the program after it has been delivered to the user. To some extent, it is the original programmer's fault for having introduced the bug into the program in the first place; on the other hand, it is the group's fault for not having found the bug during the structured walk-through. The intent here is to foster the "egoless programming" philosophy of Gerald Weinberg, as espoused in his *The Psychology of Computer Programming* (D. Van Nostrand Co., 1971).

When first exposed to the concept of structured walk-throughs, a number of programmers react rather negatively. Their primary concern is that the structured walk-through will slow down the project: It is very expensive, they feel, to have five or six programmers spending their time reviewing the work of one programmer. In fact, just the opposite is true. The structured walk-through approach generally *saves* a considerable amount of time. First of all, it should be recognized that it only takes an hour or two to review a week's work on the part of the programmer; it has probably taken him at least that long to develop his design and coding (after having thrown away several preliminary attempts). More important, by exposing his program and his design to five or six different people, each of whom probably has a slightly different way of looking at things, there is a far greater chance that most of the bugs will be eliminated before the program is ever run on the computer— including the various obscure bugs that the programmer would otherwise spend days looking for with traces and snapshots and other debugging techniques.

It seems that the *real* objection that many programmers have to the structured walk-through approach is that they prefer *not* to have other people looking at their code. "Reading someone else's program," one British programmer said to me, "is like reading his private mail—it just isn't done in polite society." Indeed, many programmers find the structured walk-through an ego-bruising experience, and some simply can't take it. A great deal of the success or failure of this approach may lie in the personalities of the programmers working together as a team. If personality clashes can be avoided or minimized, and if programmers can be made to give up their selfish attitudes toward "their" programs, the structured walk-through concept, when combined with top-down design, is usually enormously successful. One team in Australia, for example, found that they had been programming for three months without a single bug, that is, by the time any program was actually run on a computer, there were no bugs left.

2.4 Alternatives, Variations, and Problems with Top-Down Design

In the previous sections of this chapter, we have elaborated upon the philosophy of top-down design, top-down coding, and top-down testing. The important point to keep in mind is that we have been discussing *philosophies*, not a set of inviolate rules for program design. As we pointed out several times, many programmers will find it necessary from time to time to retreat somewhat from the pure approach to top-down design, coding, and testing. The purpose of this section is to discuss the nature of those compromises and the situations that cause them. The primary situations we want to examine are the following:

1. The classical approach to program development is top-down design, combined with random coding (i.e., various combinations of top-down and bottom-up) and bottom-up testing.

2. Some situations call for combinations of top-down *and* bottom-up design.

3. Some programmers prefer to approach their design in a top-down fashion, but not to begin coding or testing until the design is complete. When the design is finished, down to the most detailed level, *then* they will begin coding and testing in a top-down manner.

4. Similarly, some programmers prefer to approach design and coding in a parallel top-down fashion; however, they will not begin testing until all the coding is complete. When they *do* begin testing, it is done in a top-down fashion.

5. Management and organizational problems may make it quite difficult for the project leader to schedule the use of his people to facilitate top-down design, coding, and testing.

6. Hardware delivery problems or insufficient testing time may make it difficult to use the top-down design, coding, and testing philosophies fully.

2.4.1 The Classical Approach

As we have noted elsewhere in this chapter, the classical approach to program development is a combination of top-down design, random coding, and bottom-up testing. Several programmers have reported that even though they are personally convinced that the top-down testing concept makes more sense, they are unable to convince the rest of their organization to use it. The fact that it has *always* been done that way seems, in some organizations, to be a strong reason not to change it.

Having discussed the top-down concepts throughout this chapter, there is no need to repeat the arguments against the bottom-up approach. The important things to recognize here are that the bottom-up approach is more commonly followed and that the inertia of large companies is such that a change is rather difficult.

2.4.2   Combinations of Top-Down and Bottom-Up Design

There seems to be a number of situations where it is reasonable to combine bottom-up design with top-down design. The two most common examples of this are:

1. The programmer is aware that a number of utility routines already exist, and he tries (either consciously or unconsciously) to adapt his design to make use of them.
2. At a relatively early stage in the design of his program, the programmer anticipates that certain common or general-purpose modules will be required by several different portions of the program. Examples of this might be error routines, input/output routines, editing routines, and table lookup routines.

In both cases, the programmer may have *begun* his design in a top-down manner; however, he soon incorporates into the design a number of bottom-level modules, as shown in Fig. 2.14(a). His design then often continues simultaneously in a bottom-up *and* top-down fashion, as shown in Fig. 2.14(b). Alternatively, having established a number of bottom-level modules, he builds the rest of the program structure *down* to meet them.

There is no reason why this element of bottom-up design should be considered bad—*if* the programmer has a good feel for the design of his program. A novice or an incompetent programmer may find that, as he expands the top and bottom portions of his design as shown in Fig. 2.14(b), the two halves simply do not meet in the middle. If the interfaces between the top half and the bottom half turn out to be totally impractical, he may find himself redesigning either or both halves. Similarly, a mediocre programmer may find that he has to "bend" the design of the top half in order to make it compatible with the bottom half. An example of this is a program whose input formats are chosen solely to make the top half of the program structure compatible with an existing report-writing module—often to the great dismay and frustration of the user who finds neither the input formats nor the output reports acceptable!

If done properly, though, a small amount of bottom-up design can be extremely practical. Using general-purpose library routines usually makes good sense; anticipating the need for some general-purpose input/output routines or error-handling routines usually makes good sense. The main point we are suggesting here is that the programmer should be aware of what

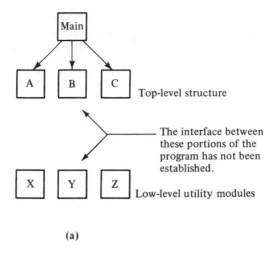

(a)

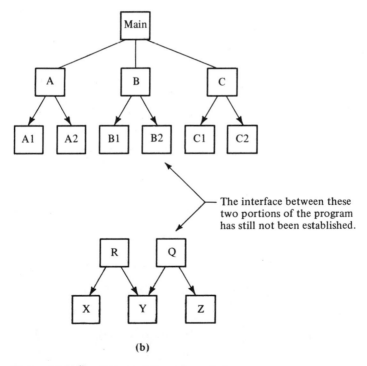

(b)

Figure 2.14. Top-down and bottom-up design.

he is doing. Many programmers do not seem to recognize *when* they are doing bottom-up design. By using some bottom-up design cautiously and deliberately, the programmer should be able to avoid the pitfalls mentioned above.

2.4.3 Top-Down Coding and Testing after Top-Down Design

It has been observed that many experienced programmers are quite reluctant to practice top-down design in its extreme form; they prefer to finish their entire design before writing any code. The two arguments that are used most frequently in support of this approach are:

1. They simply don't trust the idea of combining top-down design, top-down coding, and top-down testing. Even though the idea sounds reasonable in an academic discussion, they find that they are quite nervous about it when asked to put it into practice.
2. They are afraid that they will make a mistake, i.e., that having committed some of their design to code, they will find that they have made a mistake that will force them to redesign (and therefore recode) some of the program.

We can certainly sympathize with the first argument: people often feel nervous about trying something a new way, especially when it represents a radical departure from the accepted techniques. The second argument, though, is rather ironic: it is largely *because* of the possibility of mistakes that we are proposing the philosophy of top-down testing. There is hardly anything more frustrating than to finish a design, have it approved by management and users, document the design with elaborate flowcharts for the sake of posterity, write the code, test it thoroughly, and *then* discover that the user really wanted something else after all! Similarly, it is extremely frustrating to conceive of a design whose fatal flaws are not recognized until *after* the code has all been written. It would seem to make far more sense to design *some* of the top-level structure of the program, code it, and test it to determine whether the overall design works and whether the users will accept it.

Nevertheless, we should recognize that some organizations will adopt this approach as their compromise version of top-down design. Even though it is perhaps not as elegant as we would like, it is probably an improvement: *After* the design has been finished, we use top-down coding and top-down testing. Thus, if there are any major flaws in the design, they may well be discovered before very much low-level coding is finished.

2.4.4 Top-Down Testing after Top-Down Design and Top-Down Coding

As we saw in the previous section, many experienced programmers are reluctant to practice the extreme form of top-down design, coding, and testing. The most common expression of this reluctance is to finish the entire design first, and then to begin coding and testing in a top-down fashion. However, another common variation is to practice top-down design and top-down coding in a parallel fashion, but not to begin any testing until the design and code are complete. Once the testing begins, it is usually carried out in a top-down fashion.

Quite often, we find programmers following this approach because:

1. They lack adequate testing time on their computer, a problem that will be discussed in Section 2.4.6.
2. They are doing some top-down testing without realizing it, e.g., by performing desk-checking or structured walk-throughs at each level, though not necessarily running the skeleton of the program on a machine.

In the sense that this approach is an improvement over the basic bottom-up testing philosophy, perhaps we should not criticize it. The fact that the programmer may be carrying out some unconscious or semiconscious top-down desk-checking may also make this approach a fairly practical one.

2.4.5 Management and Organizational Problems

It seems that some project managers do not have the freedom to schedule the use of programmers on their projects as freely as they would wish; as a result, they find that they are *forced* into a bottom-up development approach against their better instincts. The most common example of this seems to be the situation where the project leader is informed by his upper management, "You have ten junior programmers sitting around doing nothing while you and the senior people are designing—*do* something with them!" In an attempt to avoid wasting the availability of the junior people, the project leader often tries to invent something for them to do, perhaps by anticipating a need for a number of bottom-level utility modules that can be coded by the junior programmers while the senior programmers continue with the top-level design.

The danger, as we have already noted, is that the top-level structure may not interface very well with the bottom-level modules when it comes time to put them together. This danger is generally increased by the fact that the junior programmers are often working in a vacuum without adequate supervision and without enough experience to anticipate exactly what their bottom-level modules ought to do.

The solution, of course, is to change the organizational structure so that the project leader is not obligated to use the junior people before he has to; unfortunately, this is not so easily accomplished in some companies. It is all the more difficult when the project leader and his managers suffer from the instinctive feeling that the major part of a programming project consists of massive numbers of low-level modules that

1. Can be written by a junior programmer without any supervision.
2. Can be written before the top-level structure is adequately defined.
3. *Must* be started as early as possible in the project in order to avoid delays.

In fact, the opposite is usually true. The low-level modules *can* be written by junior programmers, but not in a vacuum. There is hardly any point in writing random low-level modules if they are going to be thrown away due to incompatibilities with the emerging top-level structure. Finally, there is little advantage to be gained from starting the development of low-level modules early in the project if a large number of them turn out to be useless!

If the project leader is forced to make use of the junior programmers at an early stage in the project (when he would probably prefer not to have them), he may still be able to use them in the top-down development. For example, one or two junior programmers might be assigned to each senior programmer; as the senior programmer conceives of the design of a high-level module, the junior programmer could write the appropriate code to implement that module. In a sense, we are suggesting that the junior programmer could be used as an apprentice to the senior programmer. To put it very bluntly, the senior programmer would be involved in the more intellectual aspects of the design, and the junior programmer would be involved in the more menial aspects—but they would both be involved in the same module at the same time, and it would allow the design of the overall project to be carried out in a top-down fashion.

2.4.6   Insufficient Testing Time

Finally, we should note that some programmers are faced with the very practical problem of insufficient machine time to carry out adequate top-down testing. This can occur for a variety of reasons, but the following two examples seem to be the most common:

1. The design and coding are carried out long before the hardware is delivered to the programmers. This seems to occur in a number of aerospace projects and special development projects. It also occurs in computer manufacturing companies where the programmers are developing systems software for a machine that has not yet actually been produced.
2. The project may be taking place at a time when other projects are making unusually heavy demands on the available computer time in the organization. For example, if a new project is begun when end-of-year processing is taking place, it may be very difficult to schedule testing time.

Obviously, there are no magic solutions to these problems. However, both programmers and management should be aware that lack of adequate testing time at the beginning of a project can have a serious impact on the total development costs. This is generally *not* recognized now, since most organizations feel that the bottom-up testing approach is perfectly adequate. If the value of top-down testing is finally recognized, it will obviously place a higher priority on availability of adequate testing time. Among other things, it may convince management to ensure that a computer *is* available for the programmers, and that end-of-year processing does not take absolute priority over all other activities.

2.5 Case Studies and Examples: The IBM "Chief Programmer Team" Project

Unfortunately, many of the controversial aspects of top-down design are in doubt because of a lack of evidence of their success in the real world. The question of many programmers has been, "How much am I really going to gain by subjecting myself to these rules and regulations?" The answer, unfortunately, has always been, "Well, I don't know, but it should be substantial—and besides, it's a much more aesthetically pleasing approach!"

Fortunately, there is now at least one project whose success with structured programming and top-down programming can be reported—the IBM information retrieval system for The *New York Times*. By the time this book is actually published and circulated, there will hopefully be other projects that will be able to confirm this one. In the meantime, this one project should give the reader sufficient motivation to try some of the ideas discussed in this chapter.

Most of the information presented in this section is taken from a recent report on the *New York Times* project in the *IBM Systems Journal* [7]; additional information may be obtained from an internal IBM report [8]. We will give a brief description of the project's background and objectives, though the details are not relevant in this chapter. We will also give a brief description of the project management and programming library approach used in the project; then we will focus on the structured programming and top-down programming techniques used by IBM. Finally, and most important, we will attempt to show the success enjoyed by IBM with their approach.

History and Background of the Project. IBM's motivation for a structured programming approach came from their earlier experiment with the superprogrammer project [9]. One has the impression that IBM was interested in trying a variety of techniques that would allow a project to be carried out with a small group—because of the inherent advantages in group morale, group communication, and management savings. The idea of the superprogrammer was the first approach: one highly talented programmer might be able to do the work of a whole group of five or ten; similarly, a small team of three to five superprogrammers might be able to tackle a project that would otherwise require an "army of ants."

During the superprogrammer project, it became apparent that the programmer's time was too valuable to waste on a variety of clerical tasks, e.g., keypunching, coding control cards, and preparing runs on the computer. Similarly, it became apparent that there were a number of detailed technical areas that required the services of a *specialist*, e.g., someone who was extremely familiar with a particular programming language, a particular operating system, or a particular file accessing technique. All of these people could provide service to the superprogrammer, who would then be free to devote his efforts to the area where he excelled—designing and coding programs.

Much of this experimentation proved to be valuable and was formalized within the *New York Times* project. The name "superprogrammer" was changed to "chief programmer team" to reflect the feeling that the project should consist of a chief programmer, surrounded by a team of specialists and occasional junior programmers. The details of the *New York Times* project are quite interesting but beyond the scope of this discussion. It should suffice to quote briefly from Baker's description of the system [7]:

> The heart of the information bank system is a conversational subsystem that uses a data base consisting of indexing data, abstracts and full articles from *The New York Times* and other periodicals. Although a primary object of the system is to bring the clipping file (morgue) to the editorial staff through terminals, the system may also be made available to remote users. This is a dedicated, time-sharing system that provides document retrieval services to 64 local terminals (IBM 4279/4506 digital TV display subsystems) and up to one hundred twenty remote lines with display or typewriter terminals. . . .
>
> Users scan the data base via a thesaurus of all descriptors (index terms) that have been used in indexing the articles. This thesaurus contains complete information about each descriptor, often including scope notes and suggested cross references. Descriptors of interest may be selected and saved for later use in composing an inquiry. Experienced users, who are familiar with the thesaurus, may key in precise descriptors directly. When the descriptor specification is complete, inquirers supply any of the following known bibliographic data that further limits the range of each article in which they are interested:
>   · date or date range
>   · publication in which the articles appeared
>   · sources other than staff reporters from which an article has been prepared
>   · types of articles (e.g., editorial or obituary)
>   · articles with specific types of illustrations (e.g., maps and graphs)

Project Organization. As we have already described, IBM was interested in the idea of organizing a programming project around a chief programmer; in fact, this was one of the key elements in the *New York Times* project. While an overall project manager was required to deal with the various financial, administrative, legal, and reporting aspects of the project, the chief programmer was responsible for all technical aspects. As Baker puts it,

> The proposed organization is compared with a surgical team in which the chief programmers are analogous to chief surgeons, and the chief programmer is supported by a team of specialists (as in a surgical team) whose members assist the chief, rather than write parts of the program independently.

> A chief programmer is a senior level programmer who is responsible for the detailed development of a programming system. The chief programmer produces a critical nucleus of the programming system in full, and he specifies and integrates all other programming for the system as well. If the system is sufficiently monolithic in function or small enough, he may produce it entirely.

The Program Production Library. The project was assisted by a detailed set of library procedures, supervised and controlled by a trained librarian. The basic purpose of the library was to remove all clerical tasks from the programmers and to serve as a central repository for all documentation, listings, source decks, and other paperwork associated with the project. Specifically, the library consisted of the following four parts:

> 1. An *internal library* that consists of machine-readable source programs, relocatable modules, object modules, linkage-editing statements, test data or job control statements.
> 2. An *external library* that consists of all current listings of programs, as well as listings of recent versions of the programs.
> 3. A set of *machine procedures* that contains all necessary information for updating libraries, link-editing jobs and test runs, compiling modules and storing the object code, and backing up the libraries.
> 4. A set of *clerical procedures* that specify the means of accepting changes to be made to source programs, etc.; using the machine procedures; filing updated listings in the external library; and filing and replacing data in the archives of recent versions of programs.

These procedures are similar to the procedures used by a number of *maintenance departments* to control changes made to programs after they have achieved a working status. What is interesting about the IBM approach is that it has been applied from the very beginning of the project (though this is also common in other large government and military projects—or *any* large computer project, for that matter). Another interesting aspect of the program production library, as described in reference 8, was the *degree* of control exercised by the librarian. An analogy was drawn between the librarian and the *controller* (chief financial officer) of a corporation. Just as the controller has the ultimate responsibility for the accuracy of the financial records of the corporation (indeed, the controller is often legally liable for any error in the records, and as a result is usually empowered to prevent other officers of the corporation—such as the president—from making unauthorized entries or changes), the librarian has the ultimate responsibility for the accuracy and safety of the records that describe the computer project. This implies, then, that the librarian could prevent programmers—including the chief programmer—from making patches, performing test runs, or performing any other activities without going through the standard library procedures.

Structured Programming and Top-Down Programming. The structured programming and top-down programming ideas discussed in this chapter and in Chapter 4 were an important element in the IBM project. Following systems design, the programmers first wrote the job control language statements necessary to compile, load, and execute the necessary system modules. These were then combined with dummy modules and dummy files to constitute a high-level test of the system while the top-down design of actual modules then began. Though no other details were given, it seems that the approach met with success [7]:

> Top-down programming was similarly successful. System logic for one of the major programs ran correctly the first time and never required a change as the program was expanded to its full size. This was helpful in debugging, since programs usually ran to completion, and the rare failures were readily traceable to newly added functions. Top-down programming also alleviated the interface problems normally associated with multiprogrammer projects, because interfaces were always defined and coded before any coding functions that made use of the interfaces.

The structured programming concepts were the same as the ones that will be described in Chapter 4; PL/I was used as the primary programming language, and the programmers were restricted to the IF-THEN-ELSE and the DO-WHILE statements for branching and control. In addition, there was a strong attempt to use meaningful identifier names and to keep the length of modules to approximately 50 lines of source code. To make the structured programming more convenient, the programmers were allowed two extensions: a simulated ALGOL-like CASE statement (with a subscripted GO-TO and a LABEL array), and iterative DO statements with or without a WHILE clause.

The Results of the IBM Project. One of the great values of the IBM project, from the point of view of other computer scientists, was its effort to measure the productivity of its programmers in an attempt to evaluate the usefulness of its project control ideas, the program production library, and the structured programming concepts.

Table 2.1 shows the number of programming statements generated during the project; both this table and Table 2.2 were taken from reference 7. It is important to note that the project was *not* a small one; it would compare favorably with a number of medium-sized projects within industry. Another table in reference 7, which has not been repeated here, showed the man-

Table 2.1. LINES OF SOURCE CODING
BY DIFFICULTY AND LEVEL IN IBM PROJECT

	Level		
Difficulty	High	Low	Total
Hard	5034	—	5034
Standard	44247	4513	48760
Easy	27897	1633	29530
TOTAL	77178	6146	83324

The conventions used in the preparation of this table were as follows:
  Easy coding had few interactions with other system elements. (Most of the support programs were in this category.)
  Standard coding had some interactions with other system elements. (Examples are the functional parts of the conversational subsystem and the data-entry edit system.)
  Difficult coding had many interactions with other system elements. (This category is limited to the control elements of the conversational subsystem.)
  High-level coding included programs written in a language such as PL/I, COBOL, or JCL.
  Low-level coding included such languages as assembler language and linkage-editor control statements.

months spent by different members of the project. Including the project manager and a secretary, the project consumed 132 man-months of effort—again roughly the same as a number of medium-sized commercial and business computer projects.

Table 2.2 shows the productivity of the programmers, measured in several different ways. Counting only the programmers, an average of 65 debugged statements per day was generated—and this is approximately four to six times better than the average programmer can usually produce. Even when the various clerical, managerial, and support people were included in the figures, the number of debugged statements per day was 35—and this is significantly better than for most programming organizations. Note also that the effort to include a program librarian and adequate clerical help may have

Table 2.2. PROGRAMMER PRODUCTIVITY
WITHIN THE IBM PROJECT

Organization	Source lines per programmer day
Unit design, programming, debugging, and testing	65
All professional staff	47
With librarian support	43
Entire team	35

decreased the *total* productivity of the staff—but the clerical staff is generally much less expensive (in terms of salary and other fringe benefits) than the programmers.

It is not clear how much of the results are due to the project organization and the effort to remove clerical duties from the programmers, and how much was due to structured programming and top-down design. Most of the emphasis in reference 7 seems to be on the *project organization*, which is understandable. Though the top-down and structured programming ideas are acknowledged as being important, no *measure* of their usefulness could be given. Nevertheless, the success of this one project should provide sufficient motivation for others to do the same!

REFERENCES

1. W. A. WULF, "A Case Against the GOTO," *Proceedings of the 25th National ACM Conference*, Volume 2, pages 791–797.

2. N. WIRTH, "Program Development by Stepwise Refinement," *Communications of the ACM*, April 1971.

3. —— *Systematic Programming*, Prentice-Hall, Inc., 1973.

4. LARRY L. CONSTANTINE, *Concepts in Program Design*, Information and Systems Press, Cambridge, Massachusetts, 1967.

5. EDWARD YOURDON, "Call 360 Costs," *Datamation*, November 1, 1971.

6. W. P. STEVENS, G. J. MYERS, and L. L. CONSTANTINE, "Structured Design," *IBM Systems Journal*, May 1974.

7. F. T. BAKER, "Chief Programming Team Management of Production Programming," *IBM Systems Journal*, January 1972, pages 56–73.

8. ——, "Chief Programmer Teams: Principles and Procedures," Report No. FSC 71–5108, IBM, Federal Systems Division, Gaithersburg, Maryland 20760.

9. J. D. ARON, "The Superprogrammer Project," *Software Engineering Techniques*, NATO Scientific Affairs Division, Brussels 39, Belgium, pages 50–52.

10. HARLAN MILLS, "Top-Down Programming in Large Systems," from *Debugging Techniques in Large Systems*, Prentice-Hall, Inc., 1971.

PROBLEMS

1. Does your organization require a standard form of program structure of the nature shown in Fig. 2.1? Are all programmers required to use this structure? Do you think it is a reasonable requirement?

2. If you are working on commercial applications, do you think it is reasonable to suggest that all of your programs should have the form shown in Fig. 2.2? Can you think of any applications where this structure would not apply?

3. Give a brief definition of top-down design. What is the objective of this concept?

4. Is top-down design practiced by you and other programmers in your organization? If not, why not? If your management established a standard requiring you to design your programs in this fashion, do you think you would have any difficulty complying?

5. List three difficulties that programmers are likely to encounter when attempting to design their program in a top-down fashion. Do you think that you would encounter these difficulties yourself?

6. Why is it important to be very formal and very rigorous when specifying the input, the function, and the output of each module in a program being designed in the top-down fashion? Are there any techniques to aid in this formal approach?

7. Why is it important to avoid arguing about trivial details when designing a program? How can one recognize when the design effort has become bogged down in trivia? How can such a situation be avoided?

8. It is suggested in Section 2.1.3 that at each level of design, the implementation of a module should be expressed in no more than a page of coding. What is the purpose of this suggestion? What should be done if the implementation of the program cannot be expressed in a single page of primitive statements?

9. In Section 2.1.3, it is suggested that COBOL tends to be less formal in specifying the interfaces between different modules in a program. Why is this so? Do you think it is a major problem? What can be done about it? Are other languages, e.g., FORTRAN and PL/I, equally informal?

10. What is the advantage of systems like IBM's HIPO in specifying the structure of a program?

11. Why do you suppose that programmers are so informal in their attempts to break a program down into smaller modules? Is it because they lack experience in this area, or because their initial attempt at designing the program is not clearly formed in their minds? Are there any other reasons?

12. To what extent do you think the structure of your program design reflects the structure of the specification you are given? That is, have you noticed that when you are given a disorganized specification, you often end up with a disorganized program? What can be done about this? Is this problem more the responsibility of the analyst or the programmer?

13. List three reasons why analysts sometimes generate disorganized, "unstructured" specifications. Do you think the reasons you have listed are common in your organization? Are they recognized by the analysts? By the management?

14. Do you think that analysts should be given training in top-down design? Would this be difficult in your organization? Would the analysts resist the idea?

15. Give a brief definition of top-down coding. What are the objectives of this concept?

16. Discuss three advantages of top-down coding. Do you think these are significant

advantages? Do you actually believe in them yourself? Do others in your organization?

17. Why are flowcharts sometimes a poor means of communicating design ideas from one programmer to another? Do you prefer the use of flowcharts?

18. Why is code likely to be a more precise method of communicating the design of a program to another programmer? What problem might there be with this approach?

19. How do you think code should be organized in a program listing? Do you prefer the horizontal approach shown in Fig. 2.8(b) or the vertical approach shown in Fig. 2.8(c)? What are the advantages and disadvantages of each approach?

20. Give a brief definition of top-down testing. What are the objectives of this concept? What is the difference between top-down and bottom-up testing?

21. What kind of program testing is carried out in your organization? Is testing standardized? If the bottom-up approach is used, *why* is it used? Find someone who favors the approach and ask him to defend it. Do his ideas make sense?

22. One of the basic concepts of top-down testing is the use of dummy modules or program stubs for unimplemented sections of code. Give an example of a program in which each of the following *types* of dummy modules could be used:
    (a) A dummy module that exits immediately.
    (b) A dummy module that provides a constant output.
    (c) A dummy module that provides a random output.
    (d) A dummy module that prints a debugging message.
    (e) A dummy module that provides a primitive version of the final form of the module.

23. In Section 2.3.1, an example is given of a top-down testing plan for the program shown in Fig. 2.11. Pick a program that you are currently working on, or one you have completed recently, and describe a similar testing plan.

24. One of the first steps suggested in top-down testing is to develop the control cards for the program and to run a dummy version of the entire program to ensure that the control cards are correct. Do you think this is a reasonable step? Do you think everyone should be required to do it?

25. List five advantages of top-down testing. Which of these advantages do you consider the most important? Which is the least important?

26. Why does top-down testing allow us to eliminate system testing (as it is usually defined)? Do you think this is a significant point? Do you think the users and management of your organization would be willing to eliminate system testing?

27. What is the advantage of testing major interfaces of a program as early as possible? Do you think this is more significant on large projects than on small projects?

28. What are the advantages of giving the user a preliminary version of a program at an early stage in top-down testing? Do you think this may be a significant

advantage of top-down testing? Can you think of any possible disadvantages of this idea?

29. Is it common in your programming organization to be given impossible deadlines? How frequently are your programming projects behind schedule? Do you think it would help to have a portion of a program finished and demonstrable—by using the top-down testing method?

30. Why is debugging likely to be easier if a program is tested in a top-down fashion than in a bottom-up fashion? Do you think it will be *significantly* easier?

31. As an experiment, find a friend or colleague with programming skills approximately equal to yours. Pick a programming problem that you can both work on. Test your version in a top-down manner, and ask your friend to test his in a bottom-up manner. When it appears that both programs have been tested with equal thoroughness, answer the following questions:
    (a) Which program took the longest amount of elapsed time to test?
    (b) Which program took the longest amount of CPU time to test?

32. Why is programmer morale likely to be improved with a top-down testing approach? Is this likely to be a significant factor on small programming projects? On large projects?

33. Does your organization use a test harness, as described in Section 2.3.2? Do you think this approach could be replaced by a top-down testing approach?

34. What are some of the variations that we sometimes find in top-down testing? What programming situations lead to these variations? Do you think it is possible to establish standards that determine what form of top-down testing should be used?

35. List four reasons why bottom-up testing may sometimes be necessary. Do you think these situations occur frequently? Can they be avoided?

36. Give an example of a program in which it would be difficult to generate test data in a top-down fashion for adequate testing of a low-level module. Would a situation like this occur frequently in your organization? What should be done about it when it occurs?

37. What is the purpose of structured walk-throughs? Do you think it is a good idea? Is it likely to be accepted by other programmers with whom you work? If the management of your organization established a standard requiring structured walk-throughs for all projects, would you find it difficult to comply? What problems could you see occurring with this approach?

38. What is the purpose of barring the project manager from a structured walk-through? Do you think this is an important provision? Do you think your manager would be willing to abide by this suggestion?

39. Why is a structured walk-through concerned with finding flaws in an existing design, rather than attempting to generate a new design?

40. What are the major objections that programmers have to structured walk-throughs?

41. Describe a programming situation that would require a combination of top-down and bottom-up design. Is this situation likely to arise frequently? Does it require any special planning on the part of the programmer?

42. Why do some programmers insist on finishing all of their design (in a top-down fashion) before commencing their coding and testing (also in a top-down fashion)? Do you think their arguments are valid? What kind of problems are likely to result from this approach?

3
MODULAR PROGRAMMING

3.0 Introduction

Modularity in a computer program seems to be very much like honesty in a politician: everyone claims that he has it, but it seems that *nobody* knows what it is, how to instill it, how to achieve it, or how to enforce it. Every junior programmer knows that a modular program is one in which any logical portion can be changed without affecting the rest of the program. However, what on earth does that really mean? How does the programmer know when he has written a modular program? Is it a state of mind; a subtle kind of kharma? More important, how does the programmer's manager know when he has written a modular program? Is there any measure of modularity, that is, can I say that my program is 4.3 times as modular as yours?

For years, these questions have plagued programmers and computer scientists. Presumably, if we *did* know how to write modular programs, everyone would have been doing so for the past several years. Those programmers who obstinately refused to do so would have been fired and permanently blacklisted from the profession. Debugging, conversion, and maintenance problems would have been decreased by an order of magnitude, and the incidence of ulcers and divorces among the programmers would have declined sharply.

Unfortunately, this utopian world has not yet arrived, though there is now some hope that it *will* arrive in the near future. It has only been recently that a formal theory of modularity has begun to emerge, and this theory is usually couched in terms of structured programming, which we will discuss in the next chapter. Though it promises great improvements over the current ad hoc attempts to develop modular programs, structured programming is still not universally accepted. For various reasons, it seems that most programmers prefer to follow their own intuitive approach to modularity. It is not too surprising to discover that good programmers usually do a good job of achieving a modular program with their ad hoc efforts, while mediocre programmers usually produce a program that is considerably less modular than they originally planned.

We expect that structured programming will gradually become accepted as the standard method of achieving modular programs. In the meantime, though, the existing ad hoc methods are still useful, and are very much worth discussing in this chapter. We will begin by attempting to develop a definition of modularity. Next, we will discuss some of the arguments for and against modular programs—it is interesting to see some of the objections that are raised by programmers who are still violently opposed to the philosophy of modular programming.[1] Finally, and most important, we will discuss several useful techniques for achieving modular programs.

3.1   Definitions of Modularity

3.1.1   The Size of Modules Within a Modular Program

One of the most interesting ad hoc ways of defining *modularity* is by defining a *module*—since all modular programs are presumably composed of modules. In their attempts to define the characteristics of a modular program, a number of people have proposed the following standards for the *size* of the module.

1. A number of IBM users and programmers suggest that a module is anything that fits into 4096 bytes of memory.
2. Similarly, a number of Honeywell, Univac, and other programmers suggest that a module consists of any code that can fit into 512 words of memory, or 1024 words of memory, or 2048 words of memory, etc.
3. Some programming managers have suggested to me that a module is anything that can be written and debugged by one programmer in one month. Given the rule of thumb that the average programmer can generate about 10–15 debugged statements per day, this suggests a module size of some 200–300 programming statements.

[1]In December of 1972, I taught a course on advanced programming for one of the government agencies in California. During the discussion of modular programming, one of the senior programmers made the following comment: "I've been programming in COBOL for over five years now, and I've never yet used the PERFORM statement. I don't see why I should start now!"

4. A colleague of mine, Larry L. Constantine, has suggested that most good modular programs seem to consist of modules of no more than 100–200 statements.

5. Another colleague, Ron Henry, has suggested that a module should be no more than 20 high-level language statements. His feeling is that if a programmer can't program something in 20 statements, there is a good chance that he is programming more than one function—in which case it should be more than one module.

6. IBM, in its "Chief Programmer Team Management of Production Programming," (by F.T. Baker, *IBM Systems Journal*, Vol. 11, No. 2—see Chapter 4 for more details on this paper), encouraged its programmers to write modules of approximately 50 PL/I statements.

7. In 1970, the author visited a large U.S. Air Force project which involved the consolidation of several individual inventory and logistics systems. The integrated system is anticipated to have an on-line data base of approximately 22 billion characters, applications programs totaling approximately one million lines of COBOL code, and a programming staff of approximately 500. Faced with this enormous task, the project managers imposed a standard that no programmer would be allowed to develop a module of more than 500 COBOL statements.

It should be clear that imposing a *size* restriction upon a program does *not* guarantee that it will be modular. One of the Air Force programmers on the project described above made an interesting comment about the 500-COBOL-statement rule: "Heck, I get all sorts of silly restrictions like that, and most of them can be circumvented fairly easily. The modularity rule is particularly easy. I simply write my program without any regard to the 500-statement rule; then, if the final result turns out to be 3000 statements long, I simply go chop! chop! chop!—and I have six modules! Voila!"

On the other hand, there *is* an element of sense in the guidelines above. As one manager friend of mine said, "Look, I know that a modular program is supposed to be broken into several subroutines—but I have an impossible time making sure that the programmers are doing it correctly. They're likely to give me a 500-statement main program, two or three 10-statement subroutines, and call the whole mess a "modular" program! The only way I can ensure that they think about the *idea* of modularity properly, and apply the concept properly, is to impose a rather stiff standard of 50 statements per module. If they have any exceptions, they have to clear it with me first."

3.1.2 Independence

One of the more abstract concepts surrounding modularity is that of *independence*: In a modular program, each module (e.g., each subroutine, each COBOL section, or PL/I procedure) is independent of the others. This implies, of course, that it can be changed or modified without affecting other modules. However, it should be clear that the concept of independence is not an absolute one. It would be very difficult for us to say that module X is

99-44/100% independent of all other modules (if we could, perhaps we could ultimately say that program Z is 99-44/100% modular).

On the other hand, it may be reasonable to think of independence with respect to other things, e.g., the data base, a working storage area, other modules, and so forth. What we really want to ask is: If one aspect of a program is changed, how much will that affect a given module? Thus, it might be reasonable to think of the independence (and ultimately the modularity) of a module with respect to:

1. Program logic, i.e., the algorithm. If an entire program (or system) depends upon a particular approach (e.g., a network routing problem that depends upon a specific heuristic algorithm to minimize the time spent travelling through the network), how many of the modules will have to be changed if the algorithm is changed?

2. Arguments, or parameters to the module. This is an area where the independence of a module may be rather sensitive: If the number or type or format of arguments changed, it should not be too surprising if it had a major effect upon the module.

3. Internal variables, tables, and constants. Many modules depend upon global tables (e.g., the transaction data blocks or message blocks in a number of business-oriented systems and message-switching systems); if the structure of such tables changes, we would expect that the modules would change too.

4. The structure and format of the data base. To a large extent, this is similar to the global tables and variables mentioned above, except that from a practical point of view, the data base *is* considered to be separate from the program. It is interesting to note that one of the major efforts of such projects as the CODASYL Data Base Task Group has been to make the program entirely independent of the definition of the data base.

5. Flow-of-control modularity. One often writes a module without much thought as to the manner in which it will be executed. Having written a module X, suppose we were suddenly told that it must be able to execute in a reentrant fashion. How much of the logic would we have to change? Suppose the module were part of a real-time system, and that it had originally been assumed by the programmer that the module would not be interrupted as it executed. How much of it would have to be changed if it turned out that the module *was* going to be interrupted? How much trouble would there be if we suddenly wanted to use the module in a recursive fashion?

Assuming that these aspects of a program do not change, we should be able to identify the independence of individual modules within a program. If the interfaces between all of the modules have been defined, then it should be possible to replace any module with one that is functionally equivalent (i.e., one that accepts the same inputs, and generates the same outputs) without affecting any of the other modules in the program. To the extent that we can do this, it makes sense to say that we have a modular program.

Note that this concept of independence is destroyed if modules can arbitrarily branch into and out of each other—or if they can modify each other. Thus, another aspect of modularity—and one that is part of the concept of independence—is the concept of "one entry, one exit," that is, *a modular program should consist of modules that have one entry point and one exit point.* We can stretch this a bit, perhaps, and allow a module to have more than one entry point; but the main point is that the entry points are very strictly controlled, and other modules cannot enter at some arbitrary point. Furthermore, we insist that a module not be able to directly alter the instructions in another module, e.g., with the ALTER statement in COBOL.

3.2 The Advantages and Disadvantages of Modularity

Before we discuss some techniques for writing modular programs, we should first entertain some of the arguments for and against modularity.

3.2.1 The Arguments in Favor of Modularity

We have already mentioned the virtues of modularity in this chapter; at this point, it should be sufficient to merely repeat them. However, it behooves every programmer to think of each of the following points with respect to his own program—just to make sure that they *do* apply.

1. A modular program is easier to write and debug. Functional components of the program can be written and debugged separately.
2. A modular program is easier to maintain and change. Functional components can be changed, rewritten, or replaced without affecting other parts of the program.
3. A modular program is easier for a manager to control. More difficult modules can be given to the better programmers; easy modules can be given to junior programmers. By breaking a program into modules of a month's duration, the manager ensures that no programmer will become overwhelmed by the complexities of a program.

3.2.2 The Arguments Against Modularity

Having mentioned the many advantages of modularity, we might ask why more programs are not written in a more modular fashion. Indeed, you may be sure that most programs are *not* written modularly. Many large business organizations spend as much as *50% of their entire data processing budget* maintaining, modifying, and improving existing programs, and most of the modifications could have been accomplished trivially if the programs had originally been designed modularly.

Most Programmers Don't Understand Modularity. Perhaps the major reason for the lack of modular programs is that most programmers don't really know what modularity is. They have an intuitive idea of the meaning and techniques of modularity, but they seem to have no formal theorems or algorithms to draw upon. Not many programmers will admit that this is the real cause for the lack of modularity in their programs; they usually cite some of the other reasons mentioned below. Most discouraging is their feeling that modularity is an *absolute* concept and that, by introducing a few subroutines, they will have achieved it.

Modularity Requires a Great Deal of Extra Work. In order to write a modular program, the programmer must be much more meticulous in the design phase of a computer project. He must design his programs in a top-down fashion (discussed in Chapter 2), beginning with the top-level design of the entire program (or system), and then gradually work his way down to a more detailed design of individual subroutines. At each step, he must ask himself whether his design can be changed easily or modified readily. For large projects, each stage in the design should also be accompanied by appropriate documentation, so various users and managers can indicate their understanding and approval of the ongoing work.

All of this requires a great deal of patience and a moderate amount of rather tedious, painstaking work—all before the coding begins. In many cases, the programmer is under a great deal of pressure (often self-imposed!) to write the program as quickly as possible, and he may object to this extra work.

Unfortunately, the solutions to this problem are not very satisfactory. A manager who is dealing with a recalcitrant programmer can simply *order* him to write his program modularly. Alternatively, the manager can attempt to reason with him and show him that the modular approach will make the program easier to change later. However, it is often very difficult for the manager to *prove* that a modular approach will ensure easier modifications; in any case, the programmer may not be interested, for he assumes that someone else will be responsible for modifying the program.

The Modular Approach Occasionally Requires More CPU Time. This problem occurs primarily when a high degree of subroutinizing is attempted with some of the high-level languages. COBOL, FORTRAN, and PL/I seem to be the prime offenders here—one version of PL/I required 198 microseconds on a 360/50 computer just to enter and leave a subroutine! The concept of modularity may also require more CPU time if the IO portions of the program are completely separated from the computational portions; an input record may be passed through several subroutines before it even begins to be processed.

If this area seems to cause problems, then the programmer (or his manager) should use good judgment to tell whether the concept of modularity *significantly* increases the CPU time of a program. Inflexible standards that unilaterally prevent a programmer from using subroutine-calling statements (as one often finds in the COBOL standards manuals on some small computers) are generally to be discouraged. In most cases, a modular approach should not require more than 5–10% extra CPU time; this seems to be a reasonable price to pay for a program that can be changed easily—except in very special cases (e.g., some real-time applications or programs that consume several hours of machine time).

The Modular Approach May Require Slightly More Memory Space. If each subroutine is given its own area of working storage, then the total program may require slightly more memory; however, if temporary storage is allocated from a pushdown list, this need not be the case (except for deeply nested subroutine calls). Also, if the program is implemented with a large number of subroutines, extra memory may be required for subroutine linkage.

Once again, the programmer should use good judgment to decide whether a modular approach requires *significantly* more memory. In most cases, modularity should not enlarge the program by more than 5–10%. This should not cause problems, except on machines where the program size is arbitrarily limited, or on minicomputers, where there is a physical limitation on memory.

Modularity May Cause Problems in Real-Time and On-line Systems. On many large on-line and real-time computer systems, it is not sufficient to merely break the program down into several small, logical subroutines to fit into memory at one time. The programmer must also ensure that the right programs are in memory at the right time; otherwise, the entire program may be placed in a "wait" condition each time a new subroutine has to be brought into memory.

The problem is even more serious with some of the virtual memory systems, e.g., some of the newer System/370 computers. Not only must the programmer worry about breaking his program down into subroutines, but he must also make sure that the subroutines fit efficiently into the page size on the machine. Those subroutines that call each other frequently (often referred to as the "working set," a phrase coined by Professor Peter Denning) should be either in the same pages or in a set of pages that can be guaranteed to be in physical memory at the same time.

3.3 Techniques for Achieving Modular Programs

The introductory section of this chapter attempted to point out that a comprehensive theory of modularity is still developing and has not yet achieved wide acceptance. Nevertheless, there are a number of ad hoc techniques that generally seem to lead to modular programs; some of these will be explored in this section.

3.3.1 Break Your Program into Small, Independent Subroutines

As we noted earlier, one of the common definitions of a modular program states that it is one that is broken into modules of approximately 50 statements, or 20 statements, or 100 statements, etc., depending on one's preferences. The most important thing to keep in mind is that this technique is just a *means*, not an *end* in itself; specifically, breaking one's programs into 50-statement modules by no means guarantees that the result will be modular.

Another crucial element of this technique is *independence:* If the subroutines are highly dependent on one another, then they are worse than useless (because they will use extra CPU time and memory). One must continually try to emphasize the *functional* nature of a subroutine; each subroutine should have a definite purpose that is more or less independent of other subroutines in the program. Naturally, this is not always easy to achieve—but sloppy thinking and design often lead to a program that is one large network of highly interconnected subroutines, all of which are likely to be affected by a relatively minor change to any one of them.

Choosing the appropriate *size* of the "ideal" module is by no means a science. One must take into account the language, the application, and the programming ability of the original programmer and the ultimate maintenance programmer. Some organizations have chosen 50 high-level language statements as their standard, simply because they feel that such a module will fit onto one page of a computer listing. The general feeling seems to be that the average programmer can read and grasp the meaning of a module that does not extend past the end of a page. In other cases (e.g., with assembly language programs), it may be appropriate to choose a larger or smaller module size.

One final suggestion is in order here: Do not *over* modularize. There is rarely any point to breaking a program into modules of three or four statements each; such an approach will clearly add immense amounts to CPU time and memory requirements as well.

3.3.2 Use Decision Tables

In the study of switching theory in electrical engineering, we usually distinguish between two types of machines: the *combinatorial machine*, whose output is a function of the present input conditions *only*, and the *sequential* machine, whose output is a function of the present input conditions and the present state of the machine (which, in turn, is a function of past inputs). A large number of computer programs can be characterized in the same fashion: The actions taken by the program depend upon several complicated, interrelated conditions, some of which may be specified as initial conditions, and some of which may be dynamically determined as the program executes.

When viewed in this light, the comparison between switching theory and computer programming is rather intriguing. There is a vast body of theory and practical techniques to help the engineer build modular, minimum-complexity switching networks (though the theory behind all of it seems far more coherent in the case of combinatorial machines). In the case of computer programming, there is a set of techniques, loosely referred to as "decision tables," to achieve the same goals. At that point, we will see that they have a number of very significant advantages:

1. They allow for better analysis and understanding of the problem.
2. They permit more precise communication between the programmer and the user, thus avoiding many of the ambiguities that exist in a narrative description of a programming problem.
3. They allow for more comprehensive error-checking, thus avoiding the possibility of incompleteness, contradictions, or redundancies.

In addition to these virtues, a program built around decision tables is generally fairly modular, which is our purpose in discussing them in this section.

If a program is very simple, with only a few conditions, intuition will often be sufficient to do a proper job of analysis, design, and implementation; modularity is often not a concern, since the entire program can be rewritten quickly. However, when the number of inputs begins to grow, and when the interrelationships between the inputs become more complex, an intuitive approach is likely to be haphazard and "unmodular." Consider the following simple example (which, in reality, would not require the formal approach of a decision table—but then the example itself is too trivial to correspond to any real-life situation!):

> If a customer has placed an order which exceeds his credit limit, then send the order to the credit department. However, the order should always be accepted if this is one of our special customers, i.e., one who does business with us regularly. Also, if the order is less than the minimum allowable shipping quantity, it should be rejected and sent to the shipping department manager. However, the computer system should be capable of receiving exceptions to this rule, as there will be cases when a customer will insist that his order be shipped, even though it is too small.

The average programmer might attack this problem in a variety of ways, one of which is shown in Fig. 3.1. His first impulse, upon seeing the specification of the problem, is to draw a flowchart (we are ignoring those few programmers whose first impulse would be to begin coding at the keypunch!). After satisfying *himself* that the flowchart meets the specifications, he will begin coding—and to keep the program modular, he may even use as many subroutines as possible!

There are several drawbacks to this type of hurried approach. First of all, it should be apparent that the *specification*, which seems to be typical of

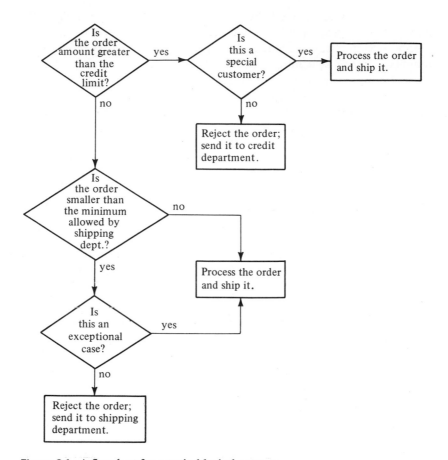

Figure 3.1. A flowchart for a typical logical program.

specifications written by non-computer-oriented people, is itself rather vague and unmodular. It seems to be following the user's train of thought, as he wanders from one condition to the next, trying to remember how he currently handles his manual order entry application. In fact, the specification above does not indicate what the program should do if an order is received that exceeds the credit limit and falls below the minimum shipping quantity—perhaps that combination of events never occurred to the user when he wrote the specification, because it happens only once every six months. It follows, of course, that if the specification is incomplete or contradictory, then the flowchart in Fig. 3.1 will be equally incomplete or contradictory; the program that implements the flowchart can only compound the foolishness.

Furthermore, given this state of affairs, it is absolutely *certain* that the user will change the specification (because the original one doesn't work!), which will necessitate a redrawing of the flowchart, and thus a recoding of the original program. Note that an abundance of subroutines is of very little help here—a minor change in the specification is likely to cause a major change in the flowchart, which will change the entire logic of the program.

A better way of attacking this problem is to construct a *decision table*. We can start by itemizing the four possible input *conditions*:

1. The dollar order amount exceeds the credit limit.
2. This is a customer with special approval from the credit department.
3. The size of the order is less than the minimum allowed for shipping.
4. The shipping department has approved this order for shipment.

Similarly, we can see that there are three possible *actions* that the program can take:

1. The order can be rejected and sent to the credit department.
2. The order can be rejected and sent to the shipping department.
3. The order can be processed normally.

A *decision table*, or truth table, can be built to show all combinations of input and output. In this example, there are $2^4 = 16$ possible *combinations* of input, as illustrated by the decision table in Fig. 3.2. The decision table can easily be rearranged so that all combinations of input conditions leading to action No. 1 are grouped together, etc.; this type of decision table is shown in Fig. 3.3; this is often a good way of developing an optimally efficient program from the decision table.

Conditions and Actions	1	2	3	4	5	6	7	8	9	10	11	12	13	14	15	16
1. Dollar amount of order exceeds credit limit.	F	F	F	F	F	F	F	F	T	T	T	T	T	T	T	T
2. Customer has special approval from credit dept.	F	F	F	F	T	T	T	T	F	F	F	F	T	T	T	T
3. Size of order is less than minimum allowed.	F	F	T	T	F	F	T	T	F	F	T	T	F	F	T	T
4. Customer has special approval from shipping dept.	F	T	F	T	F	T	F	T	F	T	F	T	F	T	F	T
1. REJECT ORDER, SEND TO CREDIT DEPT.									X	X	X	X				
2. REJECT ORDER, SEND TO SHIPPING DEPT.			X				X				X				X	
3. PROCESS ORDER, AND SHIP IT.	X	X		X	X	X		X					X	X		X

Note that this situation calls for two rejections. Is this practical, or even reasonable? For simplicity, we will proceed on the assumption that only action No. 1 is necessary.

Figure 3.2. A simple decision table.

Conditions and Actions	Rules															
	1	2	3	4	5	6	7	8	9	10	11	12	13	14	15	16
1. Dollar amount of order exceeds credit limit.	T	T	T	T	F	F	T	F	F	F	F	F	F	T	T	T
2. Customer has special approval from credit dept.	F	F	F	F	F	T	T	F	F	F	T	T	T	T	T	T
3. Size of order is less than minimum allowed.	F	F	T	T	T	T	T	F	F	T	F	F	T	F	F	T
4. Customer has special approval from shipping dept.	F	T	F	T	F	F	F	F	T	T	F	T	T	F	T	T
1. REJECT ORDER, SEND TO CREDIT DEPT.	X	X	X	X												
2. REJECT ORDER, SEND TO SHIPPING DEPT.					X	X	X									
3. PROCESS ORDER AND SHIP IT.								X	X	X	X	X	X	X	X	X

Note that we have arbitrarily decided to perform
only action No. 1 (see rule No. 11 in Fig. 3-2).

Figure 3.3. A rearranged decision table.

Note that the decision tables in Fig. 3.2 and Fig. 3.3 are exhaustive in nature, that is, they list *all possible combinations* of input conditions, even though many combinations may be impossible, erroneous, redundant, or meaningless. This has the advantage, though, of leading to a very simple programming implementation: the "indexed-branch" approach, illustrated in a general form in Fig. 3.4(a). Figure 3.4(b) shows the example above, coded in FORTRAN with the "computed GO-TO" statement; Fig. 3.4(d) illustrates

Figure 3.4(a). Implementation of the decision table with a computed GO-TO.

```
C
C     WHEN THIS SECTION OF CODE IS ENTERED, THE INTEGER K INDICATES
C     WHICH OF THE 16 POSSIBLE SITUATIONS WE ARE IN. THE COMPUTED
C     GO-TO THEN TAKES US TO THE APPROPRIATE SECTION OF CODE TO HAN-
C     DLE THAT CASE. NOTE THAT THERE ARE ONLY THREE SUCH SECTIONS OF
C     CODE - ONE FOR EACH OF THE THREE POSSIBLE ACTIONS.
C
      GO TO (3,3,2,3,3,3,2,3,1,1,1,1,3,3,2,3),K
C
C     THIS IS THE CODE TO HANDLE THE THIRD TYPE OF ACTION.
C     PROCESS THE ORDER NORMALLY.
C
3     PRINT 100,ACCTNO,PARTNO,QTY

      etc.
```

Figure 3.4(b). Implementation of the decision table in FORTRAN.

```
C    WHEN WE ENTER THIS CODE, WE ASSUME THAT THE FOLLOWING VARIABLES
C    HAVE BEEN SET UP:
C         REAL DOLLAR    THE DOLLAR AMOUNT OF THE CUSTOMER'S ORDER
C         REAL CREDIT    THE CREDIT LIMIT FOR THIS CUSTOMER
C         REAL ORDRSZ    THE SIZE OF THIS CUSTOMER'S ORDER
C         REAL ORDRMN    THE MINIMUM ALLOWED FOR SHIPPING
C
C    ALSO, WE ASSUME THAT
C         SPCRED = 0     IF THIS CUSTOMER DOES NOT HAVE SPECIAL APPROVAL
C                        FROM THE CREDIT DEPARTMENT.
C         SPCRED = 1     IF THIS CUSTOMER DOES HAVE SPECIAL APPROVAL FROM
C                        THE CREDIT DEPARTMENT.
C         SPSHIP = 0     IF THE CUSTOMER DOES NOT HAVE SPECIAL APPROVAL
C                        FROM THE SHIPPING DEPARTMENT.
C         SPSHIP = 1     IF THE CUSTOMER DOES HAVE SPECIAL APPROVAL FROM
C                        THE SHIPPING DEPARTMENT.
C
     K = 1
     IF (DOLLAR .GE. CREDIT) K = K+8
     IF (SPCRED .EQ. 1) K = K+4
     IF (ORDRSZ .LE. ORDRMN) K = K+2
     IF (SPSHIP .EQ. 1) K = K+1
     GO TO (3,3,2,3,3,3,2,3,1,1,1,1,3,3,2,3),K
```

the same techniques in COBOL, using a GO TO DEPENDING ON statement; Figs. 3.4(c), 3.4(e), and 3.4(f) show the same problem coded in PL/I, System/360 assembly language, and PDP-10 assembly language.

While the exhaustive approach is convenient when there are only a few input conditions (e.g., less than five or six), it quickly becomes unwieldy when there are a larger number of conditions. If we had to deal with fifteen conditions, our computed GO-TO statement would have 32,768 addresses! For cases like this, we might want to build a "selective" decision table, in which only certain "interesting" combinations of conditions are considered. A selective decision table for our order-entry example is shown in Fig. 3.5.

The implementation of the decision table shown in Fig. 3.5 may well look like the original flowchart that we discussed in Fig. 3.1; however, having gone through the exercise of drawing a decision table, we are now more confident that the flowchart in Fig. 3.1 actually does what the specification called for. This is perhaps the greatest value of decision tables: They force the programmer to organize his thoughts, express them in tabular form, and *then* write the flowchart. In addition, it should be apparent that the decision table approach can lead to a more modular program. This is especially true with the exhaustive decision table shown in Fig. 3.2: If the user changes his mind about the action to be taken when a certain combination of conditions oc-

Figure 3.4(c). Implementation of the decision table in PL/I.

```
/* WHEN WE ENTER THIS SECTION OF CODE, WE ASSUME THAT THE FOLLOWING
VARIABLES HAVE BEEN DECLARED APPROPRIATELY, AND THAT THEY HAVE BEEN
INITIALIZED WITH THE FOLLOWING CONTENTS:
        DOLLAR          THE DOLLAR AMOUNT OF THE CUSTOMER'S ORDER
        CREDIT          THE CREDIT LIMIT FOR THIS CUSTOMER
        ORDRMN          THE MINIMUM ORDER ALLOWED FOR SHIPPING
        ORDRSZ          THE SIZE OF THIS CUSTOMER'S ORDER
WE ALSO ASSUME THAT THE VARIABLES "SPCRED" AND "SPSHIP" HAVE BEEN
DECLARED AS BIT STRINGS WITH LENGTH OF (1), AND HAVE BEEN INITIAL-
IZED WITH THE FOLLOWING CONTENTS:
        SPCRED = 0      IF THIS CUSTOMER DOES NOT HAVE SPECIAL APPROVAL
                        FROM THE CREDIT DEPARTMENT.
               = 1      IF THIS CUSTOMER DOES HAVE SPECIAL APPROVAL
                        FROM THE CREDIT DEPARTMENT.
        SPSHIP = 0      IF THIS CUSTOMER DOES NOT HAVE SPECIAL APPROVAL
                        FROM THE SHIPPING DEPARTMENT.
               = 1      IF THIS CUSTOMER DOES HAVE SPECIAL APPROVAL
                        FROM THE SHIPPING DEPARTMENT.
NOTE THAT THIS PROGRAM COULD HAVE BEEN WRITTEN IN A NUMBER OF OTHER
WAYS, USING THE POWER AND FLEXIBILITY OF PL/I. */
        DECLARE K FIXED BINARY;
        DECLARE TABLE(16) LABEL INITIAL (PROCESS,PROCESS,REJECTSHIP,
            PROCESS,PROCESS,PROCESS,REJECTSHIP,PROCESS,REJECTCREDIT,
            REJECTCREDIT,REJECTCREDIT,REJECTCREDIT,PROCESS,PROCESS,
            REJECTSHIP,PROCESS);
        K = 1;
        IF DOLLAR > CREDIT THEN K = K + 8;
        IF SPCRED THEN K = K + 4;
        IF ORDRSZ < ORDRMN THEN K = K + 2;
        IF SPSHIP THEN K = K + 1;
        GO TO TABLE(K);
```

curs, we need only change the appropriate entry in the computed GO-TO statement shown in the programming examples.

Some programmers prefer to rearrange the basic decision table shown in Fig. 3.2 to the form shown in Fig. 3.3. Their flowchart then takes the form shown in Figs. 3.6(a) and 3.6(b). This, too, is somewhat modular: If the user decides to change the *nature* of action No. 1 (e.g., instead of rejecting the order and sending it to the credit department, the user decides to print a three-part rejection notice, with one copy sent to the credit department, one copy to the customer, and one copy to the sales department), it can be incorporated into the flowchart very simply. If, on the other hand, the user decides to change the conditions that lead to a specified action, then the flowchart shown in Fig. 3.6 will have to be completely redrawn.

Figure 3.4(d). Implementation of the decision table in COBOL.

```
NOTE EXPLANATORY NOTES. WHEN WE ENTER THIS SECTION OF CODE, WE
    ASSUME THAT THE FOLLOWING VARIABLES HAVE BEEN DEFINED AND
    INITIALIZED WITH THE FOLLOWING CONTENTS:
        DOLLAR    THE DOLLAR AMOUNT OF THE CUSTOMER'S ORDER
        CREDIT    THE CREDIT LIMIT FOR THIS CUSTOMER
        ORDRMN    THE MINIMUM ORDER ALLOWED FOR SHIPPING
        ORDRSZ    THE SIZE OF THIS CUSTOMER'S ORDER
    WE ALSO ASSUME THAT TWO FLAGS HAVE BEEN SET UP:
        SPCRED=0  IF THIS CUSTOMER DOES NOT HAVE SPECIAL APPROVAL
                  FROM THE CREDIT DEPARTMENT.
              =1  IF THIS CUSTOMER DOES HAVE SPECIAL APPROVAL
                  FROM THE CREDIT DEPARTMENT.
        SPSHIP =0 IF THIS CUSTOMER DOES NOT HAVE SPECIAL APPROVAL
                  FROM THE SHIPPING DEPARTMENT.
              =1  IF THIS CUSTOMER DOES HAVE SPECIAL APPROVAL FROM
                  THE SHIPPING DEPARTMENT.
DECISION-TABLE. MOVE ONE TO K.
    IF DOLLAR IS GREATER THAN CREDIT THEN ADD EIGHT TO K.
    IF SPCRED IS EQUAL TO ONE THEN ADD FOUR TO K.
    IF ORDRSZ IS LESS THAN ORDRMN THEN ADD TWO TO K.
    IF SPSHIP IS EQUAL TO ONE THEN ADD ONE TO K.
    GO TO PROCESS,PROCESS,REJECTSHIP,PROCESS,PROCESS,PROCESS,
        REJECTSHIP,PROCESS,REJECTCREDIT,REJECTCREDIT,
        REJECTCREDIT,REJECTCREDIT,PROCESS,PROCESS,REJECTSHIP,
        PROCESS DEPENDING ON K.
```

Figure 3.4(e). Implementation of the decision table in System/360 assembly language.

```
* WHEN THIS SECTION OF CODE IS ENTERED, WE ASSUME THAT THE FOLLOWING
* VARIABLES HAVE BEEN DEFINED AND INITIALIZED:
*           DOLLAR          THE DOLLAR AMOUNT OF THE CUSTOMER'S ORDER
*           CREDIT          THE CREDIT LIMIT FOR THIS CUSTOMER
*           ORDRSZ          THE SIZE OF THIS CUSTOMER'S ORDER
*           ORDRMN          THE MINIMUM ORDER ALLOWED FOR SHIPPING
* WE ALSO ASSUME THAT THE VARIABLES "SPCRED" AND "SPSHIP" HAVE BEEN
* DEFINED AS ONE-BYTE FLAGS WITH THE FOLLOWING VALUES:
*           SPCRED = 0      IF THIS CUSTOMER DOES NOT HAVE SPECIAL APPROVAL
*                           FROM THE CREDIT DEPARTMENT
*                  = 1      IF THIS CUSTOMER DOES HAVE SPECIAL APPROVAL FROM
*                           THE CREDIT DEPARTMENT.
*           SPSHIP = 0      IF THIS CUSTOMER DOES NOT HAVE SPECIAL APPROVAL
*                           FROM THE SHIPPING DEPARTMENT.
*                  = 1      IF THIS CUSTOMER DOES HAVE SPECIAL APPROVAL
*                           FROM THE SHIPPING DEPARTMENT.
*
```

Figure 3.4(e). Continued.

```
BEGIN      BALR  R15, 0          ESTABLISH ADDRESSABILITY OF PROGRAM
           USING *,R15
           L     R1, ZERO        INITIALIZE THE INDEX
           L     R2, CREDIT
           C     R2, DOLLAR      IS CREDIT GREATER THAN DOLLAR?
           BH    TEST2           IF SO, SKIP AROUND
           A     R1, EIGHT       OTHERWISE, INCREMENT INDEX BY 8
TEST2      CLI   SPCRED, 0       DOES CUSTOMER HAVE SPECIAL APPROVAL?
           BE    TEST3           IF NOT, SKIP AROUND
           A     R1, FOUR        OTHERWISE, INCREMENT INDEX BY 4
TEST3      L     R2, ORDRMN
           C     R2, ORDRSZ      IS ORDRMN LESS THAN ORDRSZ?
           BL    TEST4           IF SO, SKIP AROUND
           A     R1, TWO         OTHERWISE, INCREMENT INDEX BY 2
TEST4      CLI   SPSHIP, 0       DOES CUSTOMER HAVE SPECIAL APPROVAL?
           BE    DONE            IF NOT, SKIP AROUND
           A     R1, ONE         OTHERWISE, INCREMENT INDEX BY 1
DONE       IC    R1, TABLE(R1)   GET INDEX INTO BRANCH VECTOR
           B     VECTOR-4(R1)    DISPATCH TO APPROPRIATE ROUTINE
*
* TABLE FOR BRANCH VECTOR ADDRESSES
*
TABLE      DC    X'OC,OC,08,OC,OC,OC,08,OC,04,04,04,04,OC,OC,08,OC'
*
* BRANCH VECTOR
*
VECTOR     B     REJECTC         REJECT ORDER AND SEND TO CREDIT DEPARTMENT
           B     REJECTS         REJECT ORDER AND SEND TO SHIPPING DEPARTMENT
           B     PROCESS         PROCESS ORDER NORMALLY
EIGHT      DC    F'8'
FOUR       DC    F'4'
TWO        DC    F'2'
ONE        DC    F'1'
ZERO       DC    F'0'
R1         EQU   1
R2         EQU   2
R3         EQU   3
```

If we carry this idea a bit further, we can see that the selective decision table illustrated in Fig. 3.5 may not be very modular at all. If the user changes his specifications, new rules will have to be formulated, and the decision table may have to be rewritten; this in turn would lead to a complete reprogramming effort. On the other hand, if we had some mechanical means of translating the decision table shown in Fig. 3.5 *directly* into a computer program (i.e., with decision table "preprocessors"), this would not be of much concern to us. In fact, we would then *prefer* the approach shown in Fig. 3.5,

Figure 3.4(f). Implementation of the decision table in PDP-10 assembly language.

```
; WHEN THIS SECTION OF CODE IS ENTERED, WE ASSUME THAT THE FOLLOWING
; VARIABLES HAVE BEEN DEFINED AND INITIALIZED:
;           DOLLAR          THE DOLLAR AMOUNT OF THE CUSTOMER'S ORDER
;           CREDIT          THE CREDIT LIMIT FOR THIS CUSTOMER
;           ORDRSZ          THE SIZE OF THIS CUSTOMER'S ORDER
;           ORDRMN          THE MINIMUM ORDER ALLOWED FOR SHIPPING
; WE ALSO ASSUME THAT THE VARIABLES "SPCRED" AND "SPSHIP" HAVE BEEN
; DEFINED AND INITIALIZED WITH THE FOLLOWING VALUES:
;           SPCRED = 0      IF THIS CUSTOMER DOES NOT HAVE SPECIAL APPROVAL
;                           FROM THE CREDIT DEPARTMENT.
;                  = 1      IF THIS CUSTOMER DOES HAVE SPECIAL APPROVAL
;                           FROM THE CREDIT DEPARTMENT.
;           SPSHIP = 0      IF THIS CUSTOMER DOES NOT HAVE SPECIAL APPROVAL
;                           FROM THE SHIPPING DEPARTMENT.
;                  = 1      IF THIS CUSTOMER DOES HAVE SPECIAL APPROVAL
;                           FROM THE SHIPPING DEPARTMENT.
            MOVEI   1,0                 ;INITIALIZE THE INDEX
            MOVE    2,CREDIT            ;IS CREDIT GREATER THAN DOLLAR?
            CAMG    2,DOLLAR            ;IF SO, SKIP AROUND
            ADDI    1,10                ;OTHERWISE, INCREMENT INDEX BY 8
            SKIPE   SPCRED              ;DOES CUSTOMER HAVE SPECIAL APPROVAL?
            ADDI    1,4                 ;YES, INCREMENT INDEX BY 4
            MOVE    2,ORDRMN            ;IS ORDRMN LESS THAN ORDRSZ?
            CAML    2,ORDRSZ            ;IF SO, SKIP AROUND
            ADDI    1,2                 ;OTHERWISE, INCREMENT INDEX BY 2
            SKIPE   SPSHIP              ;DOES CUSTOMER HAVE SPECIAL APPROVAL?
            ADDI    1,1                 ;YES, INCREMENT INDEX BY 1
            JRST    @TABLE(1)           ;JUMP TO APPROPRIATE ROUTINE
;
; DISPATCH TABLE FOR THE 16 POSSIBLE SITUATIONS
;
TABLE:      EXP         PROCESS,PROCESS,REJECTS,PROCESS
            EXP         PROCESS,PROCESS,REJECTS,PROCESS
            EXP         REJECTC,REJECTC,REJECTC,REJECTC
            EXP         PROCESS.PROCESS,REJECTS,PROCESS
```

because a small change in the user's specifications would likely cause fewer rules in the decision table to change than in the exhaustive decision table shown in Fig. 3.2.

Once again, it should be clear that we would not require the formality of a decision table for the trivial problem posed above. However, for more complex problems, the approach can be quite useful. Naturally, there are many embellishments we may wish to add: We may wish to deal with situations where the conditions take on other than binary values; we may wish to build decision tables where the conditions are connected with a logical OR instead of (or in addition to) a logical AND; we may wish to investigate

Conditions and Actions	Rules 1	2	3	4	5	6
1. Dollar amount of order exceeds credit limit.	T	–	F	T	F	T
2. Customer has special approval from credit dept.	F	–	–	T	–	T
3. Size of order is less than minimum allowed.	–	T	F	F	T	T
4. Customer has special approval from shipping dept.	–	F	–	–	T	T
1. REJECT ORDER, SEND TO CREDIT DEPT.	X					
2. REJECT ORDER, SEND TO SHIPPING DEPT.		X				
3. PROCESS ORDER, AND SHIP IT.			X	X	X	X

Note that Rules No. 1 and 2 overlap to some extent: The situation specified by rule No. 11 in Fig. 3.2 satisfies both rules No. 1 and 2. However, since we will *first* check to see if rule No. 1 is applicable [see Fig. 3.6 (a)], this selective decision table essentially has the same effect as the one in Fig. 3.3.

Figure 3.5. A selective decision table for order-entry example.

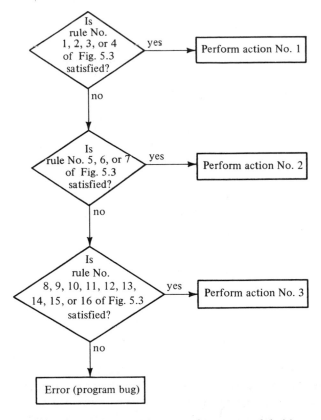

Figure 3.6(a). A flowchart based on the rearranged decision table.

110

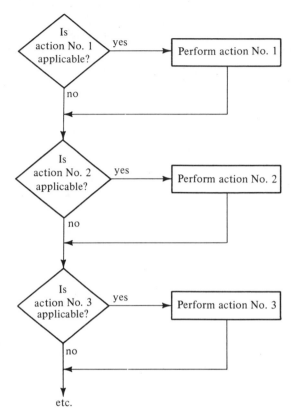

Figure 3.6(b). The general case of the rearranged decision table, the "if applicable" approach.

various techniques for optimizing the implementation of the decision table, so that the program can find the correct rule with a minimum of CPU time and/or memory; and we may wish to consider building hierarchies of decision tables.

3.3.3 Use Symbolic Parameters

As mentioned before, many programmers proceed on the premise (or even the promise) that they will never have to change their programs. As a result, many aspects of the program are coded in as *constants*; thus, when the specifications are changed, the programmer is forced to change every statement of the source program in which the obsolete constant appears.

To avoid this problem, the programmer should attempt to define as many things as possible in a symbolic fashion. In almost all programming languages, it is possible to equate a symbolic name or a constant or a "reasonable" expression. The assignment generally takes place at the time of assembly or compilation, though it may also take place when a number of separately compiled programs are link-edited (a rather ambiguous term which generally involves the resolution of global addresses between programs), or loaded into memory, or even when the program is executed. Though it may slow the compilation, assembly, or loading process somewhat, the use of symbolic parameters generally does not slow the execution of the program— and it *does* allow a characteristic of the program to be changed by changing only *one* statement in the source program.

This may seem a rather trivial form of modularity, but it should not be underestimated. In a large assembly language program, hundreds of statements may involve one of these parameter assignments; without this approach, it would be a major undertaking to change any aspect of the program —and is this not how we defined modularity? Even more important, the parameter-oriented approach helps prevent the programmer from forgetting to change all portions of the program that depend upon the parameter. By simply changing one source program statement and recompiling the program (and perhaps reloading it with other separately compiled programs), we guarantee that all affected source statements are automatically changed. Without this approach, the programmer may accidentally overlook some obscure statement that should have been changed. Some of my students have pointed out that a good text-editing package on a time-sharing system will accomplish the same thing. Though this is generally true (although not always— see the following section and Fig. 3.9), we sometimes find that a sloppy specification of the text to be changed in the source program causes some undesired changes to take place; thus, while changing all instances of CAT to DOG, we find that CATALOG becomes DOGALOG!

Some common examples of applications of parameter assignments are listed below.

The Size of a Table. The number of entries in a table, list, queue, buffer, or working storage area can be defined quite easily in a parametric fashion. Figures 3.7(a) and 3.7(b) show a FORTRAN program and an assembly language program where the size of a table has been defined symbolically; Figs. 3.8(a) and 3.8(b) show the same programs with the table sizes defined as a constant. This approach becomes particularly valuable when there are several tables (or buffers, queues, etc.), whose sizes are all related to one another; Fig. 3.9 illustrates an assembly language example of such a situation.

Relative Locations Within a Table. It is often desirable to define relative locations within a table or working storage area in a symbolic fashion. Thus, instead of referring to the third entry within a table as TABLE+3 throughout

Figure 3.7(a). A FORTRAN program with a parametrically defined table size.

```
C
C       THIS IS A SUBROUTINE THAT WILL SEARCH THROUGH ANY SINGLE-
C       DIMENSIONED ARRAY TO FIND A SPECIFIED ARGUMENT. THE ARGUMENTS
C       TO THE SUBROUTINE ARE AS FOLLOWS:
C              TABLE      THE NAME OF THE ARRAY TO BE SEARCHED
C              FIRST      THE LOWER DIMENSION OF THE ARRAY
C              LAST       THE UPPER DIMENSION OF THE ARRAY
C              ARG        THE QUANTITY BEING SEARCHED FOR
C              FLAG       INDICATES WHETHER OR NOT SEARCH WAS SUCCESSFUL
C
        SUBROUTINE SEARCH(TABLE,FIRST,LAST,ARG,FLAG)
        DIMENSION TABLE(FIRST:LAST)

        etc.
```

Figure 3.7(b). A PDP-8 assembly language program with a parametrically defined table size.

```
/ THIS IS A ROUTINE TO SEARCH THROUGH A TABLE TO FIND A SPECIFIED QUANTITY.
/
/ THE BEGINNING OF THE TABLE AND THE LENGTH OF THE TABLE ARE DEFINED SYMBOLICALLY
/ SO THAT THEY CAN BE CHANGED EASILY.
/
            BEGIN = 200
            LENGTH = 300
            *BEGIN              /SET ORIGIN TO BEG. OF TABLE
TABLE,      0
            *BEGIN+LENGTH       /MOVE ORIGIN PAST TABLE
SEARCH,     CLA                 /INITIALIZE THE ACCUMULATOR
            TAD COUNT           /INITIALIZE A COUNTER
            DCA TEMP

            etc.
```

the program, it should be given a distinct symbolic name. Figures 3.10(a), 3.10(b), and 3.10(c) illustrate the use of a parameter assignment in such a situation.

Note that this problem is avoided with the use of nested levels within the DATA DIVISION in COBOL. The use of *structures* in PL/I has essentially the same effect; some languages go even further and allow (or force) the programmer to refer to the data element itself by name, without any consideration for its physical proximity to other data elements. However, in most versions of FORTRAN and assembly language, the programmer must make a conscious effort to achieve this kind of parameterization.

Constants. Suppose we are writing a program in which we repeatedly make use of the constant 3.14159; we could code the constant into the program in

Figure 3.8(a). A FORTRAN program that does not use a parametrically defined table size.

```
C
C       THIS SECTION OF FORTRAN CODE WILL SEARCH THROUGH A TABLE TO FIND
C       A SPECIFIED QUANTITY. HOWEVER, IT IS NOT A SUBROUTINE.
C
        DIMENSION TABLE(100)
        DO 10 I=1,100
        IF (ARG .EQ. TABLE(I)) GO TO 20
10      CONTINUE
C
C       ENTER HERE IF SEARCH FAILS
C
        GO TO 30
C
C       ENTER HERE IF ITEM WAS FOUND
C
20      PRINT 100,I,TABLE(I)
```

Figure 3.8(b). A PDP-8 assembly language program that does not use a parametrically defined table size.

```
/ THIS IS A ROUTINE TO SEARCH THROUGH A TABLE TO FIND A SPECIFIED QUANTITY
/
/ NOTE, HOWEVER, THAT THE BEGINNING OF THE TABLE AND THE LENGTH OF THE TABLE
/ ARE DEFINED AS CONSTANTS.
/
            *200                    /SET ORIGIN FOR BEGINNING OF TABLE
TABLE,      0
            *500                    /MOVE ORIGIN PAST THE END OF THE TABLE
SEARCH,     CLA                     /INITIALIZE THE ACCUMULATOR
            TAD COUNT               /INITIALIZE A COUNTER
            DCA TEMP
              ⦚
            etc.
```

Figure 3.9. A program with several tables: IBM System/360 assembly language.

```
* THIS PROGRAM REQUIRES THREE TABLES; THE SIZE OF EACH TABLE IS A FUNCTION
* OF THE PARAMETER "SIZE". TO CHANGE THE SIZE OF THE TABLES, MERELY RE-
* DEFINE "SIZE"
*
SIZE        EQU     40
TABLE1      DS      CL(SIZE)
TABLE2      DS      CL(2*SIZE)
TABLE3      DS      CL(SIZE+5)
```

An application programmer is writing an assembly language program to process transactions from terminals. When a transaction is received, it is put into a *queue entry*; each queue entry has the following structure:

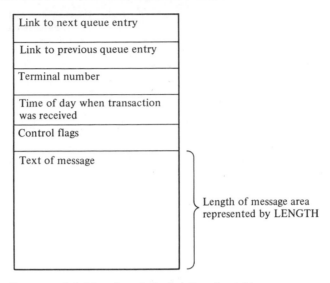

Figure 3.10(a). Parameter definitions for relative locations in a table.

Figure 3.10(b). Parameter definitions for relative locations in a table. On a word-oriented computer like the GE-435, the programmer might write the following sequence of instructions to use the queue entry shown in Fig. 3.10(a):

```
NEXT      EQU       0               *POINTER TO NEXT QUEUE ENTRY
PREV      EQU       1               *POINTER TO PREVIOUS QUEUE ENTRY
TERM      EQU       2               *TERMINAL NUMBER
TIME      EQU       3               *TIME-OF-DAY WHEN TRANS WAS RECVD
FLAGS     EQU       4               *CONTROL FLAGS
TEXT      EQU       5               *BEGINNING OF TEXT AREA
LENGTH    EQU       10              *LENGTH OF TEXT AREA, IN WORDS
*
* THIS SECTION OF CODE ASSUMES THAT THE ADDRESS OF THE QUEUE ENTRY HAS
* BEEN PLACED IN INDEX REGISTER 1.
*
BEGIN     LDS       NEXT,1          *GET ADDRESS OF NEXT QUEUE ENTRY
          STS       NXTPNT          *SAVE IT
          LDS       TERM,1          *WHICH TERMINAL SENT THE TRANSACTION?
```

Figure 3.10(c). Parameter definitions for relative locations in a table. On a byte-oriented computer like the IBM System/360, the programmer might write the following sequence of instructions to use the queue entry:

```
NEXT       EQU       0            POINTER TO NEXT QUEUE ENTRY
PREV       EQU       4            POINTER TO PREVIOUS QUEUE ENTRY
TERM       EQU       8            TERMINAL NUMBER
TIME       EQU       12           TIME-OF-DAY WHEN TRANS WAS RECVD
FLAGS      EQU       16           CONTROL FLAGS
TEXT       EQU       20           BEGINNING OF TEXT AREA
LENGTH     EQU       40           LENGTH OF TEXT AREA, IN BYTES
*
* THIS SECTION OF CODE ASSUMES THAT THE ADDRESS OF THE QUEUE ENTRY HAS
* BEEN PLACED IN GENERAL REGISTER 1.
*
BEGIN      L         R2,NEXT(R1)  GET ADDRESS OF NEXT QUEUE ENTRY
           ST        R2,NXTPNT    SAVE IT
           L         R2,TERM(R1)  WHICH TERMINAL SENT THIS TRANS?
           ⌇
           etc.
```

any one of the three ways shown in Figs. 3.11(a), 3.11(b), and 3.11(c). (The language used for this example is Burroughs B5500 ALGOL, but a variety of other languages and computers could have been used.) Note that in Fig. 3.11(a) the programmer has laboriously hand-coded the value of *pi* into

Figure 3.11(a). Parameter definitions for constants: Burroughs B5500 ALGOL.

```
AREA:= 3.14159 × RADIUS*2;
CIRCUMFERENCE:= 2 × 3.14159 × RADIUS;
IF X < 3.14159/2 THEN GO TO ERROR;
IF X > 3.14159 THEN Y:= FALSE;
```

Figure 3.11(b). Parameter definitions for constants: Burroughs B5500 ALGOL.

```
PI:= 3.14159;
AREA:= PI × RADIUS*2;
CIRCUMFERENCE:= 2 × PI × RADIUS;
IF X < PI/2 THEN GO TO ERROR;
IF X > PI THEN Y:= FALSE;
```

Figure 3.11(c). Parameter definitions for constants: Burroughs B5500 ALGOL.

```
DEFINE PI = 3.14159#;
AREA:= PI × RADIUS*2;
CIRCUMFERENCE:= 2 × PI × RADIUS;
IF X < PI/2 THEN GO TO ERROR;
IF X > PI THEN Y:= FALSE;
```

several different statements. As we pointed out earlier, this means that it will be quite inconvenient to change the value of the constant (e.g., when the programmer discovers that *pi* is more closely approximated by 3.1415926535); it also means that he may forget to change one of the source program statements because of a careless oversight.

Figure 3.11(b) certainly represents a more modular situation; the value of *pi* can be easily changed by changing the one source language statement in which PI is assigned the value 3.14159. However, this approach has the potential disadvantage that it takes effect at *execution time*; that is, after the program has been compiled and after it has been loaded, it must first execute the statement

    PI := 3.14159 ;

before PI can be used in any other statement. This generally involves the execution of one or two machine instructions *each time the program is executed*, something the programmer may wish to avoid (especially if there are several such statements in the program). On the other hand, an optimizing compiler may be able to perform this computation at compile time, since it sees that PI is assigned a value only once.

Figure 3.11(c) shows still another approach. The value of *pi* is assigned parametrically, but the assignment is done *at compile time*, and thus does not require any extra CPU time when the program is executed. The DEFINE statement works by substituting the *character string* '3.14159' for PI whenever it finds PI in the source program *during the compilation process*. A similar effect can be achieved in PL/I, and with macro facilities in many of the more sophisticated assembly languages. Note that this particular form of parameter assignment would be inefficient if it were used to define an *expression* instead of a constant, for it would cause the expression to be reevaluated (and appropriate machine instructions generated by the compiler) each time it appeared in the source program. In such a case, we would be better off with the approach shown in Fig. 3.11(b).

Note also that there are many other ways of accomplishing the type of parameter assignment shown in Fig. 3.11(c). In COBOL, for example, it is convenient to define constants in the WORKING STORAGE section of the DATA DIVISION with a VALUE clause. The same thing can be accomplished in PL/I with the INITIAL attribute in a declaration statement. Similarly, the DATA statement in FORTRAN allows the programmer to assign an initial value to a variable (or an array) at compilation time. In assembly language, the programmer usually has the option of using either a "string substitution" form of parameter assignment or a more direct form of parameter assignment, such as the one illustrated in Fig. 3.10(b). In the latter case, the programmer can usually equate a symbolic name to an *expression*, as long as the elements of the expression have already been defined.

Regardless of the programming language or the particular technique used, we must emphasize that the type of programming shown in Fig. 3.11(a) is to be discouraged. As we have seen above, virtually every programming language has at least one mechanism that facilitates a parameter-oriented approach; it remains for the programmer to find the one that best suits his needs.

Centralized Parameter Assignments and Definitions. Many of the current programming systems consist of *several* different programs, each written by a different person or group of persons. They are usually compiled or assembled separately, may or may not be link-edited and loaded together, and may or may not be executed together (e.g., even though the programs are all part of the same system, one of them may be executed on a daily basis, another on a weekly basis, another on a monthly basis, etc.). Because all of the programs are part of the same system, it is very likely that they will all make use of the same tables, lists, constants, and so forth.

Each programmer, in an attempt to make his own program more modular, could develop his own parameter assignments. However, since many of the parameters (e.g., constants, lengths of tables, etc.) are common to all of the programs, this could easily lead to an unmodular situation. For example, if we decided to change the length of a common table, we would have to change the corresponding parameter assignments of all the programs that used the table, and then recompile or reassemble all of the affected programs. Furthermore, we would again run the risk of forgetting to modify one or two obscure programs that happen to use our table.

Clearly, it would be preferable to have all of the programs make use of *common* parameter assignments. That is, if fourteen different programs have to refer to the third entry in a table (as in the example in Section 3.3.3), then there should be only *one* parameter assignment, instead of a parameter assignment in each of the fourteen programs. Similarly, if all of the programs require the same type of information from a table (a list of legal inputs, legal transaction codes, tax rates to be used in a billing program, coefficients to be used in some scientific calculation, etc.), then *all* of the programs should refer to a common table.

There are two ways of accomplishing this kind of common parameter assignment. The simplest technique is to write the parameter assignment statements on a separate source file (e.g., a separate deck of cards or a separate magnetic tape file) and then attach it to the front of each program to be compiled. This procedure is facilitated in most versions of COBOL with the INCLUDE statement, and similar procedures are provided in some versions of FORTRAN, as well as PL/I.

Another technique is to place all of the common tables, lists, queues, and so forth in a *separate* program, which is compiled independently of the others. All of the appropriate symbolic names can then be defined as *global* symbols. Similarly, the other programs that require access to the common parameters can refer to them as *external global* symbols (the terminology here is fairly widespread, but it may differ slightly from one computer system to another). The external global references are "resolved," to use another relatively standard term, when the compiled or assembled programs are link-edited or loaded together. The procedure is illustrated in Figs. 3.12(a), 3.12(b), and 3.12(c).

Figure 3.12(a). *Global parameter assignments.* Using the example from Fig. 3.10, we might have one program, which we will call PARAM, that simple consists of the parameter definitions. Thus it would consist of the following:

```
       ENTRY    NEXT       * POINTER TO NEXT QUEUE ENTRY
       ENTRY    PREV       * POINTER TO PREVIOUS QUEUE ENTRY
       ENTRY    TERM       * TERMINAL NUMBER
       ENTRY    TIME       * TIME-OF-DAY WHEN TRANS WAS RECVD
       ENTRY    FLAGS      * CONTROL FLAGS
       ENTRY    TEXT       * BEGINNING OF TEXT AREA
       ENTRY    LENGTH     * LENGTH OF MESSAGE, IN WORDS
         .
         .
         .
       any other definitions
         .
         .
         .
NEXT     EQU    0          * POINTER TO NEXT QUEUE ENTRY
PREV     EQU    1          * POINTER TO PREVIOUS QUEUE ENTRY
TERM     EQU    2          * TERMINAL NUMBER
TIME     EQU    3          * TIME-OF-DAY WHEN TRANS WAS RECVD
FLAGS    EQU    4          * CONTROL FLAGS
TEXT     EQU    5          * BEGINNING OF TEXT AREA
LENGTH   EQU    10         * LENGTH OF MESSAGE, IN WORDS
         .
         .
         .
       any other definitions
         .
         .
         .
```

Note: You should have only one ENTRY statement on each line of your source program, with a comment explaining the nature of the parameter. Do *not* put them all on one line, that is, do *not* write

```
ENTRY    NEXT,PREV,TERM,TIME,FLAGS,TEXT,LENGTH
```

for this is more awkward to read and more difficult to change.

Figure 3.12(b). *Global parameter assignments.* All other programs requiring the parameter definitions defined in Fig. 3.12(a) would be written in the following fashion:

```
        EXTERNAL    NEXT                    * POINTER TO NEXT ENTRY IN QUEUE
        EXTERNAL    PREV                    * POINTER TO PREVIOUS ENTRY IN QUEUE
        EXTERNAL    TERM                    * TERMINAL NUMBER
        EXTERNAL    TIME                    * TIME-OF-DAY WHEN TRANS WAS RECEIVED
        EXTERNAL    FLAGS                   * CONTROL FLAGS
        EXTERNAL    TEXT                    * BEGINNING OF TEXT AREA
        EXTERNAL    LENGTH                  * LENGTH OF TEXT AREA, IN WORDS
        *
        * A GE-435 PROGRAM TO PROCESS A TRANSACTION MIGHT BE WRITTEN IN THE FOLLOWING WAY,
        * ASSUMING THAT INDEX REGISTER 1 HAS THE ADDRESS OF THE CURRENT QUEUE ENTRY.
        *
        LDS     NEXT,1                      * GET POINTER TO NEXT QUEUE ENTRY
        STS     NXTPNT                      * SAVE IT
        LDS     TERM,1                      * WHICH TERMINAL SENT THIS TRANSACTION?
        .
        .
        .
LIST2   LDS     TEXT+3,1    * GET THIRD WORD OF TEXT
        .
        .
        .
LIST3   LDS     TEXT+LENGTH-1,1 * GET LAST WORD OF MESSAGE
        .
        .
        .
```

120

Note: On some computer systems, the facilities for using global symbols are somewhat limited. For example, some assemblers forbid global arithmetic of the nature shown in statement LIST3 above, that is, statements where two or more global symbols are added or subtracted. Some assemblers may even restrict global arithmetic of the nature shown in statement LIST2, that is, a global symbol plus some local symbols or con-

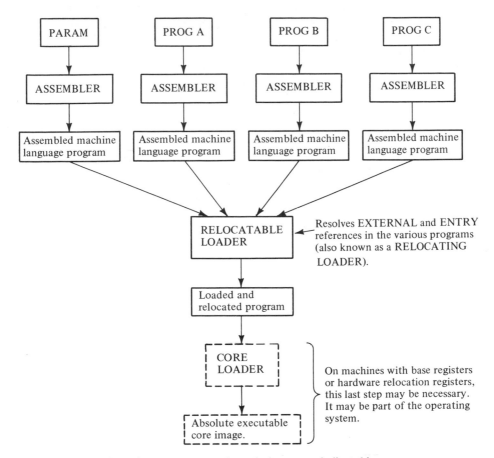

Figure 3.12(c). The various programs go through the process indicated here.

3.3.4 Separate Input/Output Functions from Computational Functions

A number of computer programs become unmodular because the input/output functions are scattered throughout the program. Since the IO portions of the program are very likely to change (because it is, by definition, the portion of the program that interfaces with the outside world), it is very important to keep them separated from the computational portions of the program. In most cases, it is convenient to write the program in such a way that the computational modules can call for an *element* of data; depending on the particular application, an element of data may be one ASCII character, a card image, a string of characters, a floating-point number, or a data base record. Similarly, the program should be written so that a single element of output data can be delivered to the output subroutines.

Some examples of activities that should be kept separate from the computational portions of the program are as follows.

The Physical Nature of the Input/Output Device. The computational portion of the program should not know or care whether the input comes from magnetic tape, cards, or a terminal; similarly, the program should not know or care whether the output is being sent to a high-speed printer, magnetic tape, or a terminal. This is especially important, because the IO devices may be changed after the program is written.

With most modern operating systems, the programmer is forced to refer to *logical* IO devices and is thus prevented from knowing the physical identification of the device. Still, the programmer can easily fall into the trap of making his program dependent on the fact that input comes from magnetic tape, as opposed to cards or terminal input. On a more trivial level, FORTRAN programmers often have several READ and WRITE statements scattered through their program, each referring to a logical unit number. If the IO device is changed (e.g., from card to tape), the programmer often has to change all of the READ or WRITE statements that referenced that unit number.

The Conventions for Initializing Input and Output. Prior to reading the first element of data or writing the first element of output, it may be necessary to open files, make certain initializing calls to the operating system, set up buffers, read or write label records, etc. These activities are likely to be changed often (e.g., if the programs are executed under a different operating system) and should thus be kept separate from the computational modules.

Buffering and Blocking Conventions. The buffering and blocking characteristics of a program may be changed to conserve memory, decrease the CPU time of the program, make better use of the physical storage medium (e.g., by reducing the number of interrecord gaps on magnetic tape), or to adapt to a different storage medium. However, the portions of the program that process the input and generate the output should not be concerned with these matters; they should only be the concern of the IO subroutines.

Error-Handling Conventions. A significant amount of programming time may be required to handle various IO errors. *Parity* errors are usually the most common problem in most programs, though there may be a variety of other types of errors. In some cases, the programmer can expect the operating system to perform all error recovery. In other cases, the programmer has the option of performing his own recovery; in still other cases, the programmer can attempt his own recovery *after* the operating system has performed its standard type of recovery. Finally, the programmer is sometimes *forced* to perform his own recovery.

However it is accomplished, error recovery is generally a very difficult and delicate part of many computer systems. It will often be modified as the programmer learns more about the nature of his hardware, his operating system, and the recovery requirements of his application. Because there are so many modifications, it is highly desirable that error recovery be performed in a modular fashion. To do this, we must usually distinguish between *recoverable* errors and *unrecoverable* errors. An example of a recoverable error is a parity error on magnetic tape, caused by a speck of dust, whereas an unrecoverable error might consist of a tape stretched, creased, and gouged by a faulty tape drive. For the purposes of modularity, it is suggested that recoverable errors be handled entirely by the IO routines, while unrecoverable errors be handled by the computational routines. In many cases, of course, the operating system will automatically handle the recoverable errors (e.g., by retrying a READ operation several times), but the IO routines may also be involved.

Figure 3.13(a) illustrates this concept with a brief section of assembly language coding from PDP-8 minicomputer; Fig. 3.13(b) illustrates the same concept with a COBOL program. Note that in both cases, the IO subroutines make an error return if an unrecoverable error is detected. At this point, the computational routines that must decide whether to ignore the unrecoverable input (or output) element, terminate all processing, print a special message for the computer operator, or take some other special action. If there are several areas where this kind of unrecoverable error processing might be required (e.g., several places where the same IO subroutines are called, and where the same kind of error return might be made), we would expect it to be handled by a common subroutine.

The Character Set Is Changed. A program may have been originally written to process ASCII input; it might have to be changed eventually to process EBCDIC, BCD, Hollerith, or perhaps a special subset of some other character set (e.g., a 64-character subset of ASCII). If these modifications are necessary, we would prefer to avoid changing all of the computational subroutines that process input characters and generate output characters.

The easiest way of accomplishing this is to define one standard *internal* character set that will be used by all of the computational subroutines—this internal character set could be ASCII, EBCDIC, a special 6-bit code (which would be useful for 12-bit, 18-bit, or 36-bit machines), etc. The IO modules should then be written to translate input into the internal character set; output should be translated from the internal character set to any desirable external character set.

Figure 3.13(a). Handling IO errors in a PDP-8 program.

```
                    .
                    .
                    .
                    .
                    .
                    .
IGNORE,     JMS READIN              /CALL SUBROUTINE FOR INPUT
            JMP ERROR               /RETURN HERE IF UNRECOVERABLE ERROR
            CLA                     /CLEAR JUNK OUT OF AC
            TAD  BUFFER             /GET FIRST WORD OF DATA
                    .
                    .
                    .
                    .
                    .
/
/ENTER HERE IF AN UNRECOVERABLE ERROR OCCURS. THIS SECTION OF CODE PUTS AN
/OCTAL 7777 IN THE ACCUMULATOR, AND HALTS. IF THE OPERATOR PUSHES THE
/CONTINUE BUTTON, THE PROGRAM WILL IGNORE THE BAD INPUT RECORD, AND GO ON
/TO READ THE NEXT ONE.
/
ERROR,      CLA CMA                 /PUT 7777 IN AC
            HLT                     /HALT WITH 7777 IN LIGHTS
            JMP IGNORE              /GO BACK AND READ NEXT RECORD.
```

Figure 3.13(b). Handling IO errors in COBOL.

```
NOTE EXPLANATORY NOTES. ASSUMING THAT THE COMPUTER SYSTEM ALLOWS
     THE PROGRAMMER TO HANDLE HIS OWN ERRORS, WE MIGHT WRITE THE
     CODE SHOWN BELOW. WE ASSUME THE EXISTENCE OF A SUBROUTINE
     CALLED "READIN", WHICH WILL PERFORM THE INPUT, AND WILL SET
     "ERRFLAG" TO THE VALUE 1 IF THERE HAS BEEN AN UNRECOVERABLE
     ERROR.
GETNEXTREC.
     PERFORM READIN.
     IF ERRFLAG = 1 THEN GO TO ERROR.
ERROR.
     DISPLAY ERRMESSAGE UPON CONSOLE.
     ACCEPT REPLY FROM CONSOLE.
     IF REPLY IS EQUAL TO YES THEN GO TO GETNEXTREC.
     STOP RUN.
```

Note that this approach is useful for a number of other character-oriented processing situations. For example, the IO modules should provide a standarized way of handling End-of-Message characters, End-of-Line characters, other control characters, multiple blanks, and so forth. Much of this will be unimportant within the computational modules; thus, the IO routines may wish to remove the control characters before passing input to the rest of the program. Similarly, some input may be nonstandard (e.g., input from teletype or paper tape may end with a Carriage Return–Line Feed *or* a Line Feed–Carriage Return, depending on the habits of the user), and the IO routines should ensure that the input has been put in some standard form before it is given to the computational modules.

3.3.5 Do Not Share Temporary Storage Locations

In Chapter 1, we pointed out that programmers often write several modules that share the same temporary storage locations or variables. Thus, we might have subroutines A, B, C, and D using variables TEMP1 and TEMP2—presumably to save memory. As we saw in Section 1.2.2, this kind of programming practice is often extremely difficult to debug.

It is usually far easier to debug a program if each module has its own dedicated temporary storage area. This is a very natural thing to do in languages such as ALGOL and PL/I, and on machines where pushdown stacks are easily implemented. Even on a simple minicomputer, it is better to set aside dedicated memory locations for each subroutine's working storage.

We must emphasize that a program *can* be written with shared working storage, and it *can* be debugged (though often with some difficulty); *however, it will not be modular.* Even though the subroutines are able to share temporary storage when the program is first written, there will probably be trouble when changes and improvements are made. Modules that were thought to be independent of one another will suddenly begin to conflict with one another and begin destroying temporary storage locations. Note that this becomes a much more serious problem with real-time, on-line, or multitasking systems. Even though module A may not explicitly call module B, it is still dangerous for them to share temporary storage locations—for module A may be *interrupted* by module B, which will then proceed to destroy the locations that were being used by module A.

3.4 General-Purpose Subroutines

One way of building modular programs is to develop a number of general-purpose "common" subroutines; these subroutines can then be used as building blocks for individual special-purpose applications. Like other aspects of modularity, the concept of writing general-purpose programs is quite popular, but it is rarely practiced with any sort of faithfulness.

Nevertheless, every programmer seems to have an intuitive notion of generality; accordingly, we will discuss generality from an intuitive point of view in this section. We will begin by discussing some of the advantages and disadvantages of general-purpose modules; we will then discuss a number of programming situations that would lend themselves to a general approach.

3.4.1 The Advantages of General-Purpose Modules

General-Purpose Modules Save Programming Time. In most cases, an average programmer will be able to find a standard version of a program before he can write it himself. Thus, if an organization keeps writing the same kind of module over and over again, it should be able to build up its own library of general-purpose modules, and its programmers should be expected to be familiar with its contents. Similarly, if as an individual programmer, you find yourself writing the same kind of subroutines over and over again, then you should try to write a general-purpose version. This will allow you to build up a "bag of tricks" that will make your next programming assignment easier and faster.

While most programmers consciously accept this argument, they subconsciously reject it. Because the general-purpose module was probably written by someone else (or, as is often the case, supplied by the computer manufacturer), the programmer usually does not want to use it. Either he doesn't trust it, or he is too lazy to find out how it works. It is much more fun, much more satisfying, from a psychological point of view, to write your own version by yourself. Writing a computer program is very much like solving a jigsaw puzzle; using someone else's general-purpose subroutine is analogous to letting someone else solve part of the jigsaw puzzle for you—it takes away some of the fun and sense of personal accomplishment.

There is also the feeling that "it will only take a few minutes to write this new subroutine, but it will take *hours* to locate a general-purpose module and find out how it works." Humbug! Poppycock! This popular fallacy is one of the many unfortunate manifestations of overestimating one's programming abilities. It does *not* take just a few minutes to write that subroutine: It probably takes an hour or so to design, a few hours to code, and an unpredictable amount of programmer time and CPU time to debug. Meanwhile, a few *days* of *real* time have elapsed!

You don't think this happens? Take a look at the last program you wrote—was it really so unique that you could not find a way of using some of the routines in the manufacturer's library? Was it *really* impossible to use a program written by someone else in your own organization? And finally, how long did it *really* take to write that unique, personally crafted subroutine of which you are so proud?

General-Purpose Modules Save Memory Space. If each programmer writes his own special-purpose subroutines, it is likely that there will be a large number of similar subroutines. Clearly, if all of these programs are executing at the same time in a computer, there will be a great deal of wasted memory space.

One of the ways of avoiding this is to use the top-down programming approach discussed in the previous chapter. When the program design is begun, no attention is paid to individual subroutines; instead, the major functional elements of the program are simply identified as a "black box." As the design proceeds, each of these black boxes can be broken into its constituent subelements; this process then proceeds until we have reached the level of individual modules. At this point, it should be fairly easy to determine which of the modules will be performing similar functions. It should also be possible to tell whether these functions could be performed by existing, previously written, general-purpose subroutines.

Alternatively, the design can begin in a bottom-up fashion by taking inventory of the *existing* library of general-purpose modules. These generally form the bottom level of modules within a system. The programmer then begins combining these modules as required to accomplish his own applications. This may not be a practical approach if there are no existing general-purpose modules that can be adapted to the application. There may also be a danger that the application may be forcibly "bent" to fit the requirements of the existing general-purpose modules—in which case, one might ask whether the modules were really so general-purpose after all!

The General-Purpose Approach Prevents Program Bugs. Finally, we should point out that a number of programming catastrophes can be avoided by using standard, general-purpose modules. The "quick-and-dirty" special-purpose modules may appear to work when they are first written, but they may have a subtle bug whose effects are not noticed for several days, weeks, or months. This is especially troublesome in the cases where the programmer writes a small program, uses it once or twice, and then throws it away. Consider, for example, a simple program to copy a magnetic tape. It may have been written by a programmer who had only one tape to copy, and in his haste to get the job done, he neglected to pay much attention to error-handling. As a result, if a parity error occurs during an attempt to read a record, that record is ignored, and the program does not even print an error message ("After all," said the programmer, "I'm only writing the program to copy this one tape—and I know that the tape is good, so there is not much chance of a parity error."). Of course, by the time someone notices that something is wrong with the copied tape, the "quick-and-dirty" program has been lost or thrown away. Consequently, nobody knows precisely what it did wrong, and it may be impossible to correct the problem.

With a general-purpose program, it is far more likely that these bugs will not exist, for the programmer will have taken the trouble to do a thorough job. If something does go wrong, it should be possible to find a program listing and other documentation to fix the problem. Thus, we have the psychologically comforting reassurance that, with a general-purpose program, we are working with a known quantity; it should give us predictable results.

3.4.2 The Potential Disadvantages of General-Purpose Programs

It would not be realistic to discuss general-purpose programs without mentioning some of their drawbacks. We implied in the previous section that the programmer's laziness and/or unwillingness to use someone else's program is a common excuse for avoiding the general-purpose approach; however, there are other valid reasons, which we will discuss next.

It May Be Difficult to Locate General-Purpose Programs. It is sometimes *very* time-consuming and frustrating to search through a library of programs to find a good general-purpose subroutine. This is more likely to be true when one depends on the local users groups (e.g., SHARE, DECUS, and GUIDE), because there is no guarantee that the program works, that it will be supported, or that the documentation will be adequate. It may also be a problem when one attempts to use the general-purpose modules provided by the computer manufacturer.

One of the main problems here is usually *documentation*. The documentation that describes what the program does and how to use it is often incomplete, incorrect, or nonexistent. In the case of a computer manufacturer's program library, which may consist of hundreds or even thousands of programs, the problem may be one of adequate cross-references, abstracts, or indexes. While it is often beyond the individual programmer's direct control, we should still point out that it is often worthwhile to engage in a little extra work to organize a well-documented, easy-to-use program library; the extra work may reap large dividends on future programming assignments.

The General-Purpose Program May Not Follow Your Programming Conventions. This can be an especially large problem if you attempt to use a general-purpose program or subroutine provided by the computer manufacturer or a user group. The programming conventions used by the author of the general-purpose module may be different than those used in your organization. Arguments may be passed to subroutines in a different way; registers and accumulators may be used differently; documentation style and content may be unacceptable, even though correct.

In some cases, the general-purpose module can still be salvaged by changing the calling sequence, changing the use of registers, etc. The important thing is to produce a practical general-purpose subroutine that can be used by you and the other programmers in your organization. Thus, even if you have to completely rewrite the manufacturer's orginal routine, it may still prove to be a wise investment of time and effort if you and your colleagues can use it again.

General-Purpose Programs May Require Significantly More CPU Time and Memory. Unfortunately this is the major drawback of many general-purpose programs. As much as the programmer would like to use them, they are simply too large and too slow. A common example of a "package" that falls into this category is the data management package provided by many computer manufacturers and software houses—one version requires as much as 300K bytes of core memory!

However, you should not be too quick to throw away general-purpose programs supplied by the vendor or user group. Especially in the area of mathematical subroutines (e.g., SIN, COS, LOG, matrix inversion, Fourier transforms), and to a lesser extent in the area of IO utility routines, the general-purpose program may have been *optimized* for fast execution and/or minimal use of memory. It may be very difficult to equal their performance with a hurriedly written special-purpose routine. If your special-purpose routine *is* faster, check to see that it does all of the error-handling that is usually provided by the general-purpose version—that is, check to see whether you did as good a job as the general-purpose program. Also, bear in mind that if the general-purpose program was well-written, it will be modular: It should be possible to remove those portions of the program that correspond to unwanted features, and thus increase the efficiency of the program.

It is often a good idea to try out the general-purpose program to see how it works. If it turns out to be too slow or too extravagant in its use of memory, disk, or IO channel time, then you may want to write your own version of the program. However, if you *do* write your own version, write it in such a way that it can be used by others. In other words, make it a general-purpose program!

3.4.3 Examples of Programs That Should Be Written in a General-Purpose Fashion

We give here only a brief list of the subroutines, programs, and packages that should be made general-purpose. This list is not intended to be complete, but it should give some idea of the approach and attitude that the programmer should have when he writes his program.

Search Subroutines and Table Lookups. A common activity in computer programming is to *search* through a table, or perhaps a file on a disk or drum, for a specified item; it is also necessary to be able to *insert* items in the table (or file) in such a way that they can be easily found again. Both functions can be accomplished by the same subroutine in most cases. To insert a new entry, we first search for it (unsuccessfully) and arrange to have our subroutine indicate the address where the new entry should be.

Unfortunately, it often seems that every programmer wants to write his own search subroutine for each new application that he works on. A standard, general-purpose search routine could easily be written to be used by all members of a programming organization. It could be written in FORTRAN, COBOL, or PL/I to meet the needs of standardization, or it could be written in assembly language for efficiency.

Input/Output Subroutines for Minicomputers. In a high-level programming language, the programmer is given powerful, convenient statements for performing input/output. On the medium- and large-sized machines, even the assembly language programmer is given convenient mechanisms for doing convenient mechanisms: On any computer with an operating system, the application programmer is generally not allowed to perform his own input/output, i.e., he is not allowed to issue the machine language instructions that actually control the peripheral device.

On the minicomputers, however, the situation is often very different. While most of these smaller computers do have operating systems, it is not mandatory to use them. Because of special applications (e.g., process control and data acquisition) or limitations on memory, the programmer may elect to dispense with the operating system and write *all* of his own software. Since he has full access to all of the IO devices, he often ends up writing his own IO subroutines. This is usually very wasteful, since the computer manufacturer or a user group invariably supplies all of the standard IO routines for the console typewriter, for the paper tape reader, paper tape punch, magnetic tape, disk, etc.

Sorts and Merges. It is now common practice for the computer manufacturers to supply a SORT and MERGE package as part of their standard software. In many cases, the package can be called directly from a COBOL, FORTRAN, ALGOL, or PL/I program. However, these vendor-supplied packages are usually tape-oriented or disk-oriented and seem to be most convenient for relatively large sorts. To sort a small number of items, such as a table consisting of a few hundred entries or less, the programmer may wish to write his own sorting subroutine. We must again warn, though, that if there are ten programmers within an organization who need a small sorting subroutine, they will each write their own; even worse, each new time that an individual programmer needs a sort routine, he will write a new one. Obviously, it should be possible to write a general-purpose sort routine.

Dumps, Traces, Snapshots, Debugging Packages, Etc. Within the high-level languages such as COBOL and FORTRAN, there is a tendency among programmers to use the built-in debugging statements; the DUMP and PDUMP statements in FORTRAN are examples, and the MONITOR statement in Burroughs B5500 ALGOL is another. In assembly language, however, the programmer is often forced to write his own traces, snapshots, etc. Aside from the simple traces and dumps, the programmer may require a variety of fairly substantial test packages: programs to generate simulated test input; programs to generate test files and data bases; DDT-type debugging programs, etc. If a number of programmers in the same organization are debugging the same kind of programs (or, equivalently, if one programmer intends to write and debug the same kind of programs over and over again), then it may be worthwhile to develop a set of general-purpose test programs. Chapters 7 and 8 discuss a number of useful testing and debugging packages.

Conversion Subroutines. In a number of applications, the programmer has to make various kinds of *conversions*: from ASCII to BCD; from ASCII to some internal character set such as the 6-bit character set used on some Honeywell and Burroughs computers; or possibly from ASCII to binary; or decimal to octal; etc. The computer manufacturer often supplies a large number of these routines, written in a reasonably general-purpose manner; a number of conversion routines can also be found in the user group libraries.

Simple Input/Output Utility Subroutines. Every computer installation must have its tape-to-printer, card-to-disk, and disk-to-tape programs; there must also be tape-copying programs, card-duplication routines, etc. Once again, these are usually provided by the computer manufacturer; because of particular labelling, blocking, buffering, or formatting conventions, however, each installation may want to write its own set of utility routines. The important thing, of course, it that we avoid the situation where each programmer writes his own utility routines; even worse is the situation where each programmer writes a new set of utility routines similar to, but slightly different from, the previous set of utility routines.

Dynamic Storage Allocation Subroutines. In a large computer system where memory, disk, or drum storage must be allocated dynamically, there should be one general-purpose subroutine that can be used by all programmers; there should also be a subroutine to release the storage when it is no longer required.

REFERENCES

1. D. A. HARDING, "Modular Programming—Why Not?" *The Australian Computer Journal*, Volume 4, Number 4, November 1972, pages 150–156.
2. M. BLEE, "Modular Programming—Innovation or Common Sense?" *Data Systems*, February 1969, pages 26–27.

3. A. COHEN, "Modular Programs: Defining the Module," *Datamation*, January 1972, pages 34–37.

4. R. JUDD, "Practical Modular Programming," *Computer Bulletin*, Volume 14, pages 4–7.

5. I. KLINGELS, "Some Thoughts on the Future of Modular Programming," *Data Processing*, Volume 13 (July–August 1971), pages 268–269.

6. D. W. PACKER, "Effective Program Design," *Computers and Automation*, July 1970, pages 37–41.

7. J. J. RHODES, "Management by Module," *Data Systems*, August 1971, pages 34–36.

8. ——, "Management by Module," *Data Systems*, September 1971, pages 36–38.

9. ——, "Management by Module," *Data Systems*, October 1971, pages 32–34.

10. R. ARMSTRONG, *Modular Programming in COBOL*, John Wiley & Sons, Inc., 1973.

11. S. MADNICK and J. ALSOP, "A Modular Approach to File System Design," *Proceedings of 1969 SJCC*, pages 1–13.

12. J. MAYNARD, *Modular Programming*, Auerbach Publishers, 1972.

13. G. J. MYERS, "Characteristics of Composite Design," *Datamation*, September 1973, pages 100–102.

14. D. L. PARNAS, "A Technique for Software Module Specification with Examples," *Communications of the ACM*, May 1972, pages 330–336.

15. ——, "On the Criteria to Be Used in Decomposing Systems into Modules," *Communications of the ACM*, December 1972, pages 1053–1058.

PROBLEMS

1. Give a brief definition of a modular program.

2. Give a brief definition of a module.

3. If you were to examine someone else's program, how would you determine whether it was modular? If you had to examine two programs A and B, how would you determine whether program A was more modular than program B?

4. What is the purpose of writing modular programs? Do you think this purpose is obvious to the user of a typical computer program or system?

5. Section 3.1.1 suggests that a modular program can be defined in terms of the *size* of a module. What are the advantages of such an approach? What are the disadvantages? Do you think this kind of definition of a modular program can be misused, and if so, how?

6. Do you think it is reasonable to restrict the size of a module to 20 program statements? Give some reasons for your opinion.

7. What is the significance of restricting the size of a module to 50 statements? Do you think this is a reasonable restriction? Would you be willing to abide by it?

8. Do you think it is reasonable to restrict the size of a module to a month's work on the part of an average programmer? Do you think it should be shorter, e.g., two weeks' work?

9. What do we mean when we say that one module is "independent" of another module? Can this be quantified? Can you tell by looking at a program whether its modules are independent of one another? Should you be able to do so?

10. How can you tell if a program is dependent upon a particular algorithm? Give an example of a program in which several modules would have to be changed if some portion of the overall algorithm changed.

11. How can you tell if a program is highly dependent upon a certain set of arguments or parameters? Give an example of a program or a module where a change of arguments (e.g., a change from a single precision format to a double precision format) would have a major effect upon the module.

12. How can you tell if a program is highly dependent upon internal tables, constants, or variables? Do you think this is a common situation? Give an example of a program that would require major changes if the format of a particular table or particular constant were changed.

13. How can you tell if a program is highly dependent upon the structure of a data base? Give an example of such a program in your organization. What can be done to reduce the dependence of a program upon the format and structure of the data base?

14. How can you tell if a program is highly dependent upon such control characteristics as reentrance, recursion, or serial reusability? Give an example of such a program in your organization. What can be done to make a program less dependent on these kinds of characteristics?

15. Discuss briefly the advantages of modular programming. Do you think these advantages are recognized and understood in your organization?

16. What are the disadvantages of modular programming? How significant are these disadvantages in your organization? What can be done to minimize the disadvantages?

17. Do you think that most programmers in your organization understand the concept of modularity? As an experiment, conduct a poll among the programmers with whom you work—ask them what they think a modular program is. Does everyone give the same answer?

18. Try to find an example of a program written by someone in your organization that was originally considered (by the author of the program) to be modular, but that eventually proved to be otherwise. What characteristics of the program contributed to its lack of modularity? Did the author of the program really understand what he was doing, that is, *why* did he think he was writing a modular program?

19. How much more development time do you think it takes to write a modular program? As an experiment, take a relatively simple programming job; find a friend or colleague whose programming abilities are roughly the same as yours; develop a modular version of the program yourself; ask your friend to develop his version of the program as quickly as possible. How much longer (if at all) did it take you to develop the program? Do you think it was worth the extra time and effort?

20. In most cases, an attempt at modular programming requires the use of subroutine-calling mechanisms, e.g., the PERFORM statement in COBOL, the CALL statement in FORTRAN, the BALR instruction in IBM System/370 assembly language. Investigate the subroutine-calling mechanism in your programming language. How many microseconds of execution time does it take? Do you think it is significant?

21. Repeat the experiment suggested in problem 19 above. How much more CPU time does the modular version of your sample program require than the "quick-and-dirty" version of the program? Do you think this is significant? If the modular version *does* require more CPU time, do you think it is justified by other advantages?

22. What can be done to minimize the extra CPU time requirements that may result from attempts at modular programming? When should these efforts be made?

23. Repeat problem 20 above; this time, however, find out how much (object code) memory is required by the subroutine-calling mechanism in your programming language. Do you think this is significant?

24. Repeat the experiment suggested in problem 19 above. How much more memory does the modular version of your sample program require than the "quick-and-dirty" version? Do you think this is a significant amount? If the modular version *does* require more memory, do you think it is justified by other savings?

25. Are decision tables used in your organization? If not, why not? How difficult do you think it would be to convince the programmers to use decision tables?

26. Why do decision tables lead to more modular programs? Is it necessary to take any special steps to ensure that the resulting programs will indeed be modular?

27. Give an example of a program where the lack of use of symbolic parameters (discussed in Section 3.3.3) contributed to its lack of modularity. Would there have been any problems introducing some symbolic parameters?

28. Why is it a good idea to describe the size of a table as a symbolic parameter? What should be done if one has a program with several tables whose sizes are related to one another (e.g., one table is always twice as long as another)?

29. What are some of the problems that can result if one does *not* use symbolic parameters to define those aspects of a program that are likely to change?

30. Discuss two different ways of defining *constants* in a program as a symbolic parameter. Which approach requires more CPU time? Which one is more convenient?

31. Why should input/output functions be separated from the computational portion of a program? Are there any disadvantages to this philosophy?

32. How can a program be designed so that the physical nature of the input/output device can be changed without affecting the logic of the program? Are there any situations where this is difficult to accomplish?

33. How can a program be designed so that the buffering and blocking characteristics can be changed without affecting the logic? Is this difficult to accomplish?

34. Why should we arrange our program so that temporary working-storage areas are not shared between modules? Describe a type of programming bug that might arise from such sharing of working storage.

35. Some programming languages make it relatively easy to avoid the problem of shared working storage. In ALGOL, for example, each module can declare its own "local" variables that are only known within the boundaries of the module itself. Thus, if module GLOP defines a local variable X, it will have a different meaning (and will be assigned to a different memory location) than a local variable X defined within module FLOP. Does your programming language offer such features? Are there any disadvantages to this feature? How can we ensure that several programmers working on the same project will use these features?

36. Some languages do not offer the "local variable" feature mentioned in problem 35 above. All of the variables and working storage declared within the program are accessible to all of the modules in the program. In such a situation, how can we ensure that different modules will be given their own unique working storage? How can we ensure that several programmers working on the same project will take the appropriate steps to obtain unique areas of working storage for their modules?

37. Do you think that general-purpose modules will save a significant amount of programming time? Have you had any cases where it was faster and easier to write your own special-purpose version of a program?

38. Do you think that general-purpose programs are likely to save memory space? If so, how much? Do you think that general-purpose programs (e.g., a square-root program offered by the hardware manufacturer) will execute more quickly than a special-purpose version you could write yourself?

39. What other advantages do general-purpose library programs have? Are these advantages recognized within your organization? Are programmers *required* to use the general-purpose programs whenever possible? If not, why not?

40. What are the potential disadvantages of general-purpose programs? Are these disadvantages significant? Are they likely to occur in an average programming situation?

4

STRUCTURED PROGRAMMING

4.0 Introduction

For several years, a number of computer scientists have been discussing and refining a relatively new approach to programming and program design—a concept known as *structured programming*. It promises great improvements over the current ad hoc programming methods, and the few experiments that have been tried with structured programming have been highly successful. Yet despite its rather extensive treatment in the literature and the controversy that still surrounds it, the vast majority of programmers, especially those in the United States, have never heard of it. When they *do* hear of it (usually in a highly oversimplified form), they tend to reject it as being unnecessarily restrictive and impractical.

Thus, one of the major purposes of this chapter will be to describe the history and background of the structured programming movement, so that its objectives may be more easily understood. The objectives have always been greater readability and clarity of the program, greater programmer productivity, and reduced testing problems. We will then focus on the techniques and theory of structured programming. Applications to the common programming languages will be given.

136

4.1 History and Background of Structured Programming

4.1.1 Early Work by Dijkstra and Others

Professor Edsger W. Dijkstra, of the University of Eindhoven, Netherlands, has been one of the driving forces in the movement towards structured programming. In 1965, he suggested at the IFIP Congress [1] that the GO-TO could be eliminated from programming languages. He is perhaps best remembered at this meeting for his statement that the quality of a programmer was inversely proportional to the number of GO-TO statements in his program![1] Despite the fact that the 1965 IFIP Congress was held in New York and was widely attended by an international audience, the impact of this statement was relatively small. Many programmers had just gotten used to FORTRAN II and were bracing themselves for an expected conversion to FORTRAN IV—one of whose mainstays is the venerable GO-TO statement. Others were painfully upgrading from RPG to COBOL; still others were engrossed in IBM's then newly released System/360.

Not to be ignored, Dijkstra repeated his ideas in a letter to the editor of the *Communications of the ACM* in March 1968 [2]. He also enunciated some of his ideas about top-down systems design (which seem to go hand in hand with the idea of structured programming) in a paper presented at the First ACM Symposium on Operating System Principles—a paper that was later reprinted in the May 1968 *Communications of the ACM* [3]. At the same time, he attended the NATO-sponsored Software Engineering Conferences and described some of his ideas in the 1969 *Software Engineering Techniques* [4]; it was in this working paper that his delightful analogy of a program being considered as a string of pearls on a necklace was first seen. Another memo describing his ideas was published at the University of Eindhoven [5].

Throughout his work, Dijkstra's objectives seem to have been relatively constant. As he points out in his paper in *Software Engineering Techniques* [4]:

> The leading question was if it was conceivable to increase our programming ability by an order of magnitude and what techniques (mental, organizational or mechanical) could be applied in the process of program composition to achieve this increase.

---

[1]Stories about Dijkstra are legion (as they are about Knuth and other superprogrammers in the field), and many of his remarks and statements are already part of the computer folklore. It is reputed that he has little interest in accepting at his university any graduate student with knowledge of FORTRAN, on the assumption that such knowledge has probably created permanent bad programming habits. Similarly, he has been heard to say that if FORTRAN can be considered an infantile disorder, then certainly PL/I would have to be classed as a fatal disease.

More than anything else, Dijkstra seems to have been concerned with the problem of proving the correctness of a computer program, i.e., developing a mathematically rigorous proof of the correctness of a program that would eliminate the necessity for costly, tedious, and largely unsuccessful ad hoc testing. As he pointed out in the same paper:

> ... I have not focused my attention on the question 'how do we prove the correctness of a given program?' but on the questions 'for what program structures can we give correctness proofs without undue labor, even if the programs get large?' and, as a sequel, 'how do we make, for a given task, such a well-structured program?' My willingness to confine my attention to such 'well-structured programs' (as a subset of the set of all possible programs) is based on my belief that we can find such a well-structured subset satisfying our programming needs, i.e., that for each programmable task this subset contains enough realistic programs.

At the same time, other workers were showing some interest in the problem, though their interest was more often directed toward programming languages and formal computability theory than towards the practical applications of structured programming. Professor Van Wijngaarden pointed out that the GO-TO statement could be removed from the ALGOL 60 language with an appropriate preprocessing algorithm [6]. Several authors introduced specialized programming languages and programming styles that eliminated the GO-TO statement; among these are Van Schorre's development of LISPX and MOL-32 [7] and Landin's ISWIM [8].

4.1.2 Work by IBM

At the same Software Engineering conference in which Dijkstra described some of his ideas on structured programming, Joel Aron of IBM described an experiment known as "the superprogrammer project" [9]. In this experiment, one programmer, Dr. Harlan Mills, was given the rather impossible task of doing in six months what appeared to be a 30-man-year project. Though the experiment was only a qualified success (Dr. Mills, for example, was shielded from the users while he worked, so they would not become confused by the fact that two groups of programmers were working on the same project!), it suggested some new ideas in project organization, system design, and program design—most notably, the idea of top-down programming that we discussed in Chapter 2. In addition, the work was done in PL/I, which, as we will see later in this chapter, has convenient mechanisms for structured programming.

The success of the first experiment prompted IBM to try the same ideas on a larger scale: an information retrieval project for The *New York Times* [10]. Once again, the major effort in this project was to develop an efficient new form of project organization and project management; however, structured programming and top-down programming also played a prominent part. What makes this project so interesting is that it was relatively large (some 83,000 source statements of code), relatively practical (a real customer paid real money for a working system), and very successful (the productivity of the programmers was approximately five times higher than that of the average programmer).

Since the successful completion of the *New York Times* project, the Federal Systems Division of IBM, in which the original "superprogrammer" idea was conceived, has begun to carry its ideas to other parts of IBM and to several large IBM users. A number of large government agencies have expressed great interest in some of the ideas (though, once again, the emphasis seems to have been on the project management aspect of the IBM approach), and there is some hope that it will soon spread to the massive number of "ordinary" IBM users.

4.1.3   Recent Developments and Current Feelings

In addition to the work mentioned above, a number of universities and research organizations have begun experimenting with "go-to-less" programming—one of the overly simplistic synonyms for structured programming. In particular, workers at Carnegie-Mellon University have developed a "systems implementation language" called BLISS that does not have a GO-TO statement. According to Professor William Wulf, the experience of three years with BLISS and its use in the development of compilers and operating systems have shown it to be a practical and useful programming language; by extension, one must assume that the experiments with structured programming have also been successful. In particular, Wulf reports [11] that

> The inescapable conclusion from the Bliss experience is that the purported inconvenience of programming without a *goto* is a myth. Programmers familiar with languages in which the *goto* is present go through a rather brief and painless adaptation period. Once past this adaptation period they find that the lack of a *goto* is not a handicap; on the contrary, the invariant reaction is that the enforced discipline of programming without a *goto* structures and simplifies the task.

Wulf's remarks were made at the 25th ACM National Conference, in 1972; his remarks were part of a session that was devoted to this one controversial aspect of structured programming—it was entitled "The GOTO Controversy." After a series of papers and panel discussions both for and against the abolition of the GO-TO statement (whose significance will become much clearer in Section 4.3), it became apparent that nobody's mind was being changed—those who came in to the meeting in favor of the GO-TO statement left in favor of it, and those who came opposing it left opposing it. In the words of Mr. Martin Hopkins [12]:

> . . . our wisdom has not yet reached the point where future languages should eliminate the *goto*. If future work indicates that by avoiding *goto* we can gain

some important advantage such as routine proofs that the programs are correct, then the decision to retain the *goto* construct should be reconsidered. But until then, it is wise to retain it.

Nevertheless, it seems that most of the data processing community is slowly becoming converted to structured programming. The December 1973 issue of *Datamation* heralded structured programming as a "programming revolution" and devoted five articles to it [33, 34, 35, 36, 37]. Dijkstra, Dahl, and Hoare have produced a book on the subject [39], as has Weinberg [38]. Several universities have begun teaching a structured approach to programming—which has proved especially successful with students who have *no* previous experience in programming. Universities, research organizations, computer manufacturers (IBM in particular, though others are working at it more quietly), and computer scientists are now striving to gain practical experience with structured programming. At the same time, they are looking for ways of using this programming approach to simplify the job of testing a computer program. In the meantime, though, many programmers continue to see only the most controversial aspect of the idea—especially the suggestion that the GO-TO statement be removed—and reject it summarily. It is expected that future research and experimentation will continue to demonstrate the greater productivity and control of programs written in this fashion; at that point, we may expect to see it accepted by the larger community of experienced programmers and analysts.

4.2 The Objectives and Motivation of Structured Programming

At this point, the reader may argue that he still doesn't know what structured programming is; even worse, he may have already come to the conclusion that it simply consists of eliminating the GO-TO statement from programming languages—and in disgust, he may have already given up on this chapter and skipped forward to Chapter 5 to see if it perhaps contains something more practical!

Indeed, there *is* more to structured programming than eliminating the GO-TO statement, and we *will* discuss it at greater length (in Section 4.3 below). However, my experience in attempting to present this subject to various groups of disinterested (and occasionally hostile!) groups of programmers has taught me that it is important to first stress the *positive* objectives of this programming approach. We have already seen one *negative* aspect of structured programming (at least from the point of view of the average programmer), i.e., the elimination of the GO-TO. In the next section, we will see that it is usually a set of programming rules and restrictions that force the program to follow a very tight form, thereby eliminating much of the randomness, unreadability, and complexity that leads to bugs and increased testing and maintenance problems. This, too, seems like a negative aspect: The programmer complains: "*More* rules and restrictions, on top of the standards that I already have to follow. Programming isn't any fun any more; I can't be creative!" While this is usually an exaggerated fear, there is some element of truth in it. On the other hand, if we can show that it allows the programmer to turn out twice as much working code per day as his "unstructured" neighbor, then it can't be all that bad!

Productivity is only one of the positive benefits to be achieved through structured programming. Several more are described below and later the details of structured programming techniques will be described.

4.2.1 Fewer Testing Problems

The original motivation of Dijkstra's work in structured programming remains the most critical one today. It represents one of the very few hopes we have of ever being able to test large programs and large programming systems thoroughly and completely. The problems are well known to many programmers and have been mentioned elsewhere throughout this book. For other excellent discussions of the problems of testing programs, the reader is referred to *Software Engineering* [13] and *Software Engineering Techniques* [14]. For the present, it will suffice to summarize the problems in the following way:

1. The effort and cost of testing large programs rise exponentially with their size. Mr. A. d'Agapayeff, in *Software Engineering* [13], estimated that "the cost of testing a change (to a large on-line system) is almost 100 times as much as the cost of producing the change." What makes this worse is the knowledge that our programs and systems are getting larger and will undoubtedly continue to get larger in the years to come.

2. It seems that bugs remain forever in large systems, especially those that require continual maintenance, improvements, and other changes. In *Software Engineering Techniques* [14], Mr. Martin Hopkins (who was quoted above as arguing in favor of *keeping* the GO-TO statement) estimated that there are approximately 1000 errors in each release of OS/360, and that the number is relatively constant. My experience and research with other vendor's operating systems shows the same phenomenon; the number of bugs per release may be higher or lower, but it seems that each vendor has his own constant.

3. The cost of untested systems is steadily growing higher as our computer systems take on more and more critical functions within society. The techniques that are used to produce process control systems and other "critical" systems are sufficient, for the most part, because many of the systems are relatively small. Even the ad hoc testing methods will suffice to exorcise all of the bugs. For the large on-line, real-time systems (by large, we mean systems with *dozens* of computers interconnected, data bases of *billions* of characters on-line at all times, *hundreds* of programmers developing in excess of one *million* lines of code), there is a very serious fear on the part of the systems analysts and programmers that an undiscovered bug

could cause a very substantial loss of life, money, or control over sensitive systems (e.g., air traffic control systems).

With these problems in mind, what hopes do we have for the future? Some of the testing techniques suggested in Chapter 7 will help reduce the randomness and lack of organization that seem to accompany most testing efforts. Some research that is currently going on in the field will help give managers a better idea of the extent of time and money that should be invested in testing. A variety of simulation packages and test-data generators may help mechanize the testing effort somewhat. Yet all of these approaches remain ad hoc in nature. The programmer picks what he thinks will be a good test case and tries it. After a sufficient number of test cases have been attempted, the programmer gives up and declares that the program is tested. As Dijkstra points out in *Software Engineering Techniques* [14], "testing shows the presence, not the absence, of bugs."

Another possible hope for salvation lies in the area of mechanical proofs of program correctness. Several workers have studied the problem of mechanically generating a proof of the correctness of an arbitrary program; some of their results may be found in references 15, 16, and 17. However, the results do not promise to have any practical applications in the near future. In one case, Hoare's proof of a twelve-statement program takes eighteen lemmas [17]. Furthermore, there is still a feeling that the number of "proof" statements is likely to increase more than linearly with the number of program statements. One of Dijkstra's objectives in the development of structured programming was that mechanical proofs might be much easier for a program expressed in some structured form. Indeed, it seems that this should be the case, but we still have no practical method today of generating a rigorous proof of a program written in *any* fashion.

Nevertheless, programs written with the structured programming approach, and with the top-down approach that will be described in section 4.5, lend themselves to an ad hoc testing approach more readily. Dijkstra, for example, describes the success in testing an operating system for the "THE" multiprogramming system, in which the top-down design approach was used (but no mention is made of structured programming):

> We have found that it is possible to design a refined multiprogramming system in such a way that its logical soundness can be proved and its implementation can admit exhaustive testing. The only errors that showed up during testing were trivial coding errors (occurring with a density of one error per 500 instructions), each of them correspondingly easy to remedy. At the time this was written the testing had not yet been completed, but the resulting system is guaranteed to be flawless.

Experience with the IBM project described above indicates the same degree of success when testing: The basic system logic had no errors, and the few bugs that were found were trivial and easy to fix.

4.2.2 Increased Programmer Productivity

While it may seem obvious, it is worth pointing out that the decrease in testing problems generally leads to an *increase* in programmer productivity, that is, the programmer is capable of generating more debugged statements per day with this approach. A number of studies have suggested the following rough figures for programmer productivity (see, for example, Aron's article in *Software Engineering Techniques* [18]):

Type of programming	Debugged statements/day
Operating systems	1–3
Systems programs—compilers	5–10
Applications programs	10–15
Structured programs	35–65
Superprogrammers	50–200

Though no experimental evidence has yet been gathered, there is good reason to believe that the increase in productivity will be even higher in the area of real-time systems (operating systems, process control systems, etc.) than it is with the non-real-time application programs. Dijkstra's enthusiastic remarks above would seem to bear this out.

The increase in productivity is more important than it may seem at first glance. If each programmer is twice as productive, then only half as many are needed to complete a project; this will often mean one less level of management and a tremendous increase in interprogrammer communication and group morale. Among N programmers, an individual programmer is likely to feel like a small cog in a large wheel; among $N/2$ programmers, he is likely to feel a much more important part of things and may end up working much harder—and learning much more about the art (or is it science?) of programming.

4.2.3 Clarity and Readability of Programs

A side benefit of structured programming is increased *readability* of the program, a subject we will discuss at greater length in Chapter 5. The behavior of many unstructured programs often resembles Brownian motion more than any kind of orderly flow. Any attempt to read the listing is frustrated by the fact that the program executes a few statements, jumps to a point several pages further down in the listing, executes a few more statements, jumps to some other random point, executes a few more statements, and so on. After a few such jumps, the reader has forgotten where he started and has certainly lost his train of thought.

A structured program, on the other hand, is more likely to proceed in a straight-line fashion. This is even truer if the program is formatted and indented properly to show nested levels of loops and IF-THEN statements. As the programmers in the IBM project discovered,

> With the elimination of GO-TOs, one can read a program from top to bottom with no jumps and one can see at a glance the conditions required for modifying a block of code.

As we will see below, structured programming rules are often accompanied by various formatting conventions and some of the modularity ideas that were discussed in the previous chapter. In the case of the IBM project, there was a strong effort to restrict the size of each module to fifty statements.

4.2.4   Efficiency

One of the common complaints *against* structured programming is that it leads to less efficient programs. Increased emphasis on subroutine-calling mechanisms as an alternative to GO-TO statements increases the CPU time of the program and may or may not add significant amounts to the memory requirements. There are other situations where the programmer finds it easier to duplicate small sections of code (rather than branching into "common" sections of code) in order to follow the rules of structured programming. Although this does not usually add to the CPU time, it clearly adds to the memory requirements.

It is now recognized that high-level language programs, e.g., ALGOL, PL/I, and COBOL, have potential for being *more* efficient with the structured programming approach. Ultimately, the efficiency of a high-level program depends on the quality of the object code generated by the compiler (ignoring, or course, the efficiency or inefficiency that is inherent in the program design itself—which is often far more significant than these coding details). Compiler-writers have begun pointing out that *global optimization* (i.e., optimization of several high-level statements at a time, or ultimately of the entire program) is much more practical with a structured program, for the program flow can be analyzed in a mechanical way. It is my personal feeling that this type of optimization will produce savings that far outweigh any inefficiencies inherent in the structured programming approach—if not with our current compilers, then certainly within the next few years.

4.3   Theory and Techniques of Structured Programming

As we have already seen, the notion of structured programming is a *philosophy* of writing programs according to a set of rigid rules in order to decrease testing problems, increase productivity, and increase the readability of the resulting program. The primary *technique* of structured programming is the elimination of the GO-TO statement and its replacement with a number of other well-structured branching and control statements. It also includes the concept of top-down program design, which was discussed in Chapter 2, and a number of other less-important programming restrictions and conventions.

This section will discuss some of the theoretical and practical aspects of structured programming in more detail. We will look at the application of the concept to such languages as ALGOL and PL/I; to less elegant programming languages like FORTRAN and COBOL; to assembly language and the so-called high-level assembly languages. We will also consider other aspects of structured programming which are usually ignored in the heated debate over the GO-TO statement. Finally, we will consider some of the tradeoffs of efficiency, convenience, etc., that still concern a number of computer scientists.

4.3.1 The Theory Behind Structured Programming

A number of writers have already noted that the formal systems of computability theory do not require the notion of a GO-TO. Thus, the Kleene general recursive functions [19], the Post systems [20], Markov algorithms [21], and Church's lambda calculus [22] are defined without the GO-TO mechanism. However, as Leavenworth points out [23], most of the programming languages that have been based on these systems, e.g., LISP, ISWIM, COMIT, and SNOBOL, *do* have a GO-TO statement. The only significance of this observation is that the GO-TO is apparently not needed to compute all computable functions (and thus solve all practicable computing problems), but it *does* seem to be convenient.

In a more practical vein, a number of researchers have been attacking the problem of writing programs in such a way that their correctness can be proved, as we have already seen in this chapter. For the pragmatic reasons enunciated by Dijkstra, the effort has been directed at programs that are developed in a top-down or "layered" fashion. In this scheme, an entire program (or system) is considered first as an independent "callable" module (and indeed, it often works out that way—any application program is often *called* as a subroutine by the operating system, and it *returns* to the operating system when it finishes or aborts). At the next stage of design, the original (level-0) program is broken into subordinate level-1 modules; these are then decomposed into level-2 submodules; and the decomposition process continues until the designer is left with building blocks that are small enough to code easily.

In order to test the entire program, it is important to be able to define the behavior of submodules at the kth level independently of the context in which they occur. This allows us to prove the correctness of the submodules at the $(k + 1)$th level independent of their context in the kth step. This in turn strongly suggests that each submodule should be designed with a single entry point and a single exit; in turn, the entire program can be described as a set of nested modules, each of which has one entry and one exit.

A classic paper by Bohm and Jacopini [24] has shown that such a structure can be composed from a language with only two basic control structures, the actual implementation of which is a function of the programming language, as we shall see in Section 4.3.2. The concept presented in the Bohm-Jacopini paper, sometimes referred to as the "structure theorem," is of fundamental importance and is the basis for much of the *implementation* of structured programming that we will develop below. Their proof that *any* proper program can be constructed with the two basic control structures is therefore of great significance, but the proof is so lengthy and complex that it will not be discussed here. It is of some historical interest that their original paper was published in Italian in 1965; the English version was published in the United States in May, 1966 and was largely ignored—as were many of the early papers of Dijkstra and others—until structured programming began to be a fad in the industry in the early 1970s.

According to Bohm and Jacopini, we need three basic building blocks in order to construct a program:

1. A process box.
2. A generalized loop mechanism.
3. A binary-decision mechanism.

The process box, shown in Fig. 4.1, may be thought of as a single computational statement (or machine language instruction) *or as any other proper*

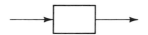

Figure 4.1. The process box.

computational sequence with only one entry and one exit—such as a subroutine. Thus, a process box might consist of a "load accumulator" instruction in assembly language, a MOVE statement in COBOL, or a typical FORTRAN computational statement. The loop mechanism, shown in Fig. 4.2(a), is often referred to in the literature as a DO-WHILE mechanism. The binary-decision mechanism is shown in Fig. 4.2(b); for obvious reasons, it is often referred to as an IF-THEN-ELSE mechanism.

Note that the constructs shown in Fig. 4.2(a) and 4.2(b) can themselves be thought of as a process box since they have only one entry and one exit. Thus, we can define a *transformation* from a looping operation to a process box, as shown in Fig. 4.3(a), and thereafter consider any such looping operation as being equivalent to a (slightly more complex) process box. Similarly, we can effect a transformation from the decision box of Fig. 4.2(b) to a process box, as shown in Fig. 4.3(b). Finally, we can transform any linear sequence of process boxes into a single process box, as shown in Fig. 4.3(c).

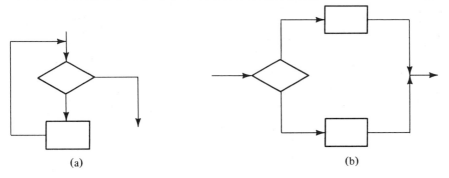

(a) (b)

Figure 4.2. Two mechanisms.
(a) The loop mechanism. (b) The if-then-else mechanism.

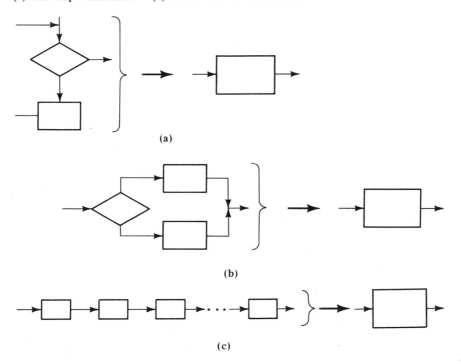

(a)

(b)

(c)

Figure 4.3 Translations.
(a) From a looping operation to a process box. (b) From a decision box to a process box.
(c) From a sequence of process boxes to a single box.

Any program that is composed of process boxes, looping operations, and IF-THEN-ELSE constructs (and according to the results of Bohm and Jacopini, it *is* possible to construct a program from these constituents alone) may be successively transformed, according to the transformations shown in Figs. 4.3(a), 4.3(b), and 4.3(c), to a single process box. As Wulf [11] points out, this sequence of transformations may be used as a guide to understanding the program and proving its correctness. Conversely, the *reverse* sequence of transformations can be used to design the program in a top-down fashion, i.e., starting with a single process box, and gradually expanding it to a complex structure of the basic components.

Note also the relationship between this "nested-structure" concept and the concept of modularity discussed in the previous chapter. A program constructed with the transformations shown above is modular in the true sense. Any of the process boxes can be replaced by a functionally equivalent one without affecting the rest of the program. Of more importance is the fact that the Bohm and Jacopini transformations can be applied to an entire program, breaking it into smaller modules which can, in turn, be broken into smaller modules, and so forth. According to this scheme, the transformation process can continue until we have reached the level of "atomic" modules, i.e., individual computational statements, IF-THEN-ELSE statements, or DO-WHILE looping constructs.

This, then, is the essential difference between structured programming and modular programming. Attempts at modular programming often begin well: The programmer decides to break a large program into modules. However, he often makes no further attempt to break each of the modules into even smaller modules; thus, the result is often a program with a large main program and a few large (e.g., several hundred statements) modules that cannot be easily subdivided. Note the importance of this: If the modules cannot be subdivided, they must be treated as a single unit—which means that any testing, debugging, maintenance, or attempts at understanding the module will be complicated by the need to comprehend a large block of indivisible coding. The situation is further complicated by the fact that the modules that are developed in the traditional attempt at modular programming are often not *independent* of one another—they alter each other's logic, share each other's working storage, etc.

4.3.2   The Implementation of Structured Programming

The theoretical basis of structured programming lends itself to implementation in many of the current programming languages. The rules are quite simple: All processing in the program must consist of straight-line statements (e.g., ordinary computational statements) or one of the following three control statements:

1. Procedure calls, subroutine calls, function invocations—any legal call to a closed subroutine with one entry and one exit. Note that subroutines are *not* absolutely necessary in order to implement structured programs; however, by the same kind of reasoning, we can implement any program on a Turing machine—and few people are doing that today!

2. IF-THEN-ELSE statements nested to any depth.

3. Some looping constructs. The most common suggestion is the **DO-WHILE** construct found in **ALGOL** and **PL/I**, though the **PERFORM-UNTIL** construct in **COBOL** is adequate.

While the foregoing mechanisms are sufficient to write any computer program, a number of organizations have found it practical to add some "extensions." Some of the more common ones are as follows:

1. The CASE mechanism. Found in many unofficial versions of ALGOL 60, and in some of the more recent ALGOL-like languages, it can take several forms; a simple version, found on Burroughs B5500 ALGOL, is

```
CASE      GLOP OF
   BEGIN
   statement1 ;
   statement2 ;
      .
      .
      .
   statementj ;
   END ;
```

If the value of GLOP is i, then the ith statement will be executed, and execution will then proceed at the statement following the CASE statement. Of course, the statements within the CASE construct can themselves be complex process boxes. Note that the CASE mechanism is itself a black-box form, as shown in Fig. 4.4. It should

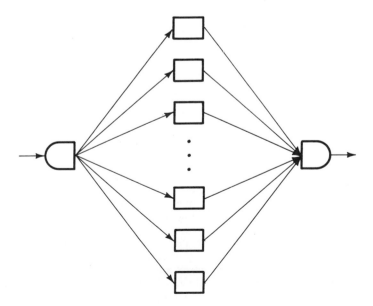

Figure 4.4. The case mechanism.

also be noted that the CASE construct can be simulated in COBOL with the GO-TO DEPENDING ON statement, as shown in Fig. 4.5; with the computed GO-TO statement in FORTRAN, as shown in Fig. 4.6; and with a variety of assembly language mechanisms.

Figure 4.5. Simulation of CASE mechanism in COBOL.

```
                           .
                           .
                  PERFORM CASE-SECTION.
                           .
                           .
                           .

        CASE-SECTION.
            GO TO A,B,C,D DEPENDING ON I.
        A.    —
              —
              —
            GO TO CASE-EXIT.
        B.    —
              —
              —
            GO TO CASE-EXIT.
        C.    —
              —
              —
            GO TO CASE-EXIT.
        D.    —
              —
              —
            GO TO CASE-EXIT.
        CASE-EXIT.
            EXIT.
```

2. Additional looping constructs. It is convenient, for example, to provide a looping construct that will execute the process box *first*, and *then* test to see if it should be repeated, as shown in Fig. 4.7. This is provided in some implementations of ALGOL, and a variety of more primitive forms in FORTRAN and assembly language. Note that the loop shown in Fig. 4.7 is a black box in the same tradition as the original Bohm and Jacopini loop. Similarly, the *iterative* loop found in most languages (e.g., the DO loop in FORTRAN and the PERFORM-VARYING statement in COBOL) are black boxes, *if used properly*.

3. Subroutines with multiple entries and multiple exits. Some programmers prefer, for example, to code a SIN and COS function in a single module with different entry points; similarly, many programmers have developed a "standard"

Figure 4.6. Simulation of CASE mechanism in FORTRAN.

```
                    .
                    .
                    .

                    .
            GO TO (1,2,3, . . . .) I
10          CONTINUE
                    .
                    .
                    .
1       —
        —
        —
        GO TO 10
2       —
        —
        —
        GO TO 10
3       —
        —
        —
        GO TO 10
        .
        .
        .
        etc.
        .
        .
        .
```

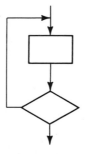

Figure 4.7. An alternative form of the basic loop mechanism.

style of providing every subroutine with a "normal" return and an "error" return. If this is handled carefully, it need not violate the black-box philosophy; in practice, though, it often does.

4. Tight restrictions on GO-TO statements. Some organizations, for example, only allow the programmer to branch forward in his program; others have developed variations on this kind of an ad hoc rule. One of the more interesting is the following: The programmer (who works in COBOL) is told that his coding must form a COBOL SECTION, which can only be entered by PERFORMing it, and from which control can leave only by executing an EXIT statement as the last paragraph in the section. Nobody else is allowed to PERFORM individual paragraphs within the section, or branch with a GO-TO statement into some arbitrary point within the section; similarly, the programmer is not allowed to use a GO-TO statement to branch outside his section. In addition, the size of the programmer's SECTION is limited to approximately 100 statements (reminding us of similar numbers in Section 3.1.1). Other than that, though, the programmer is allowed to use any GO-TO statements he considers desirable—thus leading, possibly, to the "restricted rat's nest" shown in Fig. 4.8. Though this is somewhat of a compromise with the pure structured programming theory, it may prove to be necessary when dealing with clumsy programming languages like COBOL and FORTRAN.

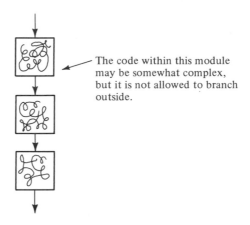

The code within this module may be somewhat complex, but it is not allowed to branch outside.

Figure 4.8. Restricted use of GO-TO statements.

A number of other modifications or compromises of the basic structured programming theory could be suggested and probably *will* be suggested as more programming organizations gain familiarity with the concept. As indicated, many of the compromises do not violate the black-box principle behind the original Bohm and Jacopini structures; other compromises *do* represent a violation and should be allowed only under extenuating circumstances, e.g., severe limitations of a programming language or extreme efficiency problems. The important point is to choose a coherent set of structured programming conventions—possibly including some of the extensions and compromises discussed above—and then to *enforce* them as programming standards.

4.3.3   Conversion of Unstructured Programs to Structured Programs

The results of Bohm and Jacopini state that *any* proper computer program can be constructed from a series of the basic building blocks discussed in the previous section. However, a number of programmers find that when they first try to write a program in this fashion, serious difficulties arise. Trivial programming applications can, of course, be coded without using the GO-TO statement (which, to many programmers, remains the test of whether structured programming has been applied properly). Those fortunate enough to be programming in PL/I, ALGOL, or other sophisticated programming languages find that they have few occasions to violate the structured programming philosophies; however, those programming in COBOL, FORTRAN, and assembly language often find that learning structured programming is even more difficult than learning a new programming language.

A great deal of the difficulty stems from the fact that structured programming requires a different approach to designing and thinking about programs. This approach is facilitated to some extent by the top-down approach discussed in Chapter 2. It comes about naturally for those experienced in the ALGOL-like programming languages; for others, though, it comes as a rude shock. To put it very simply, many of us have been programming in an unstructured "spaghetti-bowl" fashion, and it is not enough to learn that there are theorems proving the possibility of structured programs.

Fortunately, there are some techniques that can simplify that development of structured programs—though the techniques were developed for a slightly different purpose. Several computer scientists have posed the following question: Can we take any arbitrary program which has *not* been written according to structured programming rules and convert it into a structured program? The general consensus is "no": We cannot convert an arbitrary unstructured program into a structured program *that performs the same algorithm with the same primitives and no additional variables*; see Knuth and Floyd [25] and Ashcroft and Manna [26] for a discussion of this. However, we *can* make such a conversion if we are willing to introduce some redundant coding, or if we are willing to use extra state-variables or control flags. There are three common techniques for doing this: duplication of coding, the state-variable approach, and the Boolean flag approach.

Each technique will be discussed below; however, it is very important that the proper use of the techniques be noted. If we take a poorly designed, unstructured program and convert it according to the strategies listed above, we will end up with a poorly designed, GO-TO-less, structured program that will probably be just as difficult to understand and debug as the original one. Indeed, while some of the conversion research had as its objective the automatic translation of unstructured programs into structured programs, it is not clear whether any organization would want to wreak such havoc upon their existing program libraries!

On the other hand, we must remember that our traditional program design approach has typically been unstructured; with this in mind, it is interesting to note that the three conversion strategies will often help us *design* programs and *think* about programs in a more structured fashion. Thus, we are definitely *not* recommending that you should write a program using your old unstructured techniques and then convert it into a GO-TO-less form with the strategies above. Instead, you should try to use them to help develop structured thinking about programs. Once again, we should emphasize that this process is assisted tremendously with the use of top-down program design.

Duplication of Coding. Consider the program whose flowchart is shown in Fig. 4.9. Each box in the flowchart is assumed to be a group of statements corresponding to a COBOL paragraph, or a block of code in a FORTRAN main program, or a block of assembly language statements. The arrows joining the various boxes are assumed, at this point, to represent GO-TO statements.

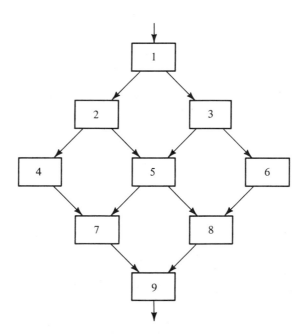

Figure 4.9. An unstructured program.

As it stands, the program is not structured; each box in the flowchart does *not* correspond to the "one-entry, one-exit" philosophy described earlier. On a very practical level, every programmer has suffered from bugs in this kind of program structure; simply stated, we are suffering here from the many dangers of "branching into common code" (note that the structure shown in Fig. 4.9 conforms to the "branch forward" use of GO-TO statements accepted by some organizations as a compromise version of structured programming).

As an example of the difficulties encountered with such a program, consider the problem of attempting to understand the processing within module 5 (such a situation typically arises in testing, debugging, and maintenance). In a typical program, we would assume that the correct execution of module 5 depends on various flags, switches, and variables having been initialized properly. These flags and variables may have been initialized properly if we entered module 5 from module 2, but may not have been if we entered from module 3. In other words, we cannot know whether module 5 is executing properly without knowing the behavior in modules 2 and 3 (and thus by extension module 1 as well). We cannot determine the proper execution of module 5 without knowing the context in which it was executed. This problem is even worse in modules 7 and 8, where there are several possible paths through which modules 7 and 8 may have been entered. Thus, if module 5 "blows up," it may be very difficult for us to tell whether the problem was due to a bug in module 5 or a bug in one of the preceding modules.

Another form of this programming problem occurs rather often. We often find that module 5 contains some coding that is absolutely necessary if we entered via module 2, but unnecessary and harmless if we entered module 5 via module 3. If indeed the program works this way, we will have no trouble; unfortunately, we sometimes find that the coding in module 5 is necessary if we entered via module 2 and *disastrous* if we entered via module 3. Such are the perils of branching into common coding; every programmer has probably suffered from it at one time or another.

Fortunately, the solution is relatively simple. In order to produce a structured program, we *duplicate* those modules that are entered from more than one place. For the example we discussed in Fig. 4.9, this leads to the modified flowchart shown in Fig. 4.10. To look at it another way, consider the original program as having the simple IF-THEN-ELSE structure shown in Fig. 4.11(a); this can be expanded to the structure shown in Fig. 4.11(b); finally, the entire program can be shown in 4.11(c). This is one of the strongest arguments in favor of the "duplication-of-coding" technique—the *thinking* and *design* process involved in the progression from Fig. 4.11(a) to Fig. 4.11(b) to Fig. 4.11(c) is considerably less complex than the lattice structure in Fig. 4.9, and thus less prone to errors.

There is little doubt that this technique can be applied to any program of the nature originally shown in Fig. 4.9. However, we should note that such a program is, in fact, extremely simple—it has no loops. The duplication-of-coding technique generally will not work for programs with loops, but rather only with network structures or lattice structures. The two techniques to be discussed below will deal with loop-oriented programs. It should be remem-

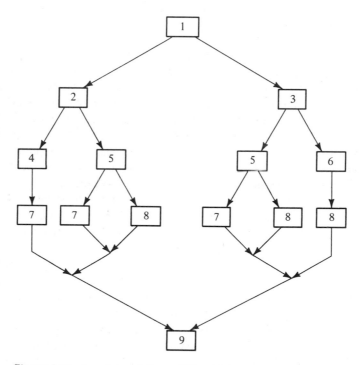

Figure 4.10. A redesigned form of Fig. 4.9.

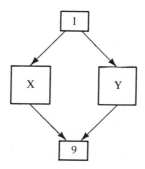

Figure 4.11(a). A simplified form of Fig. 4.10.

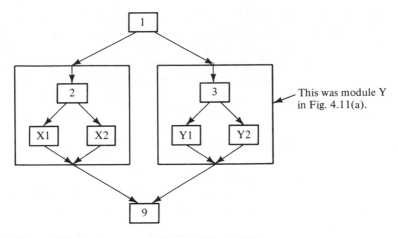

Figure 4.11(b). An expanded form of Fig. 4.11(a).

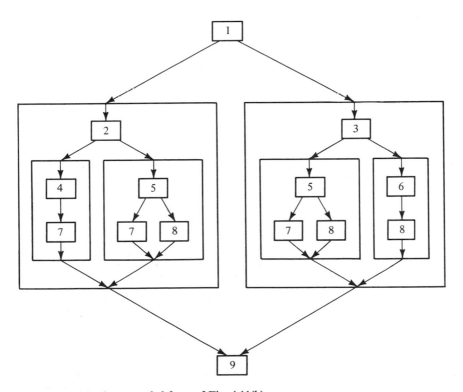

Figure 4.11(c). An expanded form of Fig. 4.11(b).

bered, though, that many of the more complex programs have lattice structures imbedded within them, and this portion of the program may be handled
in the manner shown in Fig. 4.10.

There is an obvious disadvantage to the technique of duplicating code:
It requires more memory than the original unstructured approach. However,
it is very often true that the modules (e.g., the various boxes in Fig. 4.9) in
such a program involve only two to three statements. In this case, it is well
worth the cost of duplicating the code to generate a structure that can be
broken into levels in the manner shown in Figs. 4.11(a), 4.11(b), and 4.11(c).
If the modules involve a substantial amount of coding (e.g., fifty source statements or more), then it is clear that the problem should be solved by making
them a callable subroutine. But it is extremely important that they be developed as *formal* subroutines with formal arguments, so that their correctness
can be determined without regard to the context in which they are executed.
If this approach is taken, we will have multiple calls to a single copy of a
subroutine—an approach which also involves a relatively small amount of
overhead.

It is interesting to watch the process by which the flowchart shown in
Fig. 4.9 is developed. As shown in Fig. 4.12(a), the programmer begins by
coding modules 1, 2, and 3. Having done this, he goes on to develop the
extensions from module 2, namely, modules 4 and 5, as shown in Fig. 4.12(b).
Next, the programmer begins working on the extension to module 3 and, as
illustrated in Fig. 4.12(c), it is at this point that he realizes one of the extensions (labelled 5A) is very similar to the module he has coded as an extension
to module 2. Indeed, this realization often comes about *before* any coding

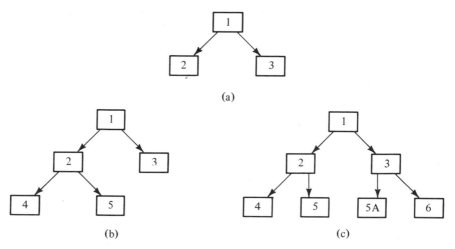

Figure 4.12. (a) The development of Fig. 4.9. (b and c) The continued development of
Fig. 4.9.

has taken place; when the programmer is *thinking* about the extensions from modules 2 and 3, he realizes that modules 5 and 5A (which are now just fuzzy ideas in his mind) are sufficiently similar that they ought to be combined— hence the flowchart shown in Fig. 4.9. In many cases, though, the modules imagined as 5 and 5A are similar but not quite the same, *and they should be left as different modules*, especially if they represent only a few lines of coding.

Many programmers argue that the structured approach shown in Fig. 4.10 is not necessarily better or similar or even easier to debug. They insist, for example, that it is just as possible for a bug to exist in module 5 of Fig. 4.10 as it is for a bug to exist in module 5 of the original program in Fig. 4.9. Naturally, this is true. It is possible for us to insert bugs in our programs regardless of how we structure them. On the other hand, we can argue that the program shown in Fig. 4.10 is logically less complex, and that there is therefore less chance of a bug creeping into our logic.

Furthermore, we can argue that the programmer should be examining his logic in a top-down fashion, and that this would tend to eliminate bugs before they actually find their way into the coding. Thus, the programmer should be able to examine the logic shown in Fig. 4.11(a) and convince himself that it is correct. He can then examine the lower levels of logic shown in Fig. 4.11(b) to convince himself that they are correct. Finally, he can examine the lowest levels of logic shown in Fig. 4.11(c) to convince himself that the entire program is correct.

It is also worth noting that many of the bugs that occur in the unstructured version of such a program (e.g., of the form shown originally in Fig. 4.9) are the result of "informal" interfaces, e.g., the programmer does not formally specify the nature of the information that must be passed to module 5 from modules 2 and 3 above it. The structured approach shown in Fig. 4.10 formalizes such interfaces, e.g., by sometimes causing module 5 to be implemented as a formal subroutine with formal arguments. In this case, if module 5 "blows up" while the program is executing, we should be able to determine whether the problem was internal (i.e., a bug within module 5) or external (i.e., incorrect information being passed across the interface).

Finally, we should deal with another objection raised by some programmers: It has been pointed out that the entire program shown in Fig. 4.9 is a black box, i.e., control enters only at module 1 and leaves only at module 9. Assuming that the entire program is rather small, e.g., that all nine modules represent a total of only twenty to thirty lines of coding, many programmers would argue that it is unnecessary to translate the program into the structured form in Fig. 4.10. While this is true, two points should be kept in mind:

    1. The program shown in Fig. 4.9 is obviously a small one. The logic found in *real* programs is often more complex, that is, the lattice structure often extends over several hundred or several thousand lines of coding.

2. Even if the logic shown in Fig. 4.9 *is* easy to follow (as some programmers claim), one of our primary purposes in this section is to show that any programming situation, including the lattice structure, *can* be handled with the basic Bohm and Jacopini structures. Thus, we might argue: While the program shown in Fig. 4.9 may be reasonable (a debatable point in any case), it represents a form of program organization that can easily be misused by mediocre programmers (or even good programmers who are having a bad day!)—and since the Bohm and Jacopini building blocks make the lattice structure unnecessary, there is no reason why we should allow it to be misused.

The State-Variable Approach. Another technique for converting unstructured programs was suggested in a paper by Ashcroft and Manna [26]. It is a slight variation on the state-variable approach used by many programmers for organizing their programs (see, for example, the discussion in Section 6.3.5). The interesting thing about this approach is that it can be applied to any program—in particular, those with loops and other complex processes—and it can be applied in a mechanical fashion.

The conversion process requires five steps; it is illustrated with the programming example shown in Fig. 4.13.

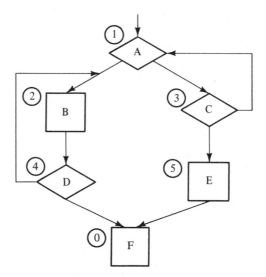

Figure 4.13. An example of the Ashcroft-Manna technique.

1. Each box in the unstructured flowchart is given a number; note that this has already been done in Fig. 4.13. The numbering scheme is completely arbitrary, but the usual convention is to give the number 1 to the first executable box and the number 0 to the last executable box.

2. A new variable is introduced into the program; for the purposes of this conversion technique, we need an integer variable. The name of the variable is arbitrary; so for this example, let us use a new variable called *i*.

3. The process boxes in the unstructured flowchart are replaced by new process boxes that perform the same computation, but also set the variable *i* to the integer that identifies the *successor* box in the original flowchart. Thus, box B in Fig. 4.13 apparently branches in all cases to box D. Since we have labelled box B as box 2, we will develop a new box 2, which we shall call box 2'; it will also perform process B, but in addition will set variable *i* to 4.

4. The decision boxes in the unstructured program are converted in a similar fashion. If the decision has the value "true," then the variable *i* is set to the integer identifying the "true" successor in the original flowchart; if the decision is "false," *i* is set to the "false" successor value. In Fig. 4.13, for example, box 1 performs the test A, which determines whether we branch to box 2 or box 3. We will replace box 1 with a new box 1', which will perform test A and set variable *i* equal to 2 if the outcome is true, and to 3 if the outcome is false.

5. We now rewrite the entire flowchart in the form shown in Fig. 4.14. The variable *i* is initialized to a value of 1, according to the conventions mentioned

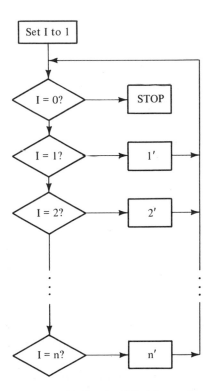

Figure 4.14. The translated form of the Ashcroft-Manna technique.

above. We then continually test the value of i, perform the required action, and then continue the testing. The example shown in Fig. 4.13 can thus be rewritten in the form shown in Fig. 4.15.

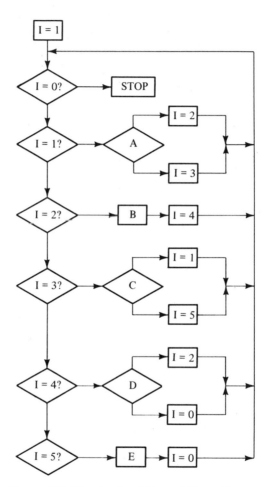

Figure 4.15. The structured form of Fig. 4.13.

This conversion process is obviously straightforward and appeals to many programmers; others, though, object to it for various reasons. One of the most common objections is that the conversion technique destroys the form and topology of the original flowchart, e.g., the flowchart shown in Fig. 4.15 bears no resemblance to the original flowchart in Fig. 4.13. The complaint is often put in somewhat stronger terms; the programmer complains that the flowchart in Fig. 4.13 is easier to understand and that the flow-chart shown in Fig. 4.15 gives very little evidence of the decisions that are being made.

In a limited sense, this complaint may be valid. However, it should be pointed out that the flowchart in Fig. 4.13 is a rather simple one—after all, it fits onto one page! Furthermore, even though it may be unstructured inter-nally, the entire flowchart is a black box, i.e., there is only one entry to the program, and only one exit. In a *real* programming situation, we are likely to find that the flowchart does *not* fit onto one page; furthermore, we are likely to find that there are multiple entries into the flowchart and multiple exits from it. The converted state-oriented form, though, has the advantage that it can be extended indefinitely (e.g., whereas there are only six states in the example shown in Fig. 4.13, we could easily imagine an example with sixty states) without increasing the overall complexity of the approach.

There is a further advantage of clarity that may not be immediately obvious. The state-oriented approach tends to encourage the programmer to provide documentation that is enormously helpful to a maintenance pro-grammer. Each box in the original flowchart corresponds to a particular *state* in the program, i.e., a situation where a decision is being made, or a process being performed. These states can be documented in a concise, compact form; even more important, the state transitions can be documented in a tabular form, as we will see in an example in Section 6.3.5.

There is also a debugging advantage to the state-oriented approach that is often overlooked. If the program does not work properly, it is relatively simple to *trace* the state variable (e.g., variable i in our example). This should give the programmer a reasonably clear idea of the flow of control through the program.

Finally, there is a question of efficiency. Many programmers assume from the flowchart in Fig. 4.15 that the state-oriented approach is intended to be programmed with a nested IF-THEN-ELSE structure. While this is pos-sible, it is more likely that it would be implemented with a combination of a DO-WHILE structure (or PERFORM-UNTIL or its equivalent in other languages) and a CASE structure (or a computed GO-TO in FORTRAN, or a GO-TO DEPENDING ON in COBOL, etc.) which, when compiled into machine language, will have the effect of using the state variable as an index into a "branch vector." It is true that each process box in the original flowchart must set the state variable, and that the state variable must be tested after the execution of each process box; but this should be a relatively small amount of overhead.

The Boolean Flag Technique. There is another programming technique that can be used to convert loop-oriented programs into a structured form; it requires the introduction of a *flag* into the program (though it may have been

present already). The flag is initialized at some point prior to the loop; a
DO-WHILE or PERFORM-UNTIL structure is used to control the execution of the loop until the flag is set appropriately; and finally, some conditions
inside the loop determine when the flag should be set. Thus, the program takes
the form

```
        .
        .
        .
FLAG  =  0
        .
        .
        .
WHILE  FLAG  =  0  DO
        BEGIN
          .
          .
          .
        IF  X  =  Y  THEN  FLAG  =  1
          .
          .
          .
        END
```

or an equivalent form in other programming languages.

This process can be generalized to some extent. One of the most common forms of an unstructured loop is that shown in Fig. 4.16(a). Note that it
contains one entry point, but two distinct exits. By introducing a new flag into
the program, we can restructure it into the form shown in Fig. 4.16(b).

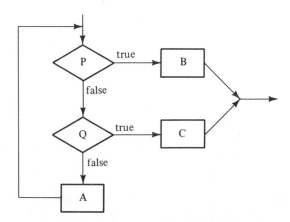

Figure 4.16(a). An unstructured loop.

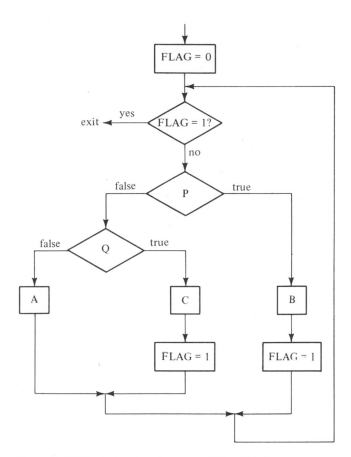

Figure 4.16(b). A structured version of Fig. 4.16(a).

Though this approach may look somewhat clumsy in flowchart form, it can be programmed rather easily by using FLAG in a DO-WHILE statement.

It is not always necessary to add a flag to the program to restructure it. For example, the unstructured loop in Fig. 4.16(a) could be restructured as shown in Fig. 4.16(c). This appears much cleaner and more elegant than the solution shown in Fig. 4.16(b); however, it becomes very clumsy if the loop contains *several* different exits instead of just two as shown originally in Fig. 4.16(a).

As an example, consider a simplified version of a master file update, shown in Fig. 4.17(a). Such an algorithm has traditionally been coded in the manner shown in Fig. 4.17(b); a more structured form is shown in Fig. 4.17(c). Note that this example involves the Boolean flag technique *and* the notion of code duplication discussed above.

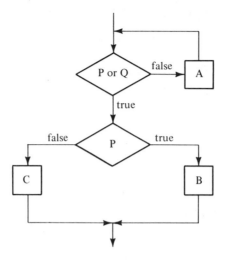

Figure 4.16(c). Another structured version of Fig. 4.16(a).

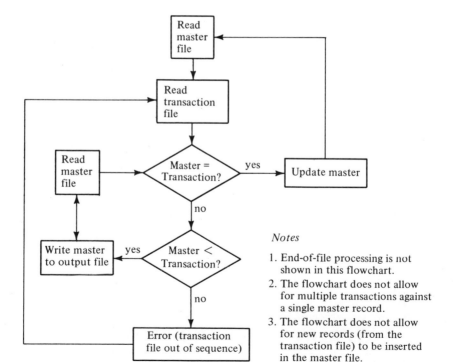

Figure 4.17(a). A simplified version of the master-file-update algorithm.

Notes

1. End-of-file processing is not shown in this flowchart.
2. The flowchart does not allow for multiple transactions against a single master record.
3. The flowchart does not allow for new records (from the transaction file) to be inserted in the master file.

Figure 4.17(b). An unstructured version of Fig. 4.16.

```
X-MASTER.
      READ MASTER.
X-TRANSACTION.
      READ TRANSACTION.
X-COMPARE.
      IF  M = T
         PERFORM UPDATE
         GO TO X-MASTER.
      IF  M < T
         PERFORM WRITE-MASTER
         PERFORM READ-MASTER
         GO TO X-COMPARE.
      PERFORM ERROR-MESSAGE.
      GO TO X-TRANSACTION.
```

Figure 4.17(c). A more structured form of Fig. 4.16.

```
      .
      .
      .
PERFORM READ-MASTER.
PERFORM READ-TRANS.
PERFORM APPLY-TRANS UNTIL M = T = 9999.
      .
      .
      .
APPLY-TRANS.
      IF  M = T
         PERFORM UPDATE-MASTER
         PERFORM READ-MASTER
         PERFORM READ-TRANS
      ELSE
         IF  M < T
            PERFORM WRITE-MASTER
            PERFORM READ-MASTER
         ELSE
            PERFORM ERROR-MESSAGE
            PERFORM READ-TRANS.
      EXIT.
READ-MASTER.
      READ MASTER AT END MOVE 9999 TO M.
READ-TRANS.
      READ TRANS AT END MOVE 9999 TO T.
```

The Boolean flag technique seems the best example of a situation where structured programming requires a complete rethinking of program design. After some practice with this technique, most programmers find that it comes rather naturally—it is the first few times that are so difficult. We must emphasize again that the examples given to illustrate the three conversion techniques are, to some extent, misleading: Each of the examples (in Fig. 4.9, Fig. 4.13, and Fig. 4.16) are extremely simple algorithms, *and they are also black-box algorithms*. The reason they were used is that they could not, in their original form, be decomposed into *smaller* black boxes.

4.3.4 Applications of Structured Programming to Common Programming Languages

Having seen that structured programming basically involves the substitution of DO-WHILE and IF-THEN-ELSE mechanisms for the GO-TO statement, we should now ask ourselves whether the popular programming languages provide the necessary facilities. We will focus on several groups of languages in the following sections.

ALGOL and PL/I. ALGOL and PL/I are the two languages that afford the easiest implementation of structured programming concepts. One of the major reasons for this is the presence of "block structures" that allow the programmer to group several individual statements together and have them treated as a *compound* statement. This, together with the powerful *nested* IF-THEN-ELSE statement in the two languages, allows such constructs as:

```
IF  BE1  THEN
    BEGIN
    statement1 ;
    statement2 ;
    IF  BE2  THEN  statement3 ;
    statement4 ;
    END
ELSE
    IF  BE3  THEN
        BEGIN
        statement1 ;
        statement2 ;
        END
    ELSE
        BEGIN
        statement1 ;
        IF  BE4  THEN  statement2  ELSE  statement3 ;
        statement4 ;
        END :
```

Another powerful statement found in the two languages is the DO-WHILE construct. This allows the programmer to perform one or more statements as long as the Boolean expression specified by the WHILE clause is true. ALGOL provides variations on this basic capability so that the Boolean variable can be tested either *before* or *after* the process box is implemented. Thus, the programmer can arrange the loop so that it is not executed at all (if the terminating conditions are satisfied upon entrance to the loop), or so that it is always executed at least once before the terminating condition is checked. As we noted above, the CASE statement in some versions of ALGOL is quite useful in building the kinds of structures described in this chapter—especially the state-variable approach discussed earlier.

Perhaps the greatest advantages of these languages, from a structured programming point of view, is the precision and conciseness of their syntax. This is especially noticeable when comparing the IF-THEN-ELSE statement of ALGOL-like languages with the IF-THEN-ELSE statement in languages like COBOL—the block structure mentioned above usually helps eliminate the ambiguity often found in a *nested* IF-THEN-ELSE structure in COBOL. Similarly, the form of the DO-WHILE statement in ALGOL and PL/I allows a loop to be coded *in-line*, instead of out-of-line (as is the case, for example, with the PERFORM-UNTIL structure in COBOL IO).

COBOL. While not as elegant and formal a language as ALGOL and PL/I, the COBOL language still includes enough features to make implementation of structured programs fairly practical. All three of the basic building blocks can be implemented directly in COBOL: process boxes, IF-THEN-ELSE structures, and DO-WHILE structures.

The IF-THEN-ELSE structure allows for nesting, though most COBOL programmers have probably been warned by their managers not to try them. Part of the reason for this is the difficulty of writing sequences of code such as

```
IF I = 1
   SUBTRACT 1 FROM J
   IF J = 2
      MOVE A TO B
ELSE
   IF I = 3
      MOVE C TO D
```

It is not clear here whether the ELSE clause corresponds to the IF $J = 2$ statement or the initial $I = 1$ statement. The point to be emphasized is not what the compiler will do with such a statement, for we assume that the compiler's actions are predictable and known (though possibly different from one vendor to another!). *The point is that the compiler will often do something other than what the programmer intended to do.*

The problem can sometimes be solved with judicious use of the ELSE NEXT SENTENCE clause in COBOL, but even this seems insufficient at times. If all else fails, we can always resort to the use of PERFORM statements; the example above, for instance, can be coded as

```
IF I = 1
    PERFORM X
ELSE
    PERFORM Y
```

where the module X contains the statements

```
X.
    SUBTRACT 1 FROM J.
    IF J = 2 MOVE A TO B.
    EXIT.
```

and module Y contains similar coding. Notice, though, how much clumsier this approach is than the corresponding ALGOL approach—sufficiently clumsy, unfortunately, to discourage some COBOL programmers from trying structured programming.

Similarly, the DO-WHILE structure is implemented directly in COBOL with a PERFORM-UNTIL statement. The general form is unfortunately rather clumsy for coding loops, since it requires out-of-line coding, that is, we require code of the form

```
PERFORM ABC UNTIL X = Y
```

where the ABC paragraph or section occurs elsewhere in the coding. We would prefer to be able to write something of the form

```
UNTIL X=Y PERFORM
    MOVE A TO B
    MOVE C TO D
    ADD 1 TO X
```

Finally, we note that the concept of block structures is not explicitly present, but it can be achieved if we combine several primitive statements (e.g., MOVE, ADD, or COMPUTE) into a single sentence. Though far less formal than the ALGOL-PL/I equivalent (a fact that occasionally causes some trouble), it has the effect of transforming several individual process boxes into a single process box.

FORTRAN. FORTRAN seems to be the one major high-level programming language (other than BASIC, perhaps) that is *not* suited to the structured programming concept. There are three major reasons for this:

1. There is no concept of block structures in the FORTRAN language, as it is presently constituted. That is, it is not possible to group several statements together and treat them as if they were *one* statement. This immediately forces the programmer to "jump" around groups of statements. While these GO-TO statements are not evil in themselves, they begin to give the programmer the ability (and the temptation) to begin building the complex structures shown in Fig. 4.9.

2. There is no nested IF-THEN-ELSE statement in the FORTRAN language. The lack of a strong IF statement is, in the author's opinion, one of the greatest weaknesses of FORTRAN.

3. While there *is* a DO statement in FORTRAN, it is not as powerful as the analogous forms in COBOL, ALGOL, and PL/I. In FORTRAN, it is difficult to use the DO statement for anything other than iterative purposes (which, of course, is a common requirement in scientific applications). The concept of a DO-WHILE or PERFORM-UNTIL is lacking.

While these points are a strong condemnation of the FORTRAN language, they do not necessarily mean that one cannot write structured programs in FORTRAN. Remember that the *real* objective of structured programs is to successively decompose programs into smaller discrete units. There is no reason why this cannot be done *with* GO-TO statements in FORTRAN—*if there was a guarantee that programmers would not use them for any other reason.* The IF-THEN-ELSE structure, for example, can be coded in FORTRAN in the same manner shown in Fig. 4.18(a); similarly,

Figure 4.18(a). The IF-THEN-ELSE mechanism in FORTRAN.

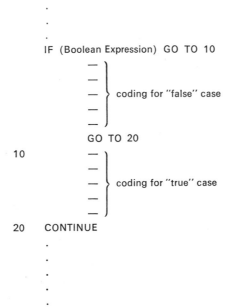

the DO-WHILE structure can be coded as shown in Fig. 4.18(b). Alternatively, it would be possible to develop a "super-FORTRAN" language that included the IF-THEN-ELSE statements, the block structures, and the DO-WHILE structures. A preprocessor could then convert these constructs into the *standard* FORTRAN statements that we all know and love. Such an approach has already been taken by at least one computer organization in Europe, a software company in the United States (see, for example, the advertisement for the IFTRAN preprocessor in the January 1974 issue of *Datamation*), and some users of Univac 1108 FORTRAN (see reference 40).

Figure 4.18(b). The DO-WHILE mechanism in FORTRAN.

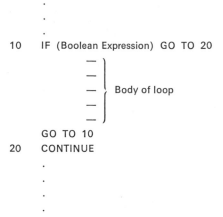

For the time being, though, FORTRAN seems a rather poor vehicle for structured programming concepts. The discipline that would have to be imposed upon programmers to ensure a structured use of GO-TO statements [by using only the forms shown in Fig. 4.18(a) and Fig. 4.18(b)] would be difficult, if not impossible, to administrate.

Systems Implementation Languages. During the past few years, a number of high-level assembly languages have been developed to give the systems programmer some of the benefits of high-level languages—convenient looping and control constructs, data structures, and error-checking—without losing the "low-level" efficiency and control of assembly language. Three of the better-known languages of this type are, at the current time, PL/S, BLISS, and PL/360. BLISS was developed by a group of researchers at Carnegie-Mellon University and has been described in the literature [29]; it has served as a vehicle for several structured programming projects. PL/360 was developed by Niklaus Wirth for the IBM System/360 and has been described in reference 30; it attempts to give the programmer the power and structure of PL/I, together with the efficiency and control of the 360 assembly language. PL/S (Programming Language for Systems) was developed by IBM as a programming language for systems software on such virtual memory machines as the 370/158. At the time this book was written, IBM considered the language proprietary property and did not provide details of the language.

These two languages, and others like it (the Burroughs B5500 ESPOL language and the Project MAC EPL language for the GE-645 MULTICS project may be considered additional examples) are generally quite amenable to structured programming concepts. In fact, one of the primary motivations for the development of these languages has been to eliminate some of the debugging and maintenance problems that are so prevalent in assembly language—and in so doing, the systems programmers have begun to realize that they must impose some structure upon their programs if they are to develop truly bug-free systems. It is interesting to note, by the way, that the BLISS language does not have an explicit GO-TO statement, while the PL/360 language *does* allow the programmer to execute an unconditional branch if he so desires.

There is one potential disadvantage of the systems implementation languages that has nothing to do with structured programming, but should be mentioned briefly in passing. The languages are almost always implemented for a specific machine and do not facilitate the development of "portable" programs. BLISS, for example, was developed for the PDP-10 computer, and it allows the programmer to interact directly with the PDP-10 instruction set and architecture. PL/360 and PL/S, of course, are equally specialized for the IBM System/360 and System/370 computers. This does not seem to be of much concern to systems programmers, who often point out that their applications —operating systems, compilers, data base management packages, etc.—are not portable anyway. The uniqueness of *any* program is usually rather exaggerated (why shouldn't we want to incorporate some of the optimization logic of the System/360 FORTRAN-H compiler on the PDP-10?), and one hopes that we will eventually see a modular systems implementation language, where the machine-dependent features can be specified separately from the high-level features.

Assembly Language. Last, we should mention assembly language as a possible vehicle for the development of structured programming. By itself, assembly language has the same weaknesses as FORTRAN: by its very nature, it lacks such things as an IF-THEN-ELSE, block structures, and the DO-WHILE construct (though, with some of the new microprogrammable machines, anything is possible!). However, with the addition of *macros*, it is possible to consider assembly language as a reasonable language for the structured programming concepts. Most of the assembly languages on the larger machines (and even a few of the minicomputers) afford the programmer the means of developing an IF-THEN-ELSE macro, BEGIN-END block structure macros, and DO-WHILE macros.

It should be remembered that the lack of the IF-THEN construct, etc., in assembly language is not a necessary deterrent to structured programming. As we pointed out earlier in the discussion of FORTRAN, the only thing that is required is strong discipline on the part of the programmer (or his manager) to use the unconditional jump instruction only in fulfillment of the constructs that are found naturally in the other structured programming languages.

4.4   Other Aspects of Structured Programming

Most of the projects that have used structured programming as an aid for program development have included a few additional rules, restrictions, and programming conventions. Although these are not *necessary* to support the theory of structured programming, they are indeed convenient. Since many of the additional programming conventions are discussed elsewhere in this book, they will be mentioned only briefly here.

1. The readability of a structured program is greatly enhanced if it is formatted properly. As we have seen, much of the basis of structured programming is the *nesting* of subroutine calls, IF-THEN statements, and DO-WHILE statements; these should all be indented appropriately for the sake of readability. For languages like PL/I, this can be done mechanically [31]; the LISP language once had a source program reformatting package called PRETTYPRINT; programmers in other languages may have to struggle along manually. Section 5.2.3 makes a number of additional suggestions concerning formatting of source programs for readability.

2. It is a good idea to continue breaking a program into smaller pieces until the remaining modules or process boxes are relatively small. Estimates of a nominal module size have varied from 20 to 200 statements, depending on the language, the application, and the predilections of the programming group. A number of examples of *size* as a measure of the modularity of a program are discussed in Section 3.1.1. The IBM structured programming project [10] strongly encouraged their programmers to develop modules of approximately 50 statements each.

3. To ensure the integrity of each module (which *is* a necessary part of the structured programming concept), no module (or process box, to use the terminology of much of this chapter) should be allowed to modify any other module. In particular, this means that we should outlaw such statements as ALTER in the COBOL language. This concept was also discussed in Section 1.2.2, and again in Section 5.1.4.

4. To further ensure the integrity of each module, local variables and temporary storage for any given module should be independent of all other modules. In other words, temporary storage should not be shared between modules. Since this seems to have been the source of a great many programming bugs in the experience of the author and his various friends, colleagues, and clients, it has been stressed repeatedly in Section 1.2.2, Section 3.3.5, and in Chapter 8.

5. To make sure that the structured programming concept is firmly imbedded within the program, make sure that the program is designed with the top-down approach; this was the subject of our discussion in Chapter 2.

4.5 Considerations of Practicality in Structured Programming

Having seen most of the major aspects of structured programming, the only remaining point is a short discussion of its practicality in everyday programming applications. There seem to be several questions that are raised whenever structured programming is discussed. Is it really worth the trouble—does it get results? Does it lead to efficient programs—what is its cost? How convenient is it—are there any practical programming situations that are *not* handled conveniently with the structured programming? Are today's programming languages really suitable for this kind of programming? All of these questions are discussed below.

4.5.1 Is Structured Programming Really Worth the Effort?

There are a number of serious programmers and computer scientists who suggest that structured programming (or the "no go-to" philosophy, as it is sometimes called) is being looked upon as a panacea for our current programming problems. A large number of programmers who have attended my courses on advanced programming have shrugged their shoulders after the discussion of structured programming and have said, "So what? I can't see that the elimination of the GO-TO statement could have a very great effect on coding time, debugging time, etc." While there is some recognition that a structured program is more amenable to rigorous proof of the program's correctness, most programmers (including the author) do not feel that this will become feasible and practical for several years. Perhaps the best summary of skepticism of the "magic" properties of eliminating the GO-TO was made by Martin Hopkins [12] (who, by the way, *does* acknowledge some of the benefits of the "anti-go-to" movement):

> A wise philosopher once pointed out to a lazy king that there is no royal road to geometry. After discovering, in the late fifties, that programming was *the* computer problem, a search was made during the sixties for the royal road to programming. Various paths were tried including comprehensive operating systems, higher-level languages, project management techniques, time-sharing, virtual memory, programmer education, and applications packages. While each of these is useful, they have not solved the programming problem. Confronted with this unresolved problem and with few good ideas on the horizon, some people are now hoping that the royal road will be found through style, and that banishment of the *goto* statement will solve all. The existence of this

controversy and the seriousness assigned to it by otherwise very sensible people are symptoms of a malaise in the computing community. We have few promising new ideas at hand. I also suspect that the controversy reflects something rather deep in human nature, the notion that language is magic and the mere utterance of certain words is dangerous or defiling. Is it an accident that "goto" has four letters?

These are serious, well-expressed thoughts, and any programmer would do well to think about them. It is indeed true that elimination of the "goto" will not perform any magic for us, and that we will still be left with more than enough problems of designing, coding, testing, and debugging computer programs—especially since our appetite for large systems seems to be growing faster than our capacity to design and implement them properly. Nevertheless, the GO-TO concept, or *structured programming* as we should continue to call it, *does* represent an improvement over our currently chaotic way of doing things. Whether it is a *significant* improvement, worthy of the attention and controversy that has surrounded it for the past few years, will not be known until we have more experience using it—including more statistics on the productivity of the programmers, the number of bugs discovered during the testing phase, and the final quality of the finished program. The most significant project to date—at least the most significant reported in literature —has been the IBM project for The *New York Times* [10]. The experiences of that project suggested an improvement in productivity of a factor of nearly 5, and *that* is definitely worth the effort that may have been put into structured programming. It is my feeling that with some practice in this area, we may yet achieve Dijkstra's goal of an order of magnitude improvement in programming productivity.

4.5.2   Is the Structured Programming Approach Efficient?

Another major complaint that has been made about structured programming is the inefficiency that it may introduce into the program. In particular, a number of researchers (Wulf [11], for example) complain that attempts to convert an unstructured program into an equivalent structured program may introduce redundant coding and extra overhead due to the introduction of a new variable. Others have pointed out that structured programming would be entirely impractical in a language such as FORTRAN, since the basis for such a structure would rest heavily on increased use of subroutine calls. Similar complaints have also been raised against ALGOL, PL/I, COBOL, the systems implementation languages, and even assembly language.

Perhaps the most eloquent argument against the emphasis on efficiency was made by Wulf [11]:

> More computing sins are committed in the name of efficiency (without necessarily achieving it) than for any other single reason—including blind stupidity. One of these sins is the construction of a "rat's nest" of control flow which exploits a few common construction sequences. This is precisely the form of

programming that must be eliminated if we are ever to build correct, understandable, and modifiable systems.

I agree with Wulf's argument—most emphatically. "Efficiency" has become a somewhat academic point in these days of large, generalized operating systems and high-level languages; one must always smile a little at complaints of inefficiency from COBOL programmers working under an operating system such as OS/360. If we were truly interested in efficiency, we would still be coding in octal on machines without operating systems.

Despite the sermon, a number of programmers continue to express serious concern over the potential inefficiencies associated with structured programming. The following comments are in order:

1. The Ashcroft-Manna technique of introducing a new variable to control looping and branching through an otherwise unstructured program is, as we have already noted, relatively cheap. *Setting* the variable to some integer value should take only one or two instructions; *testing* it and branching to the appropriate process box can often be done with something analogous to the CASE statement in ALGOL or the computed GO-TO in FORTRAN.

2. Other situations may require duplication of code to avoid the lattice structure program that was illustrated in Fig. 4.9. If large sections of code are actually duplicated, serious inefficiencies might result (in terms of memory utilization, not CPU overhead). On the other hand, if the duplication is effected by a subroutine call to a single copy of a common process box, the overhead should be tolerable.

3. Structured programming, in most implementations, places a great deal of emphasis on *subroutine calls* (e.g., the PERFORM statement in COBOL, the CALL statement in FORTRAN), which is of concern to many programmers whose managers have specifically forbidden them to use such statements because of the overhead inherent in subroutine-calling statements. The concern is legitimate in some cases. One implementation of PL/I on the 360/50 computer imposed a 198 microsecond overhead on procedure calls [32]. Many versions of FORTRAN and COBOL also suffer a great deal of overhead in this area; the subroutine call itself should require only one machine language instruction, but the instructions to pass arguments and save the general purpose registers can be expensive indeed. This is an area that must be examined with care.

4. The use of block structures in languages like ALGOL and PL/I is normally not expensive, *unless* the programmer declares local variables within the block (in which case, much of the "prologue-epilogue" overhead that is present in subroutine calls will be suffered). If the block structures are used simply to form compound statements (which is their normal use to group together a few statements in an IF-THEN construct or a DO-WHILE construct), the efficiency of the program should not be impaired.

5. The IF-THEN-ELSE construct is a potentially inefficient statement in many high-level languages, *especially* if it is nested. COBOL and PL/I are notorious in this area; the systems-implementation-language approach, being closer to the machine language level anyway, does not tend to suffer very much. This area, like the subroutine-calling overhead, should be studied carefully by the programmer.

All in all, it is likely that a structured program *will* be slightly less efficient than an unstructured program, but it is likely that greater savings can be achieved through more careful systems design. In any case, it seems that an order of magnitude increase in programmer productivity is worth a little overhead!

4.5.3   Is Structured Programming Inconvenient?

Still another common complaint about structured programming is one of *inconvenience*: Many programmers feel that programming without the GO-TO statement would be awkward, tedious, and cumbersome. For the most part, this complaint is due to force of habit. Having programmed for so many years *with* the unstructured GO-TO approach, it is natural to feel some uneasiness at the prospect of doing things in such a highly structured way. But, by the same argument, assembly language programmers in the late 1950s felt great uneasiness about the prospects of using FORTRAN (and who knows—maybe they were right!).

The only response that can be given to this complaint comes from a popular television commercial that made the rounds recently: "Try it—you'll like it!" The experience of several groups of programmers has been fairly uniform: It takes a little time getting used to the idea of thinking and design-ing in a structured manner, but having once learned the technique, it is no more difficult than any other form of programming. The learning process is greatly simplified with the translation techniques of Ashcroft and Manna that were described in Section 4.3.3. I personally had the unpleasant experience of learning to write structured programs without the benefit of these techniques, and had to discover them by myself. It has also been my experience that ex-posure to some programming languages facilitates the conversion to a struc-tured programming approach. Those who are familiar with ALGOL or PL/I usually have no difficulty learning it (in fact, I discovered that, by ac-cident, the first ALGOL program I ever wrote was structured! Needless to say, I was quite proud of myself). COBOL and FORTRAN programmers have a more difficult time, though COBOL programmers seem more willing to discipline themselves to put more emphasis on PERFORMs and com-pound statements, and less emphasis on the GO-TO statement. Those whose assembly language experience has included a healthy dose of *macros* also seem to have an easy time learning to write structured programs.

There is some feeling that there are a few programming situations that are *not* handled conveniently with the usual structured programming mecha-nisms. Wulf [11], for example, mentions the need for an escape mechanism to allow an arbitrary exit from a loop or a deeply nested subroutine. To com-pensate for this, the BLISS language, of which Wulf was one of the designers and implementers, uses a special LEAVE verb to allow an exit from any such loop or procedure. Similar additions to the basic structured program-ming mechanisms might also be convenient in languages such as ALGOL, PL/I, and COBOL.

One case that deserves special mention is the end-of-file situation. The COBOL programmer, for example, is accustomed to writing

```
READ FILEX AT END GO TO END-ROUTINE.
```

Similarly, the FORTRAN programmer knows that he should indicate in his input/output statements a statement number for EOF and a statement number for parity errors; the PL/I programmer handles this and a variety of other situations with the ON CONDITIONS facility.

The end-of-file situation and a few others are actually examples of an *interrupt* situation, that is, a situation where we know there is a possibility of normal processing being suspended. Rather than handling this with a GO-TO statement, the structured approach might involve (among other things) setting a flag that could be tested subsequently. Thus, the COBOL programmer could write

```
READ FILEX AT END MOVE 1 TO EOF-FLAG.
IF EOF-FLAG = 1 THEN PERFORM ENDROUTINE
ELSE
    MOVE A TO B
    MOVE C TO D
    .
    .
    .
  etc.
    .
    .
    .
```

Similar conventions can be established easily in PL/I and the other programming languages. The extent to which this forces clumsy coding is a matter for argument; the major point is that most situations *can* be handled in a manner that is consistent with the philosophy of structured programming.

4.5.4 Are Current Programming Languages Adequate for Structured Programming?

We have already discussed the implementation of structured programming concepts to such languages as ALGOL, PL/I, COBOL, FORTRAN, and assembly language in Section 4.3.4. There is hardly any doubt that ALGOL and PL/I are excellent candidates for use in structured programming. In fact, there is some hope among proponents of those languages that the interest in structured programming will draw programmers *away* from FORTRAN and COBOL, and *toward* ALGOL and PL/I. There are a few questions of efficiency, but they do not seem sufficiently serious to discourage the use of the languages.

COBOL, in the opinion of many structured programming proponents, lacks the formal structure that is desirable when building GO-TO-less programs. As we saw in our earlier discussion, the lack of explicit block structures, the somewhat ambiguous form of the nested IF statement, and the clumsiness of the PERFORM-UNTIL statement could occasionally make structured programming awkward. Nevertheless, it *is* possible to use the *standard* COBOL language for structured programs, as several organizations are currently doing. The experience gleaned from these projects should tell us whether the inefficiency and inconvenience of structured programming in COBOL outweighs the benefits of greater programmer productivity and reduced testing costs.

In the meantime, some COBOL groups have begun finding that *their* version of COBOL (i.e., their vendor's implementation of the COBOL language) lacks some of the features that make structured programming convenient. Some have discovered, for example, that their version of COBOL compiles nested IF statements incorrectly (i e., it generates incorrect object code); others have found that the compiler limits the number of PERFORM statements that may appear in a program; still others have found that their version of COBOL requires that the input procedure to a SORT be a single SECTION, with no PERFORMs outside the section. It has even been claimed that one version of COBOL (on a computer that shall remain anonymous) does not include the GO-TO DEPENDING ON statement; others have found that the GO-TO DEPENDING ON generates object code similar to that for a nested IF-THEN-ELSE.

FORTRAN does *not* seem a good vehicle for structured programming as it now stands. If the "anti-go-to" movement gains general acceptance, it is very likely that we will see some augmentations to FORTRAN (all of which could be handled by a preprocessor that would generate *standard* FORTRAN source code as its output, but would still force the programmer to use structured techniques). In the meantime, it seems that the predominant use of FORTRAN is by those scientists, engineers, and mathematicians who are not quite so concerned with the benefits to be gained from structured programming—though there are obviously examples to the contrary.

Assembly languages, macro languages, and the systems implementation languages should be good candidates for structured programming, and it seems that much of the work currently going on in the field is in those languages. The languages are used primarily in *systems programs* where there is a natural interest in correctness and ease of testing. The fact that the low-level languages give the programmer more direct control over the hardware eliminates most of the efficiency considerations, except for the few that are inherent in the structured programming approach itself (e.g., the need to occasionally duplicate sections of code).

REFERENCES

1. E. W. DIJKSTRA, "Programming Considered as a Human Activity," *Proceedings of IFIP Congress 65*, Spartan Books, Washington, D.C., 1965.

2. ——, "Go-To Statement Considered Harmful," Letter to the Editor, *Communications of the ACM*, March 1968.

3. ——, "The Structure of the THE-Multiprogramming System," *Communica-*

tions of the ACM, May 1968, pages 341–346. [Copyright 1968, Association for Computing Machinery, Inc., reprinted by permission.]

4. ——, "Structured Programming," *Software Engineering Techniques*, NATO Scientific Affairs Division, Brussels 39, Belgium, pages 84–88.

5. ——, "Notes on Structured Programming," EWD 249, Technical University, Eindhoven, Netherlands, 1969.

6. A. VAN WIJNGAARDEN, "Recursive Definition of Syntax and Semantics," *Formal Language Description Languages for Computer Programming*, ed. T. B. STEEL, JR., North-Holland, Amsterdam, 1966.

7. D. VAN SCHORRE, "Improved Organization for Procedural Languages," Technical Memo, System Development Corp., Santa Monica, California, August 1966.

8. P. J. LANDIN, "The Next 700 Programming Languages," *Communications of the ACM*, March 1966, pages 157–164.

9. J. D. ARON, "The Superprogrammer Project," *Software Engineering Techniques*, NATO Scientific Affairs Division, Brussels 39, Belgium, pages 50–52.

10. F. T. BAKER, "Chief Programmer Team Management of Production Programming," *IBM Systems Journal*, January 1972, pages 56–73.

11. W. A. WULF, "A Case Against the GOTO," *Proceedings of the 25th ACM National Conference*, Volume 2, 1972, pages 791–797. [Copyright 1972, Association for Computing Machinery, Inc., reprinted by permission.]

12. M. E. HOPKINS, "A Case for the GOTO," *Proceedings of the 25th ACM National Conference*, Volume 2, 1972, pages 787–790. [Copyright 1972, Association for Computing Machinery, Inc., reprinted by permission.]

13. *Software Engineering*, eds. P. NAUR and B. RANDELL, NATO Scientific Affairs Division, Brussels 39, Belgium, published in January 1969.

14. *Software Engineering Techniques*, eds. J. N. BUXTON and B. RANDELL, NATO Scientific Affairs Division, Brussels 39, Belgium, published April 1970.

15. J. KING, *A Program Verifier*, Ph.D. Thesis, Carnegie-Mellon University, 1969.

16. Z. MANNA, S. NESS, and J. VAILLEMIN, "Inductive Methods for Proving Properties About Programs," *SIGPLAN/SIGACT Conference on Proving Assertions About Programs*, January 1972.

17. C. A. R. HOARE, "Proof of a Program: FIND," *Communications of the ACM*, January 1971, pages 39–45.

18. J. D. ARON, "Estimating Resources for Large Programming Systems," *Software Engineering Techniques*, NATO Scientific Affairs Division, April 1970, pages 68–79.

19. S. C. KLEENE, *Introduction to Mathematics*, D. Van Nostrand Company, Inc., New York, 1952.

20. E. I. POST, "Finite Combinatory Processes—Formulation I," *Journal of Symbolic Logic*, Volume 1, 1936.

21. A. A. MARKOV, "The Theory of Algorithms," (translated from the Russian), U.S. Dept. of Commerce, Office of Technical Services, No. OTS 60–51085.

22. A. Church, "The Calculi of Lambda-Conversion," *Annals of Mathematical Studies*, Number 6, Princeton University Press, Princeton, New Jersey, 1951.

23. B. M. Leavenworth, "Programming Without the GOTO," *Proceedings of the 25th ACM National Conference*, Volume 2, pages 782–786.

24. C. Böhm and G. Jacopini, "Flow Diagrams, Turing Machines, and Languages with Only Two Formulation Rules," *Communications of the ACM*, May 1966, pages 366–371.

25. D. E. Knuth and R. W. Floyd, "Notes on Avoiding GOTO Statements," Technical Report CS148, Stanford University, January 1970.

26. E. Ashcroft and Z. Manna, "The Translation of 'Goto' Programs into 'While' Programs," *Proceedings of 1971 IFIP Congress*.

27. M. G. Manugian, "A Collection of Readings on the Subject of BLISS-10," *DECUS Program Library*, DECUS No. 10–118 Part II, Digital Equipment Corporation, Maynard, Massachusetts, December 1971.

28. W. A. Wulf, "Programming Without the GOTO," from "A Collection of Readings on the Subject of BLISS-10," pages 3–1 through 3–25.

29. W. A. Wulf et al., "'BLISS' a Language for Systems Programming," *Communications of the ACM*, December 1971.

30. N. Wirth, "PL360, A Programming Language for the 360 Computers," *Journal of the ACM*, January 1968, pages 37–74.

31. K. Conrow and R. G. Smith, "NEATER2: a PL/I Source Statement Reformatter," *Communications of the ACM*, November 1970.

32. R. J. Schmalz, "OS/360 PL/I-F Performance Guidelines," IBM, Dept. H74, Poughkeepsie, New York, June 1969.

33. D. McCracken, "Revolution in Programming: An Overview," *Datamation*, December 1973, pages 50–51.

34. J. R. Donaldson, "Structured Programming," *Datamation*, December 1973, pages 52–54.

35. E. F. Miller and G. E. Lindamood, "Structured Programming: Top-Down Approach," *Datamation*, December 1973, pages 55–57.

36. F. T. Baker and H. D. Mills, "Chief Programmer Teams," *Datamation*, December 1973, pages 58–61.

37. R. L. Clark, "A Linguistic Contribution to GOTO-Less Programming," *Datamation*, December 1973, pages 62–68.

38. G. Weinberg, *Structured Programming in PL/C*, John Wiley & Sons, Inc., 1972.

39. O. J. Dahl, E. W. Dijkstra, and C. A. R. Hoare, *Structured Programming*, Academic Press, 1972.

40. John Flynn, *SFTRAN User Guide*, Interoffice Computing Memorandum No. 337, Jet Propulsion Laboratory, 4800 Oak Grove Drive, Pasadena, California 91103.

41. R. C. T. Lee and S. K. Chang, "Structured Programming and Automatic Program Synthesis," *Proceedings of the ACM SIGPLAN Symposium on Very High Level Languages*, March 1974.

42. RICHARD H. KARPINSKI, "An Unstructured View of Structured Programming," *ACM SIGPLAN Notices*, Volume 9, Number 3, March 1974.

43. F. T. BAKER, "System Quality Through Structured Programming," *Proceedings 1972 Fall Joint Computer Conference*, pages 339–342.

44. HARLAN MILLS, *Mathematical Foundations for Structured Programming— Report FSC72-6012*, IBM Corp., Gaithersburg, Md., 1972.

45. DAVID L. PARNAS, "On the Problem of Producing Well Structured Programs," *Computer Science Research Review*, Carnegie-Mellon University, Pittsburgh, Pa., 1972.

46. C. L. McGOWAN and J. R. KELLY, *Top-Down Structured Programming*, Mason and Lipscomb, 1975.

47. E. YOURDON, "A Brief Look at Structured Programming and Top-Down Design," *Modern Data*, June 1974, pages pp. 30–35.

48. N. WIRTH, "On the Composition of Well-Structured Programs," *ACM Computing Surveys*, December 1974, pages 247–260.

49. D. E. KNUTH, "Structured Programming with Go-To Statements," *ACM Computing Surveys*, December 1974, pages 261–302.

PROBLEMS

1. Give a definition of structured programming in one or two brief paragraphs. What is the relationship between structured programming and the GO-TO statement commonly found in high-level programming languages? Be specific: Do not resort to the oversimplified statement that "structured programming is programming without the GO-TO statement."

2. Why do you think structured programming was not accepted for such a long period of time? Do you think that the same attitudes will mitigate against the acceptance of structured programming in your organization?

3. What are the major objectives of structured programming? Describe them briefly.

4. Why should structured programs be easier to test? What kind of testing approach is normally used on structured programs?

5. Why should it be possible for programmers to write more debugged statements per day with a structured approach? What consequence is this likely to have in a typical programming project?

6. Why are structured programs more readable than the typical unstructured program? Do you think this is a significant argument in favor of structured programming?

7. What is the difference between structured programming and modular programming?

8. What are the basic building blocks suggested by Bohm and Jacopini?

9. What is the relationship between structured programming and the concept of top-down design discussed in Chapter 2?

10. In your programming language, list the basic programming statements and "mechanisms" required to write structured programs.

11. Under what conditions may a GO-TO statement be used without violating the philosophy of structured programming?

12. Discuss one extension of the basic structured programming building blocks, and show how it does not violate the concept of structured programming.

13. Some programmers have suggested that multiple exits (e.g., a normal return and an error return) should be allowed as an extension to the basic rules of structured programming. How could this be handled in a structured (i.e., one-entry, one-exit) fashion?

14. Some programmers have suggested that GO-TO statements be allowed as long as they branch in a *forward* direction. Under what conditions might this result in a program that would be difficult to understand and debug?

15. Figure 4.19 shows a flowchart of an unstructured program. Draw a flowchart of an equivalent structured program, using the duplication-of-coding technique. Show the black boxes in the structured version of the flowchart by drawing the appropriate boundaries.

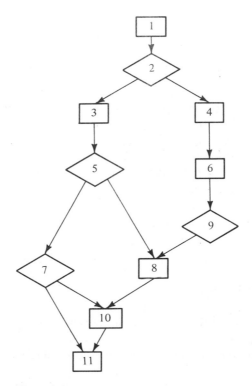

Figure 4.19.

16. Figure 4.20 shows a flowchart of an unstructured program. Draw a flowchart of an equivalent structured program, using the duplication-of-coding technique.

Show the black boxes in the structured version of the flowchart by drawing the appropriate boundaries.

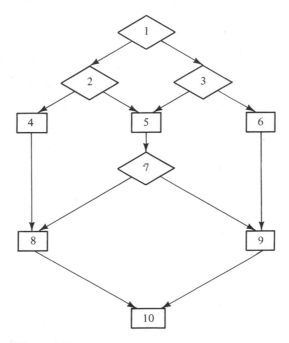

Figure 4.20.

17. Figure 4.21 shows a flowchart of an unstructured program. Draw a flowchart of an equivalent structured program, using the duplication-of-coding technique. Show the black boxes in the structured version of the flowchart by drawing the appropriate boundaries.

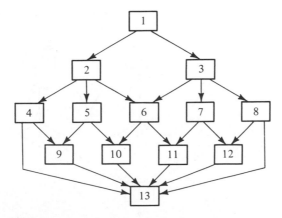

Figure 4.21.

18. Figure 4.22 shows a flowchart of an unstructured program. Draw a flowchart of an equivalent structured program, using the duplication-of-coding technique. Show the black boxes in the structured version of the flowchart by drawing the appropriate boundaries.

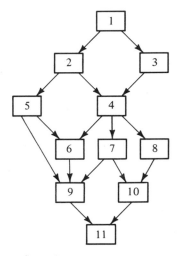

Figure 4.22.   **Figure 4.23.**

19. Figure 4.23 shows a flowchart of an unstructured program. Draw a flowchart of an equivalent structured program, using the duplication-of-coding technique. Show the black boxes in the structured version of the flowchart by drawing the appropriate boundaries.

20. Figure 4.24 shows a flowchart of an unstructured program. Draw a flowchart of an equivalent structured program using the Ashcroft-Manna technique.

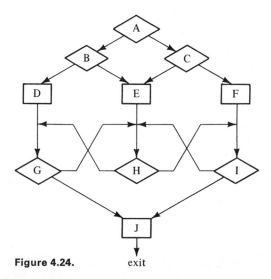

Figure 4.24.   exit

21. Figure 4.25 shows a flowchart of an unstructured program. Draw a flowchart of an equivalent structured program using the Ashcroft-Manna technique.

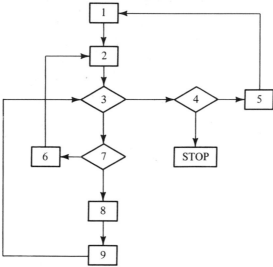

Figure 4.25.

22. Figure 4.26 shows a flowchart of an unstructured program. Draw a flowchart of an equivalent structured program using the Ashcroft-Manna technique.

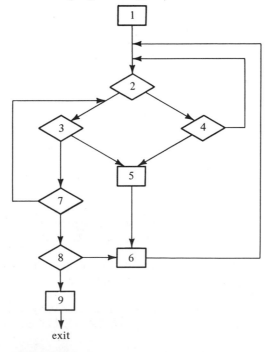

Figure 4.26.

23. Figure 4.27 shows a flowchart of an unstructured program. Draw a flowchart of an equivalent structured program using the Ashcroft-Manna technique.

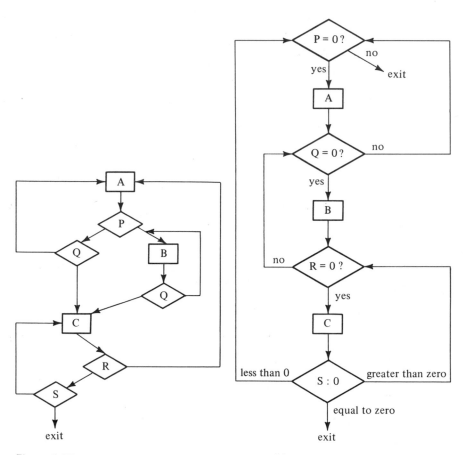

Figure 4.27.   Figure 4.28.

24. Figure 4.28 shows a flowchart of an unstructured program. Draw a flowchart of an equivalent structured program using the Ashcroft-Manna technique.

25. Figure 4.29 shows a small program written in an unstructured manner. Rewrite the program using the Boolean flag technique. The unstructured version of the program is written in a form of "computer Esperanto" whose meaning should be perfectly clear to you. When you write the structured version, do so in a specific programming language, e.g., COBOL, FORTRAN, ALGOL, etc.

Figure 4.29.

```
              Set variable I to 1.
              Set variable FLAG to 0.
LOOP.         If TABLE(I)  >  N go to GOOD.
              If TABLE(I)  =  0 go to BAD.
              Set variable I to TABLE(I + 1).
              Go to LOOP.
GOOD.         Set variable FLAG to 1.
              Go to DONE.
BAD.          Set variable FLAG to 0.
DONE.         Exit.
```

26. Figure 4.30 shows a small program written in an unstructured manner. Rewrite the program using the Boolean flag technique. The unstructured version of the program is written in a form of "computer Esperanto" whose meaning should be perfectly clear to you. When you write the structured version, do so in a specific programming language, e.g., COBOL, FORTRAN, ALGOL, etc.

Figure 4.30.

```
LOOP1.        Read disk record into FLAG.
              If FLAG ≠ 0 go to LOOP1.
              Write A into disk record.
              Read disk record into FLAG.
              If FLAG ≠ A go to LOOP1.
              Exit.
```

27. Figure 4.31 shows a small program written in an unstructured manner. Rewrite the program using the Boolean flag technique. The unstructured version of the program is written in a form of "computer Esperanto" whose meaning should be perfectly clear to you. When you write the structured version, do so in a specific programming language, e.g., COBOL, FORTRAN, ALGOL, etc.

Figure 4.31.

```
LOOP.         Set I to (START + FINISH)/2.
              If TABLE(I)  =  ITEM go to FOUND.
              If TABLE(I)  <  ITEM set START to (I + 1).
              If TABLE(I)  >  ITEM set FINISH to (I − 1).
              If (FINISH − START) > 1 go to LOOP.
              If TABLE(START)  =  ITEM go to FOUND.
              If TABLE(FINISH)  =  ITEM go to FOUND.
              Set variable FLAG to 0.
              Go to DONE.
FOUND.        Set variable FLAG to 1.
DONE.         Exit.
```

28. Figure 4.32 shows a small program written in an unstructured manner. Rewrite the program using the Boolean flag technique. The unstructured version of the program is written in a form of "computer Esperanto" whose meaning should be perfectly clear to you. When you write the structured version, do so in a specific programming language, e.g., COBOL, FORTRAN, ALGOL, etc.

Figure 4.32.

```
                    Set variable I to 1.
LOOP.               Set variable J to 1.
COMPARE.            If TABLE(J) < TABLE(J + 1) go to INCREMENT.
                    Set variable TEMP to TABLE(J).
                    Set TABLE(J) to TABLE(J + 1).
                    Set TABLE(J + 1) to TEMP.
INCREMENT.          Set J to J + 1.
                    If J < N go to COMPARE.
                    Set I to I + 1.
                    If I < (N + 1) go to LOOP.
                    Exit.
```

29. Figure 4.33 shows a program written in an unstructured manner. Rewrite the program using the Boolean flag technique. The unstructured version of the program is written in a form of "computer Esperanto" whose meaning should be perfectly clear to you. When you write the structured version, do so in a specific programming language, e.g., COBOL, FORTRAN, ALGOL, etc.

Figure 4.33.

```
                    Set variable MAX to N.
                    Set variable I to 1.
LOOP.               Set variable J to 1.
                    Set variable FLAG to 0.
COMPARE.            If TABLE(J) < TABLE(J + 1)  GO to INC.
                    Set variable TEMP to TABLE(J)
                    Set TABLE(J) to TABLE(J + 1).
                    Set TABLE(J + 1) to TEMP.
                    Set variable FLAG to 1.
INC.                Set variable J to (J + 1).
                    If J < MAX go to COMPARE
                    If FLAG = 0 go to DONE.
                    Set variable I to (I + 1).
                    Set variable MAX to (MAX − 1).
                    If I < (N + 1) go to LOOP.
DONE.               Exit.
```

30. What are the disadvantages of the duplication-of-coding translation technique? How significant are these disadvantages?

31. Why is the duplication-of-coding technique less likely to lead to program logic errors than the equivalent unstructured technique?

32. What are the objections against the Ashcroft-Manna technique of translating unstructured logic into structured logic? How significant are these objections?

33. The flowchart shown in Fig. 4.17(a) is a somewhat oversimplified version of a real master-file update algorithm. Write a *structured* version of a more comprehensive update program in which:
   (a) The first field in the record is used as a primary identification key.
   (b) The master file and the transaction file are sorted (in ascending sequence) on this key.
   (c) The second field in the transaction records is a *function code* that indicates whether the record is to be inserted in the master file, or whether the information on the record is to be used to change various fields on the corresponding master record, or whether the master record is to be deleted.
   (d) There may be multiple transactions (appearing one after the other on the transaction file) against a single master record.

34. How does the Ashcroft-Manna technique facilitate debugging?

35. It has been suggested that the unstructured program shown in Fig. 4.34(a) could be rewritten in the structured form shown in Fig. 4.34(b). Find a *different* way of writing the program, using the Boolean flag technique, *and* without introducing any new flags into the program.

Figure 4.34(a).

```
            MOVE 1 TO I.
            MOVE 0 TO FLAG.
LOOP.       IF TABLE(I) > N GO TO GOOD.
            IF TABLE(I) = 0 GO TO BAD.
            MOVE TABLE(I + 1) TO I.
            GO TO LOOP.
GOOD.       MOVE 1 TO FLAG.
            GO TO DONE.
BAD.        MOVE 0 TO FLAG.
DONE.       EXIT.
```

Figure 4.34(b).

```
            MOVE 1 TO I.
            MOVE 0 TO FLAG, DONE.
            PERFORM LOOP UNTIL DONE = 1.
            EXIT.
LOOP.       IF TABLE(I) > N
                MOVE 1 TO FLAG, DONE
            ELSE
                IF TABLE(I) = 0
                    MOVE 1 TO DONE
                    MOVE 0 TO FLAG
                ELSE MOVE TABLE(I + 1) TO I.
            EXIT.
```

36. It has been suggested that the unstructured program shown in Fig. 4.35(a) could be rewritten in the structured form shown in Fig. 4.35(b). Find a *different* way of writing the program, using the Boolean flag technique, *and* without introducing any new flags into the program.

Figure 4.35(a).

```
LOOP1.        PERFORM  READ-DISK-INTO-FLAG.
              IF FLAG = 0 GO TO LOOP1.
              PERFORM  WRITE-A-ONTO-DISK.
              PERFORM  READ-DISK-INTO-FLAG.
              IF FLAG ≠ A GO TO LOOP1.
              EXIT.
```

Figure 4.35(b).

```
              MOVE 9999 TO FLAG.
              PERFORM  OUTER-LOOP UNTIL FLAG = A.
              EXIT.
OUTER-LOOP.   PERFORM  INNER-LOOP UNTIL FLAG = 0.
              PERFORM  WRITE-A-ONTO-DISK.
              PERFORM  READ-DISK-INTO-FLAG.
              EXIT.
INNER-LOOP.   PERFORM  READ-DISK-INTO-FLAG.
              EXIT.
```

37. What features of the COBOL language make structured programming awkward?

38. What features of FORTRAN make structured programming awkward and inconvenient? With these limitations, how can one write structured programs in FORTRAN?

39. Investigate the COBOL compiler on your computer to see whether it has any special limitations that would make structured programming awkward (e.g., limitations on the number of PERFORM statements).

40. (An experiment) Choose a nontrivial program of the nature you are accustomed to working on in your organization; choose a friend or colleague whose programming ability is roughly the same as yours. One of you should write the program in a structured fashion; the other should write the program as efficiently as possible (which will probably require some violations of the structured programming philosophy). When you are finished, compare the two programs to see how much more CPU time and memory are required by the structured approach. Is it significant? Do you think you would find the same amount of overhead in other programming situations?

41. Figure 4.13 shows a small sample flowchart; Fig. 4.15 shows the same program after it has been converted by the Ashcroft-Manna technique. Note that there

is only one place in Fig. 4.15 where the state variable I is set equal to 4. This suggests that we could simplify Fig. 4.15 by rewriting it in the form shown in Fig. 4.36. Continue this process, that is, continue to simplify the flowchart shown in Fig. 4.36 by recognizing states that occur only once.

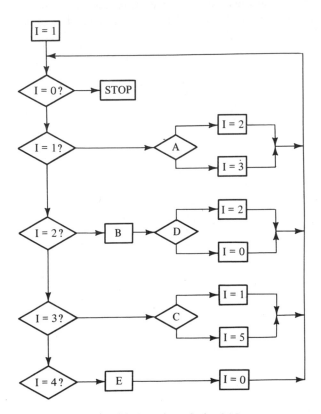

Figure 4.36. A simplified version of Fig. 4.15.

42. Using the technique described in problem 41, simplify the Ashcroft-Manna solution to Fig. 4.24 (see also problem 20).

43. Using the technique described in problem 41, simplify the Ashcroft-Manna solution to Fig. 4.25 (see also problem 21).

44. Using the technique described in problem 41, simplify the Aschroft-Manna solution to Fig. 4.26 (see also problem 22).

45. Using the technique described in problem 41, simplify the Ashcroft-Manna solution to Fig. 4.27 (see also problem 23).

46. Using the technique described in problem 41, simplify the Ashcroft-Manna solution to Fig. 4.28 (see also problem 24).

47. Figure 4.16(a) shows a common form of an unstructured look, i.e., one with a single entry and two exits. Figure 4.16(b) shows that such a loop could be restructured by introducing a new flag into the program; Fig. 4.16(c) shows an alternative method of restructuring the program without introducing a new flag. Now consider the unstructured loop shown in Fig. 4.37; note that it has two entries and only one exit. Rearrange this loop so that it is in proper structured form. The example in Figs. 4.16(a), 4.16(b), and 4.16(c) should give you a hint.

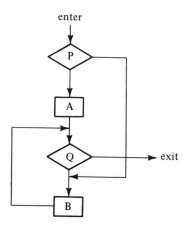

Figure 4.37. An unstructured loop.

5

PROGRAMMING STYLE: SIMPLICITY AND CLARITY

... if we use the criterion: It should be easy to explain, it is remarkable how simple the design process becomes. As soon as one tries to put into the system something that takes more than a paragraph or a line to explain, throw it out—it is not worth it.

J. W. SMITH
Software Engineering, page 71

I think we should consider patterning our management methods after those used in the preparation of engineering drawings. A drawing in a large organization is usually signed by the draftsman, or supervisor when he agrees that it looks nice. In programming efforts you generally do not see that second signature—nor even the first, for that matter. Clarity and style seem to count for nothing—the only thing that counts is whether the program works when put in place. It seems to me that it is important that we should impose these types of aesthetic standards.

M. D. McILROY
Software Engineering, page 89

Dr. R. M. McClure: I know of very few programming establishments where supervisors actually bother to read the code produced by their staff and make some efforts to understand it. I believe that this is absolutely essential.

Prof. J. N. Buxton: I know of very few programming establishments in which the supervisor is capable of reading code—some present company excepted!

Software Engineering, page 89

Chapter opening quoted from *Software Engineering*, P. Naur and B. Randell (eds.), NATO Scientific Affairs Division, Brussels 39, Belgium, January 1969 and *Software Engineering Techniques*, J. N. Buxton and B. Randell, (eds.) NATO Scientific Affairs Division, Brussels 39, Belgium, April 1970.

5.0 Introduction

By inference and innuendo, the past several chapters have attempted to point out that, as a programmer, *you often tend to overestimate your ability.* We have shown, for example, that the top-down approach suggested in Chapter 2 is usually the most logical, organized way of designing a program. Yet few programmers actually use this approach, often because they feel that they can design the entire program "on the fly"; they seem to feel (at least they *act* as if they feel this way) that they can design their program *as they code it.*

The theme of the preceding chapters has been this: *Programming should be approached in a careful, cautious, and organized fashion.* It is difficult enough to make a large program execute properly; you should not increase your problems by building in unnecessarily sophisticated, esoteric algorithms. A similar philosophy is found in many engineering disciplines; it is often referred to as the KISS philosophy (*K*eep *I*t *S*imple, *S*tupid). Again, this is only a *philosophy*; we have no theorems or statistical studies that would help prove that simplicity of design leads to better programs. Nevertheless, you will usually find that the better programmers use this philosophy, either consciously or unconsciously.

A second theme has also recurred throughout the earlier chapters: Most programs are ultimately used and modified by other programmers. An informal survey a few years ago indicated that the average American computer programmer changed jobs every 1.4 years. Though there have been no statistics, we might estimate that the average lifetime of a computer program is at least twice that, if not more.[1] This leads us to a very obvious moral: *If programs are eventually going to be read by someone else, then they should be written in such a manner that they can be read and understood.* Part of the problem, as Gerald Weinberg pointed out in his excellent book, *The Psychology of Computer Programming*, is that a number of programmers regard their programs as their own personal property.

The purpose of this chapter is to focus on the two problems raised above. First, what can we do to make programming simpler, so that fewer problems will be encountered during the coding and debugging period? Second, what can we do to make programs easier to read and comprehend by someone other than the original programmer? We will begin by quickly reviewing some of the suggestions in the previous chapters, many of which were intended to make programs simpler (so that they could be tested and debugged more quickly, etc.). We will then discuss a number of additional programming practices and techniques for developing readable programs.

---

[1]One informal survey by a major computer manufacturer indicated that, after a program was written by one person, it was typically maintained by ten generations of subsequent programmers before it was redesigned.

5.1 Review of Suggestions for Developing Simple Programs

Many of the suggestions that were made in Chapters 1, 3, and 4 were intended to make programs easier to test and debug, as well as easier to maintain and modify. It stands to reason that most of these suggestions could also make a program simpler to understand. In particular, the suggestions below are recommended for the sake of simplicity.

5.1.1 Use Structured Programming Techniques

Chapter 4 presented a discussion of a programming approach known as "structured programming." One of the primary motivations of this approach was the desire to make programs and program listings more readable. By eliminating the network structure that can easily be composed with unrestricted GO-TO statements, we make it much more likely that the programmer will be able to read his listings in a serial fashion.

5.1.2 Avoid Multitasking Features Unless Necessary

The multitasking features available in many current operating systems are extremely powerful. They are convenient for applications involving overlapped IO and computation, on-line and real-time systems, and other instances of asynchronous activities. However, the structure of most multitasking programs is very complex; there are a number of subtle bugs that will linger on long after you think the program has been debugged—and these will then become the responsibility of some unfortunate soul who will have an extremely difficult time trying to understand what is going on. Thus, unless absolutely necessary, you should try to avoid using such statements as ATTACH and DELETE in the System/360, the FORK statement in the XDS-940, and the ZIP statement in the Burroughs B5500.

5.1.3 Don't Misuse the Instruction Set or Computer Language

As we pointed out in Chapter 1, some computers have *undefined* hardware operation codes; the execution of these undefined instructions occasionally leads to obscure, undocumented, but nevertheless predictable results —but in many cases, the results are completely unpredictable. Fortunately, undefined operation codes are relatively rare on most current computers; however, some assembly language programmers still find ways of *misusing* the instruction set of the computer. It is worth repeating the moral established in Chapter 1: Don't attempt to "bend" the machine's instruction set to your own peculiar needs unless you are *very* sure of what you are doing. If you feel that you *must* pervert the original purpose of the instruction, make sure that you clearly and extensively document your actions in the program listing so that it will be clear to those who follow you.

Similar comments apply, of course, to the high-level languages. FORTRAN seems to be especially amenable to such programming tricks; COBOL programmers have developed a number of methods for accomplishing such functions as initializing the contents of a table to some constant—and most of the techniques are rather obscure, in addition to being nonportable. In most cases, it is far better to avoid such tricks and use only the standard features of the language.

5.1.4 Don't Write Programs That Modify Themselves As They Execute

Almost every programming language allows the programmer to modify his program as it executes. In an assembly language program, this practice has an obvious form; in the high-level languages, program modification is sometimes obscured by such glamorous phrases as "program switches," and so forth. Thus, in COBOL, the ALTER statement allows the programmer to actually change the code in his program as it executes; in FORTRAN, the assigned GO-TO statement has somewhat the same effect; in PL/I, the ability to define a variable as a label could be thought of as a more formal and sophisticated form of the assigned GO-TO.

Two of the disadvantages of program modification may seem rather esoteric: Such a program is generally not *reentrant*, and it is less likely to be *serially reusable*. A reentrant program is one that can be used concurrently (or simultaneously in a multiprocessing system) by two or more processes. Clearly, a program that changes itself as it executes is likely to encounter serious difficulties if it is being concurrently executed by two or more jobs or users. In theory, the assigned GO-TO statement in FORTRAN and the use of the statement label variables in PL/I need not destroy the reentrancy of the program; in most versions of COBOL, though, the ALTER statement definitely would prevent the program from being reentrant. Actually, the entire discussion is somewhat academic for FORTRAN and COBOL, since, at the time this book was written, very few of the computer manufacturers had compilers that could generate reentrant FORTRAN or COBOL *object code*—the compiler and its run-time operating system might be reentrant, but the FORTRAN and COBOL *object code* is usually not reentrant.

Another objection to programs that modify themselves is their usual inability to be executed more than once. If we wish to execute a self-modifying program a second time, we must load a fresh copy of the program into the machine. This is not necessary, of course, if the programmer takes the trouble to make his program self-initializing. Note that we can have the same problem with *variables*: If the programmer uses the DATA statement in

FORTRAN, or the VALUE clause in COBOL, then a fresh copy of the program must be loaded into the machine for each execution. (This is generally not true of PL/I: Variables declared with the INITIAL attribute are initialized upon entry to the block in which they are declared—but this adds extra overhead to the program.)

Our last objection to a self-modifying program is a more practical one and is more in keeping with the theme of this chapter: Such a program is *considerably* more difficult to comprehend and debug. This is especially true in very large programs. The instruction making the program modification may be at the beginning of the program, and the instruction being modified may be in a completely different part of the program. Thus, during the debugging process, the programmer may narrow the range of the problem down to a particular subroutine; however, if the subroutine is being modified by some other part of the program, and if the program listing is several hundred pages long, then he may find it nearly impossible to find out *how* his faulty subroutine is being altered.

If ALTER statements are bad, what about the various other forms of program modification? To put things into proper perspective (and recalling the structured programming discussion in Chapter 4), I would suggest that programmers who use a *computed* GO-TO (or GO-TO DEPENDING ON in COBOL) should be considered guilty of a minor misdemeanor (unless it is consciously being used to simulate the ALGOL CASE statement—one of the allowable black-box forms discussed in Chapter 4); programmers who use an *assigned* GO-TO statement should be considered guilty of a felony; those who use an ALTER statement should be tried for manslaughter, while those who write self-modifying assembly language programs should be charged with first-degree murder. Although the computed GO-TO makes the program unstructured and somewhat more difficult to debug, at least we are able to enumerate all of the places the program *might* go. In the case of the *assigned* GO-TO (or the use of statement label variables in PL/I), we are often unable to determine, when we look at the GO-TO statement, where it might take us in the program. The same is basically true of the ALTER statement, with the added disadvantage of making the program nonreentrant (though, in all fairness, it should be pointed out that this could be handled by the COBOL compiler). Modified instructions in assembly language programs should be considered the greatest evil, because of the almost infinite variety of ways in which the programmer can accomplish his modifications.

At this point, a logical question is: Given the many disadvantages of a self-modifying program, why are programmers so fond of this approach? The answer can usually be expressed in terms of convenience and efficiency. It often seems simpler and easier for the programmer to implement certain common programming situations with an ALTER or an assigned GO-TO; also, the programmer often feels that such a program will execute *faster* than

one using some other approach. However, if the use of program modification seems more convenient, it is usually only because the programmer has
not thought about the problem enough to find a better approach. If the
ALTER statement or the assigned GO-TO statement seems more efficient, it

Figure 5.1(a). An IBM System/360 assembly language program to search an area of
memory.

```
* THIS ROUTINE WILL PRINT OUT ALL OCCURRENCES OR NONOCCURRENCES
* OF A SPECIFIED ITEM WITHIN A SPECIFIED AREA OF MEMORY. THE CALLING
* SEQUENCE IS AS FOLLOWS:
*            BAL  R14,WSEARCH         SEARCH FOR ALL OCCURRENCES OF ITEM
*            BAL  R14,NSEARCH         SEARCH FOR ALL NONOCCURRENCES
* R1 HAS THE ADR OF THE FIRST WORD OF MEMORY TO BE SEARCHED
* R2 HAS A POSITIVE COUNT OF THE NUMBER OF WORDS TO BE SEARCHED
* R3 CONTAINS THE ITEM TO BE SEARCHED FOR
* "MASK" INDICATES WHICH BIT POSITIONS WILL BE USED IN THE COM-
* PARISON: IF THE NTH BIT OF MASK IS ONE, THEN THE NTH BIT OF R3
* AND THE MEMORY WORD WILL BE TESTED FOR EQUALITY (OR NON-EQUALITY)
WSEARCH   L     R4,SWITCH1            PICK UP THE COMPARISON INSTRUCTION
          B     SEARCH               ENTER COMMON CODE
NSEARCH   L     R4,SWITCH2           PICK UP A DIFFERENT INSTRUCTION
SEARCH    ST    R4,COMPARE           SET UP COMPARISON INSTRUCTION
          N     R3,MASK              ONLY LOOK AT BITS SPECIFIED BY MASK
          L     R4,ZERO              INITIALIZE AN INDEX INTO MEMORY
LOOP      L     R5,(R4,R1)           GET A MEMORY WORD,USING R1 AS BASE
          N     R5,MASK              ONLY LOOK AT BITS SPECIFIED BY MASK
          CR    R5,R3                COMPARE THE TWO QUANTITIES
COMPARE   BE    FOUND                *** THIS INSTRUCTION IS CHANGED ***
NEXT      LA    R4,4(R4)             INCREMENT MEMORY INDEX
          BCT   R2,LOOP              LOOP BACK TO LOOK AT ANOTHER WORD
          BR    R14                  EXIT
* ENTER HERE IF COMPARISON SUCCEEDS
FOUND     L     R5,(R4,R1)           GET THE WORD FROM MEMORY AGAIN
          STM   R1,R5,TABLE          SAVE THE REGISTERS
          LR    R1,R4                GET ADDRESS OF MEMORY WORD IN R1
          BAL   R13,PRINT            CALL SUBROUTINE TO PRINT ADDRESS
          L     R1,TABLE+4           GET CONTENTS OF MEMORY WORD
          BAL   R13,PRINT            PRINT CONTENTS OF WORD
          LM    R1,R5,TABLE          RESTORE REGISTERS
          B     NEXT                 GO BACK TO LOOK AT MORE WORDS
SWITCH1   BE    FOUND                *** THIS WILL BE USED BY WSEARCH ***
SWITCH2   BNE   FOUND                *** THIS WILL BE USED BY NSEARCH ***
MASK      DS    F                    MASK WORD
ZERO      DC    F'0'
TABLE     DS    5F                   STORAGE FOR REGISTERS
```

is usually because the programmer has failed to take into account the extra machine time that will be required to debug his program. There *are* better ways of writing programs, and they are often just as convenient; in most cases, they are just as efficient too.

Let us illustrate this point with some examples. The most common use of the self-modifying approach is to allow one module to serve many similar purposes. Thus, Fig. 5.1(a) shows an IBM System/360 assembly language sub-

Figure 5.1(b). A slightly different version of the System/360 program.

```
*  THIS ROUTINE DOES THE SAME PROCESSING AS THE ONE IN FIG. 5.1(A)
*  IT IS CALLED IN THE SAME WAY, AND USES THE SAME CONVENTIONS FOR
*  THE ARGUMENTS. HOWEVER, IT DOES NOT MODIFY ITSELF AS IT RUNS.
*
WSEARCH    LA    R6,0            USE R6 AS AN INDEX INTO A TABLE
           B     SEARCH          ENTER COMMON CODE
NSEARCH    LA    R6, 4           SET R6 TO PICK UP A DIFFERENT INST.
SEARCH     N     R3,MASK         ONLY LOOK AT BITS SPECIFIED BY MASK
           L     R4,ZERO         INITIALIZE INDEX INTO MEMORY
LOOP       L     R5,(R4,R1)      GET A MEMORY WORD, USING R1 AS BASE
           N     R5,MASK         ONLY LOOK AT BITS SPECIFIED BY MASK
           CR    R5,R3           COMPARE THE TWO QUANTITIES
           EX    0,SWITCH(R6)    EXECUTE THE APPROPRIATE BRANCH INST.
NEXT       LA    R4,4(R4)        INCREMENT MEMORY INDEX
           BCT   R2,LOOP         LOOP BACK TO LOOK AT ANOTHER WORD
           BR    R14             EXIT
*
*  ENTER HERE IF COMPARISON IS SUCCESSFUL
*
FOUND      L     R5,(R4,R1)      GET THE WORD FROM MEMORY AGAIN
           STM   R1,R6,TABLE     SAVE THE REGISTERS
           LR    R1,R4           GET ADDRESS OF MEMORY WORD IN R1
           BAL   R13,PRINT       PRINT ADDRESS OF WORD
           L     R1,TABLE+4      GET THE CONTENTS OF MEMORY AGAIN
           BAL   R13,PRINT       PRINT IT OUT
           LM    R1,R6,TABLE     RESTORE REGISTERS
           B     NEXT            GO BACK TO LOOK AT MORE WORDS
*
*  CONSTANTS AND DATA - THIS COULD BE PUT IN A DSECT FOR REENTRANCY
*
ZERO       DC    F'0'
MASK       DS    F               MASK WORD
TABLE      DS    6F              STORAGE FOR REGISTERS
SWITCH     BE    FOUND           THIS WILL BE EXECUTED IF R6=0
           BNE   FOUND           THIS WILL BE EXECUTED IF R6=1
```

routine that can be used to search through an area of memory for all *occurrences* of a specified item, or for all *nonoccurrences* of the specified item. By merely changing one conditional branch instruction, the programmer allows the subroutine to serve two different, though similar, purposes. In terms of minimizing CPU time, there is little doubt that the approach shown in Fig. 5.1(a) is fairly efficient. On the other hand, the subroutine shown in Fig. 5.1(b) is only slightly less efficient, and it has all the advantages described above: It is reentrant, serially reusable, and easier to debug and understand.

Figure 5.2(a) shows a similar situation in PL/I. The programmer wants to perform a slightly different sequence of processing, depending on the out-

Figure 5.2(a). A PL/I program with statement label variables.

```
          DECLARE ORDERFILE OUTPUT;
          DECLARE SHIPMENTFILE OUTPUT;
          DECLARE CANCELFILE OUTPUT;
          DECLARE ERRORFILE OUTPUT;
          DECLARE (TRANSCODE,DOLLAR,TOTALQ,TOTALD,QUANTITY) FIXED;
          DECLARE SWITCH LABEL;
          TOTALQ = 0;
          TOTALD = 0;
LOOP:     SWITCH = ERROR;
          GET LIST (TRANSCODE, QUANTITY, DOLLAR);
          IF TRANSCODE = 1 THEN SWITCH = ORDER;
          IF TRANSCODE = 3 THEN SWITCH = SHIPMENT;
          IF TRANSCODE = 5 THEN SWITCH = CANCEL;
          GO TO SWITCH;
ERROR:    PUT FILE (ERRORFILE) LIST (TRANSCODE,QUANTITY,DOLLAR);
          GO TO LOOP;
ORDER:    TOTALQ = TOTALQ + QUANTITY;
          TOTALD = TOTALD + DOLLAR;
          PUT FILE (ORDERFILE) LIST (TRANSCODE,QUANTITY,DOLLAR);
          GO TO LOOP;
CANCEL:   TOTALQ = TOTALQ - QUANTITY;
          TOTALD = TOTALD - DOLLAR;
          PUT FILE (CANCELFILE) LIST (TRANSCODE,QUANTITY,DOLLAR);
          GO TO LOOP;
SHIPMENT: PUT FILE (SHIPMENTFILE) LIST (TRANSCODE,QUANTITY,DOLLAR);
          GO TO LOOP;
```

Note: The purpose of this code is to read transaction cards and process them according to the *transaction code*. In this extremely simplified example, it is fairly easy to see the effect of the statement label variables; in a more realistic version of this program, the effect of the statement label variables would be obscured and effectively lost within the thousands of other statements.

Figure 5.2(b). A slightly different version of the PL/I program.

```
            DECLARE ORDERFILE OUTPUT;
            DECLARE SHIPMENTFILE OUTPUT;
            DECLARE CANCELFILE OUTPUT;
            DECLARE ERRORFILE OUTPUT;
            DECLARE (TRANSCODE,DOLLAR,TOTALQ,TOTALD,QUANTITY) FIXED;
            TOTALQ = 0;
            TOTALD = 0;
LOOP:       GET LIST (TRANSCODE,QUANTITY,DOLLAR);
            IF TRANSCODE = 1 THEN
                DO;
                TOTALQ = TOTALQ + QUANTITY;
                TOTALD = TOTALD + DOLLAR;
                PUT FILE (ORDERFILE) LIST (TRANSCODE,QUANTITY,DOLLAR);
                END;
            ELSE
                IF TRANSCODE = 3 THEN
                    PUT FILE (SHIPMENTFILE) LIST (TRANSCODE,QUANTITY,DOLLAR);
                ELSE
                    IF TRANSCODE = 5 THEN
                        DO;
                        TOTALQ = TOTALQ - QUANTITY;
                        TOTALD = TOTALD - DOLLAR;
                        PUT FILE (CANCELFILE) LIST (TRANSCODE,QUANTITY,DOLLAR);
                        END;
                    ELSE PUT FILE (ERRORFILE) LIST (TRANSCODE,QUANTITY,DOLLAR);
            GO TO LOOP;
```

come of some comparisons. While this approach may have been easier for the programmer to code, the IF-THEN approach shown in Fig. 5.2(b) represents a much better programming practice (though it might generate slightly less efficient code, depending on the particular compiler used). Figure 5.3(a) and Fig. 5.3(b) illustrate a similar situation in FORTRAN; Fig. 5.4(a) and 5.4(b) show the same problem in COBOL. In all of these examples, the preferred approach might require a little extra CPU time and a little more preliminary planning on the part of the programmer. It should be evident, though, that the resulting program is *much* better.

In summary, we can see that the various forms of self-modifying programs are generally used to handle *special cases, branching situations,* and situations where "similar" processing is carried out. From the discussion above, you should see that the many disadvantages of self-modifying programs usually outweigh the slight improvements in CPU time and memory; you should also see that there are good alternatives to such things as the

Figure 5.3(a). A FORTRAN program using assigned GO-TO statements.

```
C
C    THIS PROGRAM ACCOMPLISHES THE SAME PURPOSE AS THE PL/I PROGRAM
C    IN FIGURE 5.2(A)
C
     INTEGER TCODE
     TOTALQ=0
     TOTALD=0
10   ASSIGN 20 TO SWITCH
     READ 100,TCODE,QUANT,DOLLAR
     IF (TCODE .EQ. 1) ASSIGN 30 TO SWITCH
     IF (TCODE .EQ. 3) ASSIGN 40 TO SWITCH
     IF (TCODE .EQ. 5) ASSIGN 50 TO SWITCH
     GO TO SWITCH
C
C    ERROR ROUTINE
C
20   WRITE (3,200) TCODE,QUANT,DOLLAR
     GO TO 10
C
C    ORDER-HANDLING ROUTINE
C
30   TOTALQ=TOTALQ+QUANT
     TOTALD=TOTALD+DOLLAR
     WRITE (4,300) TCODE,QUANT,DOLLAR
     GO TO 10
C
C    CANCELLATION ROUTINE
C
40   TOTALQ=TOTALQ-QUANT
     TOTALD=TOTALD-DOLLAR
     WRITE (5,400) TCODE,QUANT,DOLLAR
     GO TO 10
C
C    SHIPMENT ROUTINE
C
50   WRITE (6,500) TCODE,QUANT,DOLLAR
     GO TO 10
```

COBOL ALTER statement and the FORTRAN assigned GO-TO statement. From a modularity point of view, perhaps the best alternative is to handle each special case with a closed subroutine; this was the approach used in Fig. 5.4(b). Equally good in many cases is the IF-THEN approach that was

Figure 5.3(b). A slightly different version of the FORTRAN program.

```
      INTEGER TCODE
      TOTALQ=0
      TOTALD=0
10    READ 100, TCODE,QUANT,DOLLAR
      IF (TCODE .EQ. 1) GO TO 30
      IF (TCODE .EQ. 3) GO TO 40
      IF (TCODE .EQ. 5) GO TO 50
C
C     FALL THROUGH TO THE ERROR ROUTINE
C
20    WRITE (3,200) TCODE,QUANT,DOLLAR
      GO TO 10
C
C     ORDER-HANDLING ROUTINE
C
30    TOTALQ=TOTALQ+QUANT
      TOTALD=TOTALD+DOLLAR
      WRITE (4,300) TCODE,QUANT,DOLLAR
      GO TO 10
C
C     CANCELLATION ROUTINE
C
40    TOTALQ=TOTALQ-QUANT
      TOTALD=TOTALD-DOLLAR
      WRITE (5,400) TCODE,QUANT,DOLLAR
      GO TO 10
C
C     SHIPMENT ROUTINE
C
50    WRITE (6,500) TCODE,QUANT,DOLLAR
      GO TO 10
```

illustrated in Fig. 5.2(b). Unfortunately, as we saw in Chapter 4, it seems that only PL/I and ALGOL have the BEGIN-END block structure necessary to implement anything other than the most trivial form of IF-THEN in a "nice" way, though COBOL is usually adequate. Once having recognized a special case in our program, we can use an unconditional branch instruction to enter some special code, as was shown in the FORTRAN example in Fig. 5.3(b); however, this is a far less desirable program structure, for it significantly reduces the clarity of the program. In this situation, the computed GO-TO should be recognized as a lesser evil. Finally, we can use program flags and various other tricks in assembly language, as we saw in Fig. 5.1(b).

Figure 5.4(a). A COBOL program with ALTER statements.

```
        MOVE 0 TO TOTALQ.
        MOVE 0 TO TOTALD.
GET-INPUT. READ TRANSACTION-CARDS.
        IF TRANSACTION-CODE=1 THEN ALTER SWITCH-PARAGRAPH TO
            PROCEED TO ORDER-ROUTINE
        ELSE IF TRANSACTION-CODE=3 THEN ALTER SWITCH-PARAGRAPH TO
            PROCEED TO CANCEL-ROUTINE
        ELSE IF TRANSACTION-CODE=5 THEN ALTER SWITCH-PARAGRAPH TO
            PROCEED TO SHIPMENT-ROUTINE
        ELSE ALTER SWITCH-PARAGRAPH TO PROCEED TO ERROR-ROUTINE.
SWITCH-PARAGRAPH. GO TO ERROR-ROUTINE.
ERROR-ROUTINE.
        MOVE TRANSACTION-CODE TO ERROR-CODE.
        MOVE QUANTITY TO ERROR-QUANTITY.
        MOVE DOLLAR TO ERROR-DOLLAR.
        WRITE ERROR-FILE.
        GO TO GET-INPUT.
ORDER-ROUTINE.
        COMPUTE TOTALQ=TOTALQ+QUANTITY.
        COMPUTE TOTALD=TOTALD+DOLLAR.
        MOVE TRANSACTION-CODE TO ORDER-CODE.
        MOVE DOLLAR TO ORDER-DOLLAR.
        MOVE QUANTITY TO ORDER-QUANTITY.
        WRITE ORDER-FILE.
        GO TO GET-INPUT.
CANCEL-ROUTINE.
        COMPUTE TOTALQ=TOTALQ-QUANTITY.
        COMPUTE TOTALD=TOTALD-DOLLAR.
        MOVE TRANSACTION-CODE TO CANCEL-CODE.
        MOVE DOLLAR TO CANCEL-DOLLAR.
        MOVE QUANTITY TO CANCEL-QUANTITY.
        WRITE CANCEL-FILE.
        GO TO GET-INPUT.
SHIPMENT-ROUTINE.
        MOVE TRANSACTION-CODE TO SHIPMENT-CODE.
        MOVE DOLLAR TO SHIPMENT-DOLLAR.
        MOVE QUANTITY TO SHIPMENT-QUANTITY.
        WRITE SHIPMENT-FILE.
        GO TO GET-INPUT.
```

Figure 5.4(b). A slightly different version of the COBOL program.

```
        MOVE 0 TO TOTALQ.
        MOVE 0 TO TOTALD.
GET-INPUT. READ TRANSACTION-CARDS.
        IF TRANSACTION-CODE=1 THEN PERFORM ORDER-ROUTINE
        ELSE IF TRANSACTION-CODE=3 THEN PERFORM CANCEL-ROUTINE
        ELSE IF TRANSACTION-CODE=5 THEN PERFORM SHIPMENT-ROUTINE
        ELSE PERFORM ERROR-ROUTINE.
        GO TO GET-INPUT.
ERROR-ROUTINE.
        MOVE TRANSACTION-CODE TO ERROR-CODE.
        MOVE QUANTITY TO ERROR-QUANTITY.
        MOVE DOLLAR TO ERROR-DOLLAR.
        WRITE ERROR-FILE.
        EXIT.
ORDER-ROUTINE.
        COMPUTE TOTALQ=TOTALQ+QUANTITY.
        COMPUTE TOTALD=TOTALD+DOLLAR.
        MOVE TRANSACTION-CODE TO ORDER-CODE.
        MOVE DOLLAR TO ORDER-DOLLAR.
        MOVE QUANTITY TO ORDER-QUANTITY.
        WRITE ORDER-FILE.
        EXIT.
CANCEL-ROUTINE.
        COMPUTE TOTALQ=TOTALQ-QUANTITY.
        COMPUTE TOTALD=TOTALD-DOLLAR.
        MOVE TRANSACTION-CODE TO CANCEL-CODE.
        MOVE QUANTITY TO CANCEL-QUANTITY.
        MOVE DOLLAR TO CANCEL-DOLLAR.
        WRITE CANCEL-FILE.
        EXIT.
SHIPMENT-ROUTINE.
        MOVE TRANSACTION-CODE TO SHIPMENT-CODE.
        MOVE DOLLAR TO SHIPMENT-DOLLAR.
        MOVEL QUANTITY TO SHIPMENT-QUANTITY.
        WRITE SHIPMENT-FILE.
        EXIT.
```

5.2 Additional Programming Techniques for Readable Programs

One of the marks of a good programmer is his reluctance to indulge in tricky code. This philosophy is not too important in FORTRAN and COBOL because of the relatively limited nature of those languages; however, in a powerful high-level language like PL/I or ALGOL, the programmer often has the opportunity to write extremely obscure, esoteric, and unnecessarily sophisticated sequences of code. In assembly language, the problem is even worse: The machine language instruction set provides an almost infinite number of means of coding a given application. It is perhaps unfair to generalize about such situations, for even the most esoteric features of a programming language can be justified at times. All we are attempting to do is to establish an *attitude*: You should always use the simplest, least-complicated, least-esoteric language features that will solve the problem adequately. Don't use an intricate sequence of code just so that you can brag to your colleagues that you finally found a way of using the XYZ instruction!

We can carry this philosophy a little further. Don't waste your time looking at programs written by your colleagues to see if you can find "dumb" sequences of code. Don't invite trouble by trying to rewrite someone else's reasonably well-written 100-statement program into a slightly more clever 99-statement program. You may possibly save a little CPU time and a little memory; on the other hand, the extra programming time, compilation time, and testing time will often negate any such savings. This point is often difficult to impress upon some programmers, especially the young, brighter, and more aggressive programmers. It often seems that their greatest pleasure in life is poring over vendor-supplied software and that of their colleagues (whom they generally consider too old, too slow, too unintelligent, and too sloppy to turn out really *good* code) for various minor inefficiencies. They may criticize that a colleague took three statements to calculate the XYZ functions when he could have done it in one, and also that the program sets the ABC variable to zero when it's *already* zero. With that, the "code bums," as they are affectionately called in some organizations, will eliminate ten microseconds of processing time from the program, spend ten minutes of compilation time inserting their improvements, fail to include any explanatory documentation of the changes they have made, and needlessly alienate their colleagues for the next several weeks.

As we have seen in the first four chapters of this book, programmers are often loath to use a number of common-sense programming practices. For example, few programmers use the top-down design approach suggested in Chapter 2, though it is intuitively the most organized approach to program design, coding, and testing. Few programmers actually *practice* modularity, though many of them preach it. Few programmers actually adhere to the philosophy of writing general-purpose subroutines, even though they agree that it is usually a good practice. Similarly, very few programmers make a conscious effort to keep their programs simple, even though they *say* that they would do anything to minimize the time needed to debug their program.

Why? The reasons seem to be largely psychological: Even though the programmer knows that he is making his program more difficult to debug and more difficult to understand, he feels *compelled* to do things in a complicated, esoteric way. A variation on this is the programmer who says, "If those (esoteric) instructions weren't meant to be used, the hardware designer wouldn't have put them into the machine—if you don't use them, you're not getting the full advantage of the computer!" Sometimes just the opposite is true: The programmer adamantly refuses to believe that multitasking, complex overlays, tricky sequences of code, and self-modifying programs could possibly be difficult to debug; one sometimes hears a programmer say, "Well, any programmer worth his salt should be capable of understanding *that* code!" Sometimes the programmer indulges in these dubious practices to improve his stature with his colleagues: "Oh, yes," he tells his dumbfounded friends, "I implemented that payroll application with a recursive procedure— it makes the tax calculation subroutine much more elegant!" These attitudes usually disappear as the programmer gains experience and maturity; unfortunately, maturity is not a universally endowed character trait, and it does not always increase in direct proportion to one's experience. In the meantime, the programming manager must be on the alert for such attitudes on the part of his programmers.

There are sometimes *valid* reasons for objecting to the simplistic approach; the major potential disadvantage is inefficiency. A "simple-minded" program may not take full advantage of the power of the programming language and the machine; as a result, the program may run more slowly or take up more memory. This was evident in the examples shown in Figs. 5.1(b), 5.2(b), 5.3(b), and 5.4(b). There certainly is a tradeoff to be established here, but most programmers fail to make the tradeoff carefully; they fail to realize that on most projects, *programmer time* and *debugging* time are much larger bottlenecks than the memory and CPU time requirements of the program. If the simplistic approach requires a truly excessive amount of CPU time and/or memory, then we might be willing to permit some trickery; however, as we have already seen in this chapter, efficiency is generally not impaired much by the simple approach.

Note the subtle difference between simple *design* practices and simple *programming* practices. You should labor to make your *design* as elegant as possible; it should be modular, general, and as elegant as required for your application. However, once you begin to write the programs, then you should do things as simply as possible. There are a number of specific programming pratices listed below that should help make the resulting program simpler and more readable by others; you may be able to add other suggestions of your own.

5.2.1   Avoid Unnecessarily Complicated
Arithmetic Expressions

Virtually every high-level programming language, and a number of assembly languages, allow the programmer to form *arithmetic expressions*; each such language specifies an *operator precedence* to eliminate ambiguity in expressions without parentheses. Thus, most programmers reading the statement

    A = B*C+3

would agree that the multiplication of B and C takes place first; the result is then added to the integer 3.

Unfortunately, some programmers—especially the scientific programmers—take rather extensive liberties with this idea. Reading the statement

    A = B*C+3**D/-3*X+Y*4

one is not even sure whether it is syntactically correct (though hopefully the compiler would tell us). In any case, it is not at all clear what operations are being performed. It is very likely that the programmer may have misunderstood the order in which the operations will be performed in that particular language (in which case he will not get the results he expected); it is even more likely that other programmers attempting to make some sense of the statement will be badly confused.

The obvious solution to this problem is to insert some meaningful *parentheses* to delimit the appropriate subexpressions and clarify the sequence and nature of arithmetic operations taking place. Such expressions are indeed redundant in the sense that the arithmetic statement can be written without them—and this seems to bother some programmers who feel that the world supply of parentheses is limited and should be conserved for those few cases where they are absolutely necessary! The pragmatic programmer realizes, of course, that the redundant parentheses slow the compilation process by only a microscopic amount and will not affect the execution time of the compiled program at all (though this may depend on the compiler). One might even argue that the parentheses are useful for the *first* example above, that is, it would not be harmful write

    A = (B*C) + 3

In the case of an expression of the complexity of the second example above, it is not clear that parentheses will make the statement more readable.

Is the following form of the example really any less confusing?

```
A = (B*C) + (((3**D)/(-3))*X) + (Y*4)
```

In such cases, it might make far more sense to break the statement into a number of simpler statements:

```
PART1 = B*C
PART2 = X*((3**D)/(-3))
PART3 = Y*4
A = PART1 + PART2 + PART3
```

The above example may or may not be the most readable form of the original complicated expression. There is a good chance that it will generate less efficient code if the compiler is not able to perform global optimization. It does, though, represent an attempt by the programmer to make his computations more legible to the reader.

5.2.2 Compound Nested IF Statements

It is interesting to note that the standards manuals in many COBOL programming shops specifically forbid the use of nested IF-THEN-ELSE statements of the form

```
IF A1 THEN B1 ELSE IF A2 THEN IF A3 THEN B2 ELSE B3 ELSE B4
```

It should not be too surprising that the statement is difficult to understand when it is written in this form; in most cases, a nested IF statement will be fairly readable if it is written in the following form:

```
IF A1 THEN B1
ELSE IF A2
        THEN IF A3 THEN B2
                ELSE B3
        ELSE B4
```

As in the case of parentheses for complicated expressions, this idea of indented (or well-formatted) compound IF statements can be carried too far. However, when there are only three or four levels of IF statements, as in the example above, careful formatting and indention should be sufficient to make the meaning clear to other readers of your program. The same comments are true, of course, in languages such as PL/I and ALGOL—but not in FORTRAN!

5.2.3 Format Your Program Listings to Make Them More Readable

In the previous section, we pointed out that nested IF statements can be made more legible by formatting them properly. Actually, this is only one example of a more general suggestion: *Your program listing should be pleasing to the eye, so that the reader will find it easy—even inviting—to follow.* Some programmers feel that this is a matter best left to keypunch operators. Others who use languages such as LISP and PL/I (and, to a lesser extent, FORTRAN, COBOL, and ALGOL) have had some success with automatic programs to help format a source program, resequence statement numbers, etc. Whatever the method, the following suggestions should be kept in mind:

1. *Do not put more than one source statement onto one line of the program listing.* While it is true that paper is valuable and that trees need to be conserved (as I have been told by several serious programmers), I feel that our programmer-ecologists could find more promising areas to attack (perhaps overly verbose computer books?). I once had the dubious honor of seeing the entire listing of a rather complex time-sharing operating system on about 15 sheets of paper; all 128 columns of the listing were covered with multiple statements, separated by semicolons. There are a few cases when it *is* more readable to have two or three statements on one line; on the PDP-8 minicomputer, for example, it is only possible to shift the accumulator two bits at a time with the RTR instruction—thus, to shift the accumulator six bits to the right, it would be reasonable to write

```
RTR; RTR; RTR        /SHIFT ACCUMULATOR SIX BITS RIGHT
```

Similar situations may be encountered occasionally in the high-level languages that permit multiple statements on one line, but this capability is usually sorely abused by programmers.

2. Use the "identification field" that usually exists in columns 73–80 of the card image form of a source program. The first four or five characters can be used as a program identification, and the remaining characters can serve as a sequence number; thus, we might see an identification field of

```
GLOP0010
```

There should be an interval of at least 10, if not 100, between the sequence numbers, so that new statements can be inserted later; such statements should be identified with the identification PATCH, or NEW, etc. As we noted above, there are usually a variety of source program maintenance packages that can help the programmer resequence the statement numbers. In addition, many compilers and assemblers check the identification field to ensure that the source statements are indeed in order. Obviously, this is neither a new technique nor a glamorous one; still, it seems to work—and it seems far more practical than the approach taken by the FORTRAN programmer who violated both this suggestion and the one above by writing FORTRAN statements in the following form:

```
10  A = B=C ; GO TO 20 ;
20  X = Y*Z ; GO TO 30 ;
30  P = Q/R ; GO TO 40 ;
```

When asked why he had included so many seemingly redundant GO-TO statements, the programmer replied, "I've had a great deal of trouble with source cards getting out of order. With this approach, the only thing necessary is to have the first card and the last card in order—everything else can be random!"

3. If a statement requires more than one line on the program listing, make sure that it is broken up in a readable fashion. Do not, for instance, break up a variable name or constant in the following absurd fashion:

```
NOAH = CAT + DOG + ALLIGA
TOR + HIPPOPOTAMUS + 3.14
159 - 2.78128
```

A little common sense will dictate the manner in which long statements or expressions may be "hyphenated" in such a way as to make them more readable.

4. Though it is a minor point, a program is often more readable if arithmetic operations ($+, -, /, *$, etc.) are preceded and followed by one or more blank characters (but be consistent about the number of characters used).

5. With the programming languages that permit "free-format" statements, try to begin each statement in the same column of the program listing. In assembly language, each component of the statement—operation code, register fields, address fields, comments, etc.—should begin in the same column. As we pointed out in Section 5.2.2, IF-THEN statements should be indented if they are nested; similar common-sense indention standards should apply to DO-loops in FORTRAN, BEGIN-END blocks in ALGOL and PL/I, and so forth.

6. There are many cases where it makes sense to arrange statement labels, procedure names, paragraph names, etc., in some ascending sequence. Thus, in FORTRAN, it is reasonable to arrange statement numbers (i.e., the numbers that generally appear in columns 1–7 of the source statement) in ascending sequence; many COBOL programmers define paragraph names of the form TAX-CALCULA-TION-ROUTINE-0010, OUTPUT-ROUTINE-0020, etc., so that the reader of the program will know where to find any given label (and its associated code) in the program listing. There are a number of ways of embellishing upon this (such as giving FORMAT statements a separate set of sequence numbers in FORTRAN), but any consistent and reasonable set of conventions should do.

7. Insert copious comments in the program listing. The importance of comments was discussed in Chapter 1; we are interested here only in the *format* of the comments. I personally have always believed in the motto espoused by Messrs. Kreitzberg and Schneiderman in *The Elements of FORTRAN Style* (Harcourt, Brace, Jovanovich, New York, 1971): "Always provide more documentation than you think you need." However, many programmers and students who have read through my program listings (both in industry and in this book) have complained that there were *too many* comments, and that the program statements were obscured by the comments. Although there is often heated controversy on this point, the following consensus seems to develop whenever this subject is discussed:

   (a) It is *extremely* useful to include a "prologue" before each subroutine, procedure, or module. This narrative description should include a brief discussion of the module's purpose, its calling sequence, the nature of its actions or outputs, other subroutines required for execution, other variables or registers used, destroyed, or otherwise affected, the author's name, date of original creation and date of last revision, and a brief description of *how* the module works.

(b) Meaningful comments should accompany critical sections of code but should not detract the reader's eye from the code itself. This is most convenient, of course, in assembly language; the problem is often solved in the high-level languages by proper formatting. It should be possible for another reader to ignore the comments if he does not trust them or prefers to work without comments.

5.2.4 Avoid Complicated Assembly Language Instructions

As we have already noted, assembly language is potentially the most dangerous of programming languages, because of the great variety with which the programmer can solve his problems. Though the warnings should be somewhat different for each machine, a few general ones should make the point:

1. Many word-oriented computers have skip instructions that allow the programmer to skip the next instruction if the accumulator is positive, negative, equal to zero, etc. It then becomes popular to construct a series of *nested* skip instructions that are all but incomprehensible to anyone other than the original programmer—if indeed *he* understands what he is doing! As an example, consider the following simple example in PDP-10 assembly language

```
SKIPL    CAT        ;SKIP NEXT INSTRUCTION IF CAT LESS THAN ZERO
SKIPE    DOG        ;SKIP NEXT INSTRUCTION IF DOG EQUAL TO ZERO
SKIPN    MOUSE      ;SKIP NEXT INSTRUCTION IF MOUSE UNEQUAL TO ZERO
SKIPG    BIRD       ;SKIP NEXT INSTRUCTION IF BIRD GREATER THAN O
```

2. Some machines have an assembly language *execute* instruction. For example, the instruction

```
EXE    SWITCH
```

might cause the instruction at location SWITCH to be performed; following that, control would normally resume at the instruction following the EXE instruction, unless the instruction at SWITCH was a jump, a subroutine call, a skip, etc. The EXE instruction is extremely useful in some programming situations, for it provides a very efficient "one-instruction-subroutine-call." Unfortunately for the cause of simplicity, some few machines allow *nested* EXE instructions, that is, the instruction at location SWITCH in the example above might itself be an EXE instruction, and the process could continue indefinitely. It is hard to think of many practical examples of such a capability; fortunately, not very many machines have it!

3. There are also a few machines that allow multiple levels of indirect addressing, often in addition to various levels of pre-indexing and post-indexing. One level of indirect addressing is common (with the notable exception of the IBM System/360 and System/370) and is usually a reasonable programming practice; two

levels are rare (thank God!), but there are a few cases when it is a very useful feature; more than two levels are rarely of interest to anyone other than what the universities and research centers sometimes refer to as the "hackers"—i.e., those who have very little else to do but find ways of using multiple levels of indirect addressing. True, it *is* useful for indexing through several levels of tables (as was done in an operating system on the GE-435, which had one of the world's most sophisticated addressing schemes)—but there are other, slightly less efficient, but much less obscure ways of doing the same thing.

Once again, proper application of these suggestions requires some common sense, and a proper analysis of the tradeoffs involved, the tradeoff usually being efficiency versus clarity. If the obscure approach is chosen, then good documentation is *absolutely* essential.

5.2.5   Miscellaneous Suggestions

For any given programming language or computer, it should be possible to add a number of additional "do's and don'ts" for developing simple programs. It is rather sad to see that these have been incorporated into *standards* in many large organizations, for that often defeats the very purpose of the suggestions. What we really want is an *attitude* of developing programs that can be read by others. Rather than give detailed discussions of any further such suggestions, we will conclude this chapter by merely listing a few miscellaneous suggestions for avoiding unreadable FORTRAN, COBOL, and other high-level language programs:

1. Avoid negative Boolean logic if possible; many programmers seem to have a hard time understanding it. For example, it should be possible to rewrite the statement

```
IF NOT FLAG THEN A=B ELSE X=Y ;
```

as the following:

```
IF FLAG THEN X=Y ELSE A=B ;
```

though there may be some cases where the readable approach will be slightly less efficient. Many compound Boolean expressions involving "not" logic can be rewritten into equivalent "positive" statements that will be easier to understand.

2. Avoid unnecessarily complicated compound Boolean expressions. This situation is often found in some COBOL applications, where the programmer has written

```
IF A AND B OR NOT C THEN PERFORM X .
```

Indeed, it is possible in COBOL to write compound Boolean expressions that are ambiguous to the reader and often quite different from the programmer's intentions.

Even without the ambiguity, such expressions are usually rather difficult for anyone other than the original programmer to understand.

3. Avoid indiscriminate use of the EQUIVALENCE statement in FOR-TRAN, the REDEFINES statement in COBOL, and similar statements in other programming languages—including assembly language. If several symbolic names have been equated to the same constant, variable, or table, the reader of the program will have a hard time remembering the meaning of the names, and the *reason* (assuming there was one—it is often done to allow the programmers to combine the source version of several different modules so that the variable names will all agree) for the redefinition.

4. Jumping in and out of loops (e.g., DO loops in FORTRAN, PERFORM VARYING loops in COBOL, etc.) should be discouraged. Many languages prohibit such antics on the part of the programmer; those programmers who insist on doing it cause great headaches for those who follow them.

5. Avoid changing the value of a loop index indiscriminately. In most languages, there is a mechanism for incrementing (or decrementing) a count N times until it has been exhausted—at which point the program begins executing statements after the body of the loop. Knuth's study of FORTRAN programs (from "An Empirical Study of FORTRAN Programs," *Software Practice and Experience*, Volume 1, Number 2, pages 105–133) showed that 95% of the DO loops had a default increment of one. It is natural to expect that the same would be true of most other programming languages. Thus, it is extremely disconcerting to find a program whose loops *normally* increment by 1, but which occasionally add 13 to the indexing variable (the unexpected addition usually takes place deep within the body of the loop). Once again, some programming languages forbid this (by moving the initialized value of the index into a special temporary register), but many make it quite easy—and tempting for those programmers who manage to find a use for such things.

REFERENCES

1. B. W. KERNIGHAN and P. J. PLAUGER, "Programming Style: Examples and Counterexamples," *ACM Computing Surveys*, December 1974, pages 303–319.

2. ——, *The Elements of Programming Style*, McGraw-Hill, 1974.

3. B. SCHNEIDERMAN and C. KREITZBERG, *The Elements of FORTRAN Style*, Harcourt, Brace, Jovanovich, 1971.

4. G. M. WEINBERG, *The Psychology of Computer Programming*, Van Nostrand Reinhold, 1971.

5. J. M. YOHE, "An Overview of Programming Practices," *ACM Computing Surveys*, December 1974, pages 221–246.

PROBLEMS

1. How often do other programmers read your programs? Is it a common occurrence in your organization? If not, why not?

2. Why is it important that other programmers be able to read your program?

3. Why does structured programming make a program easier to understand?

4. Does your computer system have any multitasking facilities? Are they used in any applications in your organization? If so, try to gather some statistics to determine whether such programs (or systems) require more debugging time and more maintenance work than nonmultitasking projects. Are there certain types of projects for which a multitasking approach would make the final program simpler and easier to understand?

5. List three programming tricks in COBOL that could be considered a programming trick. For each programming trick, give an indication of the kind of misinterpretation that would be possible on the part of another programmer. Do you think this is likely to make maintenance more difficult?

6. List three programming tricks in FORTRAN that could be considered a programming trick. For each programming trick, give an indication of the kind of misinterpretation that would be possible on the part of another programmer. Do you think this is likely to make maintenance more difficult?

7. List three programming tricks in PL/I that could be considered a programming trick. For each programming trick, give an indication of the kind of misinterpretation that would be possible on the part of another programmer. Do you think this is likely to make maintenance more difficult?

8. List three programming tricks in assembly language that could be considered a programming trick. For each programming trick, give an indication of the kind of misinterpretation that would be possible on the part of another programmer. Do you think this is likely to make maintenance more difficult?

9. Give an example of a program that modifies itself as it executes. How much CPU time does this approach save compared to an approach where the program is *not* modified as it executes? Express this as a percentage of the program's total execution time, e.g., does the use of the ALTER statement in COBOL save 1% of the program's execution time? Is this significant? Does it justify the use of program modification?

10. Why is a computation like

    A = B*C+3**D/-3*X+Y*4

    difficult to understand? How many operations (operators and/or operands) should be allowed in one computational statement?

11. Does the use of parentheses make a complex computational statement more readable? For example, do you consider the statement

    A = (B*C) + (((3**D)/(-3))*X)+(Y*4)

    more readable than the expression in problem 10? Can you think of a simple manual technique for determining whether the proper number of matching pairs of parentheses (i.e., a right parenthesis, to match every left parenthesis) are present in an expression? How many levels of parentheses do you think should be allowed in a computational expression?

12. Why do you think the nested IF statement has been forbidden in many COBOL organizations? Which of the following reasons (given by experienced programmers in several of the author's programming courses) are the most important?

(a) "The compiler generates incorrect object code for nested IF statements."

(b) "The compiler generates inefficient object code for nested IF statements."

(c) "I can't understand nested IF statements."

(d) "The COBOL manual recommended that nested IF statements not be used."

(e) "The syntax of COBOL is such that it is not always easy to tell which ELSE clause goes with each IF clause."

(f) "It is difficult to insert or delete clauses from a highly nested IF-THEN-ELSE structure."

(g) "Nobody ever taught me how to use nested IF statements."

13. It has long been recognized that ALGOL programmers and PL/I programmers (among others) are generally far more willing to use nested IF statements than COBOL programmers. Why do you think this is true? Do you think this implies that ALGOL and PL/I programs are more difficult to understand and maintain than COBOL programs?

14. It has often been suggested that nested IF statements are easier to understand if they are indented (or formatted) properly. How significant do you think this is?

15. Does your organization have any standards concerning the number of statements that can be put on one line of a listing? Are the standards enforced? Do you think they are important?

16. A number of other formatting suggestions are given in section 5.2.3. Are these standards enforced in your organization? Do you think they are important?

17. Many of the formatting suggestions in Section 5.2.3 are handled automatically in some programming languages, for example, the TIDY package provided by some vendors for FORTRAN, the PRETTYPRINT package for LISP, the NEATER2 package for PL/I, ADR's METACOBOL package, and so forth. Are any of these automated formatting packages available in your organization? Are they used? Do you think they are a significant aid? If not, why not?

18. In Section 5.2.4, it is suggested that nested skip instructions be avoided in assembly language. Do you think this is important? Can you think of any programming situations where this type of programming would be important? Can you suggest another way of programming the nested skip sequence (such as the one shown in Section 5.2.4) that would be easier to understand?

19. Does your computer allow nested execute assembly language instructions? If so, think of a programming example where some use could be made of it. If use of the nested execute were to be disallowed (on grounds of clarity), what alternative programming technique could be used?

20. Does your computer allow multiple levels of indirect addressing? Does it allow various combinations of indirect addressing and indexing (e.g., pre-indexing and post-indexing)? Are these allowed in your organization? Do you think they make programs more or less difficult to understand?

21. Section 5.2.5 suggests that positive Boolean logic is easier to understand than negative Boolean logic. Do you agree with this? Why? (or why not?)

22. Section 5.2.5 warns against indiscriminate use of the EQUIVALENCE statement (in FORTRAN) and the REDEFINES clause (in COBOL). Why is this likely to be a problem area? Should the use of such statements be restricted as part of the programming standards in an organization?

23. What kind of restrictions should be made against indiscriminate jumping in and out of program loops? Does your programming language allow you to jump out of the body of a loop? Have you ever done so? Do you think it could be justified?

24. Several programming languages allow the concept of "global" variables, e.g., through the use of COMMON in FORTRAN, the LINKAGE SECTION in COBOL, EXTERNAL variables in PL/I, and so forth. Do you think the use of global variables makes it more difficult to understand the behavior of a program? What kind of restrictions should be placed on the use of global variables?

25. Can you suggest any other programming conventions that make programs easier to understand?

6

ANTIBUGGING

6.0 Introduction

This chapter discusses "antibugging," or what I sometimes prefer to call "defensive programming." Antibugging refers to the philosophy of writing programs in such a way as to make bugs less likely to occur—and when they *do* occur (which is inevitable), to make them more noticeable to the programmer and the user. To put it another way, we assume that a program is guilty until proven innocent; on the assumption that the program is going to do something incorrectly, we build in as many error-checks as possible.

There is only one objective of this programming philosophy: *to find bugs more quickly*. As pointed out numerous times in the past several chapters, testing and debugging are among the most time-consuming activities in computer programming. While we discuss a number of useful techniques in Chapters 7 and 8 to tackle this difficult area, they all suffer from the weakness of being applied *after the program is written*. As we will emphasize in Chapter 8, debugging is often a mental activity: Though traces and core dumps are necessary and useful, many of the more subtle bugs are found only by long painstaking thought and analysis of the circumstances surrounding the bug, and long tedious checking of the "clues" found in the various dumps and traces. It is especially frustrating to watch a programmer (or perhaps an entire team of programmers, since in a large system, one often does not know whose

220

subroutine caused the error) *manually* searching for an error, when the program could have checked for the error quite easily.

All of these concepts of program design, including antibugging, are merely *philosophies.* We cannot prove that they lead to better or more efficient programs; we cannot state any deterministic algorithms for generating an antibugging type of program. All we can do is indicate an approach, an attitude, a philosophy of how to write good programs. The concept of antibugging is certainly one of the most important elements of the art of good program design; however, since many programmers seem violently opposed to it (much to my surprise when I began giving lectures and seminars on this subject), we will begin by describing the common objections to this philosophy—and hopefully presenting effective arguments against those objections. We will then discuss those aspects of a program that should be covered by the antibugging philosophy; finally, we will describe a few additional programming practices that are useful in this area.

6.1 The Arguments Against Antibugging

Having taught courses on advanced programming topics several times in dozens of countries throughout the world, I have made the startling observation that the majority of programmers are opposed to the idea of error-checking—some quite vociferously. Having listened to many such arguments, I have come to the conclusion that there are essentially three objections, each of which is dealt with below.

6.1.1 It Is Unfair to Ask a Programmer to Put Error-Checking into His Program

The most common objection to the philosophy espoused in this chapter has nothing to do with CPU time or programmer time, but rather with the concept of justice. The attitude of many programmers seems to be, "I'm going to assume that my subroutine is called with legal arguments. If some idiot gives my module bad data, then it's his fault if the system blows up. Don't put the burden of error detection on my shoulders!" A slight variation of this is the complaint: "My boss said to assume that the data received by my module would be completely 'clean,' completely error-checked—so why do you want me to do some more error-checking? Do you realize how ridiculous it would be if *everyone* did his own error-checking?"

While I can sympathize with this it's-not-my-fault-if-something-goes-wrong attitude and the corresponding the-boss-says-it-will-be-OK attitude, it doesn't help get the programming job done any faster. It may turn out that the easiest place to catch the error is in your subroutine, so why not help everyone else out? If you obstinately refuse to build any error-checks into your subroutine, then you may end up *compounding* the error: When your program receives incorrect data, it will generate incorrect results, which will be passed on to the next routine, and so forth. The original error, tiny and insignificant as it may have been, will begin to grow like a malignant cancer. After several subroutines have passed the bad data back and forth, arrays will begin to be destroyed, data-base records will be mysteriously "clobbered," and the entire system may eventually self-destruct.

I still find it surprising that so many programmers should voice such resentment at having to insert extra coding in their module (thus presumably destroying its innate elegance) to catch what they consider "somebody else's bug." Obviously, to the *user* of the computer system, a bug is a bug, and it doesn't matter who caused it. It seems natural for programmers to band together and help each other in such a situation—but they don't.

6.1.2 Antibugging Requires Too Much Extra CPU Time and Memory

Another common complaint is that the extra error-checking suggested in this chapter represents an unacceptable amount of overhead. "If I checked for *all* the things that could go wrong," the programmer will often say, "my program would spend all of its time doing error-checking, and none of its time doing useful processing." The complaint can be valid, but we usually find that a reasonable amount of error-checking doesn't really slow down the program at all—often only by a few milliseconds, which is a small price to pay for being able to catch unexpected errors. Of course, if the error-checking *does* turn out to slow the program down significantly, it can always be removed when the program is debugged; however, I feel quite strongly that most error-checking logic should *never* be removed, since most programs are *never* completely debugged.

There is an interesting psychological argument in favor of inserting the extra error-checking code at the beginning of a project. In most cases, programs seem to obey a variation of Parkinson's law: They grow to fill (and sometimes slightly exceed) the amount of available memory, and they slow down to meet the CPU time requirements. Thus, at the beginning of the project, when there is still some available memory and CPU capacity, all of the error-checking code should be inserted. Later on, when there are complaints about the size and inefficiency of the program, and when demands are made to cut it down and speed it up, *then* the error-checking can be eliminated! Remember: *It is much easier to remove some error-checking logic after a program has been debugged than it is to insert the same error-checking logic when you discover that the program doesn't work properly.* Removing error-checking statements is usually just a matter of physically removing a few cards from the source program, or setting a conditional assembly (or conditional compilation) switch to prevent the error-checking statements from being assembled in a new version of the program. *Inserting* new error-checking statements, on the other hand, can be extremely painful if the program has already grown to meet its memory capacity!

One of the most violent objections I heard in this area came from a group of programmers at a bank in Montreal. They were convinced that the error-checking and antibugging that I was suggesting would far exceed the capacity of their machine. Toward the end of the seminar I was conducting, we found that their CPU was idle nearly 80% of the time; also, large areas of memory were frequently unoccupied and could easily have accommodated larger programs! Keep this in mind: *The predominant number of computer systems in the world are under-utilized and could easily stand the extra overhead of error checking.*

6.1.3 Antibugging Takes Too Much Programmer Time

The last common objection to antibugging involves "people time": Programmers are concerned that they will spend too much time inserting extra error-checking statements into their code and that they will never finish their project as a result. It is true that if one were to check *every possible* source of error in a program, the programming process would be slowed considerably; however, if some common sense is used to judge which situations are *really* in need of some error-checking code, it should not take too much extra time. Again, keep in mind that it is far easier to insert such statements *as you write the program* than it will be to go back to the program, *after* you have written it, to attempt to insert some extra antibugging statements. As you are coding a program, all of the details of its operation (and possible weak spots) will be fresh in your mind, and it should be very little trouble to insert a few extra statements. *After* you have written the program, you will have forgotten some of the details, and the insertion of any error-checking statements will require a compilation or reassembly of the program, which is a source of errors in itself!

I once encountered great opposition to this idea from a group of programmers working for a bank in Stockholm. In fact, three of the programmers were so angry that they failed to return for the second day of my programming course. Somewhat startled at the intensity of their feelings, I asked their supervisor why they had been so upset with my sermon on antibugging. "Oh, that's not the reason why they are absent from your class today," he said. "They were called in the middle of the night to find and repair a bug in the savings account system that they were responsible for. It seems that during the last monthly run, they lost 3000 accounts from the master file, and it was just noticed by accident last night!"

6.2 Aspects of a Computer Program That Require Checking

Having hopefully gained some support for the concept of antibugging, we will now go on to a discussion of the vulnerable areas of a computer program. While common sense must determine the nature and extent of error-checking to be performed in a program, the following list should serve as a general guideline.

6.2.1 Input Data from the "Outside World"

Though it is somewhat of a generalization, it is safe to say that most programs perform their computations based on input from the "outside world," e.g., from the card reader, magnetic tape drives, or terminals. In some esoteric cases, the input may be provided by mechanical means (e.g., process control systems and data acquisition systems); however, we often expect the input to be prepared by a *user*, that is, a keypunch operator, a manager, a clerk, or perhaps the person who wrote the program.

Most programmers will agree that any such input should be checked for validity; the need for such error-checking increases if the users are untrained and unfamiliar with (or suspicious of) computers—and it should not decrease in the case where the user is the author of the program! You *must* assume that the user will provide your program with bad input, even if the keypunch operator's work has been verified by a second person. One organization thought that keypunch verification was an adequate error-check, until it discovered that the keypunch operators were saving time by *first* passing blank cards through the verifier (thus obtaining the small notch in the side of the card), and *then* punching the required data on the card!

6.2.2 Calls from Other Programs

It is equally important for a program to check internally generated arguments and data. You cannot automatically assume that your subroutine will be called with the right kind of arguments; the other fellow's subroutine may have a bug in it, and yours may be called with a "garbage" argument. The larger the system in which your module resides, the more critical this type of error-checking is.

It is this aspect of antibugging that seems to infuriate some programmers the most. They have accepted the fact that the "outside world" may provide them with bad input; the idea that their fellow programmers might do the same seems totally intolerable. The answer to this objection is really quite simple: Even programmers make mistakes.

6.2.3 Data-Base Records on Disk or Tape

The data base is another source of trouble for many programmers; the larger the data base, the more likely it is to slowly accumulate a number of minor errors. Other programs may have updated the data base incorrectly; there may have been undetected hardware errors when the record was being read from or written to the IO device; some records may have been mysteriously lost when the data base was being dumped from disk to tape; the operator might have used a slightly obsolete version of the data base when he began running the program.

One organization had severe problems in this area when it discovered that errors were being introduced into the data base by one or more FOR-TRAN programs that periodically updated the data base. Within each updated record, there were some numeric fields and some alphabetic fields. The numeric fields, in particular, were floating-point numbers that were written with a FORMAT statement (roughly equivalent to the PICTURE clause in COBOL). However, if the program attempted to output a number too large for the FORMAT statement, the FORTRAN IO routines would output a field of asterisks, *with no other error indication.* Needless to say, when some other program attempted to read the record (which, due to the cyclical nature of processing within the system, was often as much as six months later), it became very unhappy when it found asterisks instead of a floating-point number—and the program would usually abort in the middle of a three-hour run!

The programmer whose module read the data-base records was asked to insert some error-checking code, since it was not known which FORTRAN program was generating the garbage on the data base. The programmer was indignant: "Why do I have to check for those asterisks? I didn't put them there. It's not my fault that my program is blowing up!" He went on to say an extensive error-check of all the numeric fields on each of the 200,000 records in the data base would double the processing time of the program— which was probably true. After a great deal of heated debate, it was decided that a simple common-sense solution would suffice: A "data-base diagnostic" program was used on a weekly basis to check for bad numeric fields, bad alphabetic fields, records out of sequence, missing records, and various other misfortunes that were considered possible. The program took approximately 10 minutes of machine time whenever it ran (which was nearly all IO time— very little computation was done), and it saved several hours per month of reruns, lost records, operator confusion, and user unhappiness.

6.2.4 The Computer Operator

Many programmers seem to treat the computer operator as if he were an error-free input/output device. Unfortunately, while operators are normally better-trained, more conscientious, and less error-prone than other users, they *do* make mistakes occasionally. This seems to be even more true on the sophisticated multiprogramming systems, remote-batch systems, and time-sharing systems that are so prevalent today. Some operator errors cause *system* failures; however, the majority of such errors cause only one program to be aborted, or to execute with bad input—and these are the subject of our discussion here.

There are a variety of errors that can occur in this area, but they seem to fall into a few broad classes:

1. The operator may run the wrong version of your program—either an obsolete version that has since been replaced, or a new "prerelease" version that does not yet work correctly. Even worse, he may tell you (innocently, in most cases) that he executed a different version of the program than he really did.

2. He may provide incorrect "operator control" as your program executes. That is, he may supply incorrect control cards (if it is his responsibility to do so); he may give your program a priority that is too high or too low; he may give it insufficient memory to operate efficiently; he may abort the program because he thinks it is in a loop, when in fact it is executing correctly; he may fail to abort the program after it has gotten into a loop, thus wasting valuable machine time; he may forget to change the forms in the printer at the appropriate time; etc.

3. He may provide incorrect input to your program. Most programs require input from cards, tape, or disk, and it is often the operator's responsibility to put the cards into the card reader, mount the tape(s), etc. If this is done incorrectly, the program may run to completion, but with an obsolete version of the data base. Similarly, many computer programs occasionally ask the computer operator to supply certain "exceptional" parameters—such as the date (if it is not available from the operating system), or a decision about the action to be taken after an IO error has occurred. Once again, an operator error can have disastrous consequences.

As an example of the absurdities that can occur in this area, consider the following story. A programmer wrote a program that was to read approximately a thousand cards, *sorted by customer account number*; the cards would then be used to update records on a master file that was also sorted by account number. The programmer decided to break his application into two passes: The first pass read all of the cards and did a thorough job of editing (checking that all of the fields on the card were in correct account-number sequence, etc.); the second pass *reread the same cards* and used them to process the master file. Presumably, the second pass would not be run if errors were discovered in the first pass. All went well for the first six months; then the number of transaction cards slowly began to grow as more customers were added to the file, and as they became more active. One day, the inevitable occurred: The cards were read by the first pass of the program and were found to be correct. The operator took the cards out of the card reader, in preparation for the second pass—*and then dropped them.* Sensing that no great damage had been done, he picked them up, put them back together as best he could, and began running the second pass. The second pass of the program, completely oblivious to the possibility that it might be working with bad input, read transaction cards that were out of sequence, discovered that it could not find a particular customer-account record on the master file, and promptly aborted, thus wasting several *hours* of computer time! The most amazing part of the story is that the operator was severely chastised for his actions, but nobody said anything to the programmer!

Perhaps the most effective way of training programmers to write "operator-proof" programs is to force them to spend some period of time as an operator. It has been my experience that many of the most careful, thorough, and conscientious programmers began their careers as operators. I have even seen one or two organizations that periodically rotate their programmers into the computer room for a one-month stint as an apprentice operator. Failing this, the programmer should at least try to keep the following suggestions in mind:

1. Make use of as many automatic label-checking features of your operating system as possible; this is crucial, of course, for files on disk or tape (it is amazing to see how many programmers try to circumvent this—usually out of laziness), but it can be equally important to ensure that the correct version of the *program* is running. The program itself is usually a file in a library, and it is important that the operator does not run an obsolete version, or an experimental version in the programmer's private library.

2. Make your program as operator-independent as possible. Don't ask him to type the date on the computer console if you can get the information from the operating system; don't ask if this is the weekly run if there is some other way of determining it by yourself; don't ask him to make a decision about error-recovery procedures if you can design a totally automatic, deterministic procedure—for if an error does occur, it is likely that the operator will be under great pressure to rectify the situation, and he will be even more error-prone than usual.

3. Never assume that the operator has done anything correctly. If he supplies your program with input from the console typewriter, or mounts a tape, or loads a deck of cards, double-check to make sure it is correct.

4. Think carefully about the sequence of actions that will be necessary to operate your program. Are you asking the operator to change forms in the printer every five minutes? Are you forcing him to dash frantically from the printer to the tape drives, and from there to the card reader, to keep up with your program? If so, try to reorganize your program so that the operator can use his time and talents efficiently. You will find that there will be fewer errors and a happier operator.

5. At regular intervals, buy your operator a beer or a cup of coffee, and ask him for suggestions for improving your program. He will give you some good ideas and will appreciate being dealt with as an intelligent human being (which he certainly is, despite the caste system in many companies).

6.2.5   The Central Processor

It is rarely practical to insert error-checking code to test for the correct operation of the CPU; one generally has to assume that the CPU is working, or the program will not work at all. However, if things start to go wrong, and there seems to be no other reasonable explanation for the problems, it is sometimes worthwhile to check on computations (or IO operations, or whatever else seems to be wrong) that should be correct; something in the form of a trace is usually adequate. You should not wring your hands helplessly if it appears that the CPU is not working, nor should you run to the customer engineer with unfounded accusations of a faulty CPU. Good error-checking code should convince both of you that something is wrong.

6.2.6   The Operating System and Other System Software

By the same argument as in the preceding section, one should learn not to trust operating systems, compilers, or other vendor-supplied software with too much blind faith; sooner or later, they will wreak mysterious havoc upon your innocent program. If you are working with an experimental version of an operating system, or a new compiler, it may be worth including some error-checking code; in most cases, though, it is not practical to check everything the operating system is doing. However, if things start to go wrong, don't be afraid to insert some code to make sure that the operating system is returning correct information when you call it, that it is not destroying your registers and accumulators, and that other aspects of the environment that the operating system creates for you is correct.

6.2.7   The User

Though many users know far more about the application than those who program it, they should not be trusted completely. "Don't worry about *that* field," they will say. "It will never be more than three digits long." Needless to say, there will inevitably be an exceptional case where the field in question turns out to be four digits long, or *negative* when it was supposed to be only positive, and so forth. Whenever the users say something about the nature of input to the program, the type of calculations to be carried out, or the format of output, get them to write it down—and then insert some error-checking code to ensure that their statements are accurate.

6.2.8   The Boss

Last of all, don't trust your programming supervisor, especially when he tells you, "Don't worry about the input—it will be edited by the time your program gets it." When your antibugging code catches a bug, he will probably thank you; if he doesn't, perhaps you should find a new place to work!

6.3   Antibugging Programming Techniques

Many of the antibugging suggestions above are properly in the domain of *systems design*, not program design, that is, one should design any computer system with thorough error-checking at every level. In a business-oriented system, it is common to design a number of cross-totals, hash-totals, and a variety of "audit-trail" mechanisms so that everyone will be able to verify that the system is working correctly.

Much of our discussion, though, is also valid at the programming level, and even at the coding level. There are a number of general programming techniques of an antibugging variety that are useful for providing a great deal of error-checking in any program. A number of these are discussed below.

6.3.1 Scientific Subroutines Should Check Most Numeric Arguments

Most scientific routines deal with numeric quantities; therefore, it is reasonable for them to check that the numeric arguments are legal. In some cases, the error-checking is of a trivial nature. Subroutines that calculate square roots or logarithms should check that they are not working with negative arguments; subroutines that calculate e^x will usually only work properly if the magnitude of x is less than 88. This approach can be applied to most scientific applications: numerical analysis, statistics, solutions of differential and integral equations, and so forth. If, for example, you are writing a program to perform some lengthy calculations on experimental data, you may *know* either from past experience, intuition, or theory that a certain parameter should not exceed some quantity. Thus, it may be useful to make the appropriate error-check at the end of each iteration.

6.3.2 Business-Oriented Applications Should Check the Range and Type of Data

Most business-oriented programs must deal with a variety of data *types*, that is, they must deal with alphanumeric data, integer data (in binary, octal, decimal, and hexadecimal), and floating-point data. Thus, it is often important for the business-oriented program to ensure that its data is of the proper type. When the program reads a customer name from an input card, it should check to see that there are no numeric characters imbedded within the name. When it reads a character string consisting of supposedly numeric characters, it should verify that this is indeed the case. When the program reads a data-base record, it should check to see that none of the fields contain illegal fields of data.

A business-oriented program might also check the *size* of various arguments. A payroll program might check to see that the calculated taxes do not exceed the calculated salary for an employee. The order-entry program could check to see whether a negative quantity of goods has been ordered. An inventory-control program might check to see if it is working with nega-

tive Inventory. An accounts-receivable program might check to make sure
no payment exceeds a specified quantity. A personnel system might check to
see that none of the employees specified the *current* year as their year of
birth.

A large percentage of business-oriented programs seem to be written in
COBOL or PL/I; fortunately, these languages have a number of diagnostic
capabilities to help the programmer catch certain kinds of errors. In general,
the programmer can detect attempts to divide by zero, arithmetic overflow
and underflow, "size" errors, and so forth. Table 6.1 lists the common error-
checking statements in the ANS COBOL language; Table 6.2 lists the error-
checking statements in PL/I.

Table 6.1. ERROR-CHECKING STATEMENTS
IN ANS COBOL

IO Errors	file-name
USE AFTER STANDARD ERROR PROCEDURE ON	INPUT OUTPUT I/O
Arithmetic Errors	
ON SIZE ERROR imperative-statement.	

Table 6.2. ERROR-CHECKING STATEMENTS
IN PL/I

Statement	Meaning
ON CONVERSION	Conversion errors on input or output.
ON SIZE	Attempting to store a number that exceeds the size of variable.
ON FIXEDOVERFLOW	Overflow in a fixed-point arithmetic computation.
ON OVERFLOW	Overflow in a floating-point arithmetic computation.
ON UNDERFLOW	Underflow in a floating-point arithmetic computation.
ON ZERODIVIDE	Attempt to divide by zero.
ON SUBSCRIPTRANGE	Attempt to reference past the end of an array.
ON NAME	Attempt to read in an undefined variable with GET DATA.
ON UNDEFINEDFILE	Attempt to open an undefined file.
ON TRANSMIT(filename)	Transmission errors when performing I/O on (filename).
ON RECORD	Record is larger or smaller than expected.
ON KEY (filename)	Illegal key on random-access read.
ON ENDPAGE	Attempt to output more lines on a page than specified by PAGESIZE.
ON ENDFILE	End-of-file condition.

For accounting-oriented programs, or for any business-oriented programs dealing with large quantities of input and large files, additional error-checking is usually necessary. As the program processes input transactions (from cards, tape, or perhaps even terminals), it should keep a counter of the number of transactions it has received and processed. For financial applications, it may also be necessary to keep totals of monies received, monies disbursed, etc. Also, as the program reads through any input files (e.g., master file in a payroll application or a banking application), it should keep track of the number of records that have been read. These program-computed totals should be periodically compared against manually computed totals—simply so that everyone will know that the computer operator did not drop a tray of cards as he loaded it into the card reader, and so that everyone will know that the tape drive and/or the operating system did not skip an input record during processing.

For financial applications, the error-checking requirements may be rather extensive. They are often dictated by the accounting practices and requirements of the organization and will be given to the programmer as part of the specification. Nevertheless, the programmer should not abdicate his responsibility in this area: His program may have ways of generating errors that the auditors and accountants never even dreamed of!

6.3.3 Think Carefully About Input/Output Errors

One of the most difficult jobs in programming is that of handling IO errors. Although we can offer some general advice in this area, it seems that every situation must be dealt with separately. In most cases, we can distinguish between *device-oriented* errors and *transmission-oriented* errors. An example of a device-oriented error is an attempt by the programmer to use an IO device (e.g., a magnetic tape or a card reader) that does not exist, is not available, or is being used by someone else. A device-oriented error may also occur while the program is executing: The computer operator may accidentally press the POWER-OFF button on the tape drive while it is transmitting data, or there may be a "head crash" on a disk while it is in the midst of reading or writing data.

A transmission-oriented error is more common and is usually much less serious. Probably the most common transmission-oriented error of all is the *parity error*; this occurs when the CPU, an IO channel, or an IO controller detects an unsuccessful attempt to read or write data. On some IO devices, there may also be various categories of *timing errors* that are detected by the hardware. In the same category, we can also include the *illegal IO commands*: attempting to rewind the card reader, attempting to output binary data on a high-speed alphanumeric printer, attempting to write data on a write-locked tape drive or disk pack, and so forth.

The distinction between device-oriented errors and transmission-oriented errors is often important. The programmer is usually given the means of *recovering* from the transmission-oriented errors, but when a device-oriented error occurs, he is usually at the mercy of the operating system (which, in turn, is often at the mercy of the hardware!). Most high-level programming languages, for example, allow the programmer to test for end-of-file conditions; unfortunately, many versions of COBOL do *not* allow the programmer to control the recovery of parity errors. On the other hand, some languages allow the programmer to perform his own error-processing, but only after the system has executed its own error routines; this is illustrated by the ANS COBOL example in Fig. 6.1. By way of contrast, the assembly language programmer usually has a great deal of control over the handling of errors.

Input/output error-handling is an area that deserves to be closely studied when you begin writing a program. For each of the input devices and output devices, make a list of the possible types of errors that could occur; then ask yourself how this would affect your program. Finally, investigate the error-handling features of your programming language and operating system, and see whether you have an adequate degree of control over the handling of IO errors.

Figure 6.1. Handling IO errors in ANS COBOL.

```
PROCEDURE DIVISION.
DECLARATIVES:
MASTER-FILE-ERROR SECTION.
    USE AFTER STANDARD ERROR PROCEDURE ON MASTER-FILE.
MASTER-ERROR-ROUTINE.
    DISPLAY MASTER-ERROR-MESSAGE UPON CONSOLE.
    STOP RUN.
TRANS-FILE-ERROR SECTION.
    USE AFTER STANDARD ERROR PROCEDURE ON TRANS-FILE.
TRANS-ERROR-ROUTINE.
    MOVE TRANS-RECORD-NUMBER TO ERROR-RECORD-NUMBER.
    DISPLAY TRANS-ERROR-MESSAGE UPON CONSOLE.
OUTPUT-ERROR-SECTION.
    USE AFTER STANDARD ERROR PROCEDURE ON OUTPUT.
OUTPUT-ERROR-ROUTINE.
    DISPLAY OUTPUT-ERR-MESSAGE UPON CONSOLE.
    ACCEPT ANSWER FROM CONSOLE.
    IF ANSWER EQUALS NO THEN STOP RUN.
END DECLARATIVES.
```

Note: On some computers, there are nonstandard variations of these statements that allow the programmer to determine the actual nature of the IO error. For the IBM System/360, the reader is referred to *IBM System/360 Operating System: American National Standard COBOL Programmer's Guide*, Form GC28–6399.

6.3.4 Comment and Flowchart Your Program As You Write It, Not Afterward

There is simply no way of overemphasizing the importance of good program documentation. While much of the blame for poor documentation should be placed on the programmer's shoulders, his manager is also somewhat to blame. Documentation is often skipped or minimized on "rush" projects, which means that the manager may have done a poor job of estimating the manpower requirements for the project. Similarly, management may be under pressure to move the programmer on to the next project, in which case the documentation may never get done. Finally, the manager may allow himself to be overwhelmed by the ingenious excuses offered by the programmer in his attempt to avoid the dreary job of documenting.

Since we are primarily concerned with programming in this book, we will not delve any deeper into the many reasons for lack of documentation—besides, the subject has already been touched upon in Chapters 1 and 5. However, it should be pointed out that *documentation can be just as useful during the design and implementation of a program as it is afterwards.* The very act of writing documentation usually forces the programmer to re-examine the basic workings of his programs: *Why* is that XYZ variable incremented at this point of the program, anyway? What is this subroutine for, and what kind of parameters does it require? The programmer is forced to ask himself these questions as he struggles to describe his program in plain English; merely by doing so, he often exposes bugs, weaknesses, inadequacies, and redundancies in his program.

6.3.5 Try to Avoid Programs with Multiple Flags

Throughout this chapter, we have suggested that antibugging is a good way of catching errors in the act of being committed. In some cases, errors occur because the user does something that the programmer did not take into account, that is, he supplies certain combinations of input that the programmer was not expecting. This problem can occur *inside* a program, too: One subroutine or module may do something that another subroutine is quite unprepared for. It can be an especially troublesome problem if the program keeps track of its internal conditions with multiple *flags* or *program switches.*

Figure 6.2 illustrates a common situation. The programmer has seven different flags to indicate different events that have taken place during the processing of input transactions. At various times, some of the modules in the program will set (or reset) some of the flags; other modules will test the flags to determine what actions to take. The problem with flags is that the programmer rarely provides a *complete* specification of the possible states of

This program performs billing calculations for a large organization. On each run, the program reads a MASTER file consisting of all old customers; it also reads a TRANS-ACTION file consisting of new customers whose business had been acquired since the last billing run. Both files are sorted on the Social Security number of the customers; thus, the billing program merges both files as it runs, creating a new MASTER file as part of its output.

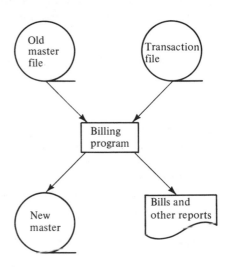

Figure 6.2(a). A flag-oriented FORTRAN program.

Figure 6.2(b). A flag-oriented FORTRAN program.

```
C
C      FLAGA = 0   IF WE HAVE NOT YET READ A RECORD FROM MASTER FILE
C            = 1   IF WE HAVE READ AT LEAST ONE RECORD FROM MASTER FILE
C
C      FLAGB = 0   IF WE ARE CURRENTLY WORKING ON A MASTER RECORD
C            = 1   IF WE ARE CURRENTLY WORKING ON A TRANSACTION RECORD
C
C      FLAGC = 0   IF WE ARE PROCESSING AN OLD CUSTOMER
C            = 1   IF WE ARE PROCESSING A NEW CUSTOMER
C
C      FLAGD = 0   IF THIS IS A NEW CUSTOMER WHO HASN'T BEEN ONE BEFORE
C            = 1   IF THIS NEW CUSTOMER HAS BEEN A CUSTOMER PREVIOUSLY
C
C      FLAGE = 0   IF ALL CALCULATIONS HAVE NOT YET BEEN DONE FOR THIS CUSTOMER
C            = 1   IF ALL CALCULATIONS HAVE BEEN DONE FOR THIS CUSTOMER
C
C      FLAGF = 0   IF NO OUTPUT RECORDS HAVE YET BEEN WRITTEN
C            = 1   IF SOME OUTPUT RECORDS HAVE BEEN WRITTEN
C
C      FLAGG = 0   IF THERE ARE NO MORE OUTPUT RECORDS TO BE WRITTEN
C            = 1   IF THERE ARE STILL SOME OUTPUT RECORDS TO BE WRITTEN.
C
```

the program. In Fig. 6.2, for example, we have seven flags; assuming that each flag can have a value of zero or one, we can have a total of 128 different combinations of those flags—and yet the programmer may only be using a dozen of those combinations. If there are bugs in the program, then it is very likely that the *wrong* combination of flags will be set at some point in the processing. Since the program looks at only one or two flags at a time, it is unlikely that the error will be detected early enough to tell where it was committed.

An alternative approach is to define each legal combination of conditions in the program as a *state*; thus, state 0 might correspond to the situation where flag A = 0, flag B = 0, and flag C = 0, while state 1 might correspond to the situation where flag A = 0, flag B = 0, and flag C = 1. There are two advantages to this scheme. First, it forces the programmer to be aware of all the legal states (he may discover, as suggested above, that certain combinations of flags are illegal); and second, it forces him to enumerate all of the legal *changes of state*. Thus, it may be meaningful for the program to change from state 0 to state 2 as it executes, but the transition from state 2 to state 0 may be meaningless and, hence, illegal. Figure 6.3 illustrates this technique by taking the original program, whose flags were shown in Fig. 6.2, and implementing it with state codes.

The overall control of the program could be implemented with two variables, OLD-STATE and NEW-STATE, and a large computed GO-TO statement (or CASE statement, or GO-TO DEPENDING ON, etc.). Each of the states listed in Fig. 6.3 would correspond to a module in the program, which would perform the processing appropriate for the associated setting of flags. Thus, if NEW-STATE = 14, we would enter module 14 (which would hopefully be given a more appropriate name!). Before module 14 began any significant processing, it would check OLD-STATE to see that it was entered from a legal module—according to Fig. 6.3, state 14 can be entered only from state 16 and state 11. When module 14 finishes its work, it will save the current state in OLD-STATE, determine what the next state should be (according to Fig. 6.3, state 14 can only lead to state 16), and store an indication of that new state in NEW-STATE. It will then branch back to the controlling computed GO-TO, which will dispatch appropriately to the next module for processing.

The state-oriented approach should appeal to those who have been exposed to switching theory and/or finite automata theory. We are suggesting that the programmer think of his program as a finite state automaton; designing the program thus includes the drawing of a state diagram. The state diagram for our sample program is shown in Fig. 6.4. For those who find the terminology and the diagram in Fig. 6.4 unfamiliar and unappealing, it may be appropriate to point out that this approach can be considered a variation of *decision tables*. The major point of this discussion is that programs with large

Figure 6.3. A state-oriented approach to the FORTRAN program.

State	FLAGA	FLAGB	FLAGC	FLAGD	FLAGE	FLAGF	FLAGG	Can Change to States
1	0	1	1	0	0	0	1	3
2	0	1	1	0	0	1	1	4
3	0	1	1	0	1	0	1	1,4,5,9
4	0	1	1	0	1	1	1	2,5,6,10
5	0	1	1	1	0	0	1	7
6	0	1	1	1	0	1	1	8
7	0	1	1	1	1	0	1	1,5,8,9
8	0	1	1	1	1	1	1	1,5,10
9	1	0	0	0	0	0	1	11
10	1	0	0	0	0	1	1	13
11	1	0	0	0	1	0	1	9,12,13,14
12	1	0	0	0	1	1	0	STOP
13	1	0	0	0	1	1	1	10,15,20
14	1	1	1	0	0	0	1	16
15	1	1	1	0	0	1	1	17,18
16	1	1	1	0	1	0	1	9,11,14,18,19
17	1	1	1	0	1	1	0	STOP
18	1	1	1	0	1	1	1	10,15,20
19	1	1	1	1	0	0	1	21
20	1	1	1	1	0	1	1	23
21	1	1	1	1	1	0	1	9,19,22,23
22	1	1	1	1	1	1	0	STOP
23	1	1	1	1	1	1	1	10,15,20

numbers of meaningless flag combinations are quite vulnerable to program bugs.

6.3.6   Check All Possible Cases of a Conditional Branch

There are many cases where a programmer tests a variable that is assumed to have one of two values—either "true" or "false," "positive" or

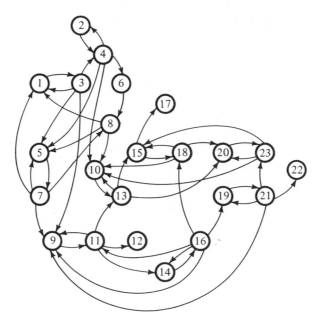

Figure 6.4. A state diagram for the FORTRAN program.

"negative," etc. If a test shows that the variable is *not* set to its first possible value, the programmer naturally assumes that it must be equal to the second possible value and takes the appropriate action. The dangers of this approach can be illustrated by recounting the experience of the computer operator who discovered that a program had typed an unintelligible message on the console typewriter, followed by the question:

DO YOU WISH TO PROCEED?

Not knowing what to do, and not knowing what the error message meant in the first place, the operator responded by typing:

HELP

Meanwhile, of course, the programmer's input routine was expecting a one-character reply of "Y" or "N." It first tested to see if the input message was a "Y," and finding that it was not, branched to the "no" routine—which promptly aborted all processing and went to end-of-job!

The moral should be clear: If you are testing a variable that may have N known values, include an $(N + 1)$th error-checking test for the none-of-the-above situation.

6.3.7   Don't Allow One Module to "Fall" into Another Module

Programmers who persist in writing unstructured programs controlled by unconditional branching statements often have a tempting situation when they find that module A exits by branching to the beginning of module B (by "module," we mean a COBOL paragraph or section, a collection of statements within a FORTRAN program, etc.). By situating module B directly after module A in the source program, the programmer can arrange for module A to "fall into" module B, and thus eliminate a redundant GO-TO statement. Thus, we might see the following hypothetical sequence of code in any programming language:

```
A:   LOAD X       COMPUTE X+Y
     ADD Y
     STORE Z      STORE RESULTS IN Z, FALL THRU TO B
B:   LOAD P       COMPUTE P+R
     ADD R
     STORE Q
       .
       .
       .
```

However, if modules A and B are relatively distinct, several disastrous things can happen during the debugging or maintenance phase of the project. A new module might be inserted between A and B in the source program; module A and/or B might be moved elsewhere in the source program (this happens quite frequently with minicomputer programs); changes to module A or B might invalidate the "falling-through" logic. Thus, it is far better to have module A *explicitly* GO-TO module B—the GO-TO statement is relatively cheap in terms of memory and CPU time. Better still, follow the structured programming suggestions of Chapter 4, and remove all of your GO-TO statements. Replace them with procedure calls, IF-THEN statements, and simple looping structures.

6.3.8   Check Array Subscripting

As we will point out in Chapter 8, one of the more common programming bugs involves subscripting past the end of arrays; such a bug can destroy code or data, and generally wreaks havoc upon the program.

Many programming languages include a test option that causes the compiler to generate extra object code to check array references at execution time. If your language has such a feature, it may be wise to use it the first few times you execute your program; if it does not, you may wish to insert your own error-checking code. Since this type of error-checking normally slows the execution of the program considerably, you may wish to remove it eventually.

6.3.9 Check Computed GO-TO Statements

FORTRAN, COBOL, and a variety of other programming languages have statements of the form

GO TO A,B,C, . . . ,Z DEPENDING ON I.

The variable I is generally assumed to be of integer type (though a conversion to integer usually takes place if it is of some other type). When the GO-TO DEPENDING ON statement is executed, I is expected to have a value between 1 and n, where n is the number of addresses (e.g., COBOL paragraph names, FORTRAN statement numbers, etc.) in the list. Of course, if there is a bug in the program, variable I may not have such a value.

The action taken when I contains an out-of-range value depends on the language and the particular implementation of the compiler. Typically, if I has a value less than 1, control will be passed to the first address in the list (e.g., to paragraph A in the coding example above) or the GO-TO DEPENDING ON statement will be ignored (i.e., control will pass to the statement following the GO-TO DEPENDING ON statement). Similarly, if I has a value greater than n, control will be passed to the last address in the list (e.g., to paragraph Z in the coding example above) or the GO-TO DEPENDING ON statement will be ignored. In any case, the execution of the program often proceeds in an entirely unexpected manner.

The remedy is very simple. Depending on the precise action of the compiler (i.e., whether the GO-TO DEPENDING ON statement is ignored when variable I has illegal values), the appropriate steps can be taken to ensure that control enters an error routine when I is out of range. This usually requires very little overhead and should perhaps be left in the program permanently.

PROBLEMS

1. Give a short definition of the concept of antibugging. What is its purpose? At what point in a programming project do you think it is likely to be most valuable?

2. Do you agree with the objection to antibugging discussed in Section 6.1.1, namely, that it is unfair to ask a programmer to insert error-checking to look for bugs in other people's code? Do others in your organization feel this way? Are their feelings allowed to dominate the feelings of others, that is, are they able to avoid such error-checking if they feel strongly enough?

3. Do you agree with the objection to antibugging discussed in Section 6.1.2, namely, that it requires too much CPU time and memory? Do you have any

estimate of the amount of extra overhead that would be required for reasonably thorough error-checking? Is it significant? Is this a common objection in your organization? Is your computer sufficiently overloaded to make it a valid objection?

4. If the addition of extra error-checking software *does* introduce a substantial amount of overhead into a program, can you suggest anything that can be done about it?

5. Many assemblers and compilers have conditional-assembly and conditional-compilation features. For example, the programmer might be allowed to write

```
%ERRORFLAG = 1
        .
        .
        .
        .
        .
%IF ERRORFLAG = 1
     X = 1
     Y = 2
     Z = 3
%ENDIF
```

Note that ERRORFLAG is a variable that exists only during assembly or compilation; no storage for it is reserved in the object program. Thus if the programmer wants error-checking code assembled into his program, he sets ERRORFLAG to 1; if he wants the error-checking code removed, he can set ERRORFLAG to zero and reassemble (or recompile) his program.

An alternate approach is to arrange the program so that the error-checking logic is *always* present in the object code. By reading a variable (perhaps from the console typewriter, under the control of the operator or the programmer), the program decides whether or not to execute the error-checking code. With this introduction, consider the following questions:

(a) Does your programming language have such a conditional assembly or compilation feature?

(b) Do you use it?

(c) For use in error-checking, is the conditional assembly approach more efficient than the alternative approach described above?

(d) Is it more convenient?

(e) Are there any other considerations that would encourage you to use conditional assembly for error-checking as opposed to the alternative approach, or vice versa?

6. Give an example of a situation where failure to check the validity of input data from the "outside world" could cause a program to abort.

7. How thorough and comprehensive should the checking of user input be? Can you think of any situations where it is possible to be *too* thorough?

8. Do you think it is necessary to check the arguments and parameters from other programs or modules to see if they are correct? How thorough should one be in this error-checking? Are there any disadvantages?

9. Do you think it is necessary to check data-base records on disk or tape for errors? What kinds of errors should one be looking for? How frequently are they likely to occur? Are there any disadvantages to this kind of error-checking?

10. How thoroughly should the programmer check for possible errors on the part of the computer operator? Do you think this is an important area?

11. Write a list of the types of errors that the operator might make—errors that could cause your program to abort or run incorrectly. For each type of error, indicate the kind of error-checking that could be done. Is it possible to prevent the operator from running your program incorrectly in all cases?

12. How can you tell whether the operator is running the right version of your program? Does this require any special programming on your part? Is it worth the effort?

13. Section 6.2.4 suggests that you should make your program as operator-independent as possible. List three examples of situations where the program could make its own decision about what to do without asking the operator. How much extra programming work would this require? Is it worth the effort?

14. Do you think it is worth the effort to put error-checking into your program to ensure that the CPU is working properly? How difficult do you think this would be? Can you think of any situations where it would be justified?

15. Under what conditions should the programmer insert error-checking code in his program to ensure that the system software is working correctly? How thorough should this error-checking be?

16. Give three examples of numeric arguments that should be checked for validity in a scientific application.

17. Give three examples of error-checking that should be carried out in a typical business-oriented program.

18. Do you think the programmer should *always* check for possible arithmetic errors in his program, e.g., division by zero, arithmetic overflow, and so forth? Under what conditions should he not bother making such error checks?

19. What sort of error-checking should be done for input/output errors? Suggest some general strategies for dealing with the following situations:
    (a) In a program that reads selected records from a master file to produce a report for management, some of the records cannot be read because of parity errors.
    (b) In a program that reads selected records from a master file, updates them, and writes them to an output master file, some of the master file records cannot be read because of parity errors.
    (c) In a program that is printing records on a report file, some of the records cannot be printed because of parity errors.

20. Do you agree with the statement in Section 6.3.4 that "documentation is just as useful during the design and implementation of a program as it is afterwards"? What do you think is the greatest value of program documentation?

21. What kind of standards do you think should be established for comments in a program listing? Do you think it is reasonable to require a comment for every source program statement? How can we ensure that the comments are accurate and meaningful?

22. Do you agree with the need for detailed flowcharts of a program? How can we ensure that the flowchart is an accurate representation of what the program is really doing?

23. What kind of documentation do you think should be provided to assist the maintenance programmer in future maintenance of a program you have written? Do you think any standards can be developed in this area?

24. What possible dangers can result from a program that contains a large number of switches and flags? Are there any general techniques for eliminating flags from programs?

25. As an experiment, find a program in your organization that contains a large number of flags. Try to redesign the program without any flags or switches; then answer the following questions:
(a) Is the new program easier to understand and easier to maintain?
(b) Does it appear that the new program will have fewer residual bugs that will eventually have to be found by the maintenance programmer?
(c) Does the new program require more memory or CPU time? If so, how much?

7

PROGRAM
TESTING CONCEPTS

In large on-line systems, the cost of testing a change is almost 100 times as much as the cost of producing the change. We cannot afford to go through this process too often.

A. D'AGAPEYEFF
Software Engineering, page 72

One can construct convincing proofs quite readily of the ultimate futility of exhaustive testing of a program and even of testing by sampling. So how can one proceed? The role of testing, in theory, is to establish a base proposition of an inductive proof. You should convince yourself or other people, as firmly as possible, that if the program works a certain number of times on specified data, then it will always work on any data. This can be done in an inductive approach to the proof. Testing of the base cases could sometimes be automated. At present, this is mainly theory; note that the tests have to be designed at the same time as the program and the associated proof is a vital part of the documentation. This area of theoretical work seems to show a possibility of practical results, though proving correctness is a laborious and expensive process. Perhaps it is not a luxury for certain crucial areas of a program.

C. A. R. HOARE
Software Engineering Techniques, page 21

Much of program complexity is spurious and a number of test cases properly studied will exhaust the testing problem. The problem is to isolate the right test cases, not to prove the algorithm, for that follows after the proper choice of test cases.

A. J. PERLIS
Software Engineering Techniques, page 21

Chapter opening quotes from *Software Engineering*, P. Naur and B. Randell, (eds.), NATO Scientific Affairs Division, Brussels 39, Belgium, January 1969 and *Software Engineering Techniques*, J. N. Buxton and B. Randell, (eds.), NATO Scientific Affairs Division, Brussels 39, Belgium, April 1970.

Testing shows the presence, not the absence, of bugs.

E. W. DIJKSTRA
Software Engineering Techniques, page 21

Programmers call their errors "bugs" to preserve their sanity; that number of "mistakes" would not be psychologically acceptable!

M. E. HOPKINS
Software Engineering Techniques, page 23

A debugged program is one for which you have not yet found the conditions that make it fail.

JERRY OGDIN
unpublished remarks

7.0 Introduction

Testing, debugging, and maintenance of computer programs is a largely ignored area. At the moment, there appears to be very little literature on the subject, little or no research, a scarcity of university courses, and very little appreciation for the scope of the problem.

One of the objectives of this chapter is to increase the level of understanding and appreciation for the magnitude of the testing effort. In addition, we will attempt to survey and discuss the current techniques and strategies that can be applied to testing. We will also point out some areas that are, at the present time, unsolved.

7.1 Definitions and Concepts

Before we discuss some approaches to testing, it is important that we try to define some of the words and concepts that we will be using. No attempt has been made here to use "official" definitions from dictionaries or other references; it is more useful to describe the words in the context in which they are used by programmers in their everyday work.

7.1.1 Module

A module is often defined in a manner similar to that of "program," that is, it is a collection of instructions sufficient to accomplish some logical function. As we saw in Chapter 3, many programmers consider the word "module" to be synonymous with "subroutine"; we also saw that a module is sometimes defined in terms of physical constraints. Some organizations specify, for example, that a module shall consist of no more than, say, fifty statements. In many cases, there is also the implicit assumption that a module is not useful unless it is combined with other modules to form a larger unit (e.g., a program).

7.1.2 Program

One is often tempted to describe a program as an undefined work of art, frequently associated with witchcraft and black magic. The more serious practitioners of that black art, though, tell us that a program is a collection of instructions which, when combined with appropriate data and control information, is sufficient to accomplish some well-defined function. A program is often regarded as the smallest such collection of instructions that can function without interacting with other programs.

7.1.3 Suites and Subsystems

To most Americans, a "suite" is a collection of rooms, as in an expensive hotel; to a large number of Europeans and Australians, though, a suite is roughly equivalent to a "subsystem." The assumption is that a subsystem is a collection of programs, organized in such a way as to accomplish a larger and more complex function than would normally be possible with a single program. One also finds that there are often *hierarchies* of subsystems, or *levels* of subsystems.

7.1.4 System

The word "system" is often used to describe any collection of programs provided by the vendor with the computer hardware, e.g., the "operating system," or the "data management system," or "the *&$¢%±¢!!! system just crashed again." In more general terms, a system is considered to be a collection of programs and/or subsystems sufficient to accomplish a significant, coherent application or function. Thus, we often hear such terms as "the payroll system," "the order entry system," etc.

7.1.5 Software Reliability

Shooman defines software reliability in reference 5 as the probability that a given software program operates for some given time period, without a software error, on the machine for which it was designed, given that it is used within design limits. Reliability is often defined in terms of MTBF (Mean Time Between Failures), MTTR (Mean Time To Repair), or in terms of data-base integrity. These terms mean much more, of course, when used in the context of a *system* than when used in the context of a single program or module.

7.1.6 Bug

In *Software Engineering Techniques* [1], Martin Hopkins describes a bug very simply as "a mistake." In common parlance, though, a bug is normally considered to be a software error—an error which may be "solid" (i.e., repeatable and consistent) or transient.

7.1.7 Glitch

The word "glitch" is one of those unofficial terms that has gained popularity in the vocabulary of the industrial/academic computer communities of Cambridge and Berkeley. Though never defined precisely, a glitch is usually thought of as an unforeseen feature of a computer program (or, in most cases, the specification and design of the program) that renders it inefficient, unelegant, or awkward to use. Note that there is a difference between a bug and a glitch. A bug implies that the program is not working to specifications, while a glitch implies that the specification itself (or some property of the program outside the scope of the specification) is awkward and clumsy.

7.1.8 Testing

Testing is defined by Hetzel [10] as a set of procedures and activities intended to demonstrate the correct operation of a program within its intended environment. Thus, the purpose of testing is to expose the existence of bugs, or to demonstrate conclusively the absence of any such bugs. It is important that we distinguish testing from the concomitant notion of debugging, which is defined below.

7.1.9 Proving Program Correctness

Within the past few years, there has been a growing interest in the development of a rigorous *proof* of the correctness of a program. That is usually done without regard to the environment within which the program operates, using a set of assertions, axioms, and theorems. There is some hope that we will eventually develop techniques for *automating* (either fully or partially) this proof process, but there remains a great deal of work to be done. As we pointed out in Chapter 4, the difficulty of proving the correctness of a program is closely related to its complexity and to the number of interactions between its components; hence, structured programming—which tends to reduce the complexity of programs—is looked upon as a highly important part of the proof process.

7.1.10 Validation, Verification, and Certification

Though not as common as "testing" and "debugging," the terms "validation," "verification," and "certification" are occasionally used in discussions of program testing. As defined by Hetzel, validation is a set of procedures and activities intended to demonstrate the logical correctness of a program *in a given external environment*. *Verification* is a set of procedures and activities intended to demonstrate the logical correctness of a program *in a given test environment*—which may or may not correspond to the actual environment in which the program will eventually run! Finally, *certification* is defined as an endorsement of the correctness and effectiveness of a program, based on personal experience, hearsay, or an organized set of procedures and activities.

7.1.11 Debugging

Debugging is a set of procedures or activities (some of which may be computer-related and some of which may not) that begin with the discovery of the existence of a bug and end when the precise location and nature of the bug has been ascertained. According to some programmers, debugging also includes the period of time during which the bug is being corrected, and does not really end until it has been demonstrated to everyone's satisfaction that the corrected bug *does* work correctly.

7.1.12 Maintenance

The word "maintenance" is normally used to describe all of the activities pertaining to the correction of errors, upgrading to maintain compatibility with new operating systems and/or compilers, and the introduction of *minor* improvements to a computer program. The distinction between a minor change and a major change is usually a qualitative one, but it should be an easy one to make in most cases. One activity is properly classed as maintenance, and the other falls into the category of development.

7.2 The Scope of the Testing Problem

Almost every programmer (or programming manager) has seen, heard, or experienced the consequences of bug-ridden computer programs; some of the stories are rather humorous, but as our computer systems take on more and more critical functions within society (e.g., air traffic control systems), the effect of poorly tested programs becomes more and more disastrous. Despite this, most programmers, many programming managers, and almost all non-technical managers drastically underestimate the amount of time, energy, planning, and money that must be devoted to testing. Similarly, they often underestimate the complexity of debugging and seem blissfully unaware of the magnitude and complexity of maintenance. It may be helpful to give a few statistics to demonstrate just how serious the problems are.

For example, the amount of time required for adequate testing of programs (and systems) has been variously estimated at 30% of the total project time, or 50%, or even higher. Indeed, it has been estimated that nearly 80% of the monies expended on the NASA Apollo project were devoted to various forms of testing. A small well-designed program could conceivably be tested in less than 30% of the total project time, of course; nevertheless, it is somewhat discouraging to continue seeing schedules that call for two years of design and implementation of a complex real-time system, and one month of system testing!

Furthermore, the number of bugs *remaining* in large programs and systems (after they have supposedly been thoroughly tested) is rather immense. It has been estimated in references 2 and 3 that each new release of OS/360 contains over one thousand errors; Tom Gilb, an EDP consultant in Oslo, Norway, claims to have counted over *eleven thousand* bugs in a recent release of OS! The author's studies of several vendor-supplied operating systems suggest that they retain a relatively constant number of system failures over a period of several years (see references 3 and 4). More quantitative studies (such as the one by Shooman in reference 5) suggest that the number of bugs in a large complex system is likely to follow an exponential decay—but it is likely that this ignores the new bugs that are constantly introduced into operational programs by ongoing maintenance and development.

As we saw in Chapter 1, testing is also a serious problem from the programmer's point of view. Sackman's classical study [6] suggested that some programmers require as much as 25 times longer to test and debug their programs than others. Since this study was based on a rather small sample, a number of observers have been tempted to conclude that things aren't really that bad in the real world; nevertheless, the author's personal observations of many EDP organizations suggest that there is at least a factor of ten difference between the best and worst programmer in the average programming group.

A similar study described by Boehm in references 2 and 7 has indicated that the programmer has a remarkably low chance of success when he attempts to modify a working program. If he attempts to change less than ten source statements in his program, he has approximately a 50% probability of making the changes correctly on the first attempt. If he tries to change as many as fifty statements, the probability of success drops to 20%.

If testing is difficult, it is not surprising to see that *maintenance*—which usually requires its own cycle of testing and debugging—also causes difficulty in many organizations. As we mentioned in previous chapters, a survey by *EDP Analyzer* [8] indicated that in the average American company, 50% of the EDP budget is spent on maintenance of existing programs; in some of the larger organizations, the figure was as high as 80%! Similarly, an informal survey undertaken by one of the major computer manufacturers turned up the following interesting observation. A typical program was written by one programmer and then maintained by ten generations of subsequent programmers before finally being scrapped and rewritten!

7.3 Levels of Testing Complexity

A discussion of testing usually elicits radically different reactions from different groups of programmers; upon further investigation, it often seems that their reactions are very much a function of the complexity of programs they are involved with. Thus, as another way of looking at the problem of testing, it is interesting to suggest a few categories of testing complexity. The categories below are somewhat arbitrary, but they seem to correspond to observable groups of applications within the computer industry.

7.3.1 Simple Programs

For the purposes of our discussion, a *simple* program is defined as a program that

1. Is less than 1000 source statements in length.
2. Is generally written by one programmer in six months or less.
3. Usually has no interactions with other programs or systems.

There is certainly a variety of such programs in the industry: small scientific applications written by engineers to solve a relatively simple numerical problem; small utility routines for a commercial environment; small report-writing programs; a vast majority of student programs developed in computer science courses; and so forth.

The significant observation about "simple" programs is that it usually doesn't matter how they are tested—it often doesn't matter whether they are tested at all! Almost by definition, these programs are performing relatively straightforward, if not utterly trivial, tasks, and often consist of straight-line coding. As a result, it becomes rather difficult for the programmer to introduce any bugs into the program in the first place. Then, too, most such programs are performing relatively noncritical functions within the organization, so if they *do* blow up, the effects are not usually so dramatic.

All of this means that there is often not much interest in the finer points of testing among that group of programmers who develop "simple" programs. They seem to sense that they can literally overwhelm the bugs in their program—almost by brute force—without resorting to any logical, organized plan of testing. In addition, they seem to know that even if a bug *does* occur after they have finished testing, there will be ample opportunity to fix it.

7.3.2 Medium-Complexity Programs

The next category of programs is defined as one that:

1. Is less than 10,000 source statements.
2. Is generally written by 1–5 programmers in less than 2 years.
3. Has few, if any, interactions with other systems.
4. Generally consists of 10–100 modules.

Informal surveys in several of my programming courses indicate that the vast majority of computer programs fall into this category. Most of the straightforward commercial applications (accounting, order entry, payroll inventory control, and so forth) seem to involve less than 10,000 COBOL statements; similarly, the majority of scientific applications consist of less than 10,000 FORTRAN statements. Even systems programs (assemblers, compilers, data management packages, teleprocessing control programs, etc.) often require less than 10,000 assembly language statements (though they may require far more than 10,000 memory locations for buffers, queues, tables, and so forth).

This is not to suggest that such programs are trivial in nature. The fact that they require one or two years of elapsed time for completion suggests that the testing effort may require 6–12 months. On the other hand, any problems that may be encountered during the testing process can usually be overcome by brute force, and the worst consequence is a somewhat delayed implementation date, e.g., the program should have been finished in 18 months, but instead requires a full 24 months. Similarly, when the finished program is put into production, the damage caused by any residual bugs is noticeable, but usually not critical. In most cases, a bug discovered during a production run on Monday can be repaired Monday night, so that the program can be put back into production on Tuesday.

It is true, of course, that some 10,000 statement programs *are* inherently complex, and it is sometimes true that bugs in these programs have catastrophic effects; nevertheless, it seems that the majority of such programs are relatively straightforward. The consequence of this, unfortunately, is that the programmers involved in such projects rarely feel a compelling need to concentrate closely on good principles of design and programming (e.g., by using top-down program design and structured programming). Similarly, they rarely feel a need to organize their testing in a careful, thorough fashion. There is little doubt that top-down design, structured programming, and some of the testing techniques suggested later in this chapter would be helpful. Unfortunately, it has been the author's experience that if such techniques are not absolutely necessary for the success of the project, they will often be ignored by programmers who are quite content with their old techniques.

7.3.3 Complex Programs

It seems appropriate to define a category of *complex* programs—programs that:

1. Have less than 100,000 source statements.
2. Are generally written by 5–20 programmers over a period of 2–3 years.
3. Consist of several subsystems.
4. Often interact with other systems.
5. Generally consist of 100–1000 modules.

Note that this category includes programs in the 10,000–100,000 statement range; while it might seem an arbitrarily large range, we should remember that the main criterion is the complexity of the final program—regardless of its size. Most programmers would intuitively agree that a program of this approximate size is likely to be complex; most managers would agree that a project that is large enough to require more than one programming team (and often more than one level of supervision) is intuitively more complex than the previous categories we mentioned. Managers also appreciate that the implementation time of such a project is long enough that (a) there is a good chance that one or more of the programmers will have left before the project is finished, and (b) the users will have had enough time to think of some desired changes and improvements to the program—and then insist that they be incorporated into the original program just as the program is beginning to be tested!

It is even more important to comment upon the effect of bugs in the "complex" category of programs. First of all, there are likely to be *more* bugs after the program has officially been put into production, simply because the program is larger and more complex, and therefore somewhat less amenable to the classical techniques of testing. Furthermore, when a *bug* is discovered (often in the middle of a production run), its effects are usually more serious than in the previous categories. More computer time will have been wasted, more users will be upset, more demands will be made to fix the bug quickly. To make matters worse, the bug often *cannot* be fixed quickly; its symptoms may be known (e.g., because the program aborts or generates incorrect output), but its nature and its location within the program may not be known. Because of the complexity of the program, it may easily take two or three days (and in some cases, weeks or months!) to find the bug and fix it.

If such bugs are discovered *before* the program is officially put into production, they will presumably be fixed. After all, that is the purpose of the systems tests, parallel runs, and acceptance tests that normally accompany such programs. However, the complex nature of the program and the elusive nature of the bugs (as well as their seemingly infinite number and variety) often extend the testing process far past the deadline that had originally been established for the project.

The consequence of these problems can be rather severe. The program is often finished substantially behind schedule, thus irritating the users and often eliminating the economies that would presumably have been realized with the program. Residual bugs (which are often a significant factor in such programs) cause large amounts of machine time to be wasted, delay production schedules, and cause great irritation to the users—and perhaps great economic loss to the organization that developed it. Indeed, we should point out that it is with this category of programs that we often see projects cancelled—simply because the organization was unable to finish an acceptably reliable program.

The moral behind this should be clear: We can sometimes afford to ignore good testing techniques (and good program design techniques) when dealing with simple programs and the medium-complexity programs; in the case of the complex programs, poor testing techniques can prevent the project from ever being implemented successfully. Since a growing number of commercial and scientific applications (as well as a number of systems programs, e.g., large compilers) are approaching this level of complexity, greater appreciation of proper testing is *necessary*, whereas it was previously only *desirable*.

7.3.4 Nearly Impossible Programs

Fortunately, there are only a relatively small number of programs that fall into the "nearly impossible" category; such a program is defined as one that:

1. Contains less than 10^6 source statements.
2. Is written by a group of 100–1000 programmers over a period of several years.
3. Requires continuing development and maintenance by people other than the original development team.
4. Generally consists of 1000–10,000 modules.
5. Generally consists of several major subsystems, with complex interactions between the subsystems; there are also likely to be complex interactions with other separately developed systems.
6. Often involves additional complexities, such as real-time processing, telecommunications, and multitasking.

Until the last few years, projects of this size were limited to the major computer manufacturers (e.g., IBM's development of OS/360) and a few ambitious government and military agencies. Recently, though, a small but increasing number of industrial organizations have begun tackling projects of this size—remember that we define this category as anything involving between 100,000 and one million lines of coding. Large banking applications, large insurance applications, "integrated" management information systems, and several other applications have the ability to approach this level of size and complexity.

It is precisely *because* of the relatively recent emergence of the nearly impossible programs and systems that we have begun seeing a healthy attitude (i.e., one of extreme apprehension and caution) taken toward testing. It has become perfectly clear to many of the organizations embarking upon such projects that there is a *significant* chance of failure if they do not insist on *both* rigid program design strategies (e.g., modular programming and structured programming) and rigid testing strategies. At the same time, the sheer magnitude of the testing effort has helped foster the development of some of the automated approaches discussed in Section 7.8.

7.3.5 Utterly Absurd Programs

Finally, we mention a category of program that can only be classed as "absurd"; such a program

1. Has between one million and ten million instructions.
2. Generally has more than 1000 programmers, working over a period of several years, often approaching a decade or more of development time.
3. Nearly always includes real-time processing, telecommunications, and other complexities.
4. Is often involved in critical processes, e.g., air traffic control or air defense.
5. Normally has an extraordinarily high requirement for reliability (e.g., one such project in Australia specified a Mean Time Between Failures for their system of 47 *years*).

Needless to say, *very* few organizations ever attempt such a project. At the current time, it seems to be limited to government and military organizations. It is the author's opinion that our current knowledge of program design and testing concepts is not sufficient to successfully produce a system of such size—and this creates a dilemma, of course, for the previously mentioned government and military agencies reply that they *must* implement such systems if they are to keep up with the ever-growing needs of society. In some cases, the success of the system is perhaps a moot point, e.g., an air defense system that will hopefully never be used; on the other hand, some systems currently being planned by civilian government agencies presumably *will* be used, and the consequences of a poorly tested system are rather staggering.

There is a certain irony to the development of such systems. Since many of them involve confidential government or military activities, the development team is often sequestered away from their colleagues in the scientific/commercial world, and thus, whatever words of wisdom might have been available from the commercial data processing community are lost. On the other hand, the vast experience of the government/military EDP community (which extends back over twenty years in complex systems—some of which have certainly been highly successful) is locked within secret file cabinets, apparently not to be shared with the commerical community that could use it. Thus, it seems almost inevitable that the civilian EDP community will suffer the same mistakes and disasters as the military community when *they* begin designing the "utterly absurd" category of programs (or systems) five or ten years from now.

7.4   Types of Errors to Be Exposed By Testing

Perhaps it is a bit of an oversimplification, but it seems that there is no point testing unless we know what we are testing *for*. As Dijkstra points out, testing shows the presence, not the absence of bugs. But what kind of bugs? To most programmers, this seems a trivial question; what else could we be looking for besides *logic* errors? If computers and computer systems can be considered as just an extension of our own human reasoning ability, then perhaps all computer bugs are, in fact, just errors in our own logic; however, it is usually more interesting to define several *categories* of bugs and adjust our testing strategies accordingly. Thus, we list below the types of errors that are normally to be found in a computer program.

7.4.1   Logic Errors

Indeed, logic errors *are* normally the most common type of computer bug—and most of our testing efforts are justifiably directed toward these bugs. For the purpose of our discussion, we can consider a logic error to be a solid, repeatable bug. If a given test input exposes the presence of a bug, then the same input, when presented to the program a second time, should expose the same bug in the same way.

7.4.2   Documentation Errors

There are some programming applications where a documentation error can be just as serious as a logic error. In most cases, we would be more concerned with errors in the *user* documentation—the documentation that tells a user how to prepare input for the program, how to operate the program, and how to use and interpret the output from the program. There are other situations, though, where errors in the *technical* documentation could be considered critical.

7.4.3   Overload Errors

It is often important to test a program to find out what happens if various internal tables, buffers, queues, or other storage areas are filled up to, or even beyond, their capacity. This is an especially critical area of testing in many on-line and real-time systems (e.g., what happens if all the terminal users type an input message simultaneously?), but it can be just as important in many batch-oriented programs.

7.4.4 Timing Errors

This is a category that is usually relevant only to real-time systems. In this case, we are concerned with logic errors that *cannot* be easily repeated; the errors are usually a function of timing conditions or coincidental combinations of events within the program. In a non-real-time program, we can usually console ourselves with the knowledge that there are a finite number of cases to be tested (even though the number is so large that we are usually quite unable to perform exhaustive testing). In a real-time system, though, the number of timing possibilities appears (at least at first glance) to be infinite.

7.4.5 Throughput and Capacity Errors

Once again, this is a category that may be relevant only for real-time systems, though it seems that more batch-oriented programs should be tested in this area. We are concerned here about the *performance* of the program; even though it generates the correct output, it may take an unacceptable amount of CPU time to do so, or it may use an exorbitant amount of memory, disk space, etc. This is critical for many on-line systems because the performance of a program is often immediately visible to the user in terms of response time. In a batch program, we might still want to specify (and then test) that the program be able to process one transaction per second, that it take no more than 100,000 bytes of storage, and so forth.

7.4.6 Fallback and Recovery Errors

For a number of programs, the concept of recovery and fallback is quite critical. If there is a hardware failure (or possibly a software failure), an unrecoverable program can cause several hours of lost machine time, or in the case of a real-time, on-line system, great confusion and chaos amongst the users. Testing in this area should ensure that the programs can be continued from some checkpoint, that files are not damaged, that the entire recovery process can be performed in a reasonable amount of time, and that users, computer operators, and other human beings are not confused by the recovery process.

7.4.7 Hardware Errors and System Software Errors

In most cases, the programmer feels that it is not his responsibility to ensure that the hardware and the vendor's operating system work correctly—

and in most cases, he does not have to. However, if the testing involves an entire *system*, and if that system is to be delivered to a non-computer-oriented user, then someone should have the responsibility of ensuring that the hardware and the vendor's operating system *do* work—for the user will generally not appreciate it when the programmer complains, "But it's not my fault that the on-line order entry system just crashed and lost the entire day's orders—it was a hardware bug!"

7.4.8   Standards Errors

Finally, some people suggest that programs should be tested to ensure that they adhere to various programming standards: that they are modular, well-commented, free of nonstandard programming statements, etc. This is of increasing concern among organizations that are beginning to realize the magnitude of the maintenance effort.

7.5   Stages of Testing

7.5.1   The Need for Stages of Testing

All but the smallest computer programs are too complex to test in one fell swoop; if we are to have any chance of success, we must test the program in stages. Good planning is essential, too: Otherwise, the programmer often proceeds in a helter-skelter fashion, and things get overlooked in the rush. Dijkstra's famous comment about testing ("testing shows the presence, not the absence, of bugs") is relevant here. If we *don't* find some bugs in the testing of a large, complex program, there is a good chance that the test was too trivial.

"Trivial testing" is a real danger in many computer projects: It can often mean that a program or computer system is installed before it is actually ready. Given our propensity for underestimating the required time and resources for a computer project (a topic that is outside the realm of our discussion), it is not surprising to see project managers and programmers sacrifice the thoroughness of a testing plan in their rush to get the program implemented on schedule.

In addition, we should point out that good planning of the stages of testing is essential to properly prepare managers, users, computer operations personnel, and others for the rigors of the testing period.

It is interesting to note that there are basically two different approaches to this concept of "testing in stages": The classical strategy is often referred to as the bottom-up approach to testing, as contrasted with the relatively new approach of top-down testing. The classical bottom-up approach is discussed in Section 7.5.2, and top-down testing is discussed in Section 7.5.3.

7.5.2 Bottom-Up Testing

The classical form of testing has recently been given the name "bottom-up" testing, primarily to differentiate it from "top-down" testing which was discussed originally in Chapter 2. For anything other than a small program, the bottom-up approach normally requires three stages: module testing, subsystem testing, and system testing; a fourth stage of acceptance is often found in commercial applications.

Module Testing. Module testing is also referred to as "unit testing," "program testing," "single-thread testing," and a variety of other terms. Regardless of its name, though, it is considered the basic level of testing; as such, it usually involves the work of a single programmer for a period of time less than one month (and, according to some EDP organizations, sometimes as short as one or two days).

Module testing implies stand-alone testing, that is, it implies that the module can be tested without the presence of other modules in the system. However, in order to make the testing practical and simple, we may have a need for a test data base and various other elements of the environment within which the program will eventually reside. It is partly because of this that we have such great use for the automated testing techniques that are discussed in Section 7.7.

To make module testing successful (and especially to make subsequent testing easier), we should strive for *exhaustive* testing. Furthermore, we should be able to *demonstrate* that the testing has been exhaustive (one of life's greatest tragedies is the programmer who says, "Well, gee, *I thought* I had tested all of the cases . . . ."). Note that this is another argument for the automated testing packages discussed in Section 7.7. Note also that exhaustive module testing implies that the program has been designed to consist of small, functionally independent modules.

In the bottom-up testing approach, thorough and comprehensive module testing is the key to success. As a consequence of this, it seems that the EDP community is in desperate need of better statistics to help it organize its testing efforts more effectively. For example, it would be extremely useful to have statistics that would tell us the average number of test shots required for the average module (normalized, presumably, to some number of test shots per thousand instructions). Similarly, we need better statistics to tell us how much real time is likely to elapse before a module has been thoroughly tested (recall here the variation in debugging and testing time found in the classical Sackman study of programmers).

Subsystem Testing. This next level of testing attempts to test the interface between the various modules in the program. What we expect to find here is a collection of *logic* errors and *interface* errors, as opposed to the relatively trivial coding errors that should have been discovered at the module testing level. In a large, complex program or system, it is common to have many levels of subsystem testing, performed in a hierarchically upward direction.

It would be desirable to perform exhaustive testing at this level, but the chances are that it will be impossible. This is another area where we would like to be able to demonstrate the extent of our testing. The programmer should be able to announce to the world just how exhaustive his subsystem testing really is—and if it is not exhaustive, he should indicate just what portions of his program have been exercised. The fact that the programmer often does not even *know* which parts of his program have been exercised is still another reason for the automated testing techniques suggested in Section 7.8.

System Testing. Obviously, at this level, we test the entire system; we expect the most subtle errors to occur at this level—for instance, interface errors, complex control and logic errors, recovery errors, throughput and capacity errors, and timing errors.

It is extremely important to establish good criteria for the success of the system testing stage, that is, we need prior agreement as to the point at which system testing can cease. Some of the criteria we might establish are:

1. The number of transactions or test cases that have been successfully tested.
2. Number of hours of successful operation.
3. Percentage of modules, or source statements, that have been exercised.

As we noted above, better statistics are needed to help EDP organizations plan the length of time required for various stages of testing; the area of system testing seems to be consistently underestimated. It is commonly felt that system testing will consume 25–30% of the total project time of an ordinary computer project, and yet there are still a number of organizations that optimistically schedule a two-month system test period for a three-year project.

Acceptance Testing. The last stage of processing commonly found in the bottom-up progression of acceptance testing; in some organizations, it is also referred to as "field testing," "user testing," "parallel testing," or other names. Its purpose is clear: Having tested the entire system in a controlled environment (often with artificially prepared test data), there is a need to test the system in "live" conditions, and to compare its output with the output of the existing computer system or manual system.

Acceptance testing obviously requires good planning coordination and liaison with various types of people within the organization to be served by the new computer system—primarily users, management (data processing management, user management, and general management), and the computer operations staff. More than one computer project has been scrapped because the acceptance testing process so disrupted the work of the user departments that they ultimately decided that they would be better off without the new system.

Also, the acceptance testing stage should have enough slack time built into it so that problems can be corrected as they are discovered. That is, it is probably a bad idea to enter into an acceptance testing period that requires continuous processing on a 24-hour-a-day basis—after all, the programmers will desperately require second and third shift computer time to fix the errors that were discovered during the first shift.

7.5.3 Top-Down Testing

As discussed in Chapter 2, top-down testing suggests that we should provide the main program and perhaps one or two levels of subroutines as a *skeleton*, and test it by itself; obviously, this means that all or most of the lower-level modules are implemented as dummy routines. Having established that the skeleton works, we proceed to add one new low-level module at a time and test it by itself. This procedure is illustrated in Fig. 7.1.

We should emphasize that top-down testing is not to be regarded as an absolutely rigid approach. It is intended as a *philosophy*, and it can be (and should be) altered as the situation requires. In most straightforward program-

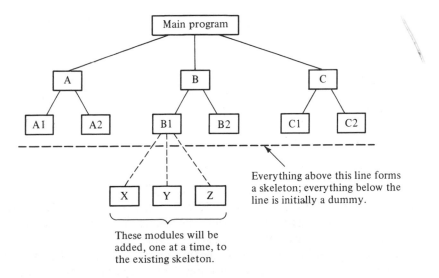

Figure 7.1. Top-down testing.

ming situations, the process shown in Fig. 7.1 can be followed without too much trouble; however, there are a number of difficult programming situations where some alteration to the strict top-down methodology is required.

It sometimes occurs, for example, that the idea of using dummy modules for the modules below the current level of testing cannot be used. Normally, the dummy modules will exit immediately without performing any real processing; alternatively, they may provide *constant* output or *random* output; in still other cases, it may be useful to have the dummy module print a message on an output file, so that the programmer will know that the module has been entered. However, there are some cases where the low-level dummy modules perform critical processing that is required for the testing of other high-level modules; examples of this are the READ and WRITE modules found in many programs.

There are several options in cases of this kind:

1. A few critical low-level modules can be designed, coded, and tested by themselves to facilitate the testing of the rest of the top-level structure of the program.

2. Some combination of top-down and bottom-up testing can be used.

3. A preliminary or primitive version of the low-level module can be implemented. In the case of a critical input/output module, for example, it may be appropriate to substitute a preliminary input/output module that performs basic IO without buffering, blocking, error-checking, optimization, or other advanced features. To the extent that those advanced features can be realized by low-level modules themselves, this idea still conforms to the basic philosophy of top-down testing.

4. Certain portions of a program may have to be tested completely before other parts, as illustrated in Fig. 7.2. Indeed, a certain amount of zigzag progress up and down the "tree structure" of the program may turn out to be the best way of testing.

It has been suggested by some programmers that a low-level module can, in some cases, determine the overall success of an entire program. If indeed this is the case, then an argument can be made for designing, coding, and testing the low-level module at the beginning of the project (or perhaps in parallel with the development of the rest of the program). Once having tested the critical low-level module, though, the rest of the testing process follows the top-down approach.

Other programmers have pointed out that a great deal of machine time might be saved if a module underwent module testing before it was inserted into the top-down structure. This would ensure that the more trivial coding errors were detected before the module was inserted into the skeleton of the program. This may indeed make sense; at the same time, it should be remembered that the existing skeleton of the program can provide an excellent environment or framework for performing the testing of the new module (in much the same sense as the test harness discussed in Section 7.8.3).

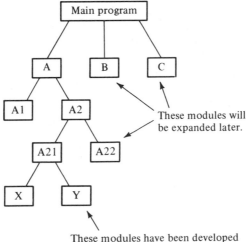

These modules will
be expanded later.

These modules have been developed
at an early stage because of some
practical considerations.

Figure 7.2. Variations in top-down testing.

This brings up another potential problem. In some cases, it may be difficult to provide adequate test data through the top-down process; this is illustrated in Fig. 7.3. A low-level module may have been specified in such a way that it is capable of receiving a wide range of inputs; for various reasons, it may be difficult to construct top-level inputs in such a way that the appropriate low-level inputs are provided to the module being tested. In a case of this nature, it would make more sense to perform extensive stand-alone testing to provide a comprehensive set of inputs to the module. It can then be inserted into the top-down structure to provide a test of the *interfaces* between the module and rest of the program.

Theoretically, module A1 should be tested by passing data from the top, e.g., from the main program to module A and from module A to module A1. However, it may be difficult to construct adequate test data that, after being transformed by module A, will constitute a sufficiently thorough test of module A1.

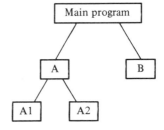

Figure 7.3. Difficulties with top-down testing.

Finally, it should be pointed out that top-down testing may not be critical for small programs, e.g., programs smaller than 500 source statements. In fact, it may be more trouble than it is worth. The same point can be made in the top-down testing of some systems. As shown in Fig. 7.4, it may be advisable to *completely* test smaller subsystems of a large complex system, and then to proceed with the top-down testing of the more complex subsystems.

Despite the qualifications above, the basic philosophy of top-down testing should remain valid. The advantages of such an approach can be summarized as follows:

1. With top-down testing, we are adding only one new piece of code at a time; if something goes wrong, the source and nature of the bug will usually be fairly obvious. With bottom-up testing, on the other hand, each new level of testing

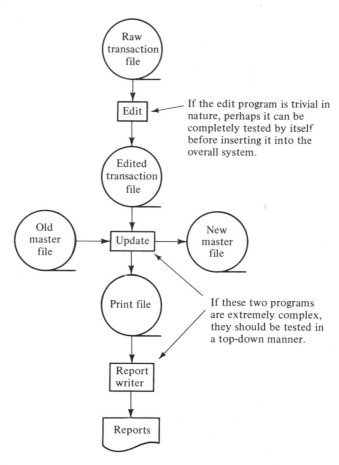

Figure 7.4. Combinations of top-down and bottom-up testing.

combines increasing numbers of modules, thereby making the *debugging* process (as opposed to the testing process) much more difficult.

2. With top-down testing, most major interface, control, and logic errors are discovered at the beginning of the testing process, and local coding errors are found at the end—instead of the other way around. In almost all cases, we would prefer to have some reassurance that the basic logic of the program is working and that the bugs that remain are merely trivial coding errors.

3. When top-down testing is combined with top-down design and top-down programming, a number of specification ambiguities and misunderstandings can be eliminated. We often find that this is the cause of many of our program bugs: Two different programmers have a different understanding of the meaning of an interface specification.

4. At a relatively early stage, a *working* program exists; despite the fact that many of its detailed features may not have been tested (or even implemented), the program can still be used, demonstrated to users, and experimented with. It is difficult to overestimate the psychological and political advantages of this approach when working on a large program that would otherwise require several months (or years) of testing with no tangible results.

It should be noted that many programmers have occasionally indulged in top-down testing without really knowing what they were doing. In many cases, the top-down testing approach is chosen out of desperation: The project is behind schedule, and the top-down approach seems to be the only way of producing a working (though incomplete) program. What we are suggesting in this section, though, is a formal, *conscious*, organized approach to top-down testing.

7.6 Designing Programs for Easier Testing

An important shift in the attitude toward computer testing seems to be taking place among many computer scientists. Many feel quite strongly that the best (and perhaps *only*) way of making testing thorough and yet economical is to design the program so that there will be no bugs in it. Actually, there are two points here. One of them is that, by the time we are actually ready to run a computer program, there should be essentially no bugs left in it, that is, most of the bugs should have been eliminated with preliminary desk-checking and visual examination of the code. More important, the design and coding approach should make it extremely difficult for bugs to creep into the code in the first place. The other point is that programs *will* have bugs in them, whether we like it or not, but our programs should be designed in such a way that the nature and source of the bugs will be immediately apparent and easily removable.

Many of the philosophies have already been stressed in earlier chapters of this book; nevertheless, it is useful to summarize them again within the context of our current discussion of testing.

7.6.1   Unambiguous Programming Languages

It has been suggested by some computer scientists that many of the most subtle and most frustrating bugs in computer programs could be eliminated by developing new programming languages (or modifying existing ones) whose syntax is more tightly defined, so that the programmer will have fewer opportunities to write something he didn't really mean. One example of this is the multitude of default options available to the programmer in PL/I. If the programmer does not explicitly declare the nature and usage of his variables, there is a nontrivial possibility that the compiler will assign a default declaration that will ultimately get the programmer into trouble. To a lesser extent, the same problem exists even in FORTRAN: Unless otherwise specified, a variable beginning with the character I, J, K, L, M, or N is assumed to be an integer.

In a completely different vein, many programmers have suggested that a number of common bugs would be eliminated if programming languages included primitive statements to implement common coding operations. To add 1 to an integer variable, for example, usually involves a statement of the form

```
I = I + 1
```

in many programming languages. A keypunching error can quite easily transform the above statement into

```
I = I + I
```

or

```
I = 1 + 1
```

both of which are syntactically correct. What makes this situation dangerous is the ease with which a programmer can overlook such a keypunching error when examining his program listing. The situation could be remedied if the programming language included a statement such as

```
BUMP  I
```

or

```
ADDONETO  I
```

While proposals of this nature are interesting and somewhat thought-provoking, they unfortunately have little relevance for the average programmer. The development of new programming languages, or modifications to existing ones, seems to be a task left to the various standards committees.

On the other hand, some data processing organizations have approached the same problem in a different way: Recognizing that some language features are ambiguous or error-prone, they have simply developed *standards* to prevent their programmers from using them. For example, many COBOL organizations forbid the use of compound Boolean expressions, so that they will not have to deal with statements of the type

IF A AND B EQUALS C OR NOT D MOVE X TO Y.

whose meaning is ambiguous to the human reader, even if it is intelligible to the COBOL compiler.

7.6.2 Antibugging as a Programming Style

This philosophy was the subject of Chapter 6. To summarize that chapter: Within your module, you should assume that everything that can possibly go wrong *will* go wrong. To paraphrase one of Murphy's laws: Even if *nothing* could possibly go wrong, something inevitably will. You should take this into account when you write your program: Be suspicious of everyone and everybody—in this fashion, when the bugs *do* occur, they will be easier to locate and remove.

Specifically, we suggested that your program should check all input from the outside world (from cards, tape, terminals, etc.), all calls from other modules (this is especially important), records read from a data base or file, input from the computer operator, and so forth. Obviously, one could spend an infinite amount of time checking for these possible errors, and that is not the objective. What we are suggesting is that you do a *reasonable* amount of checking for these potential sources of bugs.

Chapter 6 also suggested some programming practices to help reduce the number of residual bugs in a computer program. It is suggested, for example, that all cases of a branch be tested, i.e., a none-of-the-above action should be added to all decisions. Similarly, it was suggested that programs with large numbers of flags are often error-prone; this is especially true if the flags are set, reset, and tested in a random fashion throughout the program. What we are primarily concerned about here is that a large number of combinations or permutations of flags may be meaningless, and if they occur (because of a bug at some point in the program) the behavior of the program may be unpredictable.

7.6.3 Structured Programming

Structured programming was the subject of a lengthy discussion in Chapter 4, and the basic concepts need not be repeated here. It is important to emphasize again, though, that one of the major objectives of structured programming has been to sharply reduce design errors and coding errors by *forcing* the programmer to develop his program as a series of black boxes.

7.6.4 Team Programming

This idea is strongly suggested by Weinberg's "egoless" programming ideas in *The Psychology of Computer Programming* [11]. The idea itself is not very new (it was once a rather standard form of programming) but it does not seem to be very common in most large data processing organizations. The basic idea is to encourage each programmer to present his program design and his coding to *everyone* on his project team for their review and criticism. Note the difference between this approach and the more conventional idea of showing the design and the coding to just *one* person—typically the project leader or the systems analyst. In the team approach, the entire team is expected to be familiar with, and exposed to, the design and code within everyone's modules. As practiced in some organizations, the idea is carried even further by making it clear that the responsibility for success (or failure) of the entire system is with the *group*; consequently, the responsibility for success of each module rests with the group as a whole—not just with the individual programmer who designed and/or coded the module.

The original motivation for team programming—as suggested by Weinberg, and as practiced by IBM in the classic *New York Times* project [9]—was to remove bugs and subject all of the code to close scrutiny before it was ever put into the machine. The hope was that system testing would be virtually eliminated, and that the number of residual bugs would be much smaller than with the conventional approach. All of this *did* happen; in addition, though, it seemed to increase the productivity of the programmer tremendously.

Though it definitely has great promise as an adjunct to other testing techniques, there are apparently some potential psychological problems associated with the intense group scrutiny of an individual's design and coding. Many have compared this approach to the "sensitivity groups" or "T-groups" that were popular in the 1960s. As with the sensitivity groups, there is a danger that excessive destructive criticism from the group may destroy the initiative of those programmers who lack sufficient self-confidence.

7.7 Automated Testing Techniques

As we saw in the previous section, many computer scientists are beginning to feel quite strongly that the best way of eliminating bugs from a program is by not allowing them to enter the program in the first place. Some have even remarked that a number of popular testing aids exist only to compensate for programming techniques that will ultimately be regarded as obsolete. If only this were true!

Unfortunately, it does not seem likely that we will achieve this ideal objective of bug-free code; as a result, we will be forced to rely on classical testing aids and packages for at least the next few years, if not forever. On the other hand, it *is* possible to improve the process by which the programmer creates test data, feeds it into his program, and verifies the output from the test run—and that is the subject of this section.

The basic philosophy of this section is that as much testing as possible should be taken out of human hands. Perhaps the most important argument for this automated testing is that *manual* error-checking is itself an error-prone process. The major problem is that erroneous test output is likely to be overlooked as the programmer glances through reams and reams of output; it is also possible, of course, that some output may be interpreted as erroneous when in fact it is not. Another problem often occurs in testing: The programmer is often psychologically inclined to justify his output as being correct; we will make use of this problem below.

There is yet another problem with which to be concerned: Manual testing is considerably slower and more tedious than the automated techniques we will discuss below. As a result, the *volume* of testing is often insufficient; the programmer manually constructs some test input and test files, manually examines the output from the test, and after a while, he gets tired of the work involved. The usual consequence of this is an incompletely tested program.

Instead of manual testing, we propose here the use of several testing packages that will, to a large extent, automate and mechanize the testing process. Several individual packages are discussed below.

7.7.1 Automated Generation of Test Data

The primary objective of this technique is to help generate large volumes of test data in a relatively mechanical fashion. Before discussing the technique in detail, we should emphasize one point very strongly. *Volume is not the only criterion for good testing—indeed, it is likely to be somewhat dangerous.* What we are interested in is the *minimum* volume of test data that will adequately exercise our program; unfortunately, even this minimum volume is often beyond the means of manual construction.

We are therefore interested in a test-data generator (often abbreviated as TDG) that would allow us to specify formats and ranges of legal inputs and have the TDG generate large volumes of it. Since an enormous number of *possible* test inputs can usually be generated by the TDG, we often need some way of choosing a reasonable "sample" of input; this is often done by allowing the TDG to generate *random* test cases (within some range of values), or by selecting test cases at equal intervals through the range of possible values.

One of the most common problems in this area is that the program's behavior is often a function of the *sequence* of test inputs. Although the form of an individual test input may be relatively simple, the relationship between different test cases may be enormously complex. Similarly, some programs require *several* different input parameters, and it may be rather difficult to generate reasonable *sets* of test cases. Suppose, for example, we have a program that performs some relatively complex processing when given fifty different input parameters. The relationship between each of the fifty input parameters is likely to be rather complex, and it may not be meaningful to have a TDG generating sets of fifty random numbers.

A similar situation exists in the generation of test *files*; we usually require a nontrivial set of records and files in order to properly test a large program. It is often awkward to generate these test files by hand, and for various reasons, it may not be possible to develop a "live" test file. On the other hand, one of the most common techniques for generating a test file is to select a small subset of records from an *existing* file (this is often done in commercial systems when a new system is being designed to replace an existing manual or computer system).

The problem of generating test files is similar to the problem of generating ordinary test input into a program: It is often very difficult to set up complex data bases. Not only do we have to worry about generating a reasonable number of permutations and combinations of individual records (each of which presumably consists of several fields that can have a variety of

Table 7.1. SOME COMMON TEST-DATA GENERATORS

Package Name	Source
PRO/TEST	Synergetics Corporation
	One Garfield Circle
	Burlington, Massachusetts 01803
DATAMACS	Management and Computer Services, Inc.
	104 Park Towne Place East
	Philadelphia, Pennsylvania 19130
IMI/TDG-II	Information Management Inc.
	447 Battery Street
	San Francisco, California 94111
TESTPAK	Computer Methods Corp.
	470 Mamaroneck Avenue
	White Plains, New York 10605
TEST MASTER	Hoskyns Systems Research, Inc.
	600 Third Avenue
	New York, New York 10016
FILEMAKE	Synergistic Software Systems
	P.O. Box 36097
	Houston, Texas 77036
TESTGEN	Interface, Inc.
	330 Municipal Court Building
	Ann Arbor, Michigan 48108

values), but we also have to worry about meaningful *combinations* of records within a file, and possibly combinations of files within a large data base.

It should be noted that a number of software companies provide test-data generators on a commercial basis. For obvious reasons, the majority of them are oriented towards COBOL and are often implemented on IBM System/360 and System/370 hardware. Table 7.1 lists some of the more common test-data generators.

7.7.2 Automated Output Checker

The motivation for this testing package comes from a basic principle of testing: *Whenever you perform a test, you should always know what output you expect to see.* As mentioned earlier, programmers often have a subtle and unconscious inclination to find a justification or an explanation for their program's behavior (e.g., "Well, I didn't really know what kind of output I would get, but that output doesn't look terribly unreasonable."). This kind of attitude can easily lead to bugs being overlooked.

In many cases, this verification process must be done in a semimanual fashion, that is, for test input A, we manually determine (*in advance*) that the output should be X; for test input B, we manually determine that the output should be Y; and so forth. At this point, we can easily write a program that will automatically compare *anticipated* output (stored on a file) with *actual* output and list any discrepancies. This process is illustrated in Fig. 7.5.

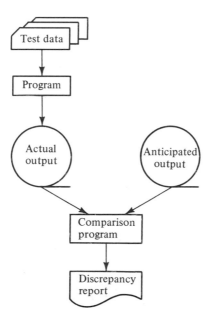

Figure 7.5. Automated output checks.

Obviously, it is only useful to have a program of this nature if we are working with fairly large volumes of test input—but in such a case, it is clear that we are saving an enormous amount of tedious and error-prone manual checking.

Sometimes we can mechanize the process of determining the expected output; if this is possible, the process of verifying the correctness of actual output can also be automated. Consider, for example, the job of testing a square-root routine; we can easily take advantage of the fact that

SQRT(X*X) = X

and

(SQRT(X))**2 = X

for any value of X. While this idea is quite straightforward (ignoring the problem of truncation and round-off problems, which in the above example may *not* be completely trivial!) and quite useful for some scientific applications, it rarely seems applicable for commercial systems. On the other hand, it can occasionally be useful for individual *modules* of a commercial application (e.g., checking the output from a module responsible for calculating interest charges on bank overdrafts, or checking the output from a module responsible for calculating withholding tax in a payroll system).

7.7.3 Automated Test Harness

A package of this type is also referred to by some as a "test monitor." The function of a test harness is shown in Fig. 7.6. Basically, it acts as a "main program": It collects test input (possibly from a program that is capable of generating it automatically), passes it to the program being tested, captures the output, prints it out, and possibly helps check that the output is correct. To some extent, a test harness can thus be combined with the idea of a test-data generator discussed above; it can also be combined with the idea of checking the correctness of test output. More important, it can be generalized that all of the programmers working on a project should be able to use

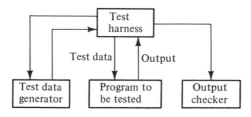

Figure 7.6. Automated test harness.

the same test harness for testing individual modules. To some extent, this should also be possible for subsystem testing as well.

7.7.4 Automated Retesting

As mentioned earlier in this chapter, studies have shown that the chances of correctly modifying a program (on the first attempt) are generally less than 50%. It is therefore usually a good idea to subject a modified program to a thorough retesting—even if it seems like an innocently small change; this is especially important once the program has entered the maintenance phase.

The basic concept of retesting is illustrated in Fig. 7.7. We begin by performing a test run, verifying the correctness of its output, and saving the output on a file. Any retest can then take the same input, perform the same processing, and hopefully generate the same output. The output can then be compared against the output file from the first test run, and any discrepancies can be listed.

In some cases, we may be making substantial changes to an existing program (possibly to fix a major bug). In such a case, it is expected that the output from a subsequent test run may be *significantly* different from the

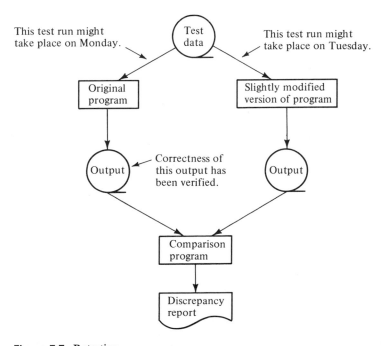

Figure 7.7. Retesting.

previous test run. Rather than allowing the retesting program to produce a massive discrepancy report, it may be possible to provide it with control information indicating which output fields are expected to be different.

A more difficult problem can occur with the testing of real-time programs. Because of timing differences, the same sequence of test inputs may generate two entirely different output files. However, it may be possible to select some test inputs whose processing is time-independent. It may also be possible to select a set of test inputs whose cumulative effect is independent of the sequence in which they were processed. While neither of these approaches could be considered a complete test of a real-time program, they may still be helpful.

7.7.5 Automated Testing Monitors

The primary idea here is to intercept the execution of each statement in a program and record the fact that it has been executed. When the program finishes, the test monitor prints a report showing which portions of the program have been exercised by the test data. The test monitor itself is a separate program that can be written in any convenient language. However, it usually requires that the problem program be executed interpretively; alternatively, a special compilation option (as in the PL/I Checkout Compiler provided by IBM) may cause extra machine instructions to be inserted with the object code generated for each high-level language statement—the effect of the extra instructions being to branch into the test monitor. As still another alternative, it would be possible for a preprocessor to insert the appropriate instructions into the source program prior to its assembly or compilation.

After the program has finished its execution, the test monitor can report any of the following types of information:

1. Modules that have been exercised (this would be especially useful for system testing).
2. Entry points to a subroutine that have been exercised.
3. IF statements that have been exercised.
4. All of the statements or instructions within a module that have been exercised.

Note that this is a good management control tool; we now have a way of seeing just how complete and thorough the programmer's test cases are. In addition, it can help us save machine time by selecting a smaller set of test inputs that will test (or exercise) the maximum proportion of coding within the program.

7.8 Other Testing Techniques

There are a variety of other techniques that are used in the field of computer testing; while many of them are not in common usage, they still deserve to be mentioned briefly. Some of the testing techniques discussed below are still experimental and require some validation and/or further research. Other techniques are relevant only for very large systems or systems with extremely high software reliability requirements (e.g., the category referred to as "utterly absurd" earlier in this chapter). Nevertheless, some of these techniques may ultimately be useful and practical for ordinary systems at some point in the future.

7.8.1 Redundant Programming

The basic idea here is to have two (or more) independently written programs for a particular application. Each version of the program would be designed, coded, and tested by separate teams who would presumably share nothing other than the original specifications.

While the concept of redundant programming may seem quite extravagant, it can be compared with the idea of providing two or more processors to guard against hardware failures. There is an interesting analogy to be drawn here: Some systems use *duplexed* CPUs, with a backup CPU used for other work unless the primary system has a failure. Other systems use *dual* CPUs, with each CPU performing the same processing and checking answers with each other. The same idea could be extended to software redundancy; despite its obvious expense, it may be justified in some cases.

7.8.2 Standardization

This is a rather obvious suggestion: Testing problems are reduced by using general-purpose subroutines and packages. Even if the general-purpose programs have some bugs, their behavior is usually predictable and known, which is usually better than living with a special-purpose program containing unknown bugs.

There is a practical disadvantage to general-purpose programs—the *large* generalized programs (vendor-supplied data-base management programs, statistical packages, order-entry systems, payroll packages, etc.) often have a large number of bugs and require continuing maintenance and development. A small, special-purpose program, on the other hand, might have fewer bugs to begin with. It is often interesting to make a distinction between a "living" system (one that requires continuing modification and improvements), and a "static" system (one whose only modifications are to remove existing bugs); we would generally expect the static system to have far fewer "crashes."

7.8.3 Simulation

In the development of large complex computer systems, it is common to see the use of *analytical* simulation. Such simulation, involving the development of *models* of a computer system prior to its actual implementation, can be extremely useful for testing throughput and capacity errors. In a few cases, it can also help discover major logic errors as well, but it certainly will not help find coding errors.

We might also mention the existence of operational simulation, where dummy inputs are used to exercise a *real* program or system. This type of simulation is quite common for large, real-time systems, especially within military and space applications. Though it is obviously quite expensive (often far more than the cost of designing and coding the operational software), there are situations where there may not be any other effective way of testing a computerized air defense system.

7.8.4   Mathematical Models of Program Reliability

The requirements of software reliability in the more complex computer systems (e.g., the air defense systems mentioned above) have recently led to a great deal of research in the development of mathematical *models* of program reliability. By gathering statistics during the testing process, the model attempts to predict, in a probabilistic sense:

1. The number of bugs remaining in the program when it is put into production.
2. The Mean Time Between Failures of the *software*.
3. The probability that the program (or software system) will run successfully for a specified period of time.

The concept of mathematical models of software reliability has been used rather successfully within the NASA space project and in one or two American defense projects. However, it must still be considered in its infancy. Many of the mathematical results are based on some rather simplistic assumptions (such as the assumption that, when a bug is found, the correction process does not introduce any new bugs). Nevertheless, there is some hope that it could be applied to "ordinary" systems in a few years; some discussion of this development is contained in Shooman's paper [5] and in recent proceedings of the IEEE Symposia on Software Reliability.

REFERENCES

1. B. RANDELL and J. N. BUXTON, *Software Engineering Techniques*, NATO Scientific Affairs Division, Brussels 39, Belgium, 1970.

2. B. BOEHM, "Software and Its Impact: A Quantitative Study," *Datamation*, May 1973.

3. E. YOURDON, *Design of On-Line Computer Systems*, Prentice-Hall, Inc., 1972.

4. ——, "Reliability of Real-Time Computer Systems," *Modern Data*, January–June 1972.

5. M. L. Shooman, J. C. Dickson, J. L. Hesse, and A. C. Kientz, "Quantitative Analysis of Software Reliability," *IEEE Symposium on Software Reliability*, January 1972.

6. H. Sackman, W. J. Erickson, and E. E. Grant, "Exploratory Studies Comparing Online and Offline Programming Performance," *Communications of the ACM*, January 1968, pages 3–11.

7. B. Boehm, "Some Information Processing Implications of Air Force Space Missions in the 1980's," *Astronautics and Aeronautics*, January 1971, pages 42–50.

8. "That Maintenance Iceberg," *EDP Analyzer*, October 1972.

9. F. T. Baker, "Chief Programmer Team Approach to Production Programming," *IBM Systems Journal*, January 1972.

10. W. C. Hetzel. (ed.), *Program Test Methods*, Prentice-Hall, Inc., 1973.

11. G. Weinberg, *The Psychology of Computer Programming*, D. Van Nostrand Company, Inc., 1971.

PROBLEMS

1. Give a brief definition of (a) a module, (b) a program, (c) a subsystem, and (d) a system.

2. Give a definition of the term "software reliability." Is it a meaningful phrase in the context of the projects you are accustomed to working on?

3. Give a definition of (a) a bug and (b) a glitch. Do you think the other programmers in your organization agree with your definitions? What is the difference between a bug and a glitch? Do you think that users and management agree with you?

4. Give a definition of "testing." What is the purpose of testing a computer program?

5. Give a brief definition of (a) validation, (b) verification, and (c) certification. Are these terms meaningful in your organization? Are they used frequently?

6. Give a definition of "debugging." What is the difference between testing and debugging? Do you think that the two terms are commonly confused by many programmers? Do you think it matters?

7. Give a brief definition of "maintenance." What is the difference between the different kind of activities that usually take place under the general heading of "maintenance"?

8. If you are using a standard vendor-supplied operating system, try to gather some statistics on the number of failures that it has contained during the last several releases. This information might be available from the vendor, from user groups, or from your computer operations department. Can you find any discernible pattern, i.e., are the number of bugs increasing, decreasing, or remaining constant? Divide the number of bugs by the number of instructions in the operating system; do you think this "bugs-per-instruction" figure is substantially higher than for the application programs you normally work on?

9. Gather some statistics concerning the amount of time spent on testing in several projects in your organization. Is it ever less than 30%? If so, do the programs seem to cause much trouble when they enter the maintenance phase? Do you find any significant correlations worthy of mention, e.g.,
   (a) between testing time and design time?
   (b) between testing time and the size of the programs?
   (c) between testing time and the experience of the programmers?
   (d) between testing time and the programming language used?
   Do you find that the amount of test time fluctuates from one project to another, or does it remain relatively constant?

10. How much of your organization's EDP budget is spent on maintenance? Is your management aware of this? Do you think much of the maintenance could be eliminated by more thorough testing?

11. Give an example of a simple program, as defined in Section 7.3.1. Are such programs common in your organization?

12. Give an example of a medium-complexity program, as defined in Section 7.3.2. Are such programs common in your organization? Do you know of any projects of this size that have been cancelled or scrapped because of testing difficulties?

13. Give an example of a complex program, as defined in Section 7.3.3. Are such programs common in your organization? Give an example of a complex program that had to be scrapped because of testing difficulties. What, in your opinion, was the fundamental problem with the project: poor design or poor testing? How could the problem have been overcome?

14. Give an example of a nearly impossible program, as defined in Section 7.3.4. Have any such programs been developed by your organization? What is the ratio of successful projects to unsuccessful projects?

15. Give an example of an utterly absurd program, as defined in Section 7.3.5. Have you ever worked on such a program? Do you know of any that have succeeded, that is, projects that did what they were supposed to do, on time, within budget, and with a reasonable degree of elegance in design?

16. Give an example of a logic error that could be exposed by testing. What proportion of all bugs do you think are logic errors?

17. Give an example of a documentation error, as discussed in Section 7.4.2. How serious do you think documentation errors are? Are they checked for in the testing procedures used in your organization?

18. Give an example of an overload error, as discussed in Section 7.4.3. Do you think this type of error is common? How can we test for such an error?

19. Give an example of a timing error, as discussed in Section 7.4.4. Do such errors ever exist in ordinary batch application programs? What proportion of the bugs in a real-time program do you think are likely to be timing errors? How can we test for timing errors?

20. Give an example of throughput and capacity errors, as discussed in Section 7.4.5. Can such errors exist in batch application programs, or are they relevant only for systems programs? How can we test for these errors? *Does* anyone test for overload errors in your organization?

21. Give an example of a fallback and recovery error, as discussed in Section 7.4.6. How can we test for such errors? Do you think this is an important area?

22. Give an example of hardware errors and system software errors, as discussed in Section 7.4.7. Do you think it is reasonable to test for such errors? How much time should be spent in such testing? How should it be done?

23. Give an example of a standards error, as discussed in Section 7.4.8. Do you think it is important to test for such errors? Is it done in your organization? How should one go about testing for standards errors? Should it be done manually?

24. Why is it important to test a program in stages? Do you think it is really necessary for simple programs? How should we determine whether a program really has to be tested in a formal fashion?

25. Give a definition of module testing. What are some of its synonyms? Why is it important that module testing be accomplished thoroughly and comprehensively? How can we ensure that this has been done?

26. Does your organization have any statistics indicating the average number of test shots required by a programmer to test individual modules? If such statistics do *not* exist, do you think the programmers would object to attempts at gathering the statistics? If so, why?

27. Give a definition of subsystem testing, as discussed in Section 7.5.2. Do the projects in your organization undergo a formal stage of subsystem testing? Do you require more than one such stage? How is this determined?

28. Define system testing. How can we tell when enough preliminary testing has been done to warrant the beginning of a system test? How do we know when to stop system testing? How much time in your project is normally spent on system testing?

29. Give a definition of acceptance testing. Does it have any other synonyms in your organization? Who controls the acceptance testing? Who develops the test data to be used in acceptance testing? Who determines when the acceptance testing will end? Do all of the projects in your organization require a formal acceptance test?

30. Give a definition of top-down testing. Why is it different from bottom-up testing? What are the advantages of top-down testing?

31. Give an example of a difficulty that can be caused by the default options that

are found in such programming languages as FORTRAN and PL/I. Have you ever experienced such difficulties in your own programs? What can be done to eliminate such problems?

32. Section 7.6.1 discusses a number of ambiguous programming situations. Give an example of such a situation in your own programming language. Can you think of any way in which it can be avoided?

33. Does your organization normally allow projects to be undertaken by the type of programming teams discussed in Section 7.6.4? Has it reduced the testing time significantly? Has it caused any other problems?

34. What is the overall objective of the automated testing techniques discussed in Section 7.7? Do you think those objectives are valid? What are the dangers of manual testing?

35. Give an example of a program that could be tested more easily with the test-data generator discussed in Section 7.7.1. Does your organization use any such generator? Is *everyone* required to use it?

36. Give an example of a program whose testing would *not* be greatly simplified by a test-data generator. Do you think such programs are common?

37. As a research project, investigate the test-data generators listed in Table 7.1. What are their advantages and disadvantages? Which one would you recommend to your organization?

38. Give an example of a program whose testing would be simplified by the use of an automated output checker, as discussed in Section 7.7.2. What is the major objective of such a package? Do you think it could be used for most of the programming projects in your organization?

39. Give an example of a program that could not be tested easily with the automated output checker. Do you think this is a common situation?

40. Give an example of a program whose testing would be simplified by the use of a test harness, discussed in Section 7.7.3. Does your organization use such a test harness? Is *everyone* required to use it? What implications does the use of a test harness have for bottom-up testing or top-down testing? Do you think this is significant?

41. What is the objective of the retesting concept discussed in Section 7.7.4? Do you think it is a valid concept? Do you think a general-purpose retesting package could be developed for use by everyone in your organization? If not, why not?

42. What is the objective of the automated testing monitor discussed in Section 7.7.5? Do you think it is a valid objective? Do you think such a package could be developed for general use in your organization?

43. What is the purpose of redundant programming? Are any of the projects in your organization developed in this manner? Do you think there might be some economic justification for such an approach to programming?

8

DEBUGGING
CONCEPTS
AND TECHNIQUES

8.0 Introduction

As we pointed out in the previous chapter, *testing* is an organized procedure that attempts to expose the presence of errors in a computer program. It is a tedious, difficult, and often unrewarding task; few programmers enjoy it, and even fewer have a natural talent for it.

This chapter discusses an activity that closely parallels testing, and one that is often mistaken for it: *debugging*. Debugging is an art: the art of finding the nature and location of an error once its existence has been established. While organized procedures and mechanical aids (e.g., memory dumps) have an important place in the debugging process, a good programmer usually finds a difficult bug through something akin to divine inspiration. As with testing, debugging is not an activity relished by the average programmer; in fact, it is usually considered the most frustrating and nerve-wracking aspect of writing a program. Most programmers do not have a talent for debugging; in most cases, they try to overwhelm a program bug with massive doses of core dumps, traces, and other brute-force approaches.

Our purpose in this chapter is twofold. First, we will examine some of the strategies and philosophies used by those who approach debugging as an art. Some strategies will involve the use of a computer, but many do not. Second, we will discuss a number of debugging packages that have traditionally been used to locate bugs in a computer program. After an explanation of some classical techniques (dumps, traces, etc.), we will concentrate our attention on a terminal-oriented package known as DDT.

It should be emphasized that a well-written program will minimize the need for the debugging techniques presented in this chapter. In Chapter 1, for example, we discussed a number of suggestions for reducing the difficulty of debugging; a review of Section 1.2 might be appropriate at this time. Chapters 3 and 4 suggested a number of techniques for writing modular programs; it was argued that, among other things, a modular program is easier to debug than an unmodular one. Chapter 5 pointed out that a simple, easy-to-understand program would be debugged much more easily than one in which the programmer went out of his way to use clever, sophisticated programming tricks. Finally, Chapter 6 discussed the idea of antibugging, that is, putting a sufficient number of error-checks into a program to catch all but the most subtle and elusive of bugs.

Even with all of these suggestions, bugs will inevitably occur in the most carefully written program; no programmer is perfect. Perhaps the best we can hope for is that our bugs (or *mistakes*, as M. E. Hopkins calls them) will be easy to find. It is with this in mind that we present the debugging techniques in the sections to follow.

8.1 Debugging Philosophies and Strategies

To many junior programmers, debugging is synonymous with core dumps, snapshots, and traces; indeed, core dumps and traces are sufficiently awkward and unintelligible on many machines that the programmer sometimes thinks of them as an end unto themselves. More than one programmer has probably muttered to himself, "If only I knew how to use that COBOL DEBUG packet properly—then I would never have any problems debugging my programs. . . ." In fact, it is not at all unusual for him to fall under this illusion by reading the chapter on debugging in his COBOL manual.

The more experienced programmer (as well as a few junior programmers who have a natural talent for such things) know that there is more to debugging a program than dumping memory. Tracking down a program bug is much like tracking down the murderer in an Agatha Christie mystery: Where massive manhunts and brute-force techniques of the local police force fail, the hero, M. Hercule Poirot, succeeds by employing the "little gray cells."

The same is generally true of computer programs. The simple, obvious bugs can be found with snapshots and traces, *but they can usually be found just as easily (and with a very noticeable savings in machine time) with a little bit of organized thinking*. The truly difficult bugs, e.g., the ones found in very large batch systems and in on-line, real-time systems, can often be found *only* with the use of some of the non-computer-oriented approaches suggested in this section. To paraphrase the method used in the detective stories, we must understand the "psychology" of the bug—and of the programmer who introduced the bug into the program. Mr. Hopkins' remark is particularly apt: A bug *is* a mistake, and if we know a little more about the kind of mistakes we make, we will be able to find them and correct them a little more easily (and possibly even prevent them from occurring in the future!).

With these thoughts in mind, we will discuss a number of strategies for finding bugs in a computer program.

8.1.1 Write Small Modules

One of the easiest ways of debugging a program is to break it into small modules. Though we lack detailed figures to support the claim, it seems that the number and subtlety of bugs increases exponentially with the number of instructions in the module; thus, by keeping modules small, we make it easier to find the bugs.

Obviously, by making the modules (or subroutines, or paragraphs of a COBOL program, etc.) small, we will usually increase the number of modules in the program. As the number of modules increases, and as the interrelationship between the modules grows more complex, we can expect more bugs in the program. However, if the program is developed in a hierarchical fashion, as described in Chapter 2, it should be possible to keep the number of interactions between modules from getting out of hand.

If a program requires 100 instructions to accomplish its purpose, it could be written as one module (or main program) consisting of 100 statements; at the other extreme, it could be written as 100 modules, each consisting of 1 statement (with some additional statements for subroutine linkage, etc.). Both extremes are bad, and it is difficult to tell which situation would be more difficult to debug. If indeed the number of bugs is an exponential function of the number of instructions in a module and the number of modules in a program, then perhaps we would minimize the number of bugs by having ten modules with ten statements each. In practice, it seems best to keep reducing the size of a module (thereby increasing the number of modules in the program) until it no longer makes any sense to make them smaller.

8.1.2 Try to Determine the Nature of the Error

Chapter 7 discussed several types of errors that could be found in a computer program. If the testing activity is done with sufficient care, it may be possible to isolate the general cause of the problem even before the programmer begins searching for the specific nature of the bug. Thus, before even beginning to find a bug, you should try to determine whether you are searching for a hardware bug, an operating system bug, a compiler error, or a bug in your own program. If a bug does appear to be in your own code, which module (or group of modules) seems to be the culprit?

PAGE 001			SALES DISTRICT 001
SALESMAN	SALES THIS MONTH	YEAR-TO-DATE	THIS MONTH LAST YEAR
BROWN	2000	6387	1998
CANNING	1720	5291	840
DENNIS	1909	6066	1837
YOUNG	1675	4280	1500
ZIMMERMAN	2100	8200	2025
TOTAL	600	423	68234

PAGE 002			SALES DISTRICT 002
SALESMAN	SALES THIS MONTH	YEAR-TO-DATE	THIS MONTH LAST YEAR
ANDERSON	2288	7254	1904
BENNET	1803	6377	1776
WATSON	1313	6281	1505
WILSON	1838	5530	1700
TOTAL	209	156	75236

Figure 8.1. Output from a sample computer program.

As an example, consider the sample output report shown in Fig. 8.1; the subtotals for each sales district are apparently consistently incorrect. Since all of the figures for individual salesmen seem to be reasonable (though there is no guarantee that they are correct), it would appear that the problem must be in the portion of the program that computes the district totals, or possibly in the subroutine that prints the totals. While it is remotely possible that the incorrect figures were due to a hardware error or some other obscure cause, it does not seem reasonable to consider them unless an investigation of the program logic proves fruitless.

Now imagine that only *one* of the district totals is incorrect, while, as show in Fig. 8.2, the remaining district totals are correct. In this case, it is still likely that the error was caused by a bug in the program logic; the nature of the individual sales reports within the district should give the programmer a clue. However, it may be worth asking a few other pertinent questions before the investigation begins in earnest (especially if it seems to be a difficult and subtle bug):

1. Could something be wrong with the high-speed printer?
2. Could the problem have been caused by an unusual error in the input cards or the master file?

PAGE 001			SALES DISTRICT 001
SALESMAN	SALES THIS MONTH	YEAR-TO-DATE	THIS MONTH LAST YEAR
BROWN	2000	6387	1998
CANNING	1720	5291	840
DENNIS	1909	6066	1837

YOUNG	1675	4280	1500
ZIMMERMAN	2100	8200	2025
TOTAL	62108	157613	57846

These figures are correct.

PAGE 046			SALES DISTRICT 042
SALESMAN	SALES THIS MONTH	YEAR-TO-DATE	THIS MONTH LAST YEAR
ABRAMS	1736	5319	1409
EDWARDS	2066	5805	1892

SMITH	1543	4212	1680
THOMPSON	2248	7227	2071
TOTAL	413	63	153814

These figures are incorrect.

Figure 8.2. A more difficult programming bug.

3. Did the computer operator notice anything unusual about the program as it executed? Does he ever notice unusual things?

4. Is the program running in the same environment as the last time it executed? That is, has the source program been recompiled or has a new operating system been generated? Could this be an explanation of the problem?

5. Has the hardware been misbehaving lately? Is it possible that there could have been a transient error in the arithmetic instructions?

In a large program (or programming system), it is not always easy to determine the nature of the error; as we pointed out in Chapter 6, an error may spread like a cancer. Also, many of the more difficult errors seem to occur at the interface between several parts of the system. On many on-line systems, for example, the programmer often has an extremely difficult time determining whether the error was caused by the user, the terminal, the communication line, the multiplexer, the computer hardware, the vendor's system software (e.g., the operating system), or his own program.

Even in such a difficult situation, it is possible to make some progress by *excluding unlikely sources of the error*. If the problem was caused by a program bug, which parts of the program can be excluded? Which parts of the hardware can be ruled out as a possible source of trouble? Except in the most difficult of situations, it is possible to narrow the field down to two or three likely candidates, and the investigation can proceed from there.

This is one of the many aspects of debugging that can be properly thought of as an *art*; some people are good at it, and some are not. However, it is also a technique that can be practiced; though you may never have a sixth sense that enables you to sniff out a bug like a bloodhound, you should be able to improve upon the random attack that many programmers make upon errors in their programs.

8.1.3 See If the Bug Is Repeatable and Consistent

Unless the bug appears to be a fairly simple one, it is a good idea to see if it is consistent and repeatable. For the bug shown in Fig. 8.1, it is probably unnecessary to reexecute the program: The nature of the bug seems to indicate that it is fairly consistent. However, the error shown in Fig. 8.2 is not quite so obvious—only one of the sales district totals is incorrect. If the error is the result of a program bug, and if it can be found easily, so much the better. On the other hand, if a diligent inspection of the program fails to uncover the bug, then it may be worth rerunning the program to make sure that the bug really exists.

There are several possible reasons why the error may *not* be repeatable:

1. The operator may have done something that caused the machine and/or the program to malfunction. He may, for example, have jostled the card reader, the high-speed printer, or the magnetic tape drive, thereby causing a one-time error (which may have been undetected by the system or ignored by the operator). Similarly, the program may have required some communication from the operator, and he may have typed the wrong input at the console typewriter (this error should be detected without rerunning the program!).

2. The program in question may be running in a real-time environment and may have become involved in what is often called a "timing error," that is, the error may have occurred because two programs attempted to update the same data-base record at the same time, or because one program unexpectedly interrupted another program and destroyed its working storage. Even if the program itself is not a real-time program, it is usually running under the control of a vendor-supplied multiprogramming operating system; it is possible for a timing error in the operating system to result in an apparent error in an innocent application program.

3. The computer hardware may suffer from a transient error. A loose cable or an overheated component might cause one of the machine language instructions to fail; undetected IO error or channel error might destroy a portion of a data-base record being read from tape or disk. Timing errors in the hardware, of the same general nature as the *software* timing errors discussed above, might cause an interrupt to be lost or data to be destroyed.

If the program is very large or very complex, it may be very difficult (or expensive) to rerun the program up to the point where it failed. This gives us yet another argument for writing small modules: Ideally, we would like to reexecute only that module that was involved in the error. While this may not always be possible, the modular approach should make it possible to avoid reexecuting the entire program.

If the error is not repeatable, it is not always clear what the programmer should do. Assuming that the error was not due to human causes (e.g., an operator error), there are a few things that can be done:

1. Rerun the program, obtain the correct results, and forget that the error occurred. While this is not recommended, it may be the only practical approach in some cases. Actually, you should never forget errors of this type, for they may some-day return to haunt you. For your own safety, you should keep a record of these mysterious, nonrepeatable, inexplicable bugs.

2. Run some hardware diagnostic programs, and hope that a hardware malfunction can be found. If the problem was caused by a transient hardware error, the diagnostics will probably not find anything wrong. A better approach is to run the diagnostics as part of the computer system, i.e., as if it were an application program running in a multiprogramming environment.

3. Assume that the bug is in your own software, and start trying to find it.

4. Assume that the operator did it, and blame it on him; he is probably low enough on the organizational totem pole that he won't be able to fight back (how-ever, don't expect any favors from the operator for the next six months!).

5. If all else fails, blame it on the vendor—either on his hardware or his software. It probably isn't his fault, but it doesn't hurt to keep him on the defensive —just be sure that the error can't be traced to a bug in your program!

8.1.4 Programmer, Know Thyself

The programmers who have the most difficulty debugging their pro-grams are often those who blame *all* of their problems on the hardware, on the operating system, on the compiler, or on someone else's program. I once had the remarkable experience of working with a programmer who, whenever he had problems with his program, complained that the computer was anti-Semitic!

You must recognize that almost all of the bugs that you encounter during your programming career will be *your* errors, *your* mistakes. By recognizing the kinds of errors you make most often, you can usually find them more easily. Some programmers, for example, find that they make the same keypunching errors over and over again (yes, some programmers do keypunch their own programs!). Others find that they consistently misuse a particular assembly language instruction or COBOL statement. Still others find that they forget to save and restore registers upon entering and exiting from an assembly language subroutine. And FORTRAN programmers often find that they have a habit of using the variables I, J, and K in several different places in a program, so that one part of the program destroys a value stored by another part of the program.

One way of learning about the errors you make is to keep a diary of your debugging progress. After you have worked on several programs, your diary should indicate a pattern of errors, which you can then use to your advantage.

8.1.5   Be Thorough, Methodical, and Logical in Your Search for Bugs

We have already mentioned that some programmers have a difficult time finding the more subtle bugs in their programs; other programmers have a knack for finding their way to a bug quickly and easily. One reason for this is the *organized* approach that the better programmers take when looking for bugs. The less-talented programmer, on the other hand, often makes random probes into his program, growing more erratic and frantic with every unsuccessful attempt to find the bug.

One example of an organized approach to debugging is the philosophy of a "binary search for bugs," as illustrated in Fig. 8.3. If we have a program that is known to have a bug lurking somewhere within it, we can examine it after it has reached the midpoint of its execution. If something has already gone wrong (and if the nature of the bug is not immediately apparent from the examination of the program at this point), then we can reexecute the program and stop it in the middle of the first half, and so forth. This technique is greatly facilitated with the DDT debugging package discussed in Section 8.3.

Any other organized approach is equally acceptable; the main thing that we want to avoid is random debugging. Every core dump, every trace,

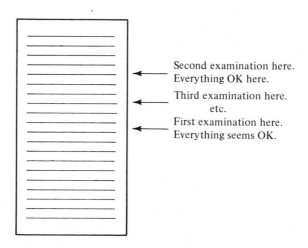

Figure 8.3. A binary search for bugs.

every investigative activity should add more information about the nature and location of the bug—either by excluding certain parts of the program that appear to be innocent, or by further confirming a previous suspicion about the location of the bug.

All of this may seem contradictory to our earlier observations about the sixth sense, or intuition, that some programmers have about their bugs; however, intuition and organization need not be mutually exclusive and should indeed be complementary. Faced with a large complicated program with a bug in it, there is nothing wrong with a programmer saying to himself, "My sixth sense tells me that the error is probably in subroutine XYZ." However, if that first guess is incorrect, then the programmer should not make a second intuitive guess entirely at random; instead, he should use the information that he has just learned to determine where to look next. That is, he might say to himself, "If something was wrong at the beginning of the program, then subroutine XYZ would have blown up; since my investigation of XYZ showed that it was doing everything correctly, it seems likely that the problem occurred somewhere *after* XYZ."

For a small program, or a simple, obvious bug, none of this caution is very necessary. In a large, complex program, on the other hand, some bugs have taken as long as three to six *months* to find. For such a situation, organization and a methodical thoroughness is of the essence. If the debugging period extends over a long period of time, it is even a good idea to keep a written record of the progress (or lack of same) that has been made, of the subroutines that have been investigated, and of the conclusions that have been drawn. In fact, since the debugging is likely to take such a long time (as much as 50% of many programming projects), a written record can also be used to convince your manager that you have not been idling your time away.

8.1.6 Investigate the Simplest Clues First

I am indebted to a student of mine, Mr. Tony Lee, for this suggestion; it is interesting that the same suggestion is given in many works of detective fiction—investigate the obvious things first.

In the case of debugging a computer program, it is usually possible to write down a list of potential "suspects" after seeing or hearing a brief description of the problem. That is, after hearing that your program has generated the wrong kind of output (e.g., an unhappy user will tell you, "When I gave your program *this* kind of input, it gave me *that* kind of output. . . ."), you should be able to say to yourself, "Well, the most obvious places where my program could have done something wrong, based on the description of the problem, are subroutines A, B, and C. Therefore, I should examine them first."

We can carry this suggestion a little further. If there are several obvious "suspects," they should be examined in order of increasing difficulty. In the example above, for instance, we decided that subroutines A, B, and C were likely suspects; however, it may turn out that subroutine A is extremely complex, B is moderately complicated, and C is relatively simple (either because it has far fewer statements, or because it is accomplishing a simpler function, or because it was documented more carefully, or simply because you have a better understanding of what it does). Thus, you might be able to estimate that it would take you 5 minutes to determine whether the bug is in subroutine C, 30 minutes to determine whether it is in subroutine B, and 3 days to determine whether the bug is in subroutine A. It should be rather clear which subroutine should be investigated first.

8.1.7 Don't Take Anything for Granted

In an earlier section, we suggested that you could assume that most of the errors in your program would be the result of your own mistakes. While this is true, there comes a time when you should cast a jaundiced eye upon everything else that might have influenced your program. This includes such things as the computer operator, the hardware, the vendor's operating system, and even the weather (lightning bolts have wreaked havoc on more than one program—could it be a message from above?).

The best example of unwarranted faith can be seen in a large program, composed of many subroutines. When something goes wrong, the innocent programmer is likely to remark, "Oh, it couldn't be *that* subroutine—it's been working for months!" And with a wave of his hand, he dismisses half of the subroutines as being unlikely sources of the error. A more experienced programmer, on the other hand, is likely to say, "Well, I don't think there's any problem with that subroutine, but have there been any changes made to it lately?" The inevitable reply is, "Well, there was one teensy weensy little change—but that couldn't have caused any problems, could it?" The experienced programmer will then go on to ask whether the subroutine in question has ever successfully processed the kind of input that was associated with the program error; subroutines that have been used successfully for years might suddenly blow up when given new input (consider a subroutine to print the Julian date—it might break down on February 29th of leap year, after having been used successfully for four years).

In most cases, the area that deserves most of your suspicious attention is software—all of the software that supplements and complements your program. If, when a bug appears in a large programming system, the finger of blame seems to point in your direction, then (after a reasonable effort to ensure that there is not a simple, obvious bug in your module) you should first check to see if there have been any changes made to the other modules. If you have recently made any changes to your own module, you should be suspicious of your own work of art as well! If you continue to have trouble finding the bug, then you and your colleagues should ask whether all of the other seemingly innocent modules in the program have truly been tested. As in the detective stories, the most obscure, innocent-looking subroutine will sometimes turn out to be the culprit in the end.

If you are still unable to find the error, you should begin casting a baleful eye upon other parts of the programming environment: the hardware, the operator, the telephone company, the data base, or even your own boss! Never forget, though, that the bug ultimately may be found in your own module; so, though you must at times be suspicious of others, be *politely* suspicious—and be appropriately humble and remorseful if the bug is found beneath your very nose.

8.1.8   Use the Little Gray Cells

The hero of many of Agatha Christie's detective stories, the fabulous M. Hercule Poirot, often remarked to his friends that the truly difficult crimes were not solved with bloodhounds and massive dragnets. While the police busily investigated clues, tracked down suspects and informants, and generally beat the bushes in search of the murderer, Poirot was content to sit back in his easy chair and *think*. The slow, laborious, and methodical techniques of the police had their place, he felt, but he personally was more interested in the psychology of the crime, of the victims, and ultimately of the murderer.

The analogy with debugging should be clear. Core dumps, traces, and snapshots—*and* that mysterious activity known as "desk-checking"—all have their place, but they are not an end unto themselves. They are a means of accomplishing an end, namely, finding a bug in a program. It is almost pitiful to watch some junior programmers exclaim, "Well, I've taken a core dump—now what?" as if they are disappointed that the bug did not leap from between the hexadecimal digits on the printer output and land on their noses!

To carry the detective analogy a bit further, it often makes sense to dispense with core dumps, traces, and snapshots. In the case of difficult bugs, much more can be achieved by putting your feet on the desk, staring at the ceiling, and thinking about the nature of the bug. Most bugs have a "psychology," that is, they seem to have a particular *behavior*. You might find yourself saying, after the second or third time a bug has reared its ugly little head, "Ah, yes, it's *that* bug again! It always seems to happen just after we open the second input file." Now is the time to sit back and think quietly: What is significant about opening the second input file? What transpired between the opening of the first and second input file? What other bugs have you encountered that were associated with file opening (another of Agatha Christie's heroines, Miss Jane Marple, always tried to relate the suspects in a murder case to people she had known in the small English village where she lived). What is the next thing the program would have done? Are there any other suspicious circumstances surrounding the untimely demise of the program?

8.1.9   Talk to Your Friends

If you have difficulty finding a bug in your program, it sometimes helps to talk to a friend. If some of your colleagues are working on the same project, they are likely to have a general understanding of your problem. In fact, this is one reason why many project leaders and programming managers try to ensure that every module is known and understood by more than one programmer (it also helps when the original programmer leaves the project).

Even if there is no one directly involved in your program, you may find it helpful to have someone else look at your code. You may be able to narrow the problem down to a particular subroutine, but then find yourself unable to detect anything wrong with the code. The more you stare at the program listing, the more convinced you become that nothing is wrong with the code. At this point, it helps to have someone else look at the program—even if he is completely unfamiliar with it. Describe the program, the nature of the problem, and the sequence of steps your program goes through. You will often find that merely talking about the program exposes a bug; in other cases, a few intelligent questions from your colleague (e.g., "Are you sure you initialized that variable before beginning your calculation?") will point out the problem. In still other cases, your colleague may be able to look at the program listing and spot an error that you have repeatedly overlooked.

A word of caution is appropriate here: Not everyone makes a good "debugging partner"; in fact, some will be worse than useless. Some of your colleagues will listen politely to a description of your problem, but will be unable to contribute any useful suggestions. Others will not even make a pretense of listening politely. You will discover that some of your colleagues have a style of programming and debugging that is so alien to yours that their assistance will only confuse you. Others will be slow to learn the nature of the problem and the extent of your progress in tracking it down; they will frustrate you with well-intentioned but hopelessly simple-minded questions. Finally, even the most intelligent and helpful of your colleagues will tire of looking at your program if you cry "wolf" too often.

The moral should be clear: Spend some time finding out which of your colleagues are willing and able to help you search for bugs. Once you have found them, use them sparingly and show your appreciation for their help. At the very least, you should return the favor when they have bugs in their programs.

8.1.10   Try Out Test Cases to Confirm Your Suspicions

At various times during your debugging activities, you will find yourself asking whether certain aspects of the hardware, the machine language instruction set, the programming language, or the operating system behave the way you think they do. Thus, you might find yourself asking, "I wonder what *really* happens when I get a parity error on a READ BACKWARD command on magnetic tape? Maybe the operating system automatically skips over the bad record before making an error return to my program—that would explain why I am having so much trouble."

In a situation like this, you might find that the documentation concerning your question is vague, inaccurate, misleading, blatantly incorrect, or simply nonexistent. Even if it is correct, you may have misunderstood it. Thus, it is often wise to write a small test program to see if your suspicions are correct. Such a small, simple test program can usually be written in a few minutes; it requires only a small amount of machine time, and it will usually not entail any testing problems of its own. If the hypothesis to be tested is a particularly complicated one, you may find it easier to modify the original program that you were attempting to debug; a core dump at the appropriate point in your program may be all that is required.

The important thing to remember is the philosophical approach that you are taking: Rather than attempting to find an error, *you are admitting to yourself that you don't know how a particular hardware feature (or operating system feature, etc.) works*—so you are trying an experiment. Whatever the outcome of the experiment, it should give you more information—and in most cases, the more information you have, the easier the debugging becomes.

8.1.11 Forget About the Problem Until Tomorrow

There comes a time when none of the suggestions in this chapter will be of any help. After a certain number of hours of staring at a program listing, after a certain number of packs of cigarettes or gallons of coffee, the brain simply shuts off—even though you may not want to admit it. At this point (which may be 3:00 in the morning or 3:00 in the afternoon), the best thing to do is drop everything, forget entirely about the program, and spend a few hours doing something relaxing—sleeping, playing golf, bird-watching, drinking beer, or any of the other strange forms of amusement known to programmers. If your supervisor has any programming experience, he will understand and approve; if not, ignore him or tell him to find the bug himself.[1]

This philosophy often has an unexpected benefit: While you are relaxing, your mind often subconsciously continues thinking about the problem; in

---

[1]An equally good technique is to begin acting slightly crazy—for no manager wants to be accused of driving his programmers stark raving mad, even though he knows that most of them are slightly neurotic even in the best of times. During a particularly hectic debugging period on one of my programming projects, I did not bother showing up for work until 3:00 one afternoon; bringing with me a can of paint and a paintbrush, I proceeded to paint my office door bright green—and then went home for the day. Nobody said a word—except for the building custodian, who was worried that some of the other programmers might want their office doors painted, too!

fact, when you go to sleep after a hard day's night of debugging, you may even dream about your program. When you return to work the next day, the bug will often leap out of the program listing and wait to be caught; if not, at least you will have gotten a good night's sleep!

8.2 Common Programming Errors and Bugs

It is probably safe to say that there are infinitely many bugs and errors that can be committed by a programmer, just as there are an enormously large number of ways of solving a problem or writing a program to solve a particular problem. Nevertheless, it seems that every programmer falls into the same traps, commits the same blunders, and has the same problems.

This would be a very valuable area for any given organization to categorize. There should be a list of the bugs that seem to be the most commonly committed, so that any programmer will first scan through the list before crying for help. We need better statistics here; someone should perform a study to find the proportion of bugs that are due to various common causes. It is not entirely clear, of course, what we would do with such a list. If we know that our program is not working properly (perhaps because it has aborted in the middle of a run), how can we tell which of the "ten most-common errors" has occurred. Similarly, how can junior programmers be trained to relate the incorrect behavior of their programs to these common bugs?

A great deal of research and study could be performed in this area. In the meantime, the list below may prove useful as a starting point.

1. *Keypunching and clerical errors.* A large number of errors are simple keypunching errors, e.g., confusion between the number zero and the letter O, transposed letters, statements left out for one reason or another, etc.

2. *Uninitialized variables.* Another of the more common errors concerns variables that were used before they were initialized. It seems that this may be an area that could be solved with better hardware, i.e., by having the compiler or operating system initialize all program variables to some value that causes an interrupt if not initialized again by the program.

3. *Sharing variables among many modules.* This was mentioned in one of the previous chapters and is, in the author's opinion, one of the most common program bugs. It occurs when module A and module B both try to use the same variable or memory location for their temporary storage. Inevitably, one of the modules will destroy the other's use of that temporary storage. The problem is considerably worse on real-time systems where module A and module B can interrupt each other in addition to, or instead of, calling each other.

4. *Control and logic errors.* I don't know how to describe this any more precisely, but it seems to be a good description of yet another common type of bug. The programmer manages to call modules that weren't meant to be called, or fails to call modules when they should have been called; he takes the wrong path of a decision branch, etc., etc.

5. *Array subscripting out of bounds.* This is an obvious type of fault, but one that seems to occur relatively often: The programmer begins to address past the end of an array, with various results. Sometimes his program aborts (if he has attempted

to address past the end of his assigned memory area), or he references data in another array, etc. This is another area that should be solved by hardware, as it is with Burroughs computers. Alternatively, some of the error-checking options in compiler languages can help eliminate this problem.

6. *Improper termination of program sequences.* Perhaps one of the best examples of this is an *N*-way merge operation. The programmer often gets into trouble when the last few records are being read, some of the files have reached an EOF condition, and so forth.

7. *Not handling exceptional cases.* It often seems that the programmer programs for the obvious case (perhaps the one that was given to him in a specification) without thinking about the exceptional case, or the erroneous case. The behavior of his program is often indeterminate.

8. *Improper linkages and interfaces.* This is another common problem, and one that is the major objective of top-down testing: incorrect information being passed from one module to another, modules forgetting to save and restore their registers, etc.

9. *Improper data formats.* Especially in a language like COBOL or PL/I, it is very easy for the programmer to make mistakes in the scale, type, or format of numerical variables in his program.

10. *Passing constants as parameters.* In many high-level programming languages, statements of the form

CALL GLOP(A,B,3)

can lead to a great deal of trouble. If subroutine GLOP thinks its third argument is a variable, it may make an attempt to change its value, thus possibly destroying the "literal" 3.

11. *Misuse of compound Boolean expressions.* We have commented elsewhere on the ease with which programmers can make mistakes with statements of the form

IF A AND B NOT EQUAL C OR D

Other expressions involving nested AND and OR operators can lead to bugs if not separated properly with parentheses.

12. *Misuse of nested IF statements.* Nested IF statements seem to lead to so many bugs that a great number of COBOL organizations forbid their use. ALGOL and PL/I programmers are presumably somewhat more familiar with such statements, but they too have trouble with them occasionally.

13. *Incorrect exit from subroutines.* This is a problem primarily in COBOL (e.g., with the use of overlapping PERFORM statements) and assembly language; it is less of a problem in languages where the subroutine structure is more formalized.

14. *Accessing data areas after WRITE statements.* One of the common problems here is that data areas or buffer areas are released by the operating system (or occasionally zeroed out) after a WRITE statement. Any attempt by the programmer to access meaningful data in those areas can thus lead to a great deal of confusion.

15. *Flag-oriented problems.* We commented on this problem in Chapter 6: If the programmer has a large number of flags, it is possible for several illegal combinations to exist, and an incorrect setting of a flag can cause the program to execute in a meaningless "state" for quite a long time before it blows up.

16. *Failing to provide for exceptional IO cases.* The most common situation here is the failure to provide for end-of-file conditions and parity error conditions on input/output operations.

17. *Failure to look at return codes.* Most IO operations and a number of other

important services are provided by the vendor's operating system. When control returns to the application program, a "return code" usually indicates whether the appropriate function has been performed successfully. Many programmers forget to look at this code, or assume that there will never be any error return; so when the error return *is* made, their program continues on as if it never existed.

18. *Counters that are too small.* Typically a problem in many commercial COBOL applications. If the programmer has allocated a limited space for a counter, it is easy for it to overflow (a possibility that he often fails to check for) and be reset to zero.

19. *Addressing problems.* In assembly language, the programmer often makes mistakes when using the indirect addressing, indexed addressing, and relative addressing features of the more sophisticated machines.

20. *Errors in complicated computational sequences.* This problem was mentioned in Chapter 5, and it seems most common in scientific/engineering applications. Even with liberal use of parentheses, programmers often end up computing something far different from what they wanted.

21. *Alignment problems.* This is typically a high-level language problem, especially in COBOL. When moving character strings, comparing character strings, or performing certain types of arithmetic, the alignment of variables can be critical. On word-oriented machines, the problems are often magnified.

22. *Pushdown overflow or underflow.* In the first case, the programmer may have a deeper level of nesting or recursion than he had originally planned (or deeper than the system allows); in the other case, a definite bug exists—an attempt is being made to exit from a subroutine when no call was made to it.

23. *Using the wrong base registers.* For obvious reasons, this is a problem that plagues assembly language programmers on such machines as the IBM System/360 and 370. It can also be a problem on other machines with multiple-base registers and relocation registers.

24. *Attempting to execute data.* This usually occurs when the program makes a "wild" transfer into a data area, or when it "falls into" some data from a sequence of coding. It can also result from the array subscripting problem mentioned above: If the program has stored data past the end of an array, it may be storing data in an area previously occupied by bug-free coding.

25. *Using the wrong version of the program.* Sooner or later, this must happen to everyone. The matter can become further confused if the programmer is dealing with a program listing, an object module, and a source program that do not correspond to one another.

26. *Forgetting a terminator.* In many programming languages, the semicolon character (;) is used to terminate a comment or a program statement; in other cases, the reserved word END is used to terminate a statement, a block of statements, a macro definition, or even the entire program. Failure to insert a semicolon or an END statement in the right place can cause enormous problems, e.g., a group of program statements may be regarded by the compiler as part of a long comment.

8.3 Classical Debugging Techniques

Having discussed some *philosophies* of debugging, we turn now to some debugging *techniques.* Although many of these techniques may already be familiar to you, there are some interesting variations of tracing and snapshots to which it is worth devoting some attention. The emphasis is not on the details of debugging packages themselves, for this information can easily be obtained from vendor-supplied programming manuals. Instead, the emphasis will be on the programming situations in which these packages might be useful.

8.3.1 Core Dumps

One of the oldest and most useful debugging packages is the simple core dump. At any time during the execution of the program, the programmer can, if he thinks it will prove helpful, print the contents of core memory (or a selected portion of memory) on a high-speed printer. Alternatively, the contents of memory can be copied onto magnetic tape, disk, or drum, to be printed later. By examining the core dump, the programmer can often get a very good idea of the nature of the bug in his program.

While the usefulness of the core dump cannot be denied, it tends to be overused to an astonishing degree. If the nature of the program error is not immediately obvious, the programmer will often dump the *entire* contents of memory, and then retire to his desk with a two-inch-thick listing and wait for a divine inspiration to occur. If it does not occur quickly, he is as likely as not to dash out to the computer room and dump core again (after all, maybe the first core dump was wrong!?!). If you, too, feel an overwhelming urge to perform core dumps, keep in mind that even in the best cases, 90% or more of the information printed out will be useless and irrelevant; in the worst case, the entire core dump will be worthless. Core dumps are very much like police dragnets: If they are done at the right time, they may net one or two useful suspects, but if they are done at the wrong time, they net nothing. In the same vein, keep in mind that core dumps are not free: They take some CPU time (admittedly a rather small amount in most cases) and a potentially large amount of IO time (i.e., IO channels, use of high-speed printer and/or tape, etc.).

When you do decide to dump core memory, make sure that the dump is formatted in a readable manner: No matter how clever one is, it becomes rather tiring trying to read a hexadecimal dump (as one programmer pointed out, if we had been meant to think in hexadecimal, we would have been given sixteen fingers). The DUMP and PDUMP packages in FORTRAN are good examples of formatted dumps. They give the programmer the capability of dumping selected areas of memory in integer, floating-point, octal, or alphanumeric format. If such a dump does not exist on your machine or in your programming language, you should consider writing a general-purpose dump subroutine that can also be used by your colleagues (remember the discussion in Chapter 3).

Another suggestion about core dumps: Save them (either in the original printed form or on magnetic tape) for future reference. If you encounter an extremely subtle bug, it may take several weeks or months to find it; you may want to refer back to an earlier dump to see if the bug exhibits any kind of noticeable pattern. Naturally, this also suggests that you should keep adequate records to indicate when the dump was taken, the circumstances under which it was taken, the magnetic tape or disk file on which it was stored, and so forth.

Finally, consider a point that was discussed in Chapter 1: If the core dump is giving you useful information, it is important that you avoid sharing the same working storage areas among several subroutines. If several subroutines use the same working storage area, then the core dump will only show the last piece of information that was stored, and any previous activity by other subroutines will be lost.

8.3.2 Traces

Another very popular debugging aid is the *trace* (or, as it is sometimes called, "snap" or "snapshot") that is provided by most of the computer manufacturers for a variety of high-level and low-level programming languages. Actually, a trace is just a variation on the core dump described in the previous section. It causes the contents of certain memory locations (variables in the program, subroutine linkages, etc.) to be printed at times, or under conditions, specified by the programmer. The information is usually recorded on a high-speed printer, or spooled onto magnetic tape, to be examined later at the programmer's leisure.

Virtually all of the suggestions that were made about core dumps apply to traces. If used indiscriminately, a trace will generate reams of paper (even more than a core dump in many cases, since the trace is a continual process in contrast to a one-time core dump) without yielding much useful information. It also tends to consume a noticeable amount of CPU time (since the faulty program keeps running and running and running. . .) and IO resources. As in the case of core dumps, some traces are printed in hexadecimal and are therefore nearly impossible to decipher (unless, of course, one has sixteen fingers. . .).

While the concept of a trace is a very general one, there are several more or less "standard" forms of traces. All of these are fairly simple to implement and are helpful in most common programming situations. The following list, though not comprehensive, should be considered a starting point for a library of debugging packages:

1. *Subroutine trace.* The purpose of this trace is to print an indication of each instance in which a specified subroutine was called. The trace would probably print

all of the arguments provided to the subroutine, and could even indicate whether or not the subroutine made a normal exit to the calling program.

2. *Variable trace*. This trace is used to print the contents of specified variables, data items, areas of working storage, arrays, etc. In most cases, it would be sufficient to trace the variable only when it changed; however, there may be cases when the programmer would like to trace *all* references to the variable.

3. *Statement trace*. This must be considered a "shotgun" trace, one that is used only when all other forms of debugging fail to locate the bug. It prints the contents of all the variables (and registers, accumulators, etc.) affected by a program statement, both before and after that statement has been executed.

4. *Macro trace*. For the programmers who have trouble interfacing their application programs with an operating system, the macro trace would indicate the contents of appropriate registers before and after a "macro," or call to the operating system. The trace might also indicate whether or not the operating system made an error return to the application program. (Failing to check for error returns is a common error in this area.)

5. *Terminal trace*. For on-line systems, message-switching systems, time-sharing systems, and other types of terminal-oriented systems, the debugging effort often requires exact knowledge of the input from a particular terminal (or group of terminals). This trace indicates all input messages and output messages from a particular terminal, or possibly groups of terminals. Since many such on-line systems already record *all* terminal messages on magnetic tape or disk for recovery purposes, the trace might simply consist of a program that could select the desired messages from a transaction tape and print them on the high-speed printer.

6. *Data-base trace*. This trace would be useful for systems involving large, complex data bases. It is especially useful in those systems that have a centralized "data-base manager" that controls all accesses to a data base, all file creations, all record deletions, *all* accesses to the data base, or any other useful combinations.

7. *Time-oriented trace*. For some real-time programming systems, it is hard to know what to trace, for the bug may be so subtle that it cannot easily be associated with a particular variable or subroutine. In this case, it may be desirable to have a trace that prints (or copies onto disk, for the sake of speed) the contents of selected areas of memory on a periodic basis. If the bug is truly impossible to find, it might even help to have the trace take place on a *random* basis.

8. *Conditional traces*. In some cases, the programmer may know that he does not want to print anything unless certain conditions are met, e.g., only if variable A is greater than zero and variable B is less than zero. This information, if not too complex, could be specified to a *conditional trace*, which could also include the properties of many of the other types of traces mentioned above.

The major problem with the trace statements in most high-level programming languages is that they are generally inserted into the program at compile time. Thus, if the programmer traces one part of the program and finds that he still has a bug, he must insert the trace statement somewhere else, *recompile his program*, and try again. This can obviously waste a tremendous amount of CPU time. A better approach in many cases is to insert *several* trace statements in the program and then use IF statements to decide which variables are to be traced. Thus, the programmer could read an input card when the program begins running, and use that to determine the portion of the program to be traced.

8.4 The DDT Debugging Package

Having discussed some of the more classical debugging aids, we turn now to a discussion of a debugging package that has had somewhat limited use in the computer field, but which is felt by many (the author included) to be far more powerful and efficient than core dumps and traces. Originally called a "dynamic debugging technique," it has come to be known by its popular initials, DDT. The similarity to the well-known pesticide is both obvious and intentional: It kills bugs.

In this section we will describe some of the different kinds of DDT packages that can be implemented. We will also describe some of the features that are common to almost all versions of DDT. Finally, we shall give some brief details on the implementation of a simple version of DDT.

8.4.1 Types of DDT Packages

There are basically three types of DDT packages which may be distinguished by the manner in which they handle terminal input:

1. *Stand-alone DDT.* This is the simplest form of DDT and is often used to debug programs on small minicomputers. As its name implies, stand-alone DDT does not depend on an operating system and does not run concurrently with any other programs; it truly stands alone.

The distinguishing characteristic of stand-alone DDT is that it handles its own terminal communication with the programmer. That is, it receives terminal input from the programmer without the aid of an operating system, and is equally adept at sending output to the programmer. Furthermore, it does not allow any processing to take place while it is waiting for input from the programmer. This is a very important point: *The machine sits in an idle loop while waiting for input from the programmer.* This implies rather inefficient use of the available machine time, since the programmer is likely to stare at the ceiling for long periods of time while trying to decide what to do next. However, such a practice is often acceptable while debugging programs on a minicomputer, because there are no other programmers waiting to use the machine. It is also occasionally useful when debugging real-time programs, since the only viable alternative is to use the hardware console switches to debug.

The important point to emphasize here, though, is not that a stand-alone DDT makes inefficient use of the CPU, but rather that it does not allow the programmer to examine and modify his program while it is actually running. Either DDT or his program may be executing at any one time; it is not possible for the two to be running concurrently.

2. *Time-sharing DDT.* The second form of DDT differs from stand-alone DDT only in that it receives its terminal input by calling the operating system, and executes along with the program being debugged, under the control of the operating system.

This means that the operating system can perform other functions while it is waiting for the programmer to provide terminal input to the time-sharing DDT program. This arrangement is very common in time-sharing systems, where several programmers can be debugging their programs concurrently, each with his own copy of DDT (or perhaps sharing one reentrant copy).

A side benefit of the time-sharing version of DDT is that it runs under the protection features of the operating system. Thus, if the user's program goes berserk (as they all do at one time or another), the operating system prevents it from executing illegal instructions or referencing an illegal area of memory. Note that, as far as the applications programmer is concerned, the DDT program does *not* run concurrently with his own program; once again, either his program is executing or the time-sharing DDT program is executing, but not both concurrently. The multiprogramming features of the system, which are usually present in the operating system, affect *other* users, jobs, or application programs.

3. *Real-time DDT*. The most complex form of DDT is the one that allows other programs to execute while it is waiting for input from the programmer's terminal. While it is possible to implement such a DDT for the application programmers, using the multitasking features available on some vendor's equipment, it is extremely uncommon. Instead, the real-time version of DDT is usually designed to help debug monitors, operating systems, and other real-time programming systems.

As we have indicated, the different forms of DDT are distinguished by the different forms of terminal input/output which they use. In the case of real-time DDT, the terminal is usually the *console typewriter*, which is located beside the computer console and connected directly to the machine; real-time DDT serves as an IO handler for the console typewriter.

Thus, while the programmer is sitting idle at the terminal, the rest of the system is free to run unhindered. When he types some input, an interrupt is generated, and real-time DDT gains control of the processor with the aid of some kind of priority interrupt structure. After it has processed the programmer's request to examine memory, change memory, etc., it releases the hardware interrupt, and the rest of the system continues to run.

In the discussion that follows, we shall describe *universal* features of DDT; when necessary, we will show how the features differ in stand-alone DDT, time-sharing DDT, and real-time DDT.

8.4.2 General Features of DDT

For the purposes of this discussion, we will assume that the program being debugged by DDT (often referred to as the "problem program") is an *assembly language program*, since most currently available versions of DDT allow only assembly language debugging. It is possible to build a DDT-like debugging aid for high-level languages such as FORTRAN, COBOL, and PL/I, and a few have been developed recently for time-sharing service bureaus; however, these high-level versions of DDT generally require that the problem program be *interpreted* rather than compiled.

In general, DDT is loaded into the machine along with the program(s) to be debugged. This leads to a memory layout as shown in Fig. 8.4. The DDT program communicates with the programmer at his terminal in one or more standard *modes*. In the simpler versions of DDT, there may be only one mode

Memory location N.

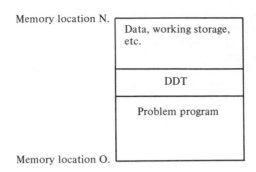

Figure 8.4. A typical core layout with DDT.

allowed, e.g., octal. Normally, though, the programmer has the option of specifying a variety of modes:

  1. Symbolic or assembly language mode.
  2. Numeric mode, in some specified format (octal, decimal, hexadecimal, or floating point).
  3. Text mode (ASCII, EBCDIC, etc.).

The mode is specified by a command to DDT; unless specifically directed otherwise, DDT operates in a standard mode (usually octal or symbolic).

  The programmer has several types of *commands* with which he can instruct DDT to help debug his program. The most common commands, which will be described in the sections below, are the following:

  1. Examining and changing memory locations.
  2. Setting and removing breakpoints.
  3. The "go" command.
  4. Search commands.

8.4.3 DDT Commands to Examine Memory

  A feature that is present even in the most primitive of DDT programs is the ability to examine and change any memory location accessible to the programmer. The memory location to be examined is indicated as an octal parameter in some versions of DDT, while other versions make use of the symbol tables generated by the assembler to allow the programmer to specify the memory location as a symbolic expression.

  The command that instructs DDT to examine a memory location is the *slash character* (i.e., the "/" character) in almost all versions of DDT. Thus, to examine memory location 234, the programmer types

234/

on his terminal. In a version of DDT that permits symbolic input, he might
type

    XYZ+3/

to examine the third location following the one symbolically defined as
"XYZ" in his program.

When it receives a command to examine a memory location, DDT
responds by typing the current contents of the memory location. Thus, when
the programmer asks to examine location 234, the following dialogue takes
place (output from DDT is underlined to distinguish it from programmer
input):

    234/ 1234

In a more sophisticated version of DDT, the dialogue might be as follows:

    XYZ+3/ ADD ABC+1

In both cases, the programmer is asking for the same type of information;
however, in the second case, DDT prints the contents of the memory location
in symbolic assembly language format.

Note that two successive "examine" commands for the same memory
location will yield the same output, if stand-alone DDT or time-sharing
DDT is used. That is, it is possible for the following dialogue to take place
between the programmer and DDT:

    234/ 1234
    234/ 1234

Since DDT and the problem program do not multiprogram with each other,
the program cannot execute while DDT is waiting for input from the programmer. Thus, location 234 is guaranteed to have the same contents from
one examination to the next.

When using real-time DDT, on the other hand, it *is* possible for the
contents of a memory location to change suddenly; the reason, as explained
above, is that the problem program continues to execute while real-time
DDT is waiting for input from the programmer. Thus, the following type of
dialogue would be possible:

    234/ 1234
    234/ 1235
    234/ 1236

Once DDT has typed the contents of a memory location, it is said to be
open or subject to modification by the programmer. At this time, he can either

make a change to the memory location or indicate that he is satisfied with the
current contents. To change memory location 234, for example, the programmer might carry on the following dialogue:

    234/   1234   4321   ↵

where ↵ is the notation for "carriage return" or "end-of-line." With a more
sophisticated version of DDT, the following dialogue would be possible:

    XYZ+3/   ADD ABC+1   SUB ABC+1   ↵

If he is satisfied with the current contents of a memory location, the programmer indicates his satisfaction with the ↵ character, leading to the following
kind of dialogue:

    234/   1234   ↵

or

    XYZ+3/   ADD ABC+1   ↵

Once the programmer has typed one of the above commands (either changing
a memory location or leaving it unchanged), the location is said to be *closed*,
i.e., no longer subject to modification without another explicit examination
command.

    The ability to examine and change memory locations is certainly the
most universal one found in different versions of DDT; there are, however,
an almost endless number of variations. Among the commands that might
supplement the basic "open" and "close" commands are:

    1. A command to open a memory location without typing its current con-
tents. This is useful when changing large sections of a program.
    2. A command to close the current memory location (with or without
changes) and simultaneously open the next sequential location.
    3. A command to close the current memory location and simultaneously
open the previous memory location.
    4. A command to close the current memory location and simultaneously
open the memory location pointed to by the effective address of the current memory
location.
    5. A command to type the contents of memory locations within a specified
range of memory locations, but without allowing modifications. This is helpful for
quickly examining a number of memory locations.

8.4.4   DDT Commands to Set and Remove Breakpoints

    It is extremely desirable to allow the programmer to stop his program
in midexecution if it reaches a specified location or instruction. This is imple-

mented in DDT with the *breakpoint* command, which the programmer issues before turning control over to his problem program. Thus, he might type the command

    456B

to tell DDT to stop his program if control ever reaches location 456. In a more sophisticated version of DDT, the command might take the following form:

    XYZ−3 $B

(the $ character is necessary to distinguish the breakpoint command from other symbolic input).

On some versions of DDT, the programmer has access to as many as sixteen different breakpoints, each of which can be referenced by number. Thus, he might say "Insert the first breakpoint at location 203" by typing the command

    203 $1 B

Similarly, he might say "Insert the second breakpoint at location 756" by typing the command

    756 $2B

If he does not care which breakpoint is used, the programmer might say "Insert the next available breakpoint at location 404" by typing the command

    404 $B

The facility for multiple breakpoints is an extremely powerful one, if used properly by the programmer. Faced with a situation where he is not certain which direction his program will take, the programmer can liberally sprinkle breakpoints throughout all the likely parts of the program.

With breakpoints inserted, the programmer normally instructs DDT to transfer control to his program (with the GO command, to be discussed in Section 8.4.6). If, during execution, his program reaches any of the specified breakpoint locations, control is returned to DDT *before that instruction is executed*, and an appropriate message is typed for the benefit of the programmer. Thus, the following message might appear if the breakpoint at location 756 were reached:

    $2B AT LOC 756

The message, though somewhat cryptic, is sufficient to tell the programmer that control reached the second breakpoint he had inserted, and that his program had been stopped just prior to the execution of the instruction at location 756. On some versions of DDT, the contents of the accumulators and/or the program instruction at the breakpoint location are automatically typed when the breakpoint is reached.

The breakpoint commands function similarly in stand-alone DDT and time-sharing DDT, but they can be rather tricky in real-time DDT. Remember that while the programmer is communicating with stand-alone DDT or time-sharing DDT, his problem program is not executing. Only when he specifically instructs DDT to transfer control to his program does the program actually begin to execute. Thus, while he is in communication with DDT, he can insert a breakpoint and then change his mind and move it elsewhere; similarly, when the breakpoint is reached, his program is suspended and DDT regains control.

With real-time DDT, we must remember that the rest of the program is running while the programmer is communicating with DDT. Thus, it is possible that while the programmer is typing the command to insert a breakpoint in a particular program, the program is executing. Furthermore, it is possible that the breakpoint might be reached an instant after DDT has inserted it; thus, the programmer might type a breakpoint command and immediately receive a message to the effect that the breakpoint was reached.

It is not always clear what action DDT should take when such a breakpoint is reached. On one hand, real-time DDT is supposed to allow the problem program to execute while it is communicating with the programmer; on the other hand, the purpose of the breakpoint, from the programmer's point of view, is to *stop everything* when the breakpoint is reached. This implies that real-time DDT should immediately disable all hardware interrupts (or establish itself as the highest priority task in the system) when a breakpoint is reached. When the programmer types a proceed command (to be discussed in the next section), DDT could turn on the interrupts (or reestablish its original priority level).

Immediately after the breakpoint is reached, the problem program is supposed to be frozen, or in a "state of suspended animation." When this is feasible, it is a tremendously useful feature, for it allows the programmer to see exactly what his program was doing, in a real-time sense, at the time of the breakpoint. Unfortunately, it is not always feasible. In a process control system, for example, such a breakpoint might result in an explosion.

Finally, we need a command to remove one or more breakpoints in the problem program. In a simple version of DDT, where only one breakpoint is allowed, the command

B

would be sufficient. In a more sophisticated version, the programmer would type

$3B

to remove the third breakpoint in his program, and

$B

to remove *all* breakpoints.

8.4.5 DDT Command to Proceed from a Breakpoint

Once a breakpoint has been reached, the programmer uses DDT to examine pertinent variables and memory locations, make any necessary patches, and in general, evaluate the progress of his program up to that point. Having satisfied himself that the program is running properly, he usually wishes to proceed with the execution of the program. This capability is provided by the *proceed* command in DDT; it is indicated when the programmer types the command

P

At this point, the programmer resumes the execution of the problem program at the point of the last breakpoint.

With some versions of DDT, it is possible to construct so-called conditional breakpoint and proceed commands. The most common form of conditional proceed instructs DDT not to stop at the current breakpoint again until control has passed through it a specified number of times. To give an example, let us suppose that a programmer is attempting to debug a section of his program that goes through a loop 100 times. He might want to insert a breakpoint to see whether the program is executing properly on the initial pass through the loop; he would then like to stop the program again on the last pass through the loop. When the breakpoint has been reached for the first time, he would type

98P

to tell DDT not to stop at the breakpoint until it has passed through an additional 98 times. On the 99th pass through the loop (which is actually the 100th, counting the initial pass), DDT will stop at the breakpoint and return control to the programmer.

With an extremely sophisticated version of DDT, the conditional proceed command is analogous to the *selective trace* discussed earlier in this chapter. That is, the programmer might be allowed to specify that a breakpoint should be bypassed until the accumulator is zero, memory location 456

contains the number 7654, and index register 3 contains a −7. This kind of
sophistication is almost unheard of, but it would not be too difficult to
implement.

8.4.6   DDT Command to Transfer Control to the Problem Program

To transfer control to his program, the programmer normally types
the following type of command:

    567G

or

    START+3 $G

8.4.7   DDT Search Commands

Though other DDT features are somewhat optional, many are quite
common in different implementations and have been found to be quite convenient. Among the most convenient features are the *search* commands found
in many DDT programs. While debugging his program, the programmer
often wants to find all references to a specific instruction, all instances of a
certain constant, all references to a particular index register, etc. These may
be accomplished with the *word search*, the *not-word search*, and the *effective-
address search*.

Suppose that the programmer wants to search through his program for
all instances of the constant 4567; to do this he types the command

    1000,2000,4567W

This command instructs DDT to search from location 1000 to location 2000,
printing out the contents of all memory locations whose contents are 4567
(it may seem redundant to print the contents of these memory locations, but
it will be justified shortly). Thus, DDT might print the following information
as a result of the above command:

1234/	4567
1456/	4567
1457/	4567
1776/	4567

With a more sophisticated version of DDT, the programmer might type a
symbolic command of the following form:

    START, END, CAT+DOG$W

Once again, the three parameters are the same: the lower and upper bounds of the search, and the item being searched for.

Suppose now that the programmer wants to search a table for all non-zero entries. In this case, he is not searching *for* a particular quantity; instead, he is searching for the *absence* of a particular quantity, namely, the absence of zero.

To effect this search, the programmer types

1000, 2000, ON

This instructs DDT to search from location 1000 to location 2000 for all memory locations whose contents are not equal to zero. As a result, it prints the following information:

1234/	4567
1324/	7654
1605/	7777
1776/	0001

Finally, the programmer might want to search through his program for all references to a specified location. This capability is sometimes provided with the cross-reference listings at the end of an assembly listing, but DDT provides a full effective-address calculation (including indirect addressing, indexing, base-register addressing, etc.) at *run time*, which an assembler cannot do.

Suppose, for example, that the programmer wanted to find all instructions that referenced location XYZ+3. With a sophisticated version of DDT, he could type the following command:

START, END, XYZ+3$E

which would result in the following printout from DDT:

START+4/	ADD XYZ+3	
LOOP+1/	SUB XYZ+3	
LOOP+6/	STORE XYZ,3	(a reference involving indexing)
ABC+14/	LOAD* PNTR	(a reference involving indirect addressing)

In many versions of DDT, there is a *mask* associated with the various search commands. When it looks at a word in memory to see if it satisfies the search condition, DDT looks only at those bits specified by the mask. Unless directed otherwise, DDT sets the mask to all ones, thus effecting a full-word search or not-search. By setting the mask with a separate command to DDT, the programmer can look for any combination of bits in a word.

Suppose, for example, that the programmer wanted to find all references

to index register 3. For the purposes of this example, let us assume that the
programmer is working with a 24-bit machine in which the index register
field is specified by bits 6–8 of the instruction. Thus, the programmer could
set the mask as follows:

    00700000M

This tells DDT to disregard everything but bits 6, 7, and 8 when making a
comparison for any of the search commands. The search itself would be accomplished with the following command:

    1000,2000,11311111W

The following command would serve the same purpose:

    1000,2000,777377777W

8.5   Implementation of a Simple Version of DDT

To complete our discussion of DDT, we provide here a brief description of
the implementation of a simple version of DDT. This DDT is intended for a
word-oriented machine, and it will accept only octal input. Furthermore, it
allows only one breakpoint to be inserted. However, this simplicity can have
advantages: The DDT presented here can be implemented in as little as 200
instructions (or even less), and it can be coded in a matter of a few hours.
Input to this simple version of DDT consists of an octal number, followed by a command character; alternatively, the input might consist of a
command character alone. Thus, legal input to DDT might consist of the
following:

    1234/
    1234G
    4321B
    B
    P

The DDT program works by simply accumulating an octal number until it
recognizes a command character; it then performs the action specified by the
command character.

8.5.1   The DDT Initialization Routine

The initialization routine is shown in Fig. 8.5 and is quite simple in
nature. It first types a carriage return (or any other suitable message) to let

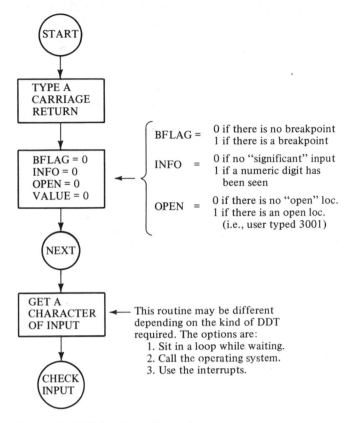

Figure 8.5. Initialization and main loop.

the programmer know that it has been started and is waiting for input. Three flags and an internal working register are then initialized: BFLAG, INFO, OPEN, and VALUE.

BFLAG is a flag that tells DDT whether the programmer has typed in a breakpoint command. If BFLAG = 0, then there is no breakpoint; if BFLAG = 1, then there is a breakpoint. BFLAG is initialized to zero when DDT begins; it is set to one, or reset to zero, when the programmer types a "B" command.

INFO is a flag that tells DDT whether it has seen any numeric information when it is accepting input. INFO is set to zero when DDT begins and is reset to zero whenever DDT begins looking for new input; it is set to one whenever DDT receives an octal digit, as will be discussed below. Thus, if the programmer types the command

1234B

then INFO will have been set to one by the time that DDT processes the "B" character. If, on the other hand, the programmer typed

B

then INFO will be zero when the "B" character is recognized by DDT.

OPEN is a flag which tells DDT whether there is an open memory location. If OPEN=0, no memory location is currently open and subject to modification; if OPEN=1, the memory location pointed to by LOC (an internal variable within DDT) is currently open. OPEN is set to zero in the initialization routine, and it is set to one by the routine that processes the *slash* character.

Finally, VALUE is an internal working variable that accumulates the value of octal input as it is typed in. VALUE is initialized to zero and is reset to zero whenever DDT begins looking for new input.

Having performed its initialization, DDT goes to its main input loop, shown in Fig. 8.6 and described below.

8.5.2   The Main Input Loop

The purpose of the main input loop is to accept one character of input from the programmer's terminal and decide what to do with it. As we discussed earlier, the "get a character" subroutine is what distinguishes standalone DDT from time-sharing DDT and real-time DDT.

Once a character of input has been received, DDT then checks to see whether it is a legal input character: an octal digit, a slash character, a carriage return, a G, a B, or a P. If it is, DDT proceeds to a routine which will process the character; if not, DDT proceeds to an error routine.

8.5.3   The Octal Digit Processor

The purpose of this routine, as shown in the flowchart in Fig. 8.7, is to accept one octal digit and accumulate it into the current VALUE. It also sets the INFO flag to one, so that DDT will later be able to remember whether a command was accompanied by octal input.

The processing in the subroutine is exceedingly simple. It simply multiplies the current VALUE by eight (which can be accomplished by shifting on most machines) and adds the new octal digit. The flowchart in Fig. 8.7 does not make any error-check. If the programmer types too large a number, VALUE simply overflows and no error indication is given. It is an easy process to add such an error-check to the routine; similarly, the routine may be easily modified to allow decimal input or hexadecimal input.

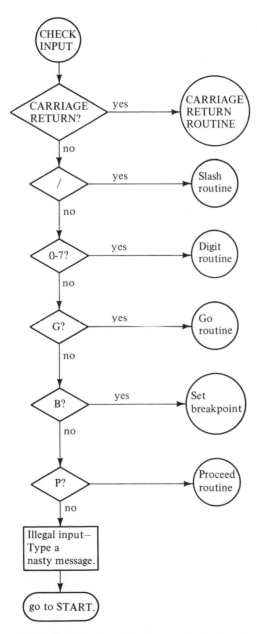

Figure 8.6. Routine to look at an input character.

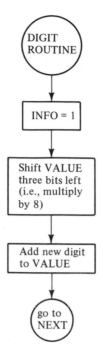

Figure 8.7. Digit routine.

8.5.4   The Slash Routine

As we saw in Fig. 8.6, the slash routine is entered when the main input loop finds a "/" character. At this point, it is apparent that the programmer must have typed something like

    1234/

and it is the duty of the slash routine, as shown in Fig. 8.8, to type the contents of memory location 1234 on the terminal.

First, though, DDT must save the current contents of VALUE. Once it types the contents of the specified memory location, DDT will go back to the main input loop to await more instructions from the programmer; consequently, VALUE will have to be reset to zero. Thus, the current contents of VALUE, which contains the address of the memory location to be examined, are saved in LOC.

Next, DDT types the current contents of the memory location, formatting its output so that it will be legible:

    1234/   7654

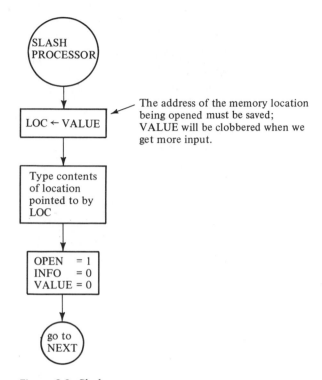

Figure 8.8. Slash processor.

At this point, DDT does not know whether the programmer will make a change to the location or not; consequently, the location is considered to be open, and DDT waits for more input from the programmer.

Before returning to the main input loop, DDT sets the OPEN flag to one, so that it will remember the open memory location. INFO is set to zero, so that DDT will be able to know whether the *next* command contained any octal digits; and VALUE is set to zero.

8.5.5 The Carriage-Return Processor

The main purpose of the carriage return is to *close* an open memory location. In so doing, it may or may not have to make a change to the current contents of that location.

The carriage-return routine, shown in Fig. 8.9, first checks the status of the INFO flag. If it is zero, the programmer must have typed the following kind of input:

1234/ <u>7654</u> ↵

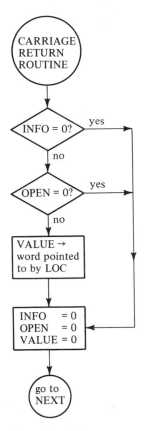

Figure 8.9. The carnage-return routine.

In other words, if the INFO flag is zero, there was no octal input immediately preceding the carriage-return character. This indicates that the programmer did not want to make a change to the memory location; DDT then resets the OPEN flag and VALUE register, and returns for more input.

If the INFO flag is set to one, it is an indication that the programmer typed a command of the following kind:

    1234/ 7654 4567 ↵

That is, if the INFO flag is one, it indicates that there *was* octal input immediately preceding the carriage-return routine. This octal input has been accumulated in VALUE by the octal digit routine, and it represents the *change* that the programmer wants to make to the memory location pointed to by LOC.

Before making the specified change, though, the DDT routine checks to see that the OPEN flag is set to one. This prevents the programmer from typing a command like

1234 ↵

preventing him from modifying a memory location without first examining it. Similar kinds of error-checking are often built into the other DDT routines, but it is critical here: An error on the part of the programmer can cause part of his problem program to be destroyed.

If everything else is proper, DDT changes the memory location as instructed by the programmer. It then clears the INFO flag, the OPEN flag, and the VALUE register; finally, it returns to the main input loop.

8.5.6 The GO Routine

The purpose of the GO routine, shown in Fig. 8.10, is to transfer control from DDT to the program being debugged. The address to which control is transferred is specified by the programmer in his command:

1234G

To be safe, the GO routine should first check the INFO flag to make sure that the programmer has not simply typed

G

For simplicity, this is avoided in our description, and such a programmer error would cause DDT to transfer control to location zero. With this philosophy, it might be better to make DDT's initial message to the programmer, "Caveat emptor."

DDT's major job is to see whether the programmer had previously inserted a breakpoint. As shown in Fig. 8.10, this is done by checking the BFLAG. If it is set to one, DDT removes the contents of the memory location at which the programmer had requested a breakpoint; it inserts a special instruction to cause a program branch to the breakpoint handler (see Fig. 8.12).

Any accumulators, index registers, or other status words that the problem program expects to be set up are then restored by the DDT program. Finally, control is transferred to the location specified by the programmer; as usual, it is contained in VALUE.

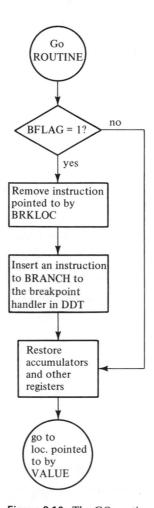

Figure 8.10. The GO routine.

8.5.7 The Breakpoint Set Routine

This routine, shown in Fig. 8.11, does not do very much; its main function is to *remember* that the programmer has requested a breakpoint, so that it can later be inserted when the GO command is processed.

The routine first checks the INFO flag to see whether the command was of the form

    1234B

or simply

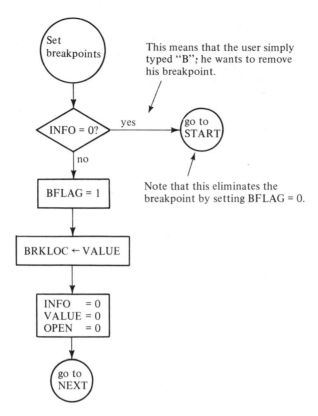

Figure 8.11. The breakpoint handler.

B

As with the past routines, if INFO=0, then the "B" character was not pre-ceded by any octal input; if INFO=1, then the breakpoint routine knows that the command consisted of an octal number followed by the "B" character.

If the programmer typed just the "B" character, it is assumed that he wants to remove his breakpoint. This is easily accomplished by having DDT transfer back to the beginning of the initialization routine, at which time all of the flags, including BFLAG, are reset.

If INFO=1, then the programmer is requesting that a breakpoint be inserted at a specified location. At this point, DDT simply sets BFLAG to one, so that it will remember that a breakpoint exists; it saves the location of the breakpoint (which, as usual, has been stored in VALUE) in an internal variable called BRKLOC. It then clears the INFO flag, resets VALUE, and returns to the main input loop.

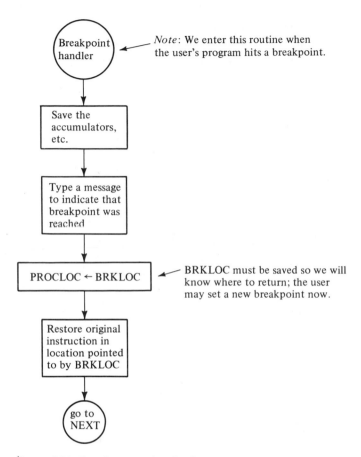

Figure 8.12. Routine to set breakpoints.

At this point, it may not be clear why DDT does not insert its special branch instruction as soon as the breakpoint command is issued by the programmer. The reason may be seen by looking at a typical sequence of commands by the programmer:

```
1234B
1234/   7654
1235B
```

In this example, the programmer decided to insert a breakpoint at location 1234. After thinking about the situation for a moment, though, he was not sure that he had put the breakpoint at the correct place, so he asked to examine location 1234. If DDT had immediately inserted its branch instruction at location 1234, the programmer would see *that* instead of his original instruction—and he would be understandably confused.

As a result, DDT's policy is to insert the breakpoint only at the instant it transfers control to the problem program, i.e., when a "G" or "P" command is typed.

8.5.8   The Breakpoint Handler

The breakpoint handler, shown in Fig. 8.11, is entered when the problem program reaches a previously specified breakpoint. Instead of executing the instruction that the programmer thinks is in that location, the program executes a branch to the breakpoint handler in DDT.

DDT's first task is to save all the accumulators, index registers, and other live registers, so that the program will never know that it has been interrupted. The registers are restored whenever a "G" or "P" command is typed.

The breakpoint handler then types a message to the programmer to let him know that the breakpoint was reached. The breakpoint message can be trivial in this version of DDT, since there is only one breakpoint.

Next, DDT must remember the fact that the problem program has been interrupted at the breakpoint location. As shown in Fig. 8.12, the breakpoint location was saved in BRKLOC: the contents of BRKLOC are now saved in another internal DDT variable called PROCLOC. This is necessary because the programmer might type the following sequence of input commands:

```
1234B
4321G
[breakpoint message]
2003B
P
```

That is, after the breakpoint has been reached, the programmer might decide to move his breakpoint to a different location. Thus, BRKLOC may receive a new value, *but DDT wants to remember to proceed from the old breakpoint*.

DDT then restores the instruction that had previously been in the breakpoint location. Once again, this allows the programmer to examine his program without finding any of DDT's special branch instructions.

8.5.9   The Proceed Routine

The PROCEED routine, show in Fig. 8.13, is very similar to the GO routine discussed earlier. It first checks to see whether a breakpoint exists and, if so, inserts the special branch instruction and saves the problem program's original instruction. It then restores the accumulators, index registers, etc., that had existed at the time of the last breakpoint.

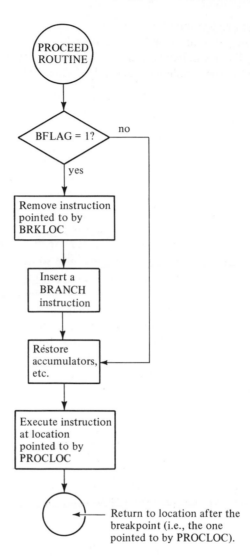

Figure 8.13. The PROCEED routine.

Finally, DDT wants to return control to the program. There is a potential problem, though, because DDT may have a breakpoint at the location to which it wants to return. For example, suppose that the programmer has typed the following sequence of commands:

```
1234B
4321G
[breakpoint message]
P
```

The breakpoint was reached just prior to the execution of the instruction at the location 1234, because DDT had inserted, without the programmer's knowledge, its own instruction in location 1234. When the programmer types "P," he assumes that his own instruction at location 1234 will now be executed, and that the program will continue until it proceeds *up to* location 1234 again, at which time the breakpoint will be invoked.

This means that DDT must execute the instruction that the programmer originally had in location 1234, and then transfer control to location 1235. In this fashion, it manages to keep its own special branch instruction in location 1234. This is fairly easy to perform on any machine with an *execute* instruction; the sequence of code at the end of DDT's PROCEED routine might look like the following:

```
EXE        SAVLOC
BRANCH     1235
BRANCH     1236
```

If the programmer's original instruction (which is presumed to be saved in location SAVLOC) is a simple instruction, like an ADD, then the instruction following the EXE instruction will be reached, that is, the BRANCH 1235 instruction will be reached. If the instruction in SAVLOC is a *skip* instruction of some type, then the BRANCH 1236 instruction will be executed, and the problem program will regain control by itself.

Note that the breakpoint situation can be rather complicated. If the machine has no execute instruction, DDT will have to store the original instruction right in its own sequence of code, that is, the PROCEED routine will look something like

```
SAVLOC     **
           BRANCH     1235
           BRANCH     1236
```

Also, if the programmer places a breakpoint at a subroutine-calling instruction in his problem program, things might go awry. The execution of the subroutine-calling instruction will generate a return address *within DDT* instead of within the problem program. This can be dealt with by making it illegal to place breakpoints on a subroutine-calling instruction, or by having the PROCEED routine recognize that it is dealing with such an instruction, and *simulate it with software.*

Finally, note that if the programmer inserts a breakpoint in a location that is modified by his program, pandemonium will result.

REFERENCES

1. E. YOURDON (ed.), *Real-Time Systems Design,* Information and Systems Press, Cambridge, Mass., 1967.

2. S. BOILEN, et al., "A Time-Sharing Debugging System for a Small Computer," *Proceedings*, Spring Joint Computer Conference, 1963.

3. T. G. EVANS and D. L. DARLEY, "DEBUG—An Extension to Current On-Line Debugging Techniques," *Communications of the ACM*, Volume 8, Number 5, May 1965.

4. R. L. VAN STEEG, "Talk—A High Level Source Language Debugging Technique," *Communications of the ACM*, Volume 7, Number 7, July 1964.

5. R. RUSTIN (ed.), *Debugging Techniques in Large Systems*, Prentice-Hall, Inc., 1971.

6. R. S. GAINES, *The Debugging of Computer Programs*, Ph.D. Thesis, Princeton University, 1969.

7. E. YOURDON, *Design of On-Line Computer Systems*, Prentice-Hall, Inc., 1972, Chapter W.

PROBLEMS

1. Give a definition of debugging. Why is it different from testing? Do you think that debugging is an art or a science? Why do you think some people are good at debugging programs and others are bad at it?

2. Why are bugs easier to find if you have broken your program into small modules? Do you really believe this? Do you think more bugs might be introduced into a program because of interface problems? What should be done about this?

3. How does one go about trying to determine the nature of the error, as is suggested in Section 8.1.2? Do you think this is a skill that can be easily taught to programmers?

4. Why does it make sense to check to see if a bug is repeatable and consistent? Give some examples of reasons why the bug may *not* be repeatable.

5. Give an example of a thorough, methodical, and logical search for bugs. Can your set of procedures be followed for most of the programs you work on?

6. Why does it make sense to investigate the simplest clues first when looking for a bug in your program?

7. What are the advantages of talking to a friend about bugs in your program? Do you think it matters which friends you talk to? Do you have any programming colleagues with whom you are particularly compatible when it comes to debugging a program?

8. Give an example of trying out a test case to confirm your suspicions about a bug in your program. Is this a strategy that can be used often?

9. Why is it often a good idea to forget about a difficult debugging problem until the next day?

10. Can you think of any other debugging strategies or philosophies?

11. Give an example of a keypunching or clerical error that caused a bug in one of your programs. Does this situation occur often? Can it be easily circumvented?

12. Give an example of a program bug caused by an uninitialized variable in one of your programs. How can such a bug be avoided? How can you tell when such a bug has occurred?

13. Give an example of a program bug caused by variables or working storage being shared among many modules. How could this bug have been avoided? How can you tell when such a bug has occurred, i.e., does it have any typical symptoms?

14. Give an example of a program bug caused by control or logic errors, e.g., modules called when they weren't supposed to be, etc. How could such an error be detected easily?

15. Give an example of a program bug caused by an array subscripting out of bounds. Does this bug occur often in your programs? How can it be avoided? How can you tell whether you have this kind of bug in your program?

16. Give an example of a program bug caused by improper termination of program sequences. Does this problem occur often in your programs? How can it be avoided? How can it be recognized when it does occur?

17. Give an example of a bug caused by not handling exceptional cases. Was this actually a program bug, or was it due to an error in the specification of the program?

18. Give an example of a bug caused by improper linkages or interfaces between modules. Is this common in your programming projects? How can it be avoided? To what extent are the antibugging ideas discussed in Chapter 6 useful in this area?

19. Give an example of a bug in one of your programs caused by improper data formats in a high-level language application. Does your compiler help you detect such errors easily? How else can they be detected?

20. Give an example of a program bug caused by passing constants as parameters to a subroutine. Does this occur often? Is there any way of recognizing the bug when it occurs?

21. Give an example of a bug in one of your programs caused by improper use of compound Boolean expressions. How can such problems be avoided? How can they be recognized when they occur? Do you think these problems occur more often in some programming languages than in others? Do you think they occur more often in cases where programmers have or have not been given certain kinds of training?

22. Give an example of a bug in one of your programs caused by improper use of nested IF-THEN-ELSE statements. Is this a common bug? Do you think there are likely to be more such bugs with the use of structured programming techniques such as the ones discussed in Chapter 4? How can such errors be recognized easily?

23. Give an example of a program bug in one of your programs caused by incorrect exit from a subroutine. Is this a common type of bug? How can it be recognized when it occurs?

24. Give an example of a bug in one of your programs caused by accessing data areas after a WRITE statement has been executed. Is this a common type of bug? How can it be avoided? How can it be recognized when it occurs?

25. Give an example in one of your programs of a bug caused by misuse of flags. Is this a common bug? Does it occur more often in batch programs or real-time programs? How can the problem be avoided? How can the problem be recognized when it occurs?

26. Give an example of a bug in one of your programs caused by not handling exceptional IO cases. Is this a common bug? How can it be recognized when it occurs?

27. Give an example of a program bug caused by failure to look at return codes. Is this a problem that occurs more often when the return codes are generated by the vendor's operating system or by a vendor-supplied software package? How can the problem be avoided? How can it be recognized when it occurs?

28. Give an example of a program bug that was caused by counters that were too small and that eventually overflowed. Can the problem be easily avoided? How can it be recognized when it occurs?

29. Give an example of a bug in one of your programs caused by an error in a complicated computational sequence. Does this type of problem occur often? Is it more likely to occur in scientific applications or business-oriented applications? How can it be recognized when it occurs?

30. Give an example of a program bug caused by alignment problems. Is this a common bug? Is it more likely to occur on word-oriented machines or byte-oriented machines?

31. Give an example of a bug caused by pushdown overflow or pushdown underflow. Is this a common type of problem? How can it be recognized when it occurs?

32. Give an example of a program bug caused by using the wrong base registers or index registers. Is this a common bug in your organization? How can it be avoided? How can it be recognized when it occurs?

33. Give an example of a bug in one of your programs caused by attempts to execute data. How can such a problem be avoided? How can it be recognized when it occurs?

34. Give an example of a program bug that was eventually traced to using the wrong version of the program. How often does this situation occur in your organization? How can it be prevented?

35. Give an example of a program bug caused by the lack of a program terminator (such as a semicolon). Is this type of bug likely to be more prevalent in certain types of languages? How can it be recognized when it occurs?

36. What is the primary use of memory dumps? What are some of the reasons for *not* using dumps?

37. Give an example of at least one type of program bug that has not been mentioned in Section 8.2.

38. What is the primary difference between a trace and a dump? When should a trace be used? When should a dump be used?

39. Give an example where a subroutine trace could be effectively used for debugging a program.

40. Give an example where a variable trace could be effectively used for debugging a program.

41. Give an example of an effective use of a time-oriented trace. Is such a situation likely to occur often?

42. Give an example of an effective use of a terminal trace. What controls should be established to ensure that the trace does not cause too much overhead?

43. Give an example of another type of trace other than the ones described in Section 8.3.

44. What are the major types of DDT packages? When should they be used? Does your organization have any such packages? Is their use encouraged?

INTRODUCTION

Class Problems and Exercises—Administrative Details

A. The Instructor's Objectives

1. The primary purpose of the class problems presented in these appendices is to illustrate the techniques and philosophies presented in the *Program Structure and Design* textbook. Though several examples are presented in the text, it was felt important to present a unified example that would involve as many different programming techniques as possible.

2. Another important objective of the class problems is to give the student a chance to apply and practice the techniques and philosophies presented in the class. Previous experience in conducting programming training courses has shown that many of the ideas presented in the classroom are not appreciated (or even understood) unless they are applied to a real problem.

3. An effort was made to choose a series of problems that would not be so trivial as to become dull and boring; at the same time, the problem is hopefully not too complex to be attacked in a reasonably thorough fashion in the limited time available in the course.

4. Finally, it is hoped that the problems will give everyone—student and instructor alike—the opportunity to experiment and learn more about the black art we call programming. In particular, we should try to carefully observe our method of attacking the problems, so we can learn more about such concepts as modularity, "simple-minded" programming, antibugging (concepts discussed in Chapters 5 and 6 of the text), structured programming (Chapter 4), and top-down design (Chapter 2).

B. Your Objectives

1. A primary objective of the programming exercises is to illustrate the concept of top-down design. You should attempt to design and code the program in a series of levels, beginning with the main program and progressing downward in a hierarchical sense until you reach the most detailed modules. Each module should be a complete functional entity, with a definite purpose, a definite beginning, and a definite ending; it should also be relatively short.

2. A second objective is to illustrate the structured programming principles discussed in Chapter 4. Assuming that you are programming in COBOL or PL/I, you should avoid all GO-TO statements and use the building blocks discussed in the class. In the case of FORTRAN or assembly language, you should be able to illustrate that any use of GO-TO statements conforms to the black-box principles that we discussed. You may not agree (yet) with the idea of eliminating GO-TO statements, but one of the purposes of the exercises is to force you to try the idea in a nontrivial fashion; therefore, any unstructured GO-TO statements that *do* appear in your program will be taken as a sign of weakness, laziness, or obstinance.

3. A third objective—and one that follows directly from the two above—is to produce a well-designed, modular, maintainable, easy-to-read program. Try to produce a program that would be easy for the instructor to read and understand; even more important, try to produce a program that you would be proud to show your friends.

4. Another objective is to finish the program, but this is not as important as the three objectives above. Indeed, the time limitations may be such that you *cannot* finish it. It is more important that you produce a top-down program whose top levels are complete and whose bottom-most levels have not been implemented (because of lack of time) than to produce a completed "rat's nest" program. On the other hand, if you design only the very top level (i.e., the main program), then no matter how structured and elegant it may appear, no one will be very impressed; a reasonable compromise is necessary.

5. The very last objective—and the least important one—is efficiency. The limitations of time will make it somewhat difficult to spend much time worrying about efficiency, and besides, that is not the point of the exercises. Obviously, you should try to avoid utterly stupid coding practices, such as repeating a computation 100 times in an in-line fashion instead of using a loop that iterates 100 times. On the other hand, do not flinch at programming practices (especially structured programming practices) that you might ordinarily avoid because of possible efficiency problems. For example, feel free to use such constructs as the nested IF statement.

C. Rules of the Game

1. The plan is to supplement the normal lectures and seminar discussion with periods of time that will be devoted to working on the problem. With some luck, students may be able to persuade the instructor to join them in their efforts.

2. The class will be broken into groups, or *teams*, that should consist of approximately three to five members. Each team should choose a *spokesman* and a *secretary* who will take notes on any interesting developments or discussions that occur in the group. Because of the limited time, and because many of the team members may not know each other well, it should not be considered imperative to choose a team leader or "chief." The team members may well prefer to consider themselves as equal members. After the exercises are finished, it may be interesting

again to consider Weinberg's discussion of teams and "egoless" programming in *The Psychology of Computer Programming*.

    3. Most important, each group should attempt to clearly identify its *objectives* as it works on a problem. For convenience, the teams will probably be selected on the basis of programming language, e.g., it is likely that we will have FORTRAN teams, COBOL teams, etc. Similarly, depending on the makeup of the class, we may wish to have an IBM System/370 team, a Honeywell team, etc. More important, though, each team should try to decide what it is attempting to maximize, and what aspect of the problem it is attempting to concentrate on. Examples follow:

    (a) One team might try to concentrate on *efficiency*, i.e., the best possible use of CPU time, memory, and other resources.

    (b) Another team might try to concentrate on simplicity and maintainability, i.e., developing a program that would have the greatest chance of being successfully turned over to a maintenance department.

    (c) Still another team might concentrate on an effort to finish the coding (and desk-checking) of as much of the program as possible. This team would have as its overriding objective finishing the entire problem by the end of the seminar.

    4. It may be very desirable to have two or three "implementation" teams that would attempt to develop and code the problems with some of the objectives listed above. Two or three other teams might act as devil's advocates to evaluate and criticize the activities of the other teams. The devil's advocate teams should spend their time developing a list of questions or acceptance criteria that they feel should be imposed on the implementation teams. They should then spend their time working with and listening to the implementation teams as they proceed in their development.

    5. Obviously, each of the teams should try to accomplish as much as possible—that is one of the purposes of the team secretary. Any notes, memos, "working papers," or any other tangible results should probably be reproduced (time permitting) for the benefit of the other people in the class.

A

THE MONEY
PROBLEM

I. Background Information

A. Financial Models

It has become quite fashionable in a number of companies to employ computer programs to assist top management as they evaluate and consider major financial decisions: changes in production, capital expenditures, advertising, and so forth. These programs are often referred to as "management information systems" (a phrase that seems to encompass a great many sins and evils), but we shall use the term "financial model."

Some of the background and motivation for such a model is given in Section 2.1.2 of the text; it should be fairly easy to see the need for and usefulness of such a program. For virtually any kind of business, a manager has a number of variables he can manipulate: sales force; production schedules; advertising and various other elements that might influence the number of customers; pricing policies that ultimately determine the revenue that can be generated; and, of course, the various costs that the company must incur.

The output from these models vary, depending on the management's needs; however, there is usually some rather basic information that any sensible manager would want to see. A profit-and-loss statement is probably the most important: Such a report would summarize the revenues, costs, profits (or losses) and cash flow (i.e., accumulated profits and/or losses) on a monthly basis. Other reports might show a more detailed picture of costs, revenues, staff growth, and so forth.

B.   Financial Models for a Time-Sharing Service Bureau

The class problem described in this appendix involves the development of a financial model for a time-sharing service bureau. In this case, there is no product per se; the major purpose of such a company is to attract customers to use its time-sharing system, for which they will pay the exorbitant rates that have become so prevalent in recent years. One of the major influences on the success of such a business is the number of salesmen touting the service, and their ability to tell a convincing story; the technical quality of the system (computational power, reliability, scope of application packages and programming languages, etc.) then determines how long a customer will stay with the system before moving on to a bigger and better (or more effectively sold) system. One can easily make assumptions about the amount of revenue that each customer will generate. Obviously, there are a number of costs associated with the computer equipment, the various communication facilities, the staff, and so forth.

As we will see in the next section, the time-sharing financial model (henceforth referred to as MONEY) will be required to read several parameter cards that describe the manager's assumptions about the number of salesmen, etc. An important concept for this problem is the notion of a "DO-loop" variable: The manager will often want to run his financial model assuming the existence, say, of 5 salesmen; he might then want to repeat the same set of computations with 10 salesmen but with all other parameters held the same; the process might then be repeated with 15 salesmen, 20 salesmen, and so forth, until we reach a specified maximum of 30. The manager might specify this by supplying a parameter card of the form

```
NSALESMEN = 5, 30, 5
```

That is, the user is specifying an *initial* value, a *final* value, and an *increment* value in the nature of a FORTRAN DO-loop or a COBOL PERFORM VARYING statement.

It is important to recognize that the user may want to vary any or all of the parameters in the program, that is, he may wish to supply input of the form

```
NSALESMEN = 5, 30, 5
NPROGRAMMERS = 1,10,1
```

In this case, the manager is indicating that he wants to perform the calculations with 5 salesmen and one programmer; then again with 10 salesmen and one programmer; and so forth, until we reach 30 salesmen and one programmer; then 5 salesmen and two programmers; 10 salesmen and two programmers; and so forth. It is important to keep in mind that, in theory, the manager may ask for all of the parameters to be varied in this nested DO-loop fashion. The number of permutations of variables (or the number of iterations through which your program must pass) is clearly equal to the *product* of the number of permutations for each individual variable. It may be a good idea to put some error-checking logic into your program to ensure that the user of your program does not ask for an unreasonably large number of permutations.

II. Specification of the MONEY Program

A. General Information

The MONEY program will be required to accept approximately fifty parameter cards that identify the manager's assumptions about the time-sharing business. For the purposes of this specification, the parameters will be identified as N1, N2, N3, etc.; however, you should feel free to identify them with slightly more mnemonic names, e.g., NUMBEROFSALESMEN.

You can assume that the input to MONEY will come from the card reader, though the management may someday insist on the ability to input their parameters directly from terminals on their desks. You are free to determine the actual, detailed format of the input parameters.

B. Customer Assumptions

1. Assume that the time-sharing business commences operations on the first day of month 1 (e.g., on January 1, 1975 or any other day you consider appropriate). On that glorious day, assume that N1 salesmen are selling the services of the company.

2. On the first day of each month thereafter, management will hire a number of new salesmen equal to the number of customers that existed in the previous month times the parameter N2. For example, assume that the company begins on January 1 with N1 *initial* salesmen; on February 1, management will hire an *additional* group of salesmen equal to N2 times the number of customers existing on January 1.

3. For various reasons, N3 % of the salesmen quit the company each month; however, assume that a salesman will stay with the company for at least one month before he thinks about quitting. Assume that every salesman in the company has an equal probability of feeling the urge to move on to greener pastures, that is, it is just as likely for a junior salesman to quit as it is for a senior salesman to quit.

4. Management has established an upper limit of N4 salesmen in the company.

5. During the first month of work, a salesman can sell N5 customers; assume that the customers begin using the system (subject to the constraints of paragraph C below) on the first day of the following month. Thus, if a salesman joins the

company on January 1, he will sell N5 customers during the month of January—and all of them will become "official" customers as of February 1.

6. In subsequent months of employment, a salesman is able to sell N6 *more* customers than he did in the previous month. Thus, the salesman sells N5 + N6 customers in his second month, N5 + 2*N6 customers in his third month, and so forth.

7. A salesman can sell a maximum of N7 customers per month.

8. For various reasons, N8% of the customers will get disgusted with the time-sharing system and stop using its services each month. This happens with equal probability to new customers and old customers alike. Thus, when a salesman sells X customers on January 1, N8% of them will get disgusted and leave even before they become official customers on February 1.

C. Revenue Assumptions

1. For the first N9 months after he becomes an official customer, each time-sharing customer spends his time converting his programs, reading his manuals, trying to find out why his terminal wasn't installed properly, and generally learning about the system. Thus, during the first N9 months, he generates no revenue.

2. In his first productive month, the customer uses N10 "units" of computer time. A "unit" is an arbitrary combination of CPU time, IO time, terminal connect time, and other resources.

3. In subsequent months, the customer uses N11 units more than he used in the previous month. Thus, in the second productive month, the customer uses N10 + N11; in the third month, he uses N10 + 2*N11; and so forth.

4. After N12 months of productive use of the system, the customer reaches his maximum revenue; from then on, he continues to use the same number of computer units each month.

5. When the company commences operations in month 1, it will charge a basic price of N13 dollars for each unit of computer time.

6. N14% of all revenue must be rebated to the customer because of poor performance, lost data, system "crashes," and other calamities.

7. The price of the time-sharing service will change by N15% each month to reflect the effect of local competition (or the lack of it). Note that N15 can be positive or negative.

8. The customer is billed on the first day of the month for the services used during the previous month. Assume that the customer does not pay his bill for N16 months after he is billed.

D. Cost Assumptions

1. The major categories of costs in the time-sharing business are:
   (a) Equipment costs
      (1) Computer—mainframe and the usual peripherals.
      (2) Communications—modems, concentrators, lines, etc.
      (3) EAM facilities—keypunches, decollators, etc.
   (b) Building and facilities
   (c) Administrative overhead (telephones, advertising, etc.)

(d) Personnel
    (1) Programmers
    (2) Operators
    (3) Customer-support technicians
    (4) Clerical
    (5) Managers
    (6) Marketing

2. Assume that the *starting* salaries of all personnel increase by N17% each year. That is, if it costs X dollars to hire an average programmer when the company commences business in month 1, it will cost X + N17% to hire an average programmer one year later.

3. Assume that each employee receives a salary increase of N18% per year. The salary increase is given after the employee has worked for the company for one year.

4. Add N19% to the basic salaries for taxes, employee insurance, and various other fringe benefits.

5. On the first day of each month, the company pays salaries to each employee for the previous month of work. The company also receives bills for computer time, rent, and administrative overhead costs incurred during the previous month; however, it delays paying these bills for one month.

E. Equipment Cost Assumptions

1. The computer rental is N20 dollars per month plus N21 dollars times the number of customers that existed in the previous month. This rental reflects the basic machine rental plus the extra disk packs, miscellaneous peripherals, computer overtime charges, and so forth, that are directly related to the number of customers on the system.

2. The communication costs are N22 dollars per month plus N23 times the number of customers that existed in the previous month.

3. The EAM costs (keypunches, etc.) are N24 dollars per month plus N25 times the number of customers that existed the previous month.

4. The building rental is N26 dollars per month plus N27 times the total number of people on the staff.

5. The cost for electricity, utilities, janitor services, etc. is N28 dollars per month plus N29 times the number of people on the staff.

6. The administrative overhead is N30 dollars per month plus N31 times the total size of the staff.

F. Staff Assumptions

1. The number of programmers on the staff is N32 plus N33 times the number of customers that existed in the previous month. If there are fewer customers in month N + 1 than there were in month N, this implies that some programmers will be fired (or turned into pumpkins, perhaps); if such an unfortunate situation does occur, you can assume that every programmer has an equal probability of being fired. Naturally, this is not the sort of thing that we tell a programmer when we hire him; by the way, the starting salary for the average programmer when the company commences business in month 1 is N34 dollars per month.

2. The number of operators on the staff is N35 plus N36 times the number of customers that existed in the previous month; if necessary, operators may be fired in the same manner that programmers are fired. The starting salary for operators in month 1 is N37 dollars per month.

3. The same assumptions exist for customer support technicians: N38 plus N39 times the number of customers in the previous month. If necessary, customer-support technicians may be fired in the same manner as programmers are fired. The starting salary for a customer-support technician is N40 dollars per month.

4. The number of salesmen has been described in paragraph B above. Their starting salary is N41 dollars per month.

5. The number of managers on the staff is equal to N42 plus N43 times the number of personnel described in paragraphs 1, 2, 3, and 4 above. The starting salary of a manager in month 1 of operation is N44 dollars per month.

6. The number of clerical people on the staff is N45 plus N46 times the number of personnel described in paragraphs 1–5 above. The starting salary for clerical people is N47 dollars per month.

G. Miscellaneous Assumptions

1. N48 is the number of months for which the model is to be run. That is, the manager will specify whether he wants a simulated profit-and-loss statement for 12 months, 36 months, 109 months, etc.

2. N49 is the maximum number of customers that the time-sharing service can support. The limitation is due to the technical features of the system itself, e.g., limitations on the number of lines or modems, etc.

B

THE MUGWUMP FERTILIZER PROBLEM

MEMO TO: Our New Superprogrammer
FROM: President, the Mugwump Fertilizer Company
DATE: March 15, 1974
SUBJECT: Management Information System

I. Introduction

    1. Congratulations! On the recommendation of an anonymous but internationally infamous American EDP consultant, I am pleased to welcome you into the EDP department of the Mugwump Fertilizer Company at the modest salary of $50,000. We have been assured that you are truly able to program faster than a speeding bullet, leap over tall reams of printout in a single bound, and generally bedazzle one and all with your programming virtuosity. As your first assignment, I would like you to develop a modest management information system that will help me, as president, to make better decisions about the current activities of the company.

    2. Your system—actually, a single program—will be concerned with information that can be found on our Open-Order File. The file is a simple magnetic tape file that contains information about the orders that have been placed by customers but not yet filled. Records are added to the file (as a result of a periodic update run) as soon as an order has been placed. Modifications may be necessary if it is later discovered that some of the information on the file is incorrect, or if the customer requests a change (e.g., if he cancels an order before it has been shipped); and, in most cases, records are deleted from the file when an order has been shipped to the

customer. More details concerning the structure of the file will be found in Section II below.

II. The Structure of the Open-Order File

1. The Open-Order File is maintained on a magnetic tape file, which may or may not involve multiple reels. The physical details of the file (recording density, blocking factor, tape label information, etc.) are of no concern to you; you may assume that one of the humble system programmers on the staff will provide you with three subroutines, which may be PERFORMed or CALLed. These three subroutines are:

XOPEN   must be called before any records are actually read. It will perform any necessary initialization, check the tape label, position the tape at the beginning of the file, and so forth.

XREAD   will read one logical record from the file. You and the system programmer will decide how to tell the XREAD subroutine where to read the record into.

XCLOSE   must be called when you are finished using the file. It will perform all necessary actions to close the file.

Each of the subroutines will set a flag before returning to the calling program. This flag, called XRESULT, will have the following value:

XRESULT = 0   requested operation was performed successfully.
          1   requested operation resulted in a nonrecoverable error, e.g., a parity error, or the tape drive exploded, etc.
          2   end-of-file condition was detected.

2. The Open-Order File contains three different types of records: a Customer record, a Purchase-Order record, and an Item record. The appropriate amount of filler, or blank characters, has been added where necessary, to ensure that all of the records are of the same length. The Customer record may be considered a master record; there may be one or more Purchase-Order records subordinate to each Customer record; there may be one or more Item records subordinate to each Purchase-Order record. If a customer has one or more orders that have not yet been shipped, he will have exactly one Customer record on the file; this record indicates the customer's account number, account name, address, and other general information. For each distinct purchase order that the customer has placed, there will be a unique Purchase-Order record *following* the Customer record; the Purchase Order record indicates the date on which the order was placed, the salesman who placed it, the shipping address, and other information pertinent to that order. Each purchase order will have one or more Item records associated with it—for example, a Purchase-Order record may be immediately followed by three Item records to indicate that it consists of a certain quantity of item X, a certain quantity of item Y, and a certain quantity of item Z. The purpose of the Item record is to identify the type of product, the quantity of the product that has been sold, the unit price prevailing on the date of the sale, and other such information.

3. Note that each Customer record may be followed by a variable number of Purchase-Order records, though there must be at least *one* Purchase-Order record. Similarly, each Purchase-Order record is followed by at least one Item record. The structure of the file may thus be summarized by Fig. B.1.

4. The record structure for a Customer record is shown in Figure B.2; the record structure for a Purchase-Order record is shown in Figure B.3; the record structure for the Item record is shown in Figure B.4. Note that all records on the file are of equal length. Note also that each record is, in a sense, self-identifying: The first field in the record indicates whether it is a Customer record, a Purchase-Order record, or an Item record.

5. The basic purpose of your program is to print selected records from the Open-Order File, so that I may receive information about all pending orders for a

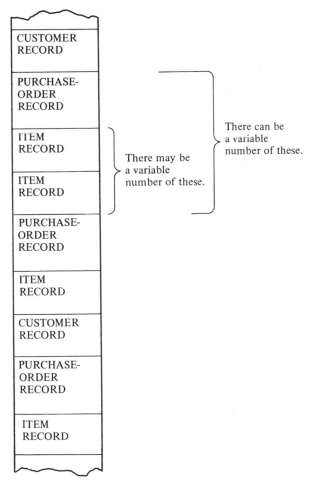

Figure B.1. The structures for the Open-Order.

particular product (e.g., decaffeinated guano), all pending orders placed by a speci-fied salesman, etc. This information will be supplied to your program in several discrete *sets* of control cards—e.g., in one execution of your program, I may wish you to print one report showing all pending orders for purple guano, followed by another report of all pending orders associated with customer 1234.

This may seem like an awkward approach to the problem, but it will allow us to select the records for several different reports with one pass through our incredibly large Open-Order File. The format of the input cards is described in more detail in Section III below.

Figure B.2. Format of the Customer Record.

RECORD TYPE CODE	1	CHARACTER
ACCOUNT NUMBER	6	
CUSTOMER NAME	30	
1ST LINE OF CUST. ADDRESS	20	
2ND LINE ″ ″ ″	20	
3RD LINE ″ ″ ″	20	
CITY	20	
STATE	20	
TELEPHONE NUMBER	10	
CUSTOMER CONTACT	20	
	167	CHARACTERS

Note: The RECORD TYPE CODE will have the value of 1 for this type of record.

Figure B.3. Format of the Purchase-Order Record.

RECORD TYPE CODE	1	CHARACTER
ACCOUNT NUMBER	6	
PURCHASE ORDER NUMBER	8	
SALESMAN ID CODE	3	
DATE OF ORDER—YYMMDD	6	
SHIPPING INFO: CUST. NAME	30	
1ST LINE OF SHIPPING ADDRESS	20	
2ND LINE ″ ″ ″	20	
3RD LINE ″ ″ ″	20	
CITY	20	
STATE	20	
REGION CODE WHERE ORDER WAS PLACED	1	
TOTAL $ AMOUNT OF ORDER	6	
FILLER (BLANK)	6	
	167	CHARACTERS

Note: The RECORD TYPE CODE is 2 for this type of record.

Figure B.4. Format of the Item Record.

RECORD TYPE CODE	1	CHARACTER
ACCOUNT NUMBER	6	
PURCHASE ORDER NUMBER	8	
ITEM NUMBER	10	
PRODUCT NUMBER	4	
SALESMAN ID	3	
DATE ORDER PLACED—YYMMDD	6	
DATE ORDER TO BE SHIPPED—YYMMDD	6	
DATE OF LAST PARTIAL SHIPMENT—YYMMDD	6	
QUANTITY	6	
UNIT PRICE, IN $	6	
TOTAL GROSS PRICE, IN $	6	
DISCOUNT PERCENTAGE	2	
NET PRICE	6	
FILLER (BLANK)	91	
	167	CHARACTERS

Note: The RECORD TYPE CODE is 3 for this type of record.

6. I am not terribly concerned about the format of the output report. I assume that each report will contain a simple "header" that will indicate the criteria used to select records from the file (i.e., the criteria that were specified in the control cards). Other than that, I assume that for each selected record, you will essentially print the magnetic tape record onto the line printer—in some readable format. However, you should be warned that I am somewhat finicky about formats of reports, and I may eventually ask you to make some minor changes in your program in this area.

III. Format of Input to the Program

1. Your program will decide which records are to be selected from the Open-Order File based on information provided in control cards. For simplicity, let us assume that these control cards are, in fact, card images; however, all of your control card input will be handled by three subroutines that will be provided to you by your humble Mugwump system programmer. These subroutines are

YOPEN	open the control card input file. This will perform any necessary initialization, checking of labels, etc.
YREAD	this subroutine will read an 80-character card image into memory. You may feel free to tell the humble system programmer the exact calling conventions of this subroutine, so that you can determine exactly where the card image will be stored.
YCLOSE	close the control card input file.

All three of these subroutines will set a flag before returning to the calling program. This flag, called YRESULT, will have the following value:

YRESULT = 0   requested operation was performed successfully.
          1   requested operation resulted in a nonrecoverable error, e.g., a
                parity error.
          2   end-of-file condition was detected.

2. Each *set* of control cards (of which there may be a variable number for any execution of the program) will contain a variable number of cards, each of which will specify a condition that must be met before a record on the Open-Order File will be selected for printing. For example, it is possible that the first *set* of control cards will contain five individual cards of the general form

A
B
C
D
E

This indicates that condition A *and* condition B *and* condition C *and* condition D *and* condition E must be met before a record will be selected for printing.

3. As indicated above, each execution of the program may involve several sets of control cards; each "packet" of cards will be separated by a single card with the word STOP occupying the first four character positions. Thus, it is possible that your program will read a set of control cards of the form

A1
B1
C1
STOP
A2
B2
STOP
A3
B3
.
.
.

Each record that is read from the file must then be matched against *each* set of control cards. For example, suppose the first record on the file satisfies conditions A1, B1, and C1; it would then be selected for printing in the first output report. Suppose the first record does not satisfy conditions A2 and B2; it would not be selected for output on the second report. Suppose it does satisfy conditions A3 and B3; the same first record would then be selected again for output on the third report—and so forth. Clearly, it is possible for one record to be printed on several different output reports.

4. Each control card consists of two fields: a transaction code and a para-

meter field. The transaction code will occupy the leftmost character positions of the control card and may take as many as ten characters. The parameter field will always begin in character position 11; it will usually consist of one or two integer numbers. For example, a typical control card format might be

CUSTOMER 123456

There is a total of eight types of control cards; each one is described in detail below. Any combination of control cards may exist in a control card packet, and they may occur in any order. However, each type of control card may appear once, at most, in a packet; thus a CUSTOMER control card may appear no more than once in a single packet of cards.

5. The CUSTOMER card requires a parameter field consisting of a single 6-digit integer. This specifies that all Customer records, all Purchase-Order records, and all Item records associated with the specified 6-digit customer account number should be included in the report that is associated with the current packet of control cards. Note that Customer records *and* Purchase-Order records *and* Item records on the file all carry the customer account number to simplify the processing of this control card. You should print an error message if this card is missing a parameter field, if it has more than one parameter field, or if the parameter field has an illegal format, i.e., anything other than a 6-digit integer beginning in column 11.

6. The PONUMBER card requires a parameter field consisting of a single 8-digit integer. This specifies that all Purchase-Order records and all Item records containing the specified purchase order number should be included in the output report. Note that this control card will *not* involve the printing of a Customer record. You should print an error message if this card is missing a parameter field, if there is more than one parameter field, or if the parameter field has an illegal format.

7. The ITEM control card requires a parameter field consisting of a single 10-digit integer. It specifies that the single Item record containing this number should be included in the output report. Note that each Item record on the Open-Order File has a unique number in this field—specifically so that each item that has been ordered by a customer can be individually referenced by a retrieval program such as the one being described here. You should print an error message if the card is missing a parameter field, if it has more than one parameter field, or if the parameter field has an illegal format.

8. The SOLDBY control card requires a parameter field consisting of a single 3–digit integer. It specifies that all Purchase-Order records and all Item records containing the specified salesman's identification number should be included in the output report. Note that when an order is initially placed by a customer, the Purchase-Order record and all subordinate Item records will contain the same salesman number. However, the subsequent updates of the file may cause certain Item records and/or Purchase-Order records to be modified, inserted, or deleted— at the direction of salesmen who receive such requests from customers whose orders have not yet been filled. Thus it is possible for the Purchase-Order records and their subordinate Item records to contain different salesman numbers; for simplicity, we can assume that the Purchase-Order record will contain the identification of the salesman who initially placed the order, and the Item records will contain the identification of the salesman who was last involved in some customer-related activity concerning that item. When processing the SOLDBY control card, we want to in-

clude *only* those Purchase-Order records and *only* those Item records that contain the specified salesman identification number. You should print an error message if this card is missing a parameter field, if it contains more than one parameter field, or if the parameter field has an illegal format.

9. The PRODUCT control card requires a parameter field consisting of a single 4-digit integer. It specifies that all Item records pertaining to the specified product (e.g., strawberry-flavored guano) should be included in the output report. You should print an error message if the card is missing a parameter field, if it has more than one parameter field, or if the parameter field has an illegal format.

10. The DATE control card requires a parameter field consisting of *two* 6-digit integers. Each integer is of the form YYMMDD, e.g., 731113 for November 13, 1973. The first such integer in the parameter field specifies a *beginning* date; it is followed immediately by a comma, followed immediately by a second 6-digit integer that specifies an ending date. The purpose of the DATE control card is to select all Purchase-Order records *and* their subordinate Item records that were placed on a date greater than or equal to the beginning date, and less than or equal to the ending date. Thus, the control card

```
DATE        730104,731113
```

indicates that we should select all records pertaining to orders (and their associated items) placed between January 4th and November 13th (inclusive), 1973. You should print an error message if the DATE card is missing a parameter field, if it contains only one parameter field, if it contains more than two parameter fields, if the specified dates are in the wrong order, or if the parameter fields are in the wrong format.

11. The REGION control card requires a parameter field consisting of a variable number of one-digit integers. These one-digit integer codes specify different sales regions, e.g., it is possible that region 1 is New South Wales. Each region code will be followed immediately by a comma, and the last specified region code must be followed by the special code 0 as an end-of-field indicator. Thus, a typical REGION card might have the form

```
REGION      1,3,2,4,0
```

The purpose of the REGION control card is to select Purchase-Orders records and their subordinate Item records that are being shipped to customers in *any one* of the specified regions. In the example above, we would include an Open-Order File record if it was being shipped to region 1 *or* region 3, *or* region 2 *or* region 4—*and* if the record satisfies all other control cards that may have been included in that packet. As many as nine region codes may be specified, and they may be specified in any order. You should print an error message if the card is missing a parameter field, if a region code is repeated more than once, if more than nine regions are specified, if the format of the parameter field is incorrect, or if the regions are not terminated by a 0.

12. The AMOUNT control card requires a parameter field consisting of a single 6-digit integer. The purpose of the AMOUNT card is to select all Purchase-Order records, and their subordinate Item records, whose total value exceeds the specified 6-digit number. Note that the amount of the purchase order is included in the Purchase-Order record itself, and that it is the sum of the "amount" fields in the

individual Item records that are subordinate to that Purchase-Order record. You should print an error message if the card is missing a parameter field, if it has too many parameter fields, or if the parameter field has an illegal format.

13. As noted before, each packet of control cards will be terminated with a single card that contains the characters STOP in character positions 1–4. The last packet of cards will be terminated with a STOP card, followed by a card with the characters END in character positions 1–3. Thus, the format of the input deck is

```
A1
B1
C1
  .

  .

  .
STOP
A2
B2
  .

  .

  .
STOP
  .

  .

  .
An
Bn
Cn
STOP
END
```

You may assume that there will be a maximum of *ten* packets of control cards in any execution of your program.

IV. Other Editing Requirements

1. In addition to the local errors that might be associated with individual cards, there are a number of global errors that your program should be looking for. These are as follows:

    (a) No control cards at all—in other words, when your program calls for input, it immediately receives an end-of-file condition.

    (b) The END card is missing.

    (c) The last STOP card is missing, but the END card is present.

    (d) The END card is not the last card in the deck. If the input deck is arranged correctly, an attempt to read a card after the END card should result in an end-of-file condition.

    (e) There are more than ten packets of control cards in the input deck.

2. In addition to the global errors mentioned above, it is possible to find a

number of errors that are associated with an individual packet of cards. These errors
are as follows:

(a) A null packet, i.e., two STOP cards in a row.

(b) More than one card of a type in a packet, e.g., more than one
    CUSTOMER card in a packet.

(c) Illegal transaction code, i.e., the transaction code in columns 1–10
    does not conform to one of the eight types described above. Note
    that this might be a mispunched END card or STOP card, which
    could lead to other error conditions.

(d) Illegal parameter field for a specific type of input card—in fact, these
    are the local errors that were described earlier.

V. Output from the Program

1. From the information already given, it can be seen that the program
might be called upon to print as many as ten different output reports. For simplicity,
we will assume that these output reports can be written to separate files on tape or
disk, and that they will be printed at some later time (by another program). Output
to any one of the output files will be performed by still another set of subroutines
that will be provided to you by your humble Mugwump system programmer:

ZOPEN   open the ith file.
ZWRITE   output one logical record to the ith output file.
ZCLOSE   close the ith output file.

Your humble system programmer will be happy to abide by any reasonable subroutine interface to specify the value of i, and to specify exactly where the output
record may be found.

All of these subroutines require an argument i to specify which of the output files
(of which there will be a variable number, but no more than ten) is involved. As
with the previous input/output subroutines, each of the three above will return with
a variable ZRESULT set to the following value:

ZRESULT = 0   the requested operation was completed successfully
          1   a nonrecoverable error occurred.
          2   available output storage space has been exceeded (this will
               only happen on rare occasions, when the output file is being
               sent to disk).

2. The format of the output report has not been specified; you are free to
print anything you consider reasonable. The report should contain a heading that
indicates the criteria that were used to select the records that follow. It should then
contain the Open-Order File records themselves, in essentially the same format as
they exist on tape.

3. In addition to the normal output reports, your program should have an
error report consisting of all errors detected during the run. Your program should
examine all of the control cards before beginning its processing; if any of the control
cards are seen to be incorrect, an appropriate error message should be printed on the
error report file, *and that control card packet should be eliminated* (however, to help

the user, it would be a good idea to analyze the entire control card packet for possible errors, and print *all* appropriate error messages, before rejecting the packet). If nonrecoverable input/output errors occur during the processing of the program, an appropriate error message should be printed on the error report file and an intelligent recovery action should be made (*you* must determine what kind of intelligent recovery is appropriate).

    4. You may assume that the error report file is the 11th output file. Thus, your output to this file may be accomplished by calling the subroutines ZOPEN, ZWRITE, and ZCLOSE with the parameter i set equal to 11.

C

THE MASTER-FILE UPDATE PROBLEM

Memo To: Horatio Superprogrammer
From: The Boss
Date: August 19, 1974
Subject: Programming Assignment

I. Introduction and Overview

Your assignment is to write a program to update selected fields in specific records of our Customer Master File. As you know, the Customer Master File is a serial file occupying several reels of magnetic tape; the file is sorted in ascending sequence on customer account number.

Updates to the Master File will be supplied to your program from cards (or card images) in a "free-field" format. Each card will specify the account number of the customer whose record is to be updated; this will be followed by a specification of one or more fields that is to be updated. For historical reasons, the user's data preparation group has always supplied us with update cards that are already ordered by customer account number.

Your program will read the cards, make certain "reasonableness" checks, and then proceed to update the Master File as specified. Your program will also print a brief report of any errors found during its processing.

II. Structure of the Master File

As mentioned before, the Master File is a serial tape file sorted on customer account number. Every customer has one record in the Master File; each record is 142 characters. The record layout is shown in Table C.1.

Table C.1. STRUCTURE OF THE MASTER FILE

Field	Type of information	Length of field	Alpha or Numeric	May be updated by update program
1	Account number	5	numeric	no
2	Customer name	30	alphanumeric	yes
3	Customer street address	30	alphanumeric	yes
4	City	20	alphanumeric	yes
5	State (abbreviated)	2	alpha	yes
6	Zip code	5	numeric	yes
7	Phone numbers (with area code)	10	numeric	yes
8	Status: active or inactive	1	alpha	no
9	Salesman handling this account	5	numeric	yes
10	Date of last transaction	6	numeric	no
11	Date of last payment	6	numeric	no
12	Current balance	8	numeric	no
13	Total volume of business this year	8	numeric	no
14	Credit limit	6	numeric	no

Each record contains 14 fields that comprise 142 characters. The nature of each field is shown above.

To a large extent, your program should be unconcerned with the details of buffering, blocking, tape labels, and other such details as it pertains to the Master File. These functions will be accomplished by subroutines that you may *call* or *perform*. These subroutines are described below:

MFOPEN	opens *both* the input Master File and the output Master File; performs label checks, initializes buffers, etc.
MFCLOSE	closes both input and output Master Files.
MFREAD	reads one record from the input Master File into an area specified by the programmer.
MFWRITE	writes one record to the output Master File from an area specified by the programmer.

Both MFREAD and MFWRITE will cause a variable called MFLAG to be set as follows:

	0	read/write completed successfully.
MFLAG =	1	unrecoverable parity error.
	2	EOF (occurs only on MFREAD).

III. Structure of Card Input

As mentioned before, updates to the Master File will be supplied from cards. Your program can access these cards by calling (or PERFORMing) the following subroutines:

CROPEN   opens the card-reader input file.
CRCLOSE   closes the card-reader input file.
CREAD   reads one 80-character card image into an area specified by the
                programmer.

In addition, CREAD will cause the variable CRFLAG to be set as follows:

$$
CRFLAG = \begin{matrix} 0 \\ 1 \\ 2 \end{matrix} \quad \begin{matrix} \text{operation completed successfully.} \\ \text{unrecoverable IO error.} \\ \text{EOF.} \end{matrix}
$$

The format of each card is as follows. Columns 1–5 will specify the account number of the record that is to be updated. Columns 6–9 are blank and should be ignored by the program. Beginning in column 10, there will be a variable number of fields of the form

xxabcd. . . .xyz*xxabc. . . .xyz* etc.

where xx represents a two-digit integer that specifies which of the fourteen fields in the record is to be updated, and abc. . . . xyz represents the variable-length character string that is to replace the corresponding field in the master record.

Note that each field is terminated with an asterisk character (*). A field may not extend past the end of a card, that is, a field may not be split between one card and the next. The last field on a card is specified by two asterisks. e.g.,

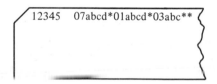

12345   07abcd*01abcd*03abc**

Note that it is possible to have multiple cards updating the same master record. That is, the following sequence is legal:

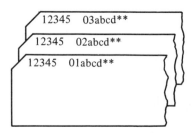

12345   03abcd**
12345   02abcd**
12345   01abcd**

IV. Editing Considerations

As your program does its processing, it should check for obvious types of errors that may be present. If errors are detected, an appropriate error message should be printed; you are free to determine the actual format of the messages. Error messages will be printed on a high-speed printer with the assistance of the following subroutines:

PROPEN   open the printer file.
PRCLOSE   close the printer file.
PRWRITE   outputs a message to the printer file from an area specified by the programmer.

The types of errors that your program should check for are as follows:

1. *Illegal account numbers.* If the account number found on the card cannot be found on the Master File or is out of sequence, the entire card should be rejected and an appropriate message should be printed.

2. *Illegal field numbers.* The field number should be in the range of 1 to 14. If it is not, the field should be ignored and an appropriate message should be printed. Subsequent fields should be processed assuming they are correct.

3. *Illegal data types.* Table 1 indicates that certain fields are required to be numeric or alphabetic or alphanumeric. Your program should check this and reject the field if it is not of the proper type.

4. *Changing fields that cannot be changed.* Table 1 indicates that the user of this program is not allowed to change certain fields; for example, the user is not allowed to change the account number. If the user *does* attempt to update such a field, that attempt should be rejected.

5. *Fields that are too long or too short.* A data field supplied on a card may be shorter than the corresponding field on the Master File, the *same* length as the Master File field, or longer than the Master File field. If the card field is too long, an error message should be generated, and the field should be ignored if the Master field is numeric. It should be truncated if it is an alpha or alphanumeric field.

D

THE TIC-TAC-TOE PROBLEM

1. Your assignment is to write a computer program that will play TIC-TAC-TOE with another player (presumably human). It is assumed that you are familiar with the rules of the game; if not, ask another student in the class.

2. You may assume that your program will be playing against an opponent who will be communicating through a time-sharing terminal. If you are familiar with time-sharing systems, you can assume any reasonable kind of interface with the user at his terminal. If you have not used a time-sharing system, you may assume the existence of two subroutines

```
INPUT (CHAR)
OUTPUT (CHAR)
```

These two subroutines may be PERFORMed or CALLed, as you see fit. CHAR is assumed to be a variable containing the single character to be displayed or accepted from a terminal.

3. That's all there is to it!

INDEX